FROM FEASTING TO FASTING,
THE EVOLUTION OF A SIN

FROM FEASTING TO FASTING, THE EVOLUTION OF A SIN

Attitudes to food in late antiquity

Veronika E. Grimm

London and New York

First published 1996
by Routledge
2 Park Square, Milton Park, Abingdon, Oxon, OX14 4RN

Transferred to Digital Printing 2005

Simultaneously published in the USA and Canada
by Routledge
270 Madison Ave, New York NY 10016

Typeset in Garamond by Routledge

British Library Cataloguing in Publication Data
A catalogue record for this book is available from the
British Library

Library of Congress Cataloguing in Publication Data
Grimm, Veronika, 1934–
From feasting to fasting, the evolution of a sin:
attitudes to food in late antiquity / Veronika Grimm.
p. cm.
1. Food in the Bible. 2. Bible. N.T. – Criticism,
interpretation, etc. 3. Food – Religious aspects –
Christianity – History of doctrines – Early church, ca.
30–600. 4. Food habits – History. 5. Fasting –
Biblical teaching. 6. Fasting – History. I. Title.
BS680.F6G75 1996 241'.dc20 95–51393 CIP

ISBN 0–415–13595–8

CONTENTS

ACKNOWLEDGEMENTS

From the time it dawned upon me that what I most wanted to do in life was to study the history of late antiquity and ancient attitudes to food, up to the completion of this project, more than ten years have passed. When I started on it I was Professor at the Hebrew University, teaching Psychology and doing research in Psychopharmacology in the Department of Biochemistry and Human Nutrition; the last five years I spent as a graduate student at Oxford University. In 1990 I embarked on this project with the understanding and generous encouragement of my Department in Israel, which even entailed on their part a granting of three years leave from my duties. The project took longer, resulting in my resignation from the Hebrew University, with great sadness on both sides.

Next, I want to express my great indebtedness to an outstanding classicist and the most perfect teacher, who not only taught me Greek and Latin, but made me fall in love with the ancient languages, Professor David Weissert of Tel Aviv University.

In Oxford, Wolfson College provided me with a warm and most stimulating intellectual home. If my competence in Greek and Latin improved at all it was because of those most challenging Friday afternoon reading sessions that Dr John Penney conducted heroically, even consenting to read Galen with me, with the anodyne of good red wine.

I had the great good fortune of having not one but two supervisors for my thesis work, two excellent scholars who each in his own ways tried to keep me from falling too hard on my face. Martin Goodman made me go through, in record time, a large part of classical literature and tried to instill scholarly discipline in an often too enthusiastic old psychologist. Mark Edwards, with his impressive erudition and quiet, unassuming manner, taught me to read ancient Christian literature with more openness and understanding than my natural inclination would grant; he was always there to help.

I want to thank Professor Norman F. Cantor of New York University, who taught me about the development of law in the Middle Ages, and who, despite his disappointment with my choice of turning from medieval history to the Graeco-Roman period, stood by me with his friendship and even read some of the early versions of this work.

One of Oxford's great attractions for scholars is its magnificent libraries. I want to thank here all the wonderful librarians who helped me unstintingly: the Librarians of the Ashmolean, the Bodleian and the Theology Faculty Library; and, last but not least, Adrian Hale, the Librarian of Wolfson College.

I also want to express my gratitude to the Harry and Abe Sherman Foundation for generously supporting my research for three years. To my beloved husband, John F. Matthews, for his unfailing encouragement, for his faith in my ability to finish this work, for keeping up my spirits when the going was rough, and for his superhuman efforts to teach me the English use of commas and semicolons, I express my love and deepest appreciation.

Veronika Grimm

ABBREVIATIONS

AJA	American Journal of Archeology
AJP	American Journal of Philology
ANRW	Aufstieg und Niedergang der römischen Welt
BT	Babylonian Talmud
CCL	Corpus Christianorum, series Latina
ExpT	Expository Times
GCS	Die Griechischen Christlichen Schriftsteller der Ersten Jahrhunderte
HR	History of Religions
HThR	Harvard Theological Review
JAC	Jarbuch für Antike und Christentum
JBL	Journal of Biblical Literature
JHL	Journal of Hellenic Studies
JJS	Journal of Jewish Studies
JRS	Journal of Roman Studies
JSS	Journal of Semitic Studies
JT	Jerusalem Talmud
JThS	Journal of Theological Studies
LCL	Loeb Classical Library
MEFRA	Mélanges de l'École française de Rome: Antiquité
NRSV	New Revised Standard Version
NS	New series
ThZ	Theologische Zeitschrift
VigChr	Vigiliae Christianae

Philo's titles

Abr.	De Abrahamo
Cher.	De Cheribum
Conf.	De confusione linquarum
Cont.	De vita contemplativa
Det.	Quod deterius potiori insidiatur
Deus.	Quod deus sit immutabilis
Ebr.	De ebrietate
Gig.	De gigantibus
Her.	Quis rerum divinarum heres sit
Leg. Alleg.	Legum allegoriarum
Op.	De opificio mundi
Som.	De somniis
Spec. Leg.	De specialibus legibus

INTRODUCTION

They devoted themselves to the Apostles' teaching and fellowship, to the breaking of bread.... Day by day, as they spent much time together in the temple, they broke bread at home and ate their food with glad and generous hearts.

(Acts of the Apostles, 2:42, 2:46)[1]

No other matron in Rome could dominate my mind but one who mourned and fasted, who was squalid with dirt, almost blinded by weeping.... The psalms were her music, the Gospels her conversation, continence her luxury, her life a fast. No other could give me pleasure but one whom I never saw eating food.

(Jerome, *Epistle* 45:3)[2]

Hospitality, loving kindness, and cheerful conviviality on the one hand and on the other contempt for the world, mortification of the flesh, weeping and groaning are held up by the authors of these passages as ideal patterns of Christian behaviour. Approximately three hundred years passed between the writing of these Christian texts and a veritable abyss seems to separate the attitudes expressed in them.[3] The two quotations above roughly bracket the turbulent history of the formation of the Christian Church, from the early appearance of groups of followers of Christ in the Roman Empire outside Palestine, to the closing years of the fourth century when it became, within a few years after the conversion of Constantine (AD 312), the ruling state religion and, even more importantly, the provider of a coherent ideology for the entire Roman Empire.[4]

This period of late antiquity has recently been receiving a great deal of scholarly attention for its importance in the foundation of medieval Europe and in consequence in the development of Western culture. Some scholars identify this period, and especially the rise of Christianity, as critical in the development of even such psychological

1

concepts as 'individuality' or 'inner life',[5] culminating in the appearance of a distinctly human 'self', an entity they define as 'an independent, autonomous, and thus essentially non-social moral being'.[6] Contrary to this and in a decidedly less optimistic vein, Foucault saw the same rise of Christianity, with its increasing insistence on rituals of public penitence, asceticism, continual confession and the demand for absolute obedience, as destroying the very idea of a 'self' that had been developing in Graeco-Roman philosophical circles.[7]

The concept of the 'self' used by writers who subscribe to the notion that it developed somehow in late antiquity, or under the influence of Christianity, does not correspond with the psychologist's concept of the same entity. Psychologists see the 'self' as the experienced core of the personality, which consists of one's assumptions about, judgements of and feelings towards oneself as a person. The 'self' is a part of a person's subjective experiential life, or what William James in his famous dictum called 'all that a person is tempted to call *me* or *mine*'.[8] The aspect of the person that increasingly became the target of both philosophical and Christian rhetoric is not so much the 'self', however, as the set of ethical or moral values that define what the person *ought to be* or *ought to do* – that is, one's *conscience*. Conscience is a partly unconscious, partly conscious internalized representation of societal constraints and prohibitions. As external societal constraints and prohibitions changed in late antiquity, internalized moral values – that is, what was acceptable for one's conscience – were expected to undergo corresponding changes, as the Christian moralizing, exhortatory literature seems to testify.

The debate concerning the role of early Christianity in the development of modern concepts of the 'self' or the 'person' continues, following the highly influential work of scholars like Peter Brown, Paul Veyne, and Foucault himself, and their followers, who all see in the period of late antiquity, if not an evolutionary leap in the history of 'inner life', at least substantial changes in a discourse that became increasingly concerned with regulating both physical and mental acts, and that brought profound changes in attitudes expressed towards the human body, its basic needs and functions.

In recent scholarship, changes in attitudes towards the body have most often been examined in terms of ideas concerning sexuality.[9] This viewpoint, that attitudes to the human body are best represented by attitudes to sex and sex only, may in itself be peculiar to the mentality of a modern well-fed culture.

That sexuality is a powerful motive upon which depends the survival of the human species is not to be doubted. The individual human body, however, is more crucially dependent for survival on adequate food supply. It is a commonplace, hence may not even need noting, that human history began in pursuit of food, and many of its later developments were fuelled by the same.[10] But there is much more to it than this. In addition to the importance of food resources in the economics and politics of a society, historians have to take into account the lesson that physicians, nutritionists and other professionals learn when dealing with health problems involving nutrition, and this is that food is more than a collection of nutrients, that people do not make their food choices on the biologically rational basis of nutritional composition, even when variety and choice are available. While food is essential for survival, the range of what various peoples of the world judge as edible is enormous.

Food is much more than just the source of nourishment. Anthropologists, following Lévi-Strauss, call attention to the fact that cooking is peculiar to humans in the same manner as language. Food habits are a language through which a society expresses itself. As Jean Soler asserts: 'there is a link between a people's dietary habits and its perception of the world'.[11] Eating is a social experience and the rituals concerning food have always played an important part in the life of human groups.[12] Food practices have established and confirmed contact and contracts of care and responsibility not only between humans but also between humans and animals, and even between humans and their gods. As W. Robertson Smith expressed it in his work, *The Religion of the Semites*: 'the very act of eating and drinking with a man was a symbol and a confirmation of fellowship and mutual social obligation .... Those who sit at meal together are united for all social effects; those who do not eat together are aliens to one another, without fellowship in religion and without reciprocal social duties'.[13] Such an observation would have had the wholehearted agreement of the author of a Pompeian graffito: *at quem non ceno, barbarus ille mihi est* ('The one with whom I do not dine, he is a barbarian to me').[14]

Psychologists regard infancy and early experience as the basis for the development of important aspects of later adult personality. Erikson sees the early feeding situation as crucial for the attachment of deep symbolic meaning to receiving and to giving, which in turn play important parts in the acquisition of attitudes of trust or mistrust of oneself and others.[15] Those who work today with patients suffering from various eating disorders (anorexia, bulimia, obesity) are confronted forcefully with proofs of the heavy psychological significance that food and eating has for the individual. The often bizarre meaning these patients attach to food reflects disturbances of 'delusional proportions in the body image and body concept' and centres on a 'paralysing sense of ineffectiveness' and powerlessness.[16] The patient suffering from eating disorders tends to perceive his or her body as distinct and alien from the 'self', as a 'thing' that he or she must fight. Often scholars interested in Late Antique Christian ascetic behaviour try to distance this phenomenon from the modern psychological disorder by dismissing anorexia as 'fashion-induced obsession with thinness'.[17] This conception of anorexia, however, is very gravely mistaken. Mara Selvini Palazzoli, writing as a psychotherapist whose understanding grew from intensive experience with sufferers of eating disorders, sees the anorexic as a person who:

> ... is prey to a most disastrous Cartesian dichotomy: she believes that her mind transcends her body and that it grants her unlimited power over her own behaviour and that of others. The result is a reification of the self and the mistaken belief that the patient is engaged in a victorious battle on two fronts, namely against: (1) her body, and (2) the family system.[18]

Most physicians and psychotherapists who treat anorexics would agree with this description of the core of anorexia. It is most instructive to compare this with Peter Brown's perception as to what motivated sexual renunciation for Christians in late antiquity. In *The Body and Society*, Brown follows the early Christians' struggle to establish the soul's transcendence over the body. It seems that by rejecting sexuality, these Christians battled on exactly the same two fronts as the anorexic today, against one's own body and against the family system and society, or as he expresses it in his characteristic language:

> By refusing to act upon the youthful stirrings of desire, Christians could bring marriage and childbirth to an end. With marriage at an end, the huge fabric of organized society would crumble like a sandcastle.[19]

Refusal of food was a part of the struggle for the Christian ascetics described by Peter Brown, just as a rejection of sexuality forms an integral part of the psychology of the present-day anorexic.

It should be recognized not only in cases of extreme or pathological behaviour that the powerful human biological drives deriving from sexuality and hunger form the bases of the network of acts and exchanges that tie the individual into a variety of social settings. In this network both sex and food acquire symbolic meanings, some shared widely by a given culture, others having significance only for the like-minded. Others again may be very private indeed.

Researchers in the sociology and psychology of nutrition have compiled lists of symbolic functions that food practices may serve, in addition to the sheer satisfaction of biological need. Food, accordingly, may be used as a gesture or a language to communicate intentions, feelings and attitudes. So a given food practice may:

1 initiate and maintain personal and business relationships;
2 demonstrate the nature and extent of relationships;
3 provide a focus for communal activities;
4 express love and caring;
5 express individuality;
6 proclaim the separateness of a group;
7 demonstrate belonging to a group;
8 cope with psychological stress;
9 reward or punish;
10 signify social status or wealth;
11 bolster self-esteem and gain recognition;
12 wield political or economic power;
13 prevent, diagnose and treat illness;
14 symbolize emotional experience;
15 display piety;
16 represent security;
17 express moral sentiments.[20]

As this list indicates, eating is an activity that can be used, consciously or otherwise, by the social group or the individual within the group, as a symbol to communicate a message, to make a statement that may extend far beyond the sheer satisfaction of the hunger need. That customs relating to food and drink can reveal the self-defining concerns and anxieties of the group has increasingly been recognized also by historians of the ancient world.[21] The fact that individual eating habits may provide insight into attitudes towards the self, towards one's nearest and dearest and towards society, has interested historians of the high middle ages, as attested by Caroline Walker Bynum's sympathetic study of the meaning of food and fasting in the piety of late medieval Christian women.[22]

Christianity was born into the Roman Empire, an empire whose 'conquests provided it with a great mixture of customs and ways of life of every kind'.[23] This great cultural 'melting pot' provided a meeting place, or a clashing ground, for at least two (if not many more) different food cultures. Christianity originated from Jewish soil, from a culture characterized by its highly defined and codified dietary rules; soon, however, the new creed parted company with most of its Jewish relations, and turned its face to the wider Graeco-Roman world, aspiring to win converts from among the inhabitants of Hellenistic cities of the immense empire, with their seemingly more relaxed, omnivorous food customs. Debate over food practices played a not insignificant role in the ensuing struggle for Christianity's self-definition. A close scrutiny of this debate as it came to be expressed in some of the surviving Christian texts of the early centuries may contribute to the social and intellectual history of this period.

Christian food practices have most often been discussed by scholars of late antiquity under the larger and more inclusive topic of asceticism. In these discussions fasting, the rejection or severe curtailment of food, is often lumped together with various other self-inflicted practices. Noteworthy exceptions to this are the studies of Rudolph Arbesmann and Herbert Musurillo, both focusing their attention on fasting.

In his studies on Greek, Roman and early Christian fasts,[24] Arbesmann surveys the literary evidence for fasting in antiquity. At the outset he makes the assumption, with little supporting evidence, that 'fasting as a religious practice is a world-wide phenomenon and can be found in the religions of almost all the peoples on earth'.[25] He is so strongly wedded to this opinion that the fact that he finds almost no evidence for Greek or Roman fasting, and has to acknowledge that not even priests were obliged to fast as preparation for liturgical function, including sacrifices, only makes him conclude that fasting *must have lost* its importance, and that it was later *revived* under the influence of Eastern cults.[26] These Eastern cults, for the fasting practices of which there is equal paucity of evidence, come in to his study conveniently, like rabbits out of a hat, to explain discrepancies between assumptions and evidence. Even his definition of the object of his extensive search through Greek and Roman literature reflects this problem. Fasting includes abstinence from food and drink for a 'longer or shorter period' or abstinence from certain articles of food and drink, which, presumably, could make a vegetarian, no matter how much he or she ate, a faster. In addition, there is included in Arbesmann's definition something he calls a 'fasting condition'. This does not imply going hungry but rather the exclusion of certain edible species from the diet.[27] All these various 'fastings' are then attributed by Arbesmann with confidence to various primitive superstitious beliefs, such as the belief that 'the act of taking food was dangerous because of the fact that demoniac forces could use this opportunity to enter into the human body and produce destructive effects'.[28] Alternatively, fasting is seen as an attempt to coerce from the gods fertility or visions; or it is claimed to be part of fertility cults arising in some unexplained ways from nature's own rhythms.[29] Since even with the greatest efforts he could find no substantial evidence for fasting as an integral part of Graeco-Roman religion, a large part of Arbesmann's interest was focused on magical papyri and on the preparation for oracular prophecy, and even these, he admits, cannot be reduced to a common denominator. He suggests that 'the point of departure . . . was the simple observation that certain articles of food produced uneasy and confused dreams'.[30] On the question of Christian fasting practices, after reviewing a wealth of literature, Arbesmann came to the conclusion that the 'dominant motive in both individual and corporate practices of fasting was asceticism'.[31] While he points to possible influences coming from philosophical, medical and Jewish sources, he does not tie any of these to any particular Christian text. Since his interest was focused on fasting as a preparation for visions, he gives undue weight in his survey of Christian fasting to this least well-substantiated aspect of it.[32] The contribution of Arbesmann is highly valuable for the wealth of material he brought together and for his innovative approach of considering both polytheistic and Christian traditions in the same work, pointing the way for further research that would study Christian ideas and practices by attempting to place them in the larger cultural and political context in which they grew. The difficulty with Arbesmann's work is, as I have already pointed out, that he had certain definite assumptions about the motives of the religious for fasting, a practice that is far from unitary but in his definition includes a very wide variety of practices. To say that the motivation for most Christian fasting was asceticism does not contribute much to historical understanding, since asceticism had different meanings for different peoples at different ages.

Herbert Musurillo followed Arbesmann and various encyclopaedic definitions in the assumption that the practice of ascetical fasting played an important role in the history of humankind's religious 'development'.[33] His article concentrates on fasting in Greek patristic writers, and attempts to assess the motivation that led to their exhortations. He concludes that it is impossible to establish a single explanation for, or even to arrive at some meaningful categorization of, all the various elements of Christian asceticism, which he regards unhelpfully as 'nothing more than the vital reaction of the Christian, in the concrete circumstances and psychological presuppositions of his milieu to the call of Jesus in the Gospels'.[34] The article brings together a rich variety of texts concerned with fasting. Musurillo, like Arbesmann, points to the various possible intellectual trends that may have played an influential role in the formation of Christian attitudes, but he too is reluctant to analyse individual texts for these possible influences or to place them into a wider political and cultural context, and prefers to see them as Christian products growing from a peculiarly Christian sensibility.

At the present there seems to be an ever-increasing interest in ascetic practices.[35] In these works the focus is no longer on fasting but on a whole collection of austerities. Scholarly opinion concerning the various early Christian practices of self-imposed torture swings widely between those who see these manifestations as serious psychopathology[36] to those who regard it with empathy as a 'deeply ethical attempt on the part of the ascetic practitioners to achieve a counter-cultural identity exhibiting the high values of the culture',[37] while still others respond with solemn reverence, seeing the same phenomena as expressions of sublime spirituality or as a source of spiritual authority.[38]

In the present work I shall attempt to trace Christian attitudes to food and drink, eating and fasting in the writings of those who shaped Christian discourse from the late first to the early fifth century AD. By taking the topic of food and fasting out of the larger problem of asceticism, whenever this can be done, it is hoped that some clarity may be gained. To emphasize the point, my purpose is to clarify the social and symbolic meanings given to food, eating and fasting, by various Christian writers. Is food for a given author a religious issue? Does he see either eating or fasting as part of what E.P. Sanders, in his powerful analysis of *Paul and Palestinian Judaism* called 'a pattern of religion'; that is to say, does either eating or fasting in the eyes of the author play a role in the processes by which one enters the religion or by which one maintains good standing in the ranks of the religious?[39] If not a part of the 'pattern of religion', is food then a social issue for the early Christians, or is it a personal, moral one? Was there a consensus concerning food practices between the various writers? What did they mean by fasting and for what reason and for what purpose did they advocate it? The analysis will focus upon the texts and upon the various possible influences, Christian or non-Christian, that may have been responsible for the opinions expressed by the particular author in question concerning food or fasting.

The survey of early Christian texts is arranged in an approximate chronological order, from the writings of the apostle Paul to those of Augustine, bishop of Hippo. It is not an exhaustive review, and it does not include all texts written during this period that may mention food or fasting but only repeat ideas already discussed. The purpose of the work is to show the *variety of attitudes* expressed by Christian writers, *changes in emphasis* that came about in time, and the *intellectual influences* that may have been responsible for or may have assisted in the formation of these. It is hoped that this kind of analysis will contribute substantially to the understanding of the meaning of food and fasting for Christians in a given historical, social or psychological context.

None of these texts can be discussed in isolation; they did not come into being against a background of homogeneous Christian ideology. Instead, all the texts reflect to some extent the 'melting pot' and battle ground of ideas that characterized late antiquity. Before turning to the Christian texts and the task outlined above, space has to be given to the description of some of the salient aspects of this background.

From its Jewish forbears the new religion claimed for itself the heritage of the Jewish Bible. It is therefore of interest to examine how far the Jewish background or heritage influenced Christian attitudes or practices relating to food. Even more than their Jewish heritage, the practices and customs of the society that surrounded the early Christian groups, and from whence came eventually the greatest number of their converts, may have coloured their attitudes. The authors of these texts were all men who were born into and lived their life in a Hellenistic culture, sharing with their non-Christian neighbours the daily experiences that characterized life in the cities of the Roman empire. Christians tried hard to ignore, and some even fought against, its pageantry and polytheistic ceremonial practices; this opposition itself, in turn, may have left some marks on their food practices and attitudes. On the other hand, not all the manifestations of the surrounding culture were shunned by Christians; the moral and ethical teachings of various philosophical schools appear to have enjoyed prestige and wide circulation, as did the writings of some medical authorities. Some of these may have exerted influence on Christian attitudes to food.

It follows from these considerations that the first task that the present work will have to address is a description of this background. The first two chapters will outline attitudes to food and fasting in Judaism and in Graeco-Roman religion, philosophy and health-care. After these background chapters I shall turn to the Christian texts. Each of the texts addressing the question of the proper Christian attitude to food will be examined for possible evidence of these various influences, for the social and symbolic uses of food that the texts emphasize, and finally, for the role these may have played in the political struggles that accompanied the spread of the new ideology.

It has to be emphasized that throughout this work we are concerned with texts, written by individuals, each with his own peculiar personality and motivation. Moreover, the texts were written to exhort, convince and often to propagandize. How much this discourse reflects actual life in ancient society is a problem that needs for its solution evidence external to the texts. Often this evidence is lacking. To fill the gap, assumptions are made derived variously from comparative history, social science[40] or from creative imagination. These practices may be valid and often enlightening. None of these approaches frame the present work. If it is informed by any single assumption, it is that the human biological organism provides the basis of, or at least puts constraints on, the range of human experience and, consequently, on any construct of the human body that we may form.

Before attempting to put ancient texts concerned with eating and fasting into a historical perspective, a short digression into some of the basic biological principles of human nutrition may be useful.[41]

The human body is a complex machine that requires energy every minute of the life span, from the moment of conception to death. It uses energy constantly, not only for work or movement but also for all the subtle internal processes without which life itself cannot be maintained, for the constant synthesis of new tissues, for nerve conduction, for secretion and detoxification, for generation of heat, and others. To provide this energy the tissues of the body oxidize glucose (from carbohydrate), non-esterified fatty acids and ketone bodies (from fat) and amino acids (from protein). These substances are provided by food, which is the *only* source of energy for the human organism. If food in excess of the energy requirements of the body is ingested the surplus will be stored as body fat. This, then, is turned into energy when the food intake does not match the work output. When food intake is inadequate and the stored fat has been depleted, the body will burn protein by breaking down its own muscles to provide energy for the brain and central nervous system, the remaining muscles, the abdominal organs, and the circulating blood cells, in this order. In a 24-hour period the tissues of a normal fasting human male will utilize for the upkeep of their own function about 1,800 kilocalories, derived from about 75 grams of protein (mainly muscle) and 160 grams of fat from adipose tissue.[42] Of the 180 grams of glucose released from the liver, about 144 grams will be totally oxidized by nervous tissue, mainly the brain, while other tissues use fatty acids and ketone bodies in fasting. With continued fasting the combined effects of loss of fat and protein produce changes in body composition, with a reduction of lean body mass in relation to body water. In initial starvation the rapid weight loss is largely due to loss of sodium and water; however, with prolonged starvation, body fluid volume declines less than that of lean tissue and sodium is conserved. The continued breakdown of lean tissues is associated with increasing urinary excretion of potassium and zinc, with disturbances in the normal electrolyte ratios. As starvation continues, energy requirements also fall, not only because of the reduction of physical and mental activity but also because of changes in hormone secretions resulting in slowing metabolic activity. Reduced resistance to infections accompanies all forms of undernutrition together with apathy, reduction in spontaneous activity, loss of social interests, loss of mental concentration, the disappearance of menstrual periods in women, loss of sexual potency in men, and loss of sexual interest in both. The feeling of hunger disappears and appetite for food is lost in prolonged starvation. Chronic undernutrition – that is, a prolonged intake of food insufficient for the needs of the body – leads to progressive weight loss and reduced resistance; how long the body can keep alive will depend upon the environment in which the person lives, since it provides the range of noxious agents that, with rapidly dwindling resources, the body will need to withstand.

Adequate nutrition, the daily intake of the basic nutrients, is essential to life. Humans evolved as omnivores, which in principle at least, would maximize their chance for adequate nutrition. However, many forms of edible matter are not used as food; the decision to include or exclude a particular edible substance in the diet depends on many social, religious and economic factors and may bear no relation to its nutritive value.

The diet of most people consists of a staple food, which is most easily obtained and is characteristic of an area or culture, and another form that may be called 'prestige' food, since it is harder to obtain and more expensive and therefore usually constitutes a smaller proportion of the diet. Foods belonging to the staple category are nearly always vegetable in origin (cereals, bulbs, etc.), the prestige food is usually meat. Since meat is the most efficient source of essential nutrients, humans may have a natural preference for it.

Undernutrition, seriously compromising the body's ability to function efficiently, can result not only from starvation but also from unvaried, monotonous diets based upon a narrow band of staples. For example, iron deficiency and anaemia, with the consequent reduction in work capacity, are common in communities whose food is predominantly of vegetable origin. In terms of caloric intake a one-staple diet, consisting of only vegetable matter, would necessitate the daily intake of rather enormous quantities, since vegetables contain a large amount of water. It is calculated that an average sized-man (height 168 cm, weight 66 kg) requires daily from 2,300 to 3,700 kilocalories, depending upon the work he does: the lower figure indicates the needed caloric intake for light work and sedentary occupation; the higher figure shows the same for heavy physical labour. If our average-sized man, for example, were to subsist on nothing but lentil porridge, he would need about 2.25 kg of it daily; if his diet was bread only, again, he would need to ingest more than 2 kg of it a day. If he lived solely on green vegetables and fruit the impossible weight of about 13.5 kg per day would be necessary to see him through a day of light work. The sheer impossible bulk could be reduced by adding oil to the food, since 100 g of olive oil (about ten spoonfuls) would provide 900 kilocalories. If our hypothetical 'average man' would try to follow a routine of eating intermittently only every other day, or every fourth day or only once a week, he would have to find room in his gastro-intestinal system for a two, four or sevenfold increase in the vegetables or bread he ate. The internal machinery would be unable to cope with the bulk and that is the biological reason that people hunger and eat every day and ordinarily more than once a day.

Given adequate water supply, one may be able to survive without food for some time, depending on the pre-fasting state of the body, since, as was pointed out above, during starvation the body feeds on itself by breaking down stored fat, and when that is finished will burn its own muscle tissue for fuel. Therefore a well-muscled fat person will take a longer time to starve to death than a thin undernourished one. Water deprivation, on the other hand, kills much faster. The human body consists of 50 to 60 per cent water. It constantly loses water through evaporation from the skin, exhalation through breathing and through elimination in urine and faeces. The body cannot manufacture water, but it is able to conserve some through the regulation of urine outflow. This mechanism, which is quite efficient for dealing with short term water shortage, has the disadvantage of concentrating salts within the body. Total water deprivation kills in a few days; length of survival within this time depends on environmental factors, like heat and humidity.

In the following chapters, the reader will have occasion to recall some of these biological principles.

The human organism cannot survive long if its bodily needs are not satisfied. Consequently, texts that describe feats of self-torture and self-starvation that a biological organism would be most unlikely to survive will be regarded firmly as *texts*; the concern will be with clarifying the reasons for writing these texts, rather than speculating about how these superhuman acts could have been accomplished.

In summary, the purpose of the present work is to study a set of ancient texts, to place them as precisely as possible in their intellectual, social and historical context. If successful, this would not only contribute to our understanding of aspects of ancient 'mentality' but also may hold up a 'distant mirror' to some of our modern conflicts concerning food, eating and our bodies. As Peter Brown so rightly pointed out at the end of his book, we are still heirs to some of the ideas expressed by these texts. The fact that the modern Western world 'grew out of the Christian world that replaced the Roman Empire ... has ensured that, even today, these notions still crowd in upon us, as pale, forbidding presences'. The historian must bring to them, not so much 'their due measure of warm, red blood'[43] as Brown would have it, but an attempt at a clear and objective analysis.

1

THE JEWISH BACKGROUND

Jesus of Nazareth was born a Jew and spent his entire life among Jews.[1] In his lifetime his friends and detractors, his followers and admirers, were Jews. The early Christians carried their message through Jewish contacts in Palestine and in and around synagogues in the Jewish Diaspora that spread through the Hellenistic cities of the Mediterranean basin, Asia Minor, and even to Rome itself.[2] When the two faiths parted ways, the new religion took with itself a substantial part of Jewish literature, claiming the holy books as its due inheritance. An examination, then, of this inheritance, and the way in which it was being understood by the Jews themselves in the early centuries of Christianity, when contact and even competition with Judaism figured significantly in the growth of the movement, may aid our understanding of Christian attitudes to food and fasting. This chapter will attempt to give a short survey of a very complex and large topic: Jewish thought and practice concerning eating and fasting as these are expressed in biblical and extra-biblical Jewish writings and in some non-Jewish sources that may testify to Jewish thought and custom in the time of the Roman Empire, both in the Land of Israel and in the far-flung Jewish communities of the Diaspora.

FOOD AND FASTING IN THE TORAH

The Jews saw themselves, from ancient times, as a unique society that functioned on the basis of a set of written laws.[3] Important aspects of life were regulated by laws in many other ancient societies; however, the giver of the Jewish Law was not a wise human ruler, a Hamurabbi or a Solon, to the likes of whom other societies attributed the creation of their laws, but an all-seeing, all-powerful god,[4] who created the whole universe, including humankind, who gives generously but can

14

also take away, who blesses and curses, and who can be pleased and displeased by the minutest actions of his creatures – a ruler from whose sight there is no escape. This all-powerful god elected His people and made a contract with them. Jewish society, in principle, is based upon a charter, a covenant[5] offered by Yahweh to the sons of Israel and their descendants, whom he had chosen from all the peoples of his creation. All who share in the covenant for all time to come wear a visible, indelible mark as a sign of it: all male Jewish children to this day are circumcised.[6] Yahweh liberated his chosen people from bondage and then gave them his laws. As long as they worshipped Him and together with their households, including slaves and even beasts of burden, obeyed Him by observing the laws, He promised to provide them with peace and prosperity. The Jews' perception of their god as their liberator from slavery, as giver of land and political sovereignty, has tied the religious and political life of the nation inseparably together.[7]

The Law of God, regarded as the Law of the Jewish nation, covered all conceivable aspects of life from the behaviour of the individual to that of the whole community of Israel. Community life centred on the service in the Temple while this existed; where and when it did not exist, as in the Diaspora, the Torah still informed the lives of the widespread Jewish groups, whose distinct identity it helped to maintain. Whatever way it was interpreted, whether strictly observed or not, the Torah was ever present, a part of the definition and self-definition of the Jew.

This Law, the written Torah, tolerates with equanimity the human body with its fundamental biological requirements, including the need for food, drink and sexual intercourse. The manner of satisfaction of these needs, however, is subject to elaborate rules and regulations, which, while aiming to provide amply for these needs, clearly exclude certain ways to their satisfaction as prohibited by God, either as 'impurity' and unacceptable in those wishing to enter God's Sanctuary or as 'abomination' in the eyes of God in all times and all places. The most salient precepts of the Law with relevance to the life of each individual, and which together distinguish it from the laws of the Graeco-Roman surroundings, were the following: it ordered the circumcision of all males, as mentioned above; it required the setting aside of every seventh day as consecrated to God, a day of rest for all; and finally, it set out the dietary laws that regulate what Jews may eat.[8] The Law lists the animals the flesh of which is for consumption and prohibits the eating of pork and a large number of other species designated as 'unclean'.[9] The Law also forbade Jews the eating of blood,[10] and the boiling of a kid in its mother's milk,[11] which by the first century came to be interpreted as a prohibition on the mixing of meat with dairy products.

The dietary laws in Leviticus and Deuteronomy list the permitted and forbidden species among the quadrupeds, the birds and the fish, and in addition provide the principle by which the edible can be clearly separated from the inedible in each of these categories. A point worth noting is that the elaborate list of dietary regulations set out in the Pentateuch presupposes a meat-eating population. If, as is often claimed by modern historians, meat was a negligible part of the ancient diet and most people only ate meat on sacrificial occasions,[12] one may wonder why the Law enumerates a large number of animal species, both in the permitted and the forbidden categories, that were definitely not suitable for sacrifice. Yahweh, like most other ancient deities, demanded only domestic animals for the altar, from the herd and from the flock, but the people of Israel were permitted to hunt and eat 'the deer, the gazelle, the roebuck, the wild goat, the ibex, the antelope, and the mountain sheep',[13] not to mention the locust and the cricket.[14] Rather than addressing a largely vegetarian society, the only meat protein of which came from the occasional sacrifice of its highly priced working beasts, the Law appears to confront a human society that in order to obtain its necessary nutrients in a most efficient form would eat, if not regulated, just about anything that moved.[15] In the eyes of the law-makers this was not fitting for the people of Israel. The reasons for this are not known but through the ages many hypotheses have been put forth to account for the choice of permitted meat, ranging from various hygienic to separatist ones. There is not a shred of evidence for the hygienic claims; a lot is to be said, however, for the separatist ones. Whether it was knowingly intended by the framers of the Law or not, the dietary rules of the Jews have kept the observant from eating the food of others, and therefore, to a greater or lesser degree, have always separated the Jews from the surrounding world.[16]

The Torah that embodied the core of Jewish religious life, as we have seen, gave explicit permission for meat eating.[17] It is conceivable that this clear and unequivocal permission in the written Law is responsible for the dearth of exhortations to vegetarianism[18] as an expression of piety among the ancient Jews. The arguments, and there were many, among the pious concerned the purity of food,[19] while the eating of God-given and God-permitted meat seems to have been seldom questioned. Not even the pietist parties or sects are known to have urged vegetarianism; the Pharisees, who, according to Josephus, 'despised delicacies in diet',[20] and who may have seen themselves as experts and guardians of the purity laws,[21] ate meat; so too did the Essenes, sectarians who regarded themselves as the true Israel and adhered to all the precepts of the Law of Moses and observed all the biblical feasts, which entailed the eating of meat.[22] Even the proverbially frugal diet of John the Baptist included locusts, an animal permitted for consumption by the Law! Among ancient Jewish writers whose work is extant, the only one who valued alimentary self-denial and a meatless diet very highly is Philo of Alexandria. About him and his Therapeutae we shall have more to say below.

The aim of the purity laws set out in the Hebrew Bible is to safeguard the proper worship of God in his Sanctuary. The God of Israel demanded daily worship amidst exacting rules of ritual purity, and since, in addition to the priestly castes, all males in Israel were potentially partakers of the temple worship, the laws of purity encompassed all aspects of life. Consequently, the Law made no distinction between private and public domain. As E.P. Sanders so rightly emphasized, the peculiarity of Judaism was to bring all life under divine law, to treat deceiving one's neighbour as being just as serious as accidentally eating food that should have gone to the priests or the altar.[23]

The God of Israel, like other gods of his age, required sacrifice: offerings from all edible agricultural produce and, outstanding among these, a large number of animals daily in a variety of different rites. In addition to holocausts, in which the whole animal was burned on the altar on behalf of the community, there were first-fruit offerings as a token given back to God for his great bounty;[24] sacrifices were offered as atonement for the sins of the community, accompanied by public confession, and also oblations for private sin. Sin was any action on the part of the community or the individual, committed or omitted, wilfully or even inadvertently, that displeased Yahweh. Importantly, there were also sacrifices offered as a part of reparation for damage caused to one's fellows and many voluntary votive offerings. Only 'clean' and unblemished animals could be used, and the participants in the sacrifice and all who entered the Temple had to be purified. Jewish thinkers often insisted that purification meant cleansing both body and soul.[25] Despite the fact that the commandments and provisions ordained for the sacrificial worship of God in the Mosaic code clearly indicate a central Temple cult, the dietary laws definitely, and to a large extent the other laws concerning ritual purity, were extended beyond the Temple and were understood by the ancient sources and later by the rabbis to encompass all of Israel. Purity was an ideal in ancient Judaism.[26] God's command of his people, 'You shall be holy for I the Lord your God am holy!',[27] was interpreted as a command addressed to all Israel, and not only to its priests, to keep away from defilement, and from all that was regarded as abomination in the eyes of God.

In the mind of the shapers of the Jewish Law, three things endangered ritual purity, and these were contact with dead bodies, (skin) disease and sexual discharges (including childbirth).[28] As all three of these were part of life they were not in themselves regarded as wrong, sinful or forbidden, but they conveyed a condition, a temporary one removable by the appropriate ritual cleansing, that prevented entrance to the Temple and eating consecrated food lest they cause defilement of the holy place, which constituted a most grievous sin. As a consequence of this, the ritual of worship was carried out only by healthy males, without blemish on their bodies, who had no contact with dead bodies and were purified of all seminal discharge. Women were excluded from the ritual worship, presumably on account of the 'impurity' of their menstrual flow, or on account of their sexual behaviour when not menstruating and, finally, on account of the impurity brought upon them by childbirth. Sexual behaviour, while generally regarded as God-given legitimate pleasure, was, however, strictly regulated and limited to married partners; all sexual discharge that could not, potentially at least, result in the conception of legitimate offspring was considered in the class of 'abominations', with homosexuality,[29] prostitution[30] (both capital offences) and masturbation heading the list.

Feasting was an integral part of the Temple cult. The various sacrifices, with the exception of the total burnt offerings, were accompanied by a communion meal, the priests as representatives of the people taking part in the holy food of Yahweh, or the community present at the Temple all taking part, while in private votive sacrifice the offerer and his family ate, after giving the priests the portion due to them.[31] The aftermath of the solemn ceremony was a joyous feast.

In the presence of the Lord your God ... you shall eat the tithe of your grain, your wine and your oil, as well as the firstlings of your herd and flock ... spend the money for whatever you wish – oxen, sheep, wine, strong drink or whatever you desire. And you shall eat there in the presence of the Lord your God, you and your household rejoicing together.[32]

Whatever may have been the theological interpretations of the sacrifices, as communion with the deity and communion and fellowship with the people who shared in the festive meal or identification with the whole people whose customs these followed, the feasts were seen by ancient Jewish writers as an important aspect of the cult. Philo of Alexandria in the first century AD, writing about the Temple cult in Jerusalem, observed that by eating their portion of the sacrificial feast the people shared in God's own food and thus entered a holy 'partnership'.[33] Furthermore, these festivals strengthened social cohesion by encouraging the formation of new friendships, 'the sacrifices and libations – writes Philo – are the occasion of reciprocity of feeling and constitute the surest pledge that all are of one mind'.[34] Philo, an Alexandrian Jew who may or may not have had firsthand experience with the Temple sacrifices in Jerusalem,[35] is supported in this view by Josephus, the historian who, as a member of a priestly family, had ample opportunities to take part in and witness the Temple cult, and who similarly claimed that the feasting following the sacrifices leads to 'feelings of mutual affection'.[36] Jewish festivals, as Sanders points out, partly created and partly reflected the feeling of solidarity of the people.[37]

Food and feasting were regarded as God's blessing by the Jews. Various parties or sects may have had their peculiar interpretations of purity rules, and there may even have been some 'food extremists', some worried about the distance to which dishes containing the sabbath meal could be carried in order to be shared with neighbours, others who would rather starve than eat unclean food, but they all celebrated Israel's festivals with eating and drinking and regarded food with respect as a gift and a part of the great good that was God's creation. What is more, God expected that in return for his bounty his people would also show generosity by feeding the needy.[38]

Jewish wisdom literature advised moderation and good manners and preached against adultery, laziness, greed and drunkenness.[39] Generosity with food was highly valued.

> People bless the one who is liberal with food and their testimony to his generosity is trustworthy.
> The city complains of one who is stingy with food and their testimony to his stinginess is accurate.[40]

Depriving one of food without cause was a sign of greed and wickedness; by some it was used as stern and harsh punishment for certain offences. The Qumran sectarians, whose perfectionist views on what constituted true purity seem to have separated them from their Jewish contemporaries, lived a communal life and shared their daily meals. These meals were of utmost importance for the participants. Exclusion from the common 'Pure Meal' was used by the community as stern punishment for insubordination of its members.[41] That food deprivation was regarded as punishment and that it was often used as self-punishment, and not only by sectarians but by many Jews, will be seen in the following discussion of fasting.

As noted above, holiness for the Jews consisted in observing strictly all the commandments, while sin was any transgression of the Law. God's Law was to be observed diligently, as the writer of Deuteronomy instructs, 'so that it may go well with you, and so that you may multiply greatly in a land flowing with milk and honey'.[42]

Jews of later ages also generally expected their reward and punishment to be justly meted out by God in this world. As Josephus testifies, 'People who conform to the will of God, and do not venture to transgress laws that have been excellently laid down, prosper in all things beyond belief',[43] but those who transgress end up in disaster. The promise is often spelled out in detail: 'He will bless the fruit of your womb and the fruit of your ground, your grain and your wine and your oil, the increase of your cattle and the issue of your flock.'[44] The land of the promise was a good land, 'a land of wheat and barley, of vines and fig trees and pomegranates, a land of olive trees and honey, a land where you may eat bread without scarcity.... You shall eat your fill.'[45]

The rewards for living according to God's laws are explicitly spelled out in the Bible[46] together with the dire consequences of their transgression. A thundering storm of curses is promised to descend upon Israel for disobedience. Famine, infertility, plagues, pestilence and dispersion among the nations and more will fall upon them for not keeping God's commandments.[47]

FASTING AMONG THE JEWS

As was seen above, the concept of sin in the Mosaic Law is unambiguous; any transgression of the Law is an abomination in the eyes of the all-seeing God, whose vengeance strikes terror into the whole community. The wages of sin is death! Death by stoning, chopping off of limbs, and excision of the individual from the community were the Biblical punishments for intentional transgressions. Sacrifice and public confession with a contrite heart were required to atone for sins inadvertently committed. God, the giver of the Law, inspired fear, but did not require self-denial or mortification of the flesh.[48]

There is only one fast ordained by God in the Mosaic Law:

> Now, the tenth day of this seventh month is the day of atonement; it shall be a holy convocation for you: you shall *deny yourselves* and present the Lord's offering by fire; and you shall do no work during that entire day; for it is a day of atonement, to make atonement on your behalf before the Lord your God.... from evening to evening you shall keep your sabbath.[49]

Although the Hebrew does not use the word for fasting, צֹום (*tzom*), but the expression עִנּוּיְפֶשׁ (*inui nephesh*) that is here translated, not very exactly, as 'deny yourselves' ('constrict' or 'humble' your 'person' or your 'self' may express the Hebrew better), it seems that the command was interpreted from earliest times[50] by the Jews to mean a total fast, the strictest abstaining from all food and drink from sundown to sundown.[51]

In addition to the God-ordained Day of Atonement, there are numerous fasts recounted in the narrative of the Old Testament, which seem to be spontaneous or ritualized responses to collective or individual misfortune. There are some notable exceptions. Moses while receiving the Law from God goes without eating and drinking for forty days.[52] This is often seen as a conscious preparation for prophecy, a method for inducing a state of susceptibility to visions.[53] A closer reading of the text gives a different impression. The first forty days' abstention of Moses signifies that for this time he was in the actual presence of God; lifted out of normal human experience he needed no food or water.[54] He did not use the fast as a method for producing the theophany. His second fast on Mount Horeb, after he had smashed in anger the tablets of the Law, is of a different nature: 'Then I lay prostrate before the Lord .... I neither ate bread nor drank water, *because of all the sin you had committed*.'[55] Superhuman effort as it was, the motivation for it was similar to most other fasts in the Bible: the expiation of sin.

The fasts of the Israelites express feelings of guilt, sorrow, fear and suffering. David and his men mourned and fasted on receiving the news of the deaths of Saul and Jonathan.[56] The men who burned the bodies and buried the bones of the king and his son fasted seven days as a communal ritual of mourning. Upon the killing of Abner, David commanded Joab and all the troops who were with him, and were thus implicated in the murder, to 'tear your garments, put on sackcloth and mourn before Abner'.[57] David also fasted till sundown to demonstrate remorse for Abner's death.

David fasted and lay all night on the ground and pleaded with God for the life of his sick child. When the child died he did not fast any more but rose, anointed himself, worshipped God, ate and went to console his wife and made love to her. When his lack of fasting for the dead child gave rise to comment he explained:

> While the child was still alive, I fasted and wept; for I said, 'Who knows? the Lord may be gracious to me and the child may live.' But now he is dead, why should I fast? Can I bring him back again? I shall go to him, but he will not return to me.[58]

The sentiment so simply and touchingly expressed here will later inform the rabbis, who advised against fasting and other extreme expressions of grief in mourning, as we shall see below.

The rending of garments, the wearing of sackcloth and covering the head with dust or ashes were not ordained for the Day of Atonement but were added to fasting when the purpose of the fast was to cry out for God's help, to catch his attention and beg for forgiveness or for his direct intervention in terminating calamity or averting disaster. Ahab, when realizing that he did what was evil in the sight of the Lord, 'tore his clothes and put sackcloth over his bare flesh; he fasted, lay in sackcloth and went about dejectedly.' His self-humiliation achieved its goal, for the Lord did not bring disaster in his days.[59]

Fasting in wartime is aimed at gaining God's direct intervention or guidance.[60] Fasting is connected with other ritual expressions of repentance, such as weeping and public confession, and was often followed by sacrifice, a custom that may have become ritualized in the Temple sacrifice of sin-offering, although there is no mention of fasting before the sacrifice, except for the Day of Atonement in Leviticus or Deuteronomy.

In addition to touching God this kind of pious self-abasement not infrequently made a significant and forceful impression on the bystanders. Ezra prayed and made confession, weeping and throwing himself down before the house of God, and thus compelled the men of Israel to swear to divorce their foreign wives.[61] On occasion, fasting could be used for illicit purposes and even for mischief. Saul fasted to compel the spirit of the dead Samuel to rise, after he himself forbade the use of this sort of magic as displeasing to God.[62] Jezebel plotted the downfall of Naboth by having the elders and nobles of the city declare a fast.[63]

In the later biblical period, other regular community fasts may have been instituted, among these the one on the 9th of Av to commemorate the destruction of the Temple.[64]

In contrast to fasting motivated by guilt and fear of disaster, habitual abstinence as an ascetic routine for the pious seems to be a late development, attested only in post-biblical literature of the Second Temple period, in the Apocrypha and pseudepigrapha.[65] The impulse giving rise to the protracted or habitual fasting varies from an exaggerated need to prolong mourning,[66] to show total dedication to the service of God,[67] to controlling the appetites in order to prevent sin and to purify the soul.[68] This last type reflects dualistic conceptions that emphasize the dichotomy of body and soul and urge disdain for the material world. As Fraade, who perceives the presence of 'ascetical tensions' in ancient Judaism, argues, the dualism expressed in some of the Apocryphal writings is not as radical as certain Greek forms that influenced it; nevertheless it 'does presuppose a "spirit" that links humans with God and a "body" that links them with the earth'.[69] This view would imply that in ascetic fasting, consciously aimed at subduing normal bodily impulses, this earthly part of the personality is punished while the 'spiritual' one is seen as somehow liberated. In all dualistic conceptions, whether mild or radical, the two aspects into which the personality is split are never equal; the higher the 'spirit' is valued the worse treatment the 'body' can expect. Fasting bouts tend to get longer and more pronounced in apocryphal writings,[70] but the overwhelming emphasis still seems to be put *not* on constant 'mortification of the flesh' for the sake of the spirit, but, as in the Biblical literature, on mourning, on repentance and on supplication to God for forgiveness. As M.E. Stone writes in his commentary on Fourth Ezra, it is difficult to regard the fasting and abstinence in this work as due to ascetic ideas about the need to purify the body, or even as an apocalyptic visionary discipline. It should rather be seen as related to repentance, which, by common Jewish practice, was signalled by prayer, lamentation and fasting.[71]

Fasting when facing serious trouble seems to have remained an ingrained, habitual reaction of the Jews, both as individuals and as a community, following the great national upheavals in the first and second centuries that destroyed the Temple and irretrievably ended all hope of political independence from Rome. The reorganization of Jewish community life after these disasters, when Torah scholars and teachers portrayed themselves as the leaders and central figures of Jewish self-government, is known as the rabbinic period. We turn now to an examination of attitudes to fasting reflected in the literary products of this period, which will take us far beyond the first century AD into late antiquity. The Mishnah and the Talmud were compiled between 200 and 600 AD, long after Christianity had parted from Judaism. However, Christian writers of late antiquity like Origen, Jerome and others often claimed to have had converse with Jewish religious experts. Moreover, as will be seen in later chapters, the Church throughout the period of late antiquity was frequently disturbed by so-called Judaizers, Christians who wanted to follow some Jewish customs. It is often unclear whether these Judaizers were impressed by the customs of their Jewish contemporaries or only by the Jewish Bible or whether they were indeed Jews who had turned to Christ. For this reason it may be of interest to follow Jewish attitudes to food and fasting into the rabbinic literature and to see if and how these differed from those expressed in the earlier Biblical works.

It has often been pointed out that the use of rabbinical literature for the purpose of building an accurate historical picture is fraught with danger.[72] As H.L. Strack and G. Stemberger point out in their *Introduction to the Talmud and Midrash*, this body of literature represents the testimony of a single group within Judaism, a group that in all probability ascended slowly to a position of recognized leadership, and their party's literature only gradually became the near canonical literature of Judaism. Thereafter, the self-understanding of the rabbis shaped all tradition, since no other contemporary party of Judaism has left any literary evidence.[73]

ATTITUDES TO FASTING IN RABBINIC LITERATURE

It appears that by the time the Mishnah and the Talmud were being compiled, in the early centuries of the common era, fasting as part of the ritual of mourning lost its importance and may even have been actively discouraged.[74] It retained importance, however, for averting disaster and for repentance.

In the Mishnah, the late second-century AD compilation of accumulated Oral Law,[75] there are two tractates devoted to matters related to fasting; the first, *Yoma*, is concerned with matters pertaining to the Day of Atonement, the second, *Taanith*, with other fasts. In addition to these there are scattered references to fasting in other tractates.

Taanith[76] deals with the special fasts decreed upon the community by its leaders on account of the failure of the autumnal rains. In an agricultural community the continued drought, a disaster, was regarded as a sign of God's anger evoked by some transgression of the community. To expiate for the sin and to avert calamity, a mild, three-day fast is ordered, each of the three fast days separated from the next one by non-fast days; thus as a rule, the fast was to start on a Monday, was then taken up again and continued on Thursday and was finally concluded on the following Monday. Fasting on all three days meant abstaining from food and drink from sunrise to sundown of the same day. Working, bathing and anointing the body, the wearing of shoes and marital intercourse were all permitted to the fasters at this stage. If this did not suffice to placate God and to bring down the rain, then increasingly more severe fasts were introduced, during which working, bathing, wearing of shoes and sexual intercourse were also forbidden.[77] If all these did not bring rain then the ark was carried out into the open place of the town, dust sprinkled on it and on the heads of the people,[78] twenty-four benedictions were to be said over the community and sermons on repentance preached by the most pious of the elders.[79]

The communal public fast on the 9th of Av was now to commemorate not only the destruction of Solomon's Temple[80] but also that of the Second Temple and a number of other disasters that befell the People of Israel in their long history.[81] By the time of the completion of the Babylonian Talmud, fasting as a substitute for the sacrificial sin-offering is explicitly acknowledged:

> When Rab Shesheth[82] kept a fast, on concluding his prayer he added the following: Sovereign of the Universe, Thou knowest full well that in the time when the Temple was standing, if a man sinned he used to bring a sacrifice, and though all that was offered of it was its fat and blood, atonement was made for him therewith. Now I have kept a fast and my fat and blood have diminished. May it be Thy will to account my fat and blood which have been diminished as if I had offered them before Thee on the altar, and do Thou favour me.[83]

The rabbis generally insisted on the nature of the sabbath as a joyous feast and did not allow any fast to encroach upon it,[84] with the exception of the Day of Atonement. Fasting was also prohibited on the eve of festivals and the festivals proper, on the eve of New Moon and on the New Moon.[85] Fasting was forbidden to the inhabitants of a city under siege or one endangered by floods, to those on board a ship, 'for a person pursued by Gentiles or by brigands or by a demon, for all these it is not right to afflict themselves by fasting, otherwise they would not conserve their strength'.[86] The concern with saving life and health generally overrode the wish for fasting. Children, pregnant women and nursing mothers fasted lightly or not at all.[87]

In addition to these communal fasts, rabbinic literature attests to the extensive use of private fasts undertaken by extremely pious individuals, with the purpose of strengthening their prayer, trying to avert disaster and for atonement for sins. Some of these offences for which the pious rabbis fasted until their 'teeth were blackened' were so minor that the self-induced punishment for it seems out of all proportion.[88] For example, R. Elazar b. Azariah[89] for voicing a dissenting opinion,[90] R. Joshua[91] for using insulting words about an opinion of the school of Shammai[92] and R. Shimon[93] for making derogatory remarks about R. Aqiba,[94] all fasted 'until their teeth were black'.[95] The story of Rab Hiyya b. Ashi[96] is worth relating for it may throw some light on Jewish ascetic piety. The hero of the story appears at first glance as a fully fledged pious ascetic, devoted to guarding his chastity, who metes out upon himself extreme punishment when he loses it. The first impression, however, is deceptive. Like most Talmudic tales, Rab Hiyya's story acquires depth of meaning on a closer look. As the story is told, Rab Hiyya, motivated by excessive piety, lived apart from his wife for years. Presumably to test his resolve, his wedded wife visited him one day, dressed as a harlot. Needless to say she succeeded in seducing him. Even after realizing her identity, he was tormented by a sense of guilt and kept repeating: 'But I intended to sin!' He starved himself to death, trying to expiate his sin!'[97] The story makes a very fine moral point indeed. The pious Jew, who stayed away from the bed of his wife in order to be able to pray constantly in ritual purity, did not punish himself for embracing his own wife. Rab Hiyya knew the Law according to which marital embrace was both a God-granted pleasure and a God-commanded duty. The ritual impurity it purveyed was temporary and removable by immersion. Sexual intercourse with one's wife was most certainly not a sin; and a Torah-scholar like Rab Hiyya knew it. On the other hand, he also knew it well enough that whoring and adultery were most grievous sins indeed. He punished himself, not for embracing his own wedded wife but for the sinful fantasy he entertained of embracing a harlot![98]

Alongside the reverence for the fasting of some extremely pious rabbis, there are strong objections in both the Jerusalem and Babylonian Talmud against the practice. 'Too many fasts trouble the community unduly'; 'Whosoever fasts (for the sake of self-affliction) is termed a sinner'; 'How could then a man who fasts be called holy seeing that he humiliates God (who dwells within him) through fasting.'[99] The sages declared that one should not fast since fasting may cause illness, and in addition one may become a public burden. Scholars, especially young ones, were denounced for fasting.[100] The fasting of the biblical heroine Esther was highly respected; however, some rabbis strongly disapproved of ascetic women of their own time, condemning especially abstemious widows and 'fasting maids'.[101]

The rabbis objected also to the habitual rejection of meat and wine as an ascetic practice, even if it was motivated by the best of intentions, by mourning for the destruction of the Temple.

> From the day on which the Temple was destroyed, it would have been reasonable not to eat meat and not to drink wine. But a court does not make a decree for the community concerning things which the community simply cannot bear....
>
> After the last Temple was destroyed, abstainers became many in Israel, who would not eat meat or drink wine, for they were offered in the Temple and now they are not. He said to them 'But if so, we also should not eat bread, for from it did they bring the Two Loaves and the Show-Bread. We also should not drink water, for they did pour out water offering on the festival of Atseret ...' They fell silent. He said to them 'My children, to mourn too much is not possible.'[102]

The two rabbinic views given here both face up to the immensity of the disaster that befell the Jews and their need for mourning. Both are concerned, however, with the life of the community and as a consequence discourage practices of extreme self-punishment.

That fasting could be substituted for the sin-offering sacrifice, expressed so poignantly by a third-century rabbi, as we have seen above, may have been recognized also in earlier times. Fasting had the obvious advantage over the sacrifice that it could be done in any place, while sacrifice was offered only in the Temple. If so, then fasting could be expected to grow in importance in the Diaspora for Jews who could not reach the Temple in Jerusalem, and for all Jews after the destruction of the Temple, which put an end to sacrificial ritual.

FOOD AND FASTING AMONG JEWS IN THE DIASPORA

Many ancient authors indeed attest that fasting was a conspicuous feature of Diaspora Judaism. Philo testifies that in Alexandria the fast on the Day of Atonement: 'is carefully observed not only by the zealous for piety and holiness but also by those who never act religiously in the rest of their life'.[103]

Greek and Roman writers often describe Jews as fasting; more than that, they write as if fasting were a peculiarly Jewish trait. They often claim that the Jewish sabbath is a fast day, which is rather curious, since rabbinic Law expressly forbids fasting on the sabbath.[104] Jewish fasting is mentioned by Tacitus,[105] Suetonius,[106] Fronto,[107] Strabo[108] and others.[109] The fasting Jewish woman must have been a figure familiar enough among the readers of Martial for the poet to use it to evoke a vivid, if unflattering, olfactory image: the odour of the breath of fasting Sabbatariae.[110]

Fasting, the keeping of the sabbath[111] and circumcision were regarded by the ancient witnesses as the customs that identified and defined the Jews. Few of these writers show any depth of interest or understanding of Jewish customs and many of them are disdainful of or downright hostile to the Jews. On the other hand, ancient evidence also testifies to a considerable interest and attraction that Judaism evoked in peoples coming in contact with the Jews. These sources seem to suggest that the Jews both attracted and accepted proselytes and that there were sizeable crowds of 'God-fearers' around Jewish communities. Modern scholars disagree on the presence or absence of a strong missionary proselytizing zeal in Judaism of the ancient world.[112] Whether they actively recruited followers or just accepted those who came fired by their own quest, the Jews must have made attempts to explain their way of life to those interested to follow, or at least to counter the many misconceptions and unfriendly opinions manifested on the part of some educated pagans. In service of either of these needs one would expect the Jews to respond and defend or explain their customs.

The only written evidence for this kind of apologetic effort on behalf of Jews comes from Philo of Alexandria (c. 20 BC – c. AD 50) and Flavius Josephus (c. AD 38 – after 100). For the topic under consideration, Jewish attitudes to food, Philo is the more interesting of these two writers. Philo was a wealthy Alexandrian Jew, who had the benefit of the best of Greek education.[113] As a Hellenized Jewish theologian he attempted to harmonize the Pentateuch with Greek philosophy. Philo was deeply and passionately committed to two cultures; his lifelong aim, to which all his efforts were mobilized, was to unite in a harmonious and blissful marriage Hellenistic philosophy and *paideia* with Jewish religion and morality. Taking the tool of allegorical interpretation, invented to give new meaning to the Homeric pantheon, he tried to invest the Jewish Scriptures with the spirit of Platonic theology and Stoic ethics.[114] Allegorizing the Law, however did not release the Jew from the keeping of its literal meaning. Philo insisted on the meticulous observance of the letter of the Mosaic Law as the infallibly revealed will of God. The allegorical method, a clever sophistical device, enabled him to evade the difficulties caused by some parts of the Bible that he thought unpalatable for educated Greek sensibilities. By this method he rationalized what he deemed superstitions and claimed that the best of Greek thought was learned from Moses. As will be seen in later chapters, Philo's influence on Christianity was substantial;[115] on his fellow Jews it seems negligible. With the exception of Josephus, there is no evidence that either Jews or Greeks paid any attention to him, until the early Christians discovered him as a kind of 'fellow traveller'.

Unfortunately there is no way of telling how characteristic Philo's attitudes, especially those that concern us here, are of Diaspora Jews of his age. His attitudes to food are quite distinct from all that we have discussed so far in this chapter. Since his influence is more discernible on Christians than upon Jews, specific aspects of his thought will be discussed in more detail in the chapters dealing with Alexandrian Christians. Here only a few general points need to be mentioned about him and what he may reveal to us about attitudes to eating or fasting in Philo's Alexandria.

Philo's ethical writings are steeped in a radically dualistic, Platonic conception of the universe, and consequently often express an ascetic world-negating view according to which the 'flesh' is a hindrance to the spirit,[116] the soul dwells in the body as in a tomb, or as a variant, the soul carries the body around as a corpse,[117] which is 'the dwelling place of endless calamities'.[118] The sharp antithesis of soul and matter is an attitude more congenial to Pythagorean or Platonist dualism than to Biblical Judaism, which Philo aimed to explain to his readers.

The purpose of man, as Philo sees it, is to rise to the eternal world of mind (or intellect or God), which can only be achieved by suppressing all responsiveness to the pull of the sensible world.[119] Added to his devotion to Platonic dualism, Philo's thought is gripped by an obsessive concern with personal piety; these in combination lead him to take rather large liberties with the Biblical text, forcing meanings where they actually do not belong.

From Platonic philosophy Philo took the idea of the separation of the world into a lower, material and a higher or intelligible realm. Truth can be attained only in this upper realm of reason and ideas. From the Stoics he took the doctrine of the four passions: anger, grief, fear and pleasure. Despite the elaborate Stoic trappings in his writing the basic tenets of Stoicism were abhorrent to Philo. His Jewish piety did not square with the idea that the aim achieved by controlling the passions is godlikeness and superior power. The Stoic ideal that Horace expressed so succinctly: 'a man is master of his fate and captain of his soul' was, in Philo's eyes, a vain and dangerous delusion. For him the aim of controlling the passions was to leave the material realm and arrive at the highest spiritual plane in total slave-like submission to God: 'To be the slave of God is the highest boast of man, a treasure more precious not only than freedom, but than wealth and power and all that mortals most cherish.'[120]

Philo's main motive force was extreme piety. Contemplation of the deity, he thought, could be achieved only by the soul in a disembodied state, which demanded the suppressing of all passions in the living person. The control of the 'passions' and the disdain for the pleasures of the flesh were common moralizing topoi, shared by Cynics, Stoics and Platonists in the Hellenistic world.[121] In Philo's religious piety the 'passions' were to be eliminated and the body rejected. Curiously the 'passions' against which he struggled most were not the Stoics' anger, fear or pity but mainly those of 'the belly and what is underneath it'. The amount of space and emphasis that the dangers of gluttony receive in Philo's work reveals an obsessive fear of overeating and fatness that is remarkable and rare in ancient Jewish sources.[122] For Philo the pleasures of the table 'produce drunkenness, daintiness and greediness. These causing the cravings of the belly to burst out and fanning them into a flame, make the man a glutton, while they also stimulate and stir up the stings of sexual lusts.'[123] He preached ceaselessly against the pleasures of the senses, against gluttony, and venery. Sometimes his sensibilities, however, were offended by the more ostentatious accompaniments of ascetic discipline. So he writes:

> If thou observest anyone not taking food or drink when he should, or refusing to use the bath and oil, or careless about his clothing, or sleeping on the ground ... and on the strength of all this fancying that he is practising self-control, take pity on his mistake ... for all these practices of his are fruitless and wearisome labours, prostrating soul and body by starving and in other ways maltreating them.[124]

These external trappings of the Cynic way of life did not please an ardent Platonist like Philo; he deplored in such ostentatious self-mortifying practices the lack of prominence that should have been given to learning. True asceticism for Philo was embodied in a community of religious Jews, the Therapeutae. In his treatise, *On the Contemplative Life*, he describes their solitary but still communal life of total dedication to study and meditation on the Jewish Law and philosophy. This ideal community is both vegetarian and celibate:

> none of them would put food or drink to his lips before sunset since they hold that philosophy finds its right place in the light, the needs of the body in the darkness. ... Some in whom the desire for studying wisdom is more deeply implanted even only after three days remember to take food. Others so luxuriate and delight in the banquet of truths which wisdom richly and lavishly supplies that they hold out for twice that time and only after six days do they bring themselves to taste such sustenance as is absolutely necessary.[125]

His highly idealized and mostly imaginary communities share many of those physical austerities that he found ostentatious in others who, presumably, indulged in these for reasons other than philosophy. Their long-term endurance without physical sustenance is certainly more severe than that which the Cynics advocated, namely, to live on the simplest food that could be obtained without effort by begging.[126] In his more restrained and realistic moods, Philo too would grant the satisfaction of the actual necessities of life which enable us to live in health and free from sickness.[127]

Even the highly valued contemplative life, which meant for him the total withdrawal from the world of 'sense perception', he would only recommend to those over the age of fifty, for the duty of the Jewish man before this age is to marry and raise a family and attend to his business, therefore to live in the world, in the realm of the senses.[128]

Despite the occasional allowances he made for the satisfaction of needs without which the life of the individual and the community could not proceed, by high-handedly reinterpreting the Bible, Philo proposed an ethics that turned its back on the biological nature of the human being, and in this he remains quite unique in the Jewish tradition that we have surveyed. The high values he attributes to virginity and celibacy, the worshipful picture he paints of the holy philosopher who is nourished by the Law and needs no food more than once a week, and then only bread and water, all these conflict with Jewish custom. He himself was often aware of this conflict. And so were, in later ages, those who preferred to regard him as a Christian.

CONCLUSIONS

As this review of Jewish literature shows, fasting for the purpose of atonement came to the Jews together with the concept of an all-seeing God, the God-given Law and the concept of sin as transgression of the Law. Where there is sin there is need for means of expiation. The main attested function of fasting in Jewish literature was penitence, expiation for transgression, the humbling of the self in order to arouse the pity of the Deity. Fasting was also used as an expression of mourning for disasters that befall the nation and thus as a means of reinforcing national cohesion. Both eating with gratitude for God's bounty and fasting with a contrite heart thus became a code of communication between God and humankind, symbols in a language that communicated to God the people's acceptance of His rule and their need for His mercy. This same language of food laws and fasting applied not only to the discourse with God but also in the discourse between men, symbolizing community, belonging or exclusion. Food and fasting was, and to many Jews still is, a part of what Sanders defined as a 'pattern of religion'.[129] One of the signs of entering the Jewish religion and staying in it is the keeping of the food regulations and fasting on the Day of Atonement. Food and fasting in antiquity thus played an important part in the definition and self-definition of the Jew. Fasting, whether communal or individual, meant total abstinence from food and drink, both in the Bible and in the Talmud. The duration of most fasts was from sunrise to sunset, that on the Day of Atonement lasted from sunset to sunset.

Individual fasting had many motives from simple piety to the ostentation of holiness. Fasting may have provided a new arena for competition, in which even those with little learning and humble status in the community could compete in holiness with the high and mighty.[130] Special fasts may, on occasion, have been employed by women, who were excluded from most cultic practice in Judaism, as an exhibition of piety or a means of avoiding some burdens of married life, even as a weapon in domestic squabbles. This seems to be suggested by clauses in the Law that empower fathers and husbands to annul the vows of their womenfolk, if these displease them.[131] There is no evidence that fasting was widely employed as a means of bringing on dreams or prophecy,[132] or to communicate with the spirits of the dead;[133] nor for fasting as purification or as a response to fear of demonic invasion of the body through food.[134]

Even the extended and habitual fastings that appear in post-Biblical sources seem to have either atonement or mourning for national disasters as their motivation rather than a pronounced negative valuation of 'the flesh' based upon a radical dualism. It seems safe to conclude that the ethics taught by most Jewish literature of antiquity is based on a clear acceptance of the biological aspects of the human being. Philo's voice sounded a different note. Under the influence of Platonic dualism, this Hellenized Jew of monumental piety felt the body to be a hindrance in the soul's progress toward the divine, but most often even he advised strict self-control rather than active mortification of the flesh.

2

THE GRAECO-ROMAN
BACKGROUND

The Christian message was carried from Roman Syria-Palestine through cities and towns of the eastern Mediterranean and inland Asia Minor. As evidenced by the extant texts, it seems to have been carried in its beginnings and for some time to come by Greek-speaking apostles to Greek-speaking peoples. Even when it reached Rome and the West, the language of Christianity remained predominantly Greek until the late second century or the beginning of the third, the time of the first surviving Christian writings in the Latin language. However varied the ethnic and cultural character of the vast areas through which the early Christian messengers travelled,[1] they shared two conditions: the Greek language, which carried with it, at least potentially, shared cultural habits and assumptions; and Roman rule. The more Christianity distanced itself from the Jews, the more it became pressed by the Graeco-Roman cultural milieu. Christian converts born into this culture shared with their non-Christian neighbours experiences, ideas and customs that the adoption of a new faith did not touch directly or, even if it did, could not eradicate completely or change. Early Christian sources reveal the various strategies Christians developed that would allow them to reject some of these cultural influences and to acknowledge others, and in both instances to demonstrate their own superiority.[2] The present chapter will focus attention on ideas and practices concerning food and drink in this Graeco-Roman 'pagan'[3] milieu. First the role of food in religion and civic ceremonial will be examined; then we shall survey ideas concerning the importance of food in health and the 'good life' in the discussions of philosophers, sophists, physicians and other self-appointed guardians of public health and decency.

FOOD AND FASTING IN GRAECO-ROMAN RELIGION

The divine power that gave life was also believed to provide sustenance for it; food, upon which all life depends, has played an important role in all ancient religions. Unlike the Jews, whose jealous god demanded exclusive allegiance, most other inhabitants of the Empire were free to worship supernatural forces in a rich variety of forms and shapes.[4] The central act in the worship of all deities was the sacrifice. This awesome ceremony of bloodshed and fire, relating food to life and life to food, was the heart of religious ritual not only for the Jews but to all ancient religion.

As in the Temple cult of the Jews, so too in polytheistic sacrifice something of life was solemnly given over to the superhuman power, who in turn would give continuing life to the worshipper. Walter Burkert, in his anthropological study of ancient Greek sacrifice and myth, puts the origin of the sacrificial ritual long before Jews or Greeks appeared on the scene, even before agriculture. He sees the sacrifice as an attempt to expiate guilt of bloodshed in early prehistoric hunting groups:[5] 'Sacrifice as an encounter with death, an act of killing that simultaneously guarantees the perpetuation of life and food, grew out of the existence of the Palaeolithic hunter and remained the formative core of the sacred ritual.'[6] Most of the ancient sources upon which our knowledge of sacrificial rites are based, however, are products of settled agricultural communities.

Gods were plentiful in the ancient world, and their nature and form of representation varied with each city, locality or tribe. The expression of human desire to reach towards the deity, on the other hand, was universally limited to about three general categories: ascertaining the will of the god, entreaty, and thanksgiving. Divination, the ascertaining of the will of god, could be executed by watching the flight of birds, by observing prodigies, the occurrences of various rare, unexpected or 'unnatural' phenomena, but most often as a part of a sacrifice, where the liver and other internal organs of the newly slaughtered victim were inspected by the adept for what they would reveal of the will of the gods. Sacrifice was used both as an entreaty and as thanksgiving, while prayer was ubiquitous on the part of the devout.[7] Libation, sacrifice, first-fruit offering, these acts that defined piety, all had to be accompanied by the right words, the invocation and entreaty. There is rarely a ritual without prayer and no important prayer without ritual. As Burkert argues from Greek literary sources, prayer with sacrifice is an ancient and fixed conjunction.[8]

Holidays break up the monotony of the endless succession of nights and days and invest time with meaning. Calendars come into being in order to define time, to separate it into units, to make some days or nights different from others. Time is made meaningful by the things that are observed to happen in time. The happenings that were significant to early agrarian communities were the seasonal changes in nature. Early calendars, and even later ones, reflected the works and days of the agricultural year. Once the year has been divided into smaller units, important events in the life of the community could be kept in mind and milestones in the life of the individual remembered and celebrated. Among pagans, just as among the Jews (and among Christians too, later, after they were forced by the need that seems to be universal to recognize the importance of 'days'), the marking of time, the separation of the holy day from the everyday, was a religious function in the hands of those officials whose task it was to mind the deities and minister to them. Cicero was only describing what he knew to be the custom in Rome when he prescribed that 'whoever plans the official year ought to arrange that these festivals shall come at the completion of the various labours of the farm', while the dates of the festivals should be arranged so that:

> the offering of first fruits and offering of the flocks ... may be maintained ... and so that no violation of these customs shall take place, the priests shall determine the mode and the annual circuit of such offerings; and they shall prescribe the victims which are proper and pleasing to each of the gods.[9]

Pagan holidays generally included colourful processions, pageantry and sacrificial offerings to the gods. In both Greek and Roman usage, sacrifice meant offerings of animals, cereals or vegetables, most commonly those kinds that were highly valued by humans for their own sustenance. Garlands of flowers and tree leaves were often used as festive decorations on cult statues and altars but in themselves they were not considered sacrificial offerings and neither were wild animals, no matter how rare or exotic, nor the prey of the huntsman.[10] Sacrifice meant communion between the god and the worshippers, which culminated in the consumption of food and drink with the god or in the presence of the god. The gods wanted for their part the same as what mortals liked to eat, cakes of wheat and barley, salt, fruits and honey, but, like their mortal devotees, they too preferred most of all, meat and wine.[11]

From the time of Homer, when these rites were practised by small agrarian communities, through the centuries of Greek and Roman history up to the eventual suppression of the ritual by the Christian authorities in the late Empire, the basic structure of the sacrificial rite remained surprisingly constant. Some complex rituals, like the Greek Thesmophoria or the Roman Bona Dea[12] left room for a great variety of symbolic interpretations. The sacrificial act itself, however, did not deviate significantly from Cato's prescription, which is clear and straightforward as to its purpose, and simple and homely as to its manner of execution. The celebrants should be clean; hands should be washed before the offering. After the solemn killing of the animal its entrails are examined for omens, then some wine is poured and the prayer said, the meat is then cut up, the portion for the god is burnt on the altar, the rest is 'roasted or cooked and the feast is consumed by all those present, with the god as the guest of honour.'[13] Whether the sacrifice was carried out in public on a grand scale by emperors or high officials or on a smaller scale by guilds, burial societies or private households, this structure remained constant.[14]

The god, invited as guest of honour to take part in the human banquet, did not always get the choicest pieces of the meat, as Menander the Greek poet complained, for the humans, 'after giving the end of the spine and the gall bladder to the gods – because unfit to eat – gulp the rest themselves!'[15] The rules of some rites explicitly ordered that the meat was to be consumed at the site of the sacrifice. The solemn rites were then followed by the setting up of couches and banqueting tables, and by eating, drinking and merriment. As Mommsen wrote:

> The practical side of the Roman priesthood was the priestly cuisine; the augural and pontifical banquets were as it were the official gala-days in the life of a Roman epicure, and several of them formed epochs in the history of gastronomy: the banquet on the accession of the augur Quintus Hortensius for instance brought roast peacocks into vogue.[16]

Banquets were, however, not restricted to priestly *collegia*, but were a customary part of sacrificial offerings by private individuals or by groups such as professional or cult associations. The people liked the *feriae*, the temples and the ceremonies, and when some gods lost popularity other gods with new rites and holy days took their place. As

R. Lane Fox rightly remarked, at a basic level the pagan cults did indeed satisfy the emotions; they allayed hunger,[17] for the natural aim and outcome of a festival was feasting.[18]

What happened to the meat of the hundreds of animals that were sacrificed in regular yearly public festivals, in supplications and in the occasional triumphs is not immediately obvious. The sources are distinctly uncommunicative about the organization of the distribution of the sacrificial meat. One reason for the silence of the ancient writers concerning this problem may be its sheer banality.[19] The generosity or the wastefulness of an emperor in sacrificing hecatombs or in providing entertainment could be a useful literary device to describe character and to express approbation or derision. Giving an account of how the cow was cut into pieces, how the blood and gore was cleaned up, how the pieces were distributed and to whom, seems to have been a less interesting topic. Consequently, speculations abound. Some claim that the meat of these sacrifices was sold off by the questors for the benefit of the treasury,[20] or that the meat was not distributed among the crowds present but probably reserved for the senators.[21]

In an empire where *liberalitas* and *beneficia* were the self-expressed claim of the aristocracy to fame and legitimacy, and where the emperor's well-orchestrated propaganda presented him as the *pater-familias* with the whole Empire as his *familia*, the keeping up of the role of the ancient head of the household who sacrificed to the gods with the participation of his extended family, the Roman people, necessarily included distribution of some food or gifts as tangible tokens of this participation.[22] As P. Veyne points out, a special, technical vocabulary came into being:[23] sacrifice was followed by an *epulum*, the banquet, a *visceratio*, a distribution of meat, while *crustum* and *mulsum* meant distribution of sweets and cakes. It appears from the sources that when the occasion called for it, Rome and other cities of the Empire could and did include a wider range of the population than just senators in sacrificial feasting.[24]

Feasting was in all ways an integral and deeply satisfying aspect of pagan religious celebrations. Even the dead, scrupulously honoured by the ancients, were treated to it. Not only were they remembered, but their hungry spirit was fed. Food was put in with the corpse at the funeral; food was also sacrificed to the Manes on the anniversary of the parents' death. The scale of this family sacrifice, in most cases, may have been somewhat less grand than the one described by Virgil, where Aeneas fed the ghost of his father, Anchises, with two goblets of unmixed wine, two of fresh milk and two of the blood of the victim, by way of a first course; after which 'two sheep he slays, as is meet, two swine, and as many dark-backed heifers, while he poured wine from bowls and called great Anchises' shade and ghost released from Acheron', while his comrades helped with the slaughter and the roasting of the meat for the feast.[25] According to another poet, Ovid, the Manes were not greedy gods, they could be satisfied with 'a tile wreathed with votive garlands, a sprinkling of corn, a few grains of salt, bread soaked in wine', or some larger offering.[26] For the great and wealthy families, funerals, with portraits of ancestors displayed and carried in procession, were opportunities to affirm their dynastic longevity and social importance. These great funerals also provided opportunity for public feasting. In the words of P. Veyne, 'the life of the plebs in Rome was punctuated by free banquets in memory of the illustrious departed'.[27] Funerals of the rich were public occasions not only in Rome but in Greek cities too,[28] some of which had to control by law the extravagance of these benefactions.[29] Some of the wealthy aspired to be honoured long after their death and left funds and instructions for this purpose. Funerary foundations were common in the Imperial period. Donors who wanted to be remembered donated money or property to groups who came together regularly to sacrifice and feast, forming a community as devotees of a particular deity. The members of these clubs celebrated in their banquets their patron's memory and themselves contributed funds that ensured them decent funerals when they died.[30]

In addition to the public holidays the gods were involved in a number of family events. They were present at all the milestones that mark life's basic pattern: birth, adolescence, marriage and, as we have seen, death.[31] The domestic Genius, a kind of personal guardian who watched over the fertility and continuation of the family, was worshipped, together with various other Immortals, on wedding days and birthdays, on the *dies lustricies* after childbirth, upon reaching adolescence, or full manhood. On these festive family occasions, wine and honey cakes, pigs and lambs were customarily sacrificed and partaken of by the household, the guests and the god.[32]

It seems fair to conclude that eating and drinking were central to pagan religious life, whether in grand public celebrations given by a triumphator or an emperor, or more modest festivities of a club or a family holiday. Food was a part of the religious ceremony, whether only the officiants and their rich guests tasted the meat and the wine while the onlookers got only some small token, or the whole people got sated and drunk.

Despite the often repeated claim that fasting is a universal religious practice,[33] neither Greek nor Roman religious life made much use of it.[34] The general sense of the Greek word νηστεία, as that of the Latin *ieiunium*, is 'not having eaten', 'being without nourishment' or 'suffering hunger'. While both terms are often understood to have the special meaning of abstention from food for religious purposes,[35] neither is limited to this. Even a fish can be described as 'fasting', as Athenaeus testifies (by misquoting Aristotle) about a certain type of mullet believed to be a vegetarian, that 'eats no live bait, nor can he be lured or pulled by meat or by any other living thing'.[36]

And this highlights the other difficulty with both these terms, whether used in religious or non-religious contexts: they may denote anything from complete lack of food and drink to abstinence from just one particular thing. In Jewish literature, as we have seen, fasting was clearly understood as abstaining from all food and drink for a specified period of time.[37] In translations of the Jewish Bible νηστεια or *ieiunium* generally mean total abstention, most often for religious reasons. The same cannot be assumed for Greek and Latin literature.

The second day of the ancient Greek festival, the *Thesmophoria*, was called νηστεία, because it is believed that the Athenian matrons who celebrated the Thesmophoria fasted on this day.[38] But since the women's festival in honour of Demeter and Kore was secret and forbidden to spectators, the nature of their fast is a matter for speculation; this second day may have been a total fast or just an abstention from the 'gifts of Demeter'.[39]

Philo of Alexandria, admittedly not a friendly witness to the pagan customs of his city, did not think the Greeks fasted at all. When describing the strict observance of the Jewish fast day, he points to the Greek 'holy month' as a religious practice that would be comparable in solemnity. The Jewish fast for Philo, however, is highly superior in piety since, in the 'holy month' of the Greeks, 'the untempered wine flows freely, and the board is spread sumptuously and all manner of food and drink are lavishly provided'.[40]

In Rome, following the instruction of the Sibylline Oracles in 191 BC, a *ieiunium* was to be held every fifth year in honour of Ceres. This cult is believed to have been imported from or at least influenced by the Greek rites of Demeter.[41] In the days of Augustus the *ieiunium Cereris* was celebrated on the 4th of October every year. Who abstained, from what and for how long, is not known, but it is most likely that the *ieiunium* consisted of abstaining from 'the gifts of the Goddess', that is cereals. Another extremely hostile witness, the

Christian Jerome, lends support to this, writing at the end of the fourth century that the worshippers of Isis and Cybele, 'in gluttonous abstinence gobble up pheasants and turtle doves all smoking hot, of course to avoid contaminating the gifts of Ceres'.[42]

Fasting had no part in the preparation of priests for sacrifice or for other liturgical functions in Latin and Greek city cults,[43] and neither were the priests and priestesses of the Imperial cult obliged to go without food. Ritual purity necessary for approaching the deity for worship was understood among the pagans, as it was among the Jews, to consist of being free of any defilement contracted by birth, death and sexual discharge.[44] Purification was accomplished most often by bathing and the wearing of special garments and not by fasting. Fasting as a sign and accompaniment of mourning for the dead was probably as common among pagans as we have seen that it was among the Jews.[45]

If austerities, fasts and other self-mortifying practices had no place in state or city cults, they have often been attributed to mystery cults: the religions of Isis, Magna Mater, Cybele and Mithras.[46] Death and rebirth, the celebration of the great cycle of life, were central to the theologies of these.[47] Their ceremonies enacted yearly the life, death and resurrection of a god. Self-mortifications and fasting, when they were present, were in all likelihood associated with the commemoration of the suffering of the god and with mourning for his death, while the usual sacrifice and feasting celebrated his resurrection. Being mysteries, the most important rituals of these religions, like the initiation of the neophytes, were secret. Much of what is said about them in ancient literature comes from their detractors,[48] and from gossip.[49] C.R. Phillips cautions against taking this testimony too seriously by pointing out that their authors tended to identify with antiquity's socio-economic elite, a group that 'regularly disparaged the religious systems of the masses, often as a prelude to grinding their own particular theological axes'.[50]

The most extensive description of the Isiac religion from a sympathetic source is in the eleventh book of Apuleius's *Metamorphoses*, which however provides no evidence for either fasting or other self-mortification on the part of the devotees of Isis. When Lucius, the much-tried hero of Apuleius's novel, is finally allowed to undergo the longed-for initiation into the mysteries of the great goddess Isis, he is asked only to abstain from animal meat and wine and from sexual intercourse[51] for ten days. It should be noted that this regimen did not require him to go hungry, consequently he did not find the purification difficult or stressful. The initiation itself, like any pagan rite, culminated in sacrifice and a sumptuous banquet.[52]

In the same work, Apuleius also acquaints his readers with a group of eunuch priests of the Syrian Goddess.[53] Here he goes along with the upper-class Romans, who generally expressed suspicion and supercilious scorn for these 'half-men'. Lucius, in his asinine form, is sold to a group of these eunuch priests, who soon enough prove themselves to be an abominable bunch of scoundrels. Their main occupation is the procuring of suitable objects for their insatiable lusts by exploiting the credulity and generosity of pious folk. They succeed in fooling rich and poor alike by producing an oracular prophecy that would fit all occasions, and to inspire awe by their frenzied processions accompanied by the rhythm of beating cymbals and flute, their wild shrieking, the rolling of their heads, all culminating in slashing their own flesh with knives and self-flagellation after loud public confession of some religious sin. The spectators were so impressed with what seemed like a most painful expression of religious devotion that they showered them with coins and supplied them with generous quantities of food and wine. The unholy 'priests' then demanded the fattest ram for sacrifice, and prepared a great feast for themselves.[54] So much for austerities!

As Burkert perceived it, the mysteries did not constitute a separate religion outside the public one; they represented a special opportunity for dealing with gods within the multifarious framework of the polytheistic religion of the polis.[55] As noted earlier, the various deities of the Empire seem to have lived side by side in remarkable peace. Being initiated in a new cult did not mean one had to convert and leave behind the old. All the religions shared the common conviction that through sacrifice a sacred communion is reached between the worshipper and the god. Sacrifice was the central feature of pagan religion, purification before approaching the god was generally interpreted as bodily cleanliness: thus one was obliged to wash before offering sacrifice. Some of the priests or priestesses of the oracular temples may have abstained from food before prophesying.[56] Other priests, like those of Isis, in order to 'undertake austere and difficult services in sacred rites' followed a 'continuous and temperate regimen' and abstained from 'many foods and pleasures of love',[57] but habitual fasting was seldom required of the devotees of the gods. Certain old formulas for curing eye disease or sickness of cows were sometimes thought to be more potent if administered on an empty stomach,[58] and the gods may have preferred to appear in the dreams of those who did not overindulge in food and drink before bedtime.[59] In general, however, total fasting did not play any significant part in Graeco-Roman religion. Even a meatless and wineless diet appears to be quite rare in pagan religious practice. Vegetarianism, advocated in some philosophical circles, was generally supported by various arguments that ranged from the religious through the moral to the sheerly practical ones, as will be discussed below.

FOOD AND FASTING IN HEALTH AND THE 'GOOD LIFE'

It appears that the most common entreaty addressed to the gods asked for 'health and strength'.[60] 'Orandum est ut sit mens sana in corpore sano', wrote Juvenal,[61] repeating the age old topos, common to all, that health is the most important boon one can pray for, without which nothing else has much value.

In a world rife with infectious and parasitic disease, war and pestilence, where death was ever present, prayer for *mens sana in corpore sano* was more than just a pious turn of phrase and must indeed have been heartfelt. Diseases, periodic food shortages, malnutrition, urban overcrowding and the lack of even the most rudimentary notions of public hygiene made health indeed a state to pray for. For us today it is hard to conjure up what it was like to live without vaccines, antibiotics, effective pain relievers, even without disinfectants, or soap.[62]

What did the ancients pray for when, bringing votive offerings, they sang paeans to the healing gods and goddesses? Was health in their thoughts only the absence of pain or freedom from the threat of death, or was it something more? Did they wish for it only when it was quite palpably gone, or was it a positive state worthy of constant cultivation? Since modern attitudes to food are often strongly affected by health considerations, it seems reasonable to look for the same in antiquity. An understanding of Graeco-Roman concepts of health may provide some insights into their attitudes to food. In what follows I shall try to explore ideas concerning health and the healthy body, based on texts written during the early centuries of the Roman Empire, and on some that were written much earlier but were still discussed vigorously in this period.

As will be seen, the majority of the texts that are relevant to the topic were written in Greek. Those writing in Latin, like Celsus or Seneca, were familiar with Greek literature. The mental world of those who left us the written evidence was characterized furthermore by an orientation toward the past, more precisely, toward the glorious past of the Greek intellectual heritage.[63]

In particular, the lives and thoughts of ancient Greek philosophers were still of great interest amongst the educated circles of the Roman Empire. Witness to this is the fact that a fair number of books were written about them; one of these, the *Lives of Eminent Philosophers*, written in the early decades of the third century AD by Diogenes Laertius, still survives. How accurately this work represents the views of its subjects may be debated. It must be assumed, however, that any inaccuracies that exist reflect the writer's attempt to cater to the concerns and interests of his contemporaries, and this is what we are interested in.

Diogenes's presentation of the ancient Greek sages shows that the human body, its nature and its health, were topics central to philosophical discourses both in Ethics and Physics. Health played an important role in what the ancient philosophers considered to be the 'good life'. So Plato held that virtue in itself was sufficient for happiness; but it needed, in addition, as instruments for use, bodily advantages like health and strength, and external advantages, such as wealth, good birth and reputation.[64] Both Plato and Aristotle, Diogenes Laertius reminds us, used to divide things in the following manner: 'Goods' are in the mind, or in the body, or external. For example, justice, prudence, courage, temperance, and suchlike, are in the mind; beauty, a good constitution, health and strength are in the body; while friends, the welfare of one's country and riches are among external things.[65] Good health and strength in both mind and body were accorded importance even among the moral precepts of Diogenes the Cynic, who strove for extreme self-sufficiency, and was said to have preferred liberty to anything.[66] Zeno and the Stoic philosophers considered the purpose to be 'life in agreement with nature'. Virtue, which they claimed to be perfection in anything, may be non-intellectual like health and strength, or intellectual like prudence. Health was thought by the Stoics to attend upon and to be coextensive with the intellectual virtue of temperance.[67] Some maintained that health and wealth are 'goods'; others claimed that they are morally indifferent but belong to the class of things 'preferred'. They agreed, however, that the duty incumbent upon man is to live in accordance with virtue and to take proper care of his health.[68] Health of body and tranquillity of mind were the *summum bonum* and the aim of a blessed life for the Epicureans.[69] The Pythagoreans believed in the transmigration of souls and regarded the body as the prison of the soul. But even they preferred to live to a ripe old age in health, for according to their tenets, if they did not take care of this present 'prison', then, as a punishment, their soul would be incarcerated in an inferior one next time. Pythagoras himself was reported to give instruction concerning diet and comportment, the aim of which was to ensure a healthy body and clear mind.[70]

It appears then, from this conspectus of views reported by Diogenes Laertius, that in the High Empire the revered ancient philosophers of Classical Greece were remembered as holding health of the body in high esteem. Moreover, health was for most of them something more than just the absence of pain.[71] The words they use are suggestive. In these writers, as reported by Diogenes, health is almost always coupled with strength, vigour, robustness of constitution, acute senses, and often with beauty. They deemed health indeed worthy of cultivation.

Health meant strength, and strength, robustness and beauty of the body all went together and constituted a state that had to be achieved, cared for and guarded. Ancient writers also pointed to the means by which this blessed state could be achieved:

> From food which being too strong, the human constitution cannot assimilate when eaten, will come pain, disease and death, while from such as can be assimilated will come nourishment, growth and health.[72]

> But eating alone will not keep a man well, he must also have exercise. For food and exercise, while possessing opposite qualities, yet work together to produce health.[73]

These and similar sayings attributed to Hippocrates, the 'father of rational medicine', were well known and often repeated. Inspired by these, a lot of effort was expended both on inquiries into the 'nature' of foodstuffs and arguments about what constitutes the best exercise. Health care thus became not only a concern urged on the individual, but a field of professional expertise, in which physicians, athletic trainers, cooks, bath attendants or massagers, compounders of drugs, and possibly others, competed. Among all these only the medics left written evidence. The others apparently did not advertise themselves by the written word or their writings did not survive. We can only get a glimpse of them and of the techniques they used indirectly from the writings of others.

Athletic trainers turn up in literature all over the Greek-speaking world from the time of Classical Athens up to the Christian Empire. The athletic trainer's job involved the training and care of athletes – that is, boxers, wrestlers, runners, etc. – who from very early times became professionals.[74] Gymnastic training was a part of the general education of the young in Classical Greece, not only for those who were destined to become professional athletes but as a means of maintaining a good constitution. The practice seems to have spread to many parts of the empire with the Greek influence.[75] To gymnastic exercise the Roman institution of the bath was added, and some combination of these two constituted the basic body culture of the empire.

Now as far back as the writing of the Hippocratic treatise *On Ancient Medicine*, a concern with proper diet was seen to be a part of the trainer's expertise, for we read here that 'those who study gymnastics and athletic exercises are constantly making some fresh discovery by investigating ... what food and what drink are best assimilated and make a man grow stronger'.[76]

A more elaborate picture of the profession of the trainer is gained from a rather unexpected source: Philo of Alexandria.[77] It appears that despite his Jewish piety and dualistic disdain for the flesh,[78] Philo held the profession of the athletic trainer in high esteem. The skill of the trainer, he wrote, 'is a sister skill to medicine',[79] and this skill produces 'fitness and good condition'.[80]

Many Greek writers from Euripides onward mention athletic diets only to satirize the heavyweight boxers and wrestlers for overeating. Philo is aware of this literary topos but still he shows respect for the athletic regimen;[81] the diet of athletes produces 'strength and vigour, not pleasure to the senses'.[82] Trainers, according to Philo, not only prescribed for their charges what they should eat, but also how they should eat: 'Trainers urge athletes not to gobble, but to chew slowly so that they may gain strength ... to chew one's food is an important part of one's training'.[83]

The athletic trainer whom we glimpse in Philo's widely scattered remarks is a professional engaged in health care. He prescribes an exercise schedule together with a training diet; he varies both of these as the condition and the progress of his charges demand and he augments the benefit of these by anointing and massage. His indeed is a sister art to that of medicine, since he does to healthy bodies what the physician does to the sick ones.

Another profession with some claim to health care is that of the cook. Cooks are the earliest stock characters in European drama.[84]

Cooks were highly paid and sought-after professionals. From the fifth century BC many cookbooks were written by philosophers, physicians, cooks and gourmets for the instruction of philosophers, physicians, cooks and gourmets.[85] Unfortunately, with the exception of a compilation of recipes that survived in two manuscripts from the late fourth or early fifth centuries under the name of Apicius, and the massive work of Athenaeus from the end of the second or the beginning of third century, none survived. The *Deipnosophistae* of Athenaeus is, on the other hand, a treasure trove of information, gossip, legend, literary quotation, ethnography, potted history, philosophical and medical lore and the like, all centred around dining, food and drink. The massive work is organized on the pattern of the symposium that was a favoured setting for learned relaxation and a popular literary device since Plato and Xenophon. The many cooks that appear in the pages of the *Deipnosophistae* all protest their expertise – some not only in making tasty dishes but also in the various sciences and arts and the care of good health. They claim that the good cook must penetrate nature, know something about medicine, about the seasons, the setting and rising of the stars, in order to be able to prepare food that is nourishing and will be 'properly digested and exhaled' with the 'juices ... distributed evenly in all the passages', for food takes on a different flavour at different times 'in the revolution of the universal system'. In addition, it is useful for him to be skilled also in architecture and the military art of strategy![86] Food prepared without science, warns another cook on the pages of Athenaeus, could result in 'colic and wind ... and make the guests behave with impropriety'.[87] On a less exalted plane, cooks claimed to know 'what was good for digestion, for promoting regularity, and for averting all sort of sicknesses and plagues and chills'.[88]

Guarding health meant guarding the stomach and exercising the muscles. What underpinned the *diaita* or *regimen* of these caretakers of health was the popular conception of the body whose most imperious organ was the stomach, derived not so much from medical lore as from the common experience of its relentless demands, for the fulfilment of which all the rest of the organs of the body were enslaved.[89] To add to this, queasy feelings from the same organ often signalled the end of health and strength. Judging from the frequency they appear in Celsus and other medical writers, stomach upsets and other gastro-intestinal symptoms were very common, possibly due to reasons mentioned earlier, and these were often the forerunners of more serious complaints and the need for the physician.

Ancient science regarded humankind as a privileged but organic part of the universe. The universe, according to some speculations in ancient Physics, was composed of elements. The number and identity of these were matters for debate. Fire, Air, Water and Earth – one, two or all four in combination – were favourite candidates. But there were also dissenting opinions, positing just one basic element, the atom. In medicine there were followers of both views.[90] The four element theory,[91] however, gained the most vociferous adherents, and most surviving texts.

Health, according to most medical philosophies, was some kind of balance, *isonomia* or *symmetria*. For some it was the free, 'balanced' movement of fluids within the body, an 'equilibrium of corpuscles and pores',[92] for others it was the balance of hot and cold, wet and dry,[93] or of the four humours, blood, phlegm, yellow bile and black bile, regarded as 'opposites'.[94]

According to this theory, the body was visualized as a series of interconnecting receptacles for the production and maintenance of the humoral equilibrium, at one end of which food was put in, distilled inside to become blood and the other humours in good measure; if all went well, the undesirable residue came out peacefully at the other end. But if things did not go well and the works got stopped up inside, then the remedy called for the emptying of the system.[95] Blood circulation was not known. Humans were seen to be a part of nature and their dependence on their surroundings was anxiously affirmed.

Seeing health as a precarious balance, the physician shared the common conviction that it was affected first of all by the food one ate, by physical activity, by geographical location and by the climate. The ancient physician, setting himself to the task of combating disease, had to take into account all these factors, together with the age, gender and type of physique of his patient – and 'fight opposites with opposites'. This was the basic rule of Hippocratic therapy, which means that 'diseases due to repletion are cured by evacuation', and, vice versa, that 'those due to exercise are cured by rest, and those due to idleness are cured by exercise'.[96]

While various methods of 'evacuation' were put forward, the physicians in general were not in favour of fasting, even as a treatment of disease. The Hippocratic treatise *On Ancient Medicine* states the general principle firmly:

If a man takes insufficient food, the mistake is as great as that of excess, and the harm just as much. For abstinence has upon the human constitution a most powerful effect, to enervate, to weaken, and to kill. Depletion produces many other evils, different from repletion, but just as severe.... If a man is accustomed to taking two meals a day, *even abstaining from one of these may bring dire consequences*, symptoms of prostrating weakness, trembling, faintness, hollowness of the eyes; his urine becomes paler and hotter, his mouth bitter, his bowels seem to hang; there come dizziness, depression and listlessness. When next he attempts to dine his food is less pleasant, he cannot digest what formerly he used to dine on when he had lunch. The mere food, descending into the bowels with colic and noise, burns them, and disturbed sleep follows, accompanied by wild and troubled dreams.[97]

This vivid and horrifying picture of starvation describes a man who only missed his lunch![98]

The Hippocratic physician felt himself called upon to guard his patient not only in disease but in health as well. The treatises on regimen, especially the *Regimen in Health*, give advice as to the manner of life in each of the four seasons according to age and type of constitution. Food takes up a very large part of the recommendations and so does exercise. In order to protect health and cure disease not only the nature of the body but the nature of the various foodstuffs had to be known. It seems to have been generally held that, just as everything in nature, foodstuffs may also be categorized as 'hot' or 'cold', 'moist' or 'dry'. As such they could be used to good advantage in opposing the dominant attributes of the patient: a hot person may be treated with cooling food, whereas a dry person could be 'moistened' by a judicious choice of diet.[99] To make things somewhat more complicated, foodstuffs were believed to vary also according to a continuum of strength, which it was advisable to match carefully to the constitution of each individual. 'Strong' foods were believed to be most nourishing but hard to digest, 'weak' foods least nourishing but easy to digest. Among the strong foods were counted generally beef and other large domesticated quadrupeds; all large game such as the wild goat, deer, wild boar, wild ass; all large birds, such as the goose, the peacock and the crane; all 'sea monsters', such as the whale and the like; all pulses and bread-stuffs made of grain, honey and cheese. Among foods belonging to the class of medium strength were counted: the hare, birds of all kinds from the smallest up to the flamingo, fish, and root and bulb vegetables. Finally, to the weakest class were thought to belong snails and shellfish, all vegetable stalks, gourds, cucumbers and capers, olives and all orchard fruits. There were differences of opinion as to the categories to which certain items belonged.[100]

Food was seen to affect all aspects of bodily functioning, including sexuality. Food provided the body with the material from which blood was distilled. Semen was thought to be the most highly distilled and 'best blood' produced by the body's 'vital heat', mixed with pneuma, the 'vital spirit'.[101] These in turn were regarded as finite, or at least limited in quantity. Squandering sperm in sexual activity was feared to deplete blood and heat, even the 'vital spirit', causing, at best, fatigue. Strong foods, in addition to being most nutritious, were also 'heating', and for both these reasons thought to be aphrodisiacs: the harder they were to digest, the more they were supposed to increase sexual potency, or at least the desire. In thinking that relied heavily on analogy, 'strong' and 'weak' were loaded with meaning that, while having little to do with nutrition, became attached to food and drink. Thus 'strong' food was also masculine food, food fit for a free man as opposed to 'effeminate' food. Homer's heroes, in the good old days, ate strong food, which they prepared with their own hands; but ever since Lucullus introduced luxury to the Romans, fancy banquets prepared by professional cooks consisted mainly of luxurious 'effeminate' food, according to the fulminations of upright moralists.[102]

The Hippocratic *Regimen in Health* concerns itself with all aspects of life in minute detail. In addition to its attention to the type and quantity of foods, it discusses the qualities and dangers of the seasons of the year, the age groups and the various body constitutions. It regulates exertions, baths, sexual activity, type of clothing and the beds in which one sleeps. All these in turn have to fit the seasons and each individual constitution. Following this view implies that there is no state of health, but only a continuous struggle to become healthy. People are almost completely helpless in the face of all the dangers unless they keep a constant vigil over the state of their bodies and all their activities, or, better yet, if they put themselves in the hands of the physician.

This so-called Hippocratic view dominated medicine in the time of the empire and a very long time thereafter; however, not everyone shared its pessimism regarding the maintenance of health. An important Latin exponent of Greek medicine was Celsus, the author of *De Medicina*, who wrote his work probably during the reign of the emperor Tiberius.

There is a striking and salutary change from the Greek attitude in the views of Celsus concerning the healthy. Contrary to the Hippocratic doctors, the Roman writer is a firm believer in a state of health. A healthy and vigorous man:

> should be under no obligatory rules and have no need, either for a medical attendant, or for a rubber and anointer. His kind of life should afford him variety; he should be now in the country, now in town, and more often about the farm; he should sail, hunt, rest sometimes, but more often take exercise; for whilst inaction weakens the body, work strengthens it; the former brings on premature old age, the latter prolongs youth.[103]

A healthy man can eat as much as he wants, avoiding no kind of food in common use; he can go to banquets, he can overeat sometimes or eat less than usual. While exercise and food are both necessary, the regimen of athletes is not recommended because it is a too demanding routine which interferes with civic life. Sexual intercourse in moderation is not to be feared: 'seldom used it braces the body, used frequently it relaxes'. If no fatigue or discomfort follows it, good. Nature and not number should be the standard of frequency![104]

The reader of Celsus, a busy man, who has been engaged in the day, whether in domestic or in public affairs, is advised that he 'ought to keep some portion of the day for the care of the body. The primary care in this respect is exercise'.[105]

Celsus sees no need for any 'health-care professionals', he encourages a kindly regard for one's own body, which should be free from exaggerated anxiety even in the case of those who are not so strong.[106]

The mechanics of the body, the shape and working of the internal organs, are envisioned by Celsus along the lines of the Hippocratic writers. We should turn now to this strange physiology on which medical practice rested not only in antiquity but even long after it. The writer who is responsible for its longevity is the physician Galen.[107] Galen was born in Pergamum, practised medicine in Rome and in Pergamum, travelled much, argued with and vituperated against many of his fellow physicians, regardless of whether they were alive or long dead. He experimented on animals and cut up corpses, but claimed to have learned his medicine from Hippocrates, Diocles, Praxagoras, Plato, Aristotle and Theophrastus. Aristotle's influence is clearly visible in Galen's system of physiology.[108] With Aristotelian concepts he reworked the Hippocratic heritage into a logical but imaginary physiology based on the four humours and the four 'qualities'. Disease was seen as a state of the body that is not in accordance with Nature, i.e. *cacochymia* resulting from inadequate coction[109] and mixing. The common disorder present in all the diseases is 'plethos' which is an excess of bad blood, blood mixed with 'residues', with too much of phlegm or black or yellow bile. The residues, if not excreted, would wander about in the body, settle in weak parts and there cause putrefaction. The physician's task is to aid Nature's healing power by vigilantly guarding against and eliminating everything that is contrary to Nature. The medical practice that grew up on this intellectual soil presents a picture of constant tension between a priori tenets that had little or no foundation in reality, and acute empirical observations of the practising physician.[110]

Concerning health, Galen admits that 'whenever there is no impediment in any of the activities of all their body parts, people say that they are healthy and think that they have no need for doctors', and that 'the business of the therapeutic method is to bring about health in bodies that are diseased'.[111]

But still he seems to share the view characteristic of Hellenistic medicine that those who hope to attain health must live an extremely orderly life, take upon themselves to follow complicated and irksome rules. They may not do what they want, but what is good for their constitution. The rules that apply to one person may not apply to another. If people want to keep out of harm's way the best thing is to put themselves in the hands of the physician and obey his orders faithfully. In his treatise on *Hygiene*, Galen states that those with the 'most perfect constitution' may follow their own inclination in diet and exercise; 'if the functions of his mind have been well trained' a person can be trusted not to overindulge in either of these. By writing this treatise as advice to a trainer he implies, however, that without the specialized knowledge he is imparting and the trainer's implementation of it, even the ideal perfect constitution is in danger of deterioration.[112]

The contrast between the Roman writer Celsus and the Greek physicians with respect to the healthy is indeed striking.[113] No Greek fleet could have sailed nor the Roman army marched far had their commanders decided to follow the Greek doctors' regimen. That this medical ideal of the 'healthy' life was not accepted without criticism by the ancient Greeks is suggested by Plato's comment in the *Republic* that medicine cures the sick by regimen, but may make the wealthy invalids and indolent who devote their whole life's effort to the preservation of health.[114]

It is more likely, however, that this striking difference in outlook concerning the healthy is due simply to the different social and professional position of these writers. Those who were practising physicians, in order to secure for themselves steady occupation, tended to overstate the lurking dangers and to advertise their own importance. As I.M. Lonie points out, the development of elaborate dietetic systems in medicine had, among others, a professional value: 'the possession of a technique which was not only complex in itself but which could also be rationally justified, would serve to increase both the confidence of the patient in the physician and the physician's confidence in himself'.[115]

If we add to this the fact that taking care of the healthy rich may have been more lucrative and less dangerous than trying to cure the seriously ill with the skills available for them, we may then begin to understand the jealous care with which the ancient physicians regarded their 'techne', their art, and the territory they carved out for themselves in caring for sick and healthy alike.

Celsus, on the other hand, is believed by historians of medicine to have been an upper-class educated layman, not a practising physician.[116] Those who believe that he was an encyclopaedist and not a doctor, I think, are supported in this view, among other things, by his singular lack of enthusiasm for medics, especially for treating the healthy.

One would like to know a lot more about the extent to which these medical notions were accepted and how popular they were among the Roman public in comparison with the Greeks. Galen's own enormous social success in Rome (the evidence for which largely comes from his own writing, and he could not be accused of modesty) prompted Glen Bowersock to attribute a 'popular hypochondria' to the Antonine age 'that welcomed medicine, philosophy and rhetoric all together and enthusiastically'.[117] Physicians aspired to the status of philosopher, and the philosopher liked to think of himself, in the words of Musonius, as 'the teacher and leader of men in all the things which are appropriate for men according to nature', including the care of his health.[118] Many of Galen's own writings are organized as transcriptions of public debates and demonstrations. Medical lectures and demonstrations, like any other oratory, were part of public entertainment. The easy use of medical terminology by the public, just like the widely shared commonplaces of the sophists, attest to the popularity and sheer entertainment value of public speeches. Physicians, like rhetors and sophists, moved in a highly competitive world. The successful and famous among them acquired great wealth and prestige, and with these many envious detractors among their colleagues.[119] In this competitive world the physician naturally tried to persuade the public that his services were indispensable. Not only was he needed when illness struck, his complex art based on his all-embracing knowledge was most useful – he protested – also for the maintenance of health. Galen, who found it hard to tolerate competition from fellow physicians, certainly was not going to put up with puffed-up athletic trainers and others who claimed expertise in health care! In *Thrasybulus*, a treatise on whether health care belongs to medicine or gymnastics, Galen concludes that there is a single comprehensive science of the care of the body, which is divided into therapy for the ill and maintenance of well-being in the healthy, all within the expertise of the physician.

In addition to those who saw themselves as professionals involved in health care, and probably influenced by the popularity of these, many orators and writers showed great interest in health and its cultivation. The sophists too saw the healthy body as one that is strong, vigorous and beautiful. Inactivity and a sedentary life were regarded by most as injurious and not fit for a free man, the notion of exercise was widened to include other activities in addition to gymnastics. While the physicians saw work as distinctly un-healthy,[120] a threat to the perfectly balanced life, some of the orators seemed to think differently. The important principle was not to feed an inactive body. All should work their body, each according to their station in life. Those who work at trades ought to use their body in heavy physical labour. Those who own land should toil at farming before they eat. City dwellers should find some 'honest toil', and the leisured class should frequent the gymnasia to run on track or wrestle or indulge in some non-competitive exercise. In order to find 'his meat and drink wholesome' a man of good sense should be physically active, concludes Dio of Prusa at the end of the first century AD.[121]

It appears from the foregoing that in the early centuries of the empire, as in earlier periods, there was a lively interest in health. Sometimes this interest indeed may have bordered on neurotic self-absorption, as in the case of Aelius Aristides, but more often it was a reflection of a realistic concern with the care of the body and a response to, and justified fear of ever-present disease. Health was seen as the condition of a strong, vigorous and active body that deserved constant cultivation. The well-conditioned, healthy and strong body was beautiful and was considered as a positive good. The cultivation of health was the duty of each individual aided by various experts, who would call themselves today 'health-care professionals'. Food and drink were used to combat diseases and it was firmly believed that they were of general assistance in preserving health as well.

The guardians of public decency preached temperance, self-restraint and self-sufficiency. The ethical ideal of the Greek philosophers, the 'self-controlled' free man who is 'not slave to his passions', was elaborated, for it fit well with Roman moral conservatism.[122] Gluttony and venery headed the list of temptations that would endanger not only the 'philosophic life' but also the *auctoritas* and *gravitas* demanded in political life. The Stoic moralists of the early empire, like Seneca or Musonius Rufus, felt themselves called upon to teach and give example of the 'philosophic life'. Those who followed the ethical teaching of the philosophers and had learned to control themselves through strenuous training were promised superiority over the merely rich and powerful. The ranks of an 'aristocracy of virtue'[123] were thought to be open to any man who trained himself in the 'philosophic life'. The aspiring disciples who undertook the necessary *askesis* were encouraged to adapt themselves to 'cold, heat, thirst, hunger, plain food, a hard bed, abstinence from pleasure and endurance of strenuous labour'.[124] Musonius Rufus, the Stoic philosopher and contemporary of the Apostle Paul, taught that a man of dignity would not indulge in homosexuality or in sexual intercourse with slaves; that sexual intercourse was proper only in marriage and that the love between man and wife was the 'highest form of love',[125] for the couple hold everything in common, body, soul and possessions. With respect to eating he held that a free man should choose food not for enjoyment but for nourishment, not to tickle his palate but to strengthen his body! He saw many dangers lurking in a meal:

> First of all, the man who eats more than he ought to does wrong, and the man who eats in undue haste no less, and also the man who wallows in the pickles and sauces, and the man who prefers the sweeter foods to the more healthful ones, and the man who does not serve food of the same kind or amount to his guests as to himself.[126]

The Stoic philosophers generally did not preach self-mortifying fasts or very stringent abstinence; instead they asserted that a free man should eat in order to live, and not live for eating.[127] Seneca admired Sextius, a Pythagorean, who believed that 'we should curtail the sources of our luxury', and argued that a varied diet was contrary to the laws of health[128] and was unsuited to human constitution. Under his influence, Seneca in his youth even experimented with vegetarianism for a short time.[129] The Cynics[130] went further; by ostentatiously rejecting the comforts of life, by refusing baths, beds and elaborate food, they claimed to be leading a 'simple life', the only kind of life that was in 'accordance to nature'. As a consequence, they felt free to censure and ridicule their contemporaries who feasted on 'effeminate' and 'luxurious' food, and were thus slaves of the 'passions'.[131] The audience in turn often resented these exhortations, seeing them, as they often were, as attacks on society, and attempts to claim moral superiority over the ordinary man. Comedy and satire, from the time of Aristophanes to the dialogues of Lucian, abound with caricatures of the moralizing philosopher who preaches temperance but stuffs himself with food and wine until he is about to burst.[132]

The moralizers, as they tend to do in all ages, saw their own time as corrupted and as a sad decline from a golden age of fortitude and virtue of a distant past. Culinary extravagance, often depicted in riotous colours in their writing, could serve as a literary metaphor for conveying unease over social and political complexities, especially those engendered by the phenomenal expansion of Rome.[133] Evocations of simple or luxurious eating were often employed as a convenient literary device for the praising or attacking of character. Since temperance and moderation were highly praised as the foundations of virtue, other persons' eating and drinking habits and love-making were of interest to everyone, including the historians, who were clearly aware of the great potential food had for projecting an individual's moral and cultural values. While the ancient physician correlated food with the physical constitution of the person, the historian, like the satirist, insisted on the connection between the type of food a man ate and his character. Heroes were most often characterized as frugal eaters and villains as gorging themselves on 'luxurious' food (which went hand in hand with debauching boys or women, often both together!).

Much of Greek and Roman literature reflects a tension of conflicting attitudes with respect to food. It was generally acknowledged that food was essential to life, to health and to conviviality but at the same time the need for food was felt to be a somewhat trivial and embarrassing need, a constant reminder of one's baser 'animal nature'. While life itself was dependent on eating and drinking, these most fleeting of pleasures were thought unworthy of pursuit by free men of *gravitas*.[134]

None of this literature, however, advocated self-mortification by fasting. There were no great acrobatic feats of abstinence among the ancient philosophers described by Diogenes Laertius, despite the commonly shared determination to 'subdue the pleasures'. The exceptional behaviour of Heraclitus of Ephesus – who

> became a hater of his kind and wandered on the mountains, and there he continued to live, making his diet grass and herbs. However, when this kind of life gave him dropsy, he made his way back to the city[135]

– was not held up for admiration, but recognized for what it was; according to Diogenes Laertius he was thought to be melancholy mad!

Self-starvation, however, was employed by a number of the aged philosophers as a way of ending their long life. Democritus, Dionysius and Cleanthes were all said to have died in ripe old age, quietly after refusing to take nourishment.[136] Self-starvation could be used as protest against injustice or as a consequence of shame, as Gylippus the liberator of Syracuse was reported by Athenaeus to have starved himself to death because he was convicted of embezzlement.[137] This elegant exit from life was chosen quite often also by upper-class Romans. And then there is in Dio's *Roman History* an episode that looks very much like an economically or politically motivated hunger strike, which, like many subsequent public displays of self-starvation in history, seems to have accomplished its purpose:

> Nerva, who could no longer endure the Emperor's society, starved himself to death, chiefly because Tiberius had reaffirmed the laws on contracts enacted by Caesar, which were sure to result in great loss of confidence and financial confusion, and although Tiberius repeatedly urged him to eat something, he would make no reply. Thereupon Tiberius modified his decision regarding loans and gave one hundred million sesterces to the public treasury.[138]

By turning the rage that he felt towards the powerful emperor whom he could not touch against his own self the senator gained the attention he needed; his murderous 'self-control' evoked admiration and shamed the dour Tiberius into giving way. Self-starvation as a weapon will have a long history in political struggles. It is usually resorted to by the less powerful of the adversaries, who by using it gain a propaganda victory. More about this later.

Awe-inspiring as this kind of 'fortitude' may have been to some, it was not generally recommended; instead Aristotle's dictum that the best in everything consisted in the mean between extremes was shared by many, which meant moderation when it came to food and drink. The philosophers saw temperance and moderation as prerequisites of philosophical inquiry. Temperance and moderation required for the pursuit of philosophy were achieved by training, *askesis*, just as the physical prowess of an athlete was achieved by strenuous and consistent physical training. The Stoics and even the Cynics were concerned in their ethical teachings with the way in which the person should conduct himself in this life, in the present physical world; the benefits accruing from the training would be enjoyed by body and soul together. Some philosophies, on the other hand, immortalized the soul as a divine particle entrapped by the earthly body and taught that man should strive to reach toward perfection which is his true divine nature. These tended to have negative views of the body. In Neoplatonic and Pythagorean circles the focus of inquiry turned away from science and the observation of nature to the contemplation of the soul and a search for the divine,[139] bringing with it an increasingly harsh asceticism and hostility to the physical body. 'Likeness to God' became the slogan for the Neoplatonist philosopher, replacing the Stoic emphasis on 'conformity with Nature'.[140] Neoplatonic and Pythagorean training or ascesis often put strong emphasis on curtailing the desires of the flesh,[141] and those who practised this ascesis and succeeded in distancing themselves from the pleasures of the flesh were regarded by their followers as 'divine men'. In accounts of their lives their miraculously frugal living excited admiration no less than their uncanny ability to predict future events and other superhuman accomplishments. The biographies of 'godlike' wise men and holy philosophers seem to have enjoyed some popularity in late antiquity.[142] The Pythagorean and Neoplatonic divine men held that purity is required of those who want to approach the divine, and that nothing material is pure to God who is immaterial. The eating of meat, which, as we have seen, was widely considered as 'strong' and 'heating' food, and as such an aphrodisiac, was thought to impede ascetic progress. Consequently some held a vegetarian diet to be a necessary prerequisite for the contemplative philosopher whose aim was personal ascent to the divine.

There seem to have been three classes of arguments put forward for vegetarianism in Graeco-Roman antiquity:[143] the religious one based on belief in the transmigration of souls, held by Empedocles[144] and Pythagoras;[145] the moral one, on the conviction that animals as rational beings deserved justice, held by Plato, Carneades and some other members of the Academy, against whom the Stoics held that animals were created for man's profit; and, finally, the argument that a meat diet is unhealthy or expensive or both,[146] held usually by self-appointed guardians of morality like Plutarch.[147] Vegetarianism, however, was not a widespread practice even among the philosophically minded. Porphyry, a late third century Neoplatonic philosopher and learned opponent of Christianity, wrote a treatise *On Abstinence from Animal Food*, in which he elaborates in detail all the reasons for abstinence from meat.[148] His aim was not to recommend vegetarianism for everyone but only to philosophers who, having 'abundant leisure', engaged in the quiet contemplative life and not in heavy physical work, do not need to eat meat to keep up their strength and superfluous weight.[149]

As this survey of views and attitudes would indicate, food and feasting was an integral part of Graeco-Roman religion, just as it was, as we have seen, of the religion of the Jews. There was a crucial difference, however, between pagans and Jews. Pagan gods expected worship and sacrifice, just like the God of the Jews, but they showed little interest in regulating the daily life of people, in what they ate or with whom they slept. The God of the Jews, on the other hand, watched closely the bedrooms and dining rooms of his people. Among the Jews, both food and sex were part of an ethical conduct for which the rules were given by God; among the pagans food and sex were not regulated explicitly by the gods, so it was up to the people to work out the rules for themselves. The doctors and other caretakers of health proposed guidelines for these that would safeguard the health of the body. Philosophers interested in the 'good life', and social critics, in chastising those who had more access to the good things in life than others, engaged in discussions concerning proper human conduct and the nature of virtue. Proper human conduct and virtue in the eyes of most of these accommodated the human body with its survival needs. Excess was frowned upon. Food was regarded as fuel necessary for living. Most importantly, all the rules of conduct put forward by the philosophers were proposed as products of human thought and consideration, not divine command; even the most serious ascesis of the Neoplatonic philosopher was not demanded by his God, since his God was perfection with no needs and no wants. The philosopher's desire to be 'godlike' was his own human desire, his way to achieve it was not imposed on him by God; consequently he might try to persuade but could not impose this way of life on others.

3

FOOD AND FASTING IN THE PAULINE EPISTLES

After reviewing both Jewish and pagan attitudes to food, I shall turn now to the Christian texts, starting with those parts of the New Testament that contain clear and explicit instructions about personal conduct fitting for Christians. Rules concerning proper Christian attitudes to food in daily life are most explicitly stated in the Epistles, attributed to the authorship of Paul. These, or the interpretation of these by later Christians, have greatly influenced Christian values. Through the ages these letters were read by theologians, who searched in them for 'Paul's Gospel', or his Christology, while leaders of Christian congregations looked in them for guidelines for their flock. Some of the sayings of Paul have been claimed by later generations to be the foundation of Christian asceticism.[1] It is the purpose of this chapter to concentrate on the instructions that Paul gave concerning the everyday life of Christian communities, and through these to examine Paul's attitude to food.

Food and eating are mentioned in Romans, (14:2–3; 14:6; 14:14–15; 14:17; 14:19–22), 1 Corinthians, (5:11; 6:13; 8:8–13; 10:16–21; 10:25–7; 10:31–2; 11:20–9; 11:33–4), Ephesians, (5:18; 5:29), Colossians, (2:16-17; 2:20-23), 2 Thessalonians, (3:8–10), and in 1 Timothy, (4:1–5; 6:8). In these texts the question of food arises in three general contexts. The first context is the argument that in the Christianity preached by Paul food as such is of no religious concern. In Paul's religion neither holiness nor sin is engendered by what one eats. Food and eating are of social importance and may give rise to concern if they cause dissension and quarrelling in the Christian brotherhood. Hospitality is urged. Eating together, even with one's pagan neighbour, is fine if it contributes to peace and mutual understanding; not so fine if food becomes a matter for argument, rivalry and a cause for social tension. The only warning given is that one should not eat (meaning in this context to associate) with a brother who is a fornicator.

The second context concerns meat sacrificed to idols. Paul's answer here is that all meat is clean; Christians should not make a question of conscience out of food as long as they do not participate or make others believe that they participate in pagan cults. Again the emphasis is on not endangering the faith or the peace of mind of a fellow Christian.

The third context in which food appears has to do with the conducting of the community meal and the meaning of the Lord's Supper. There is warning against drunkenness but no recommendation or even mention of fasting as a Christian religious practice in any of the letters.[2]

ABOUT THE TEXT AND ITS AUTHOR

The thirteen letters attributed to Paul play a role in the formation of Christianity that may rival in importance even that of the canonical gospels, which some at least, if not all, of these letters predate.[3]

'The fullest possible understanding of Paul's letters must rest on the fullest possible understanding of the factors which caused Paul to write. For each of Paul's letters we desire to know not simply the meaning of the words Paul used, but the situation which evoked them and the effect Paul intended them to have in the minds of those to whom they were addressed.' So writes J.C. Hurd, expressing the commonly shared aspiration of New Testament scholars.[4] To reach this goal, first and foremost we would have to know who the man was whom – as he himself tells us – his contemporaries viewed as a person whose 'letters are weighty and strong, but his bodily presence is weak, and his speech of no account'.[5] The volumes of studies written about Paul throughout the ages may fill libraries, but modern scholars still have to reach consensus on his biography, his personality and on the identity and nature of his audience or of his 'opponents' against whom he aimed his polemics.[6] What is commonly acknowledged is that Paul was central to the establishment of a creed that centred on the death and resurrection of the Messiah, and that he was the originator and the driving force of the transplantation of the Christian movement into Gentile soil.[7] Writings attributed to him take up a large part of the Christian holy scripture and, as noted above, may constitute the earliest Christian writings included in the biblical canon. In order to understand Paul's views on food, I believe that some thought must be given to his personality.

Only two sources of biographical information relate to Paul: the

Acts of the Apostles, and the Pauline Epistles, only seven of which are usually accepted as authentic: Romans, 1 and 2 Corinthians, Galatians, Philippians, 1 Thessalonians and Philemon.[8]

It has often been pointed out that the biography of Paul drawn by the author of the Acts of the Apostles does not fit easily with the autobiographical details found in Paul's own epistles.[9] Actually two different personalities and two different religious emphases emerge from these two sources. Basing the reconstruction of Paul's life and his background mainly on Acts, one school of thought claims that Paul originated from a prominent family in Tarsus, the son of a Pharisee and Palestinian Jew, who at the same time had Roman citizenship. Furthermore, it postulates that he grew up and was educated in Jerusalem at no lesser a place than the school of Gamaliel I, the son or grandson of the sage Hillel. As a consequence of his family background and his Pharisaic and scribal education, this version claims, he became an important member of the Jerusalem 'establishment', distinguishing himself further by his zealous persecution of the new Christian heresy. His sudden conversion to Christianity, which completely lifted him out of the social milieu in which he was so well integrated, indeed came as unexpectedly as a thunderbolt from summer skies. The story makes wonderful theological sense. The resurrected Christ himself appears to his violent persecutor and changes his sworn enemy into a follower, the 'chosen vessel' of his gospel. Miracles and theology apart, this account, however, is highly unlikely; it makes neither social nor psychological sense for a devout Pharisee, son of an important family, well integrated in Jerusalem society, to be an active and violent persecutor of a heretical group one day, an equally vehement apostle of the same heresy the next. Most importantly, it does not square with the testimony contained in Paul's own letters.[10]

He himself is reticent about his background. There is no mention of his father's name, nor of his relations in Jerusalem or elsewhere. This is rather unusual in autobiographical accounts in ancient society, especially in Jewish society, where a person was identified with his or her father's name and where family connections often defined the person and his or her standing in society.[11] Paul claims no social prominence for his family;[12] he barely mentions it, and when he does so it is only to claim a Jewish background when this seems to be expedient. It is commonly accepted that he was born in a Hellenistic city of Asia Minor,[13] into a Jewish family that counted its descent from the tribe of Benjamin and had Pharisaic connections.[14] His family may not have been very observant and exclusive in its Judaism, if so, this would explain the obvious ease with which Paul mingled with and felt at home in the company of gentiles. His use of the Greek language and preference for the Septuagint version of the Jewish Bible, possibly even when this mistranslates the Hebrew, would suggest that Greek and not Hebrew or Aramaic was his first language.[15] In his youth he may not have been very religious, as he said: 'I was once alive apart from the Law.'[16] If that is so, then he may have had not one but two conversions. In his adolescence or young adulthood he turned to the religion of his forebears and became a 'born-again Jew', ('*hazar be' teshuva*' as the experience of turning to religion is called in Hebrew).[17] He studied the Law with great dedication, as he says in Galatians: 'and I advanced in Judaism beyond many of my own age among my people, so extremely zealous was I for the traditions of my fathers'.[18]

The immersion in Pharisaic Judaism does not seem to have eased his deep-seated pessimism. His letters, all, of course, written after he turned Christian, reveal a troubled, conflict-ridden man experiencing his own self as split into two irreconcilable and constantly warring forces: the decaying flesh with its devastating passions and against it the sublime spirit with its longing for another world.

> I do not understand my own actions. For I do not do what I want, but I do the very thing I hate. . . . For I know that nothing good dwells within me, that is, in my flesh. I can will what is right, but I cannot do it. For I do not do the good I want, but the evil I do not want is what I do. Now if I do what I do not want, it is no longer I that do it but sin which dwells within me.[19]

Paul absorbed the notion of sin from his zealous study of Judaism: 'if it had not been for the Law, I should not have known sin'.[20]

But his understanding of sin went beyond the letter of the Law; he felt it as an overwhelming evil power that resides in the 'flesh', splitting the human personality into those two eternally antagonistic forces:

> for I delight in the law of God in my innermost self, but I see in my members another law in war with the law of my mind and making me captive to the law of sin which dwells in my members. Wretched man that I am! Who will deliver me from this body of death? . . . I of myself serve the law of God with my mind, but with my flesh I serve the law of sin.[21]

He projects the evil force that his anxiety and guilt cannot bear within himself onto all flesh: all humans are hopeless sinners. In Paul's mind the Jewish Law, which affirms a disciplined satisfaction of human carnal desires, instead of liberating one from the burden of sin, tempts one even more to indulge the flesh: 'sin finding opportunity in the commandment, wrought in me all kinds of covetousness'.[22]

Adherence to Pharisaic Judaism did not resolve Paul's struggle against sin and guilt; the attempt to externalize inner turmoil by violent persecution of heretics did not accomplish its aim. Finally he underwent a second and more profound conversion, which enabled him to repudiate completely the 'workings of the flesh', to overthrow the Law of his fathers and consequently to build and propagate a new religion. His conversion finally illuminated for him a way out of his sense of defeat through the absolute submission of self to God – through faith in Christ. Experiencing Christ as living in his own body,[23] he fashioned his whole self into the 'chosen vessel' for the gospel. This identification with the resurrected Christ empowered him to impose his conception of the faith on the followers of Jesus and to fight with great vehemence against all differing views.

For Jews, as was discussed earlier,[24] the meaning of sin was transgression of the God-given Law; the 'flesh' was not a power whose dominion one must escape, it was neither good nor evil but only weak and mortal.[25] Paul, in contrast, felt the power of sin 'in the flesh', which for him meant in the sexually charged body.[26] Modern Christian commentators often contest this view and try to sublimate Paul's pronouncements concerning sexuality.[27] Even those who admit that πορνεία (fornication) is one of the most important key words in Paul's moral exhortations like to understand it as referring not specifically to sexual but general immoral or unethical behaviour, or assert that Paul's views on the subject are 'in line with the tradition of Jewish sexual ethics'.[28] They point to the many warnings in the Old Testament against fornication but do not cite any particular Jewish ethical writing that parallels or in any way explains Paul's sexual attitudes as expressed in Romans 6:6–8; 7:15–25; 1 Corinthians 5:9–12; 6:9–14; Galatians 5:16–20, and many other places. In the Old Testament, expressions like 'fornication', 'whoring', 'adultery' and the like most often relate to one of two things: either to adultery in the strict ancient sense, which takes account only of actions involving married women, or, in a far greater measure, not to sexual misdeeds but to a religious one: the worship of gods other than the God of Israel, that is, to idolatry.[29] For Paul, however, fornication did not mean idolatry, nor was it limited to adultery. His often repeated list of sinners who would surely be excluded from Heaven is headed by πόρνόι (fornicators); the same list also includes three other categories of explicitly sexual offenders, μοιχοὶ (adulterers), ἀρσενοκοῖται (sodomites) and μαλακοὶ(effeminates) as separate items in addition to idol worshippers, thieves, robbers and other common criminals.

Other exegetes (see n. 16) take great pains to explain away passages such as chapter 7 in Romans, claiming that the 'I', the first person singular pronoun, implies the use, stylistically, of a rhetorical figure with general significance, 'ego means mankind under the shadow of Adam'. And if the sin must be named, then be it covetousness. 'Sin, here defined as the power and reality of covetousness, is both stimulated and unmasked by the law as the divine commandment', argues E. Käsemann.[30] That commandment, if indeed it is what Paul had in mind, itself refers first of all to sexual transgression: You shall not covet your neighbour's wife! In a similar vein, Bultmann sees the 'I' passages in Romans as a non-autobiographical stylistic device to expose 'the plight of mankind'.[31]

The many attempts to bring Paul's message in line with the sensibilities of various modern Christian groups[32] underline the fact that a historical understanding of Paul may not necessarily coincide with any theological interpretation of his words, for as Sanders cogently argued, 'what Paul concretely thought cannot be directly appropriated by Christians today. The form of the present world did not pass away, the end did not come and believers were not caught up to meet the Lord in the heavens'. It is understandable that those who wish to make Paul's gospel relevant today may choose and emphasize the more 'easily appropriated language of trust, obedience, renunciation of one's striving, and the like'; these, however, cannot be claimed as the real or exhaustive interpretation of what Paul himself meant.[33]

In an attempt to concentrate on a historical understanding, rather than the theological significance of Paul, one should rigorously follow Sanders's dictum: 'It seems to be best to understand Paul as saying what he meant and meaning what he said'.[34] This principle is observed in what follows.

FOOD AND FASTING IN PAUL'S TEACHING

The new faith preached by Paul embodied his conviction that 'man is sinful, incapable of obeying God, potentially damned and lost without the saving grace of Christ's atoning death', and that 'Christ's sacrificial blood is essential to the cleansing of his sins'.[35] The most readily identifiable convictions governing Paul's 'gospel' may be summarized in the following: that Jesus Christ, who died and rose again, is Lord; that in him God has provided for the salvation of all who believe; that death is nullified, Christ will soon return and bring the present world to an end; and that he, Paul was called to be the apostle to the Gentiles.[36] His ethical teaching aimed to show the way his hearers could participate in the 'saving action' of Christ.

Participation 'in Christ' Paul saw as the only way to escape the dominion of sin that ruled and overwhelmed men and women and under which all humanity was bent. Only the believer's union with Christ could liberate the Christian from being thus enslaved.[37] The union with Christ that Paul envisaged involved the Christian's body and soul,[38] and consequently it excluded any other bodily union, intercourse with prostitutes, homosexuality, even a too passionate embrace of one's own wife. Christ is 'in' the Christian's body, therefore the body should be kept as a temple; the believer, in turn, is 'in' the body of Christ, and consequently should not tolerate contamination, such as that which would result from eating with demons at pagan sacrificial feasts.[39] Paul's message to Gentiles and Jews was that Christ came to be the Lord of all, that salvation rested on faith in Christ, and that any other way to assure salvation, including reliance on the Law, was wrong. He certainly did not come to fulfil the Law but indeed to overthrow it![40] Salvation of the believers and the destruction of the unbelievers he envisaged to be imminent, when the true believers among his hearers will be taken up by Christ to heaven, and this world will end.[41] His ethical teaching and pastoral concerns focused on a community of 'participants in Christ'.

As was mentioned earlier,[42] Sanders, in his brilliant analysis of Palestinian Judaism, defined a method that makes possible a comparison of religions, not on the basis of polemics but on the basis of a description of how a religion is perceived by its adherents to function. What he calls 'the pattern of religion', includes more than soteriology usually does: it includes the logical beginning-point of the religious life, what it takes to enter into it, as well as what one must do to remain in it.[43] As we have seen earlier, in order to 'get into' Judaism a man entered the Covenant, as a sign of which he was circumcised; in order to 'stay in' Judaism he was expected to live according to the Law.[44] Paul changed both the requirement for getting in and staying in, thus making a complete break with Judaism. The rules for 'getting into' Christianity were made literally less painful by the abolition of circumcision; however, as the early Christian literature amply testifies, the rules for 'staying in' were not always clear and the abolition of the Law may have left a void that was, for some Christians, difficult to fill.

Paul's pronouncements about food should be understood in light of his conception of the Christian's participation in 'the body of Christ' on the one hand and his hostility to Judaism on the other.

The epistles were meant not for individual recipients but for circulation and public reading in the various Christian groups. H. Koester argues that these earliest written documents of Christianity were directed to communities that understood themselves as 'founded by the activity of the spirit', that is, by religious enthusiasm, and that the documents themselves are to be seen as 'political instruments designed to organise and maintain the social fabric and financial affairs of these communities'.[45] If so, one must assume that the topics treated in these were of importance either for the writer or for his intended audience or both. Questions relating to food clearly appear to have been initiated by the communities to which he wrote. The problems of the composition of these communities, and of the identity of Paul's opponents, no less than that of his hearers, have engaged a long line of interpreters. The solution of these problems would of course take us closer to the understanding of the historical background of early Christianity. The task, however, is made difficult by the lack of external evidence; the communities are usually reconstructed by some imaginative use of Paul's own letters, with or without reference to Acts. Scholarly consensus on the topic is minimal,[46] and this must be borne in mind in the following discussion.

Paul's major pronouncements concerning food are concentrated in the Epistle to the Romans and in I Corinthians. In Romans Paul asserts that food in itself should not be a religious issue, 'For the kingdom of God is not food and drink but righteousness and peace and joy in the holy spirit.'[47] The letter assumes that among its recipients there are those who believe that they may eat anything, a belief that Paul shares and whose proponents he calls 'the strong', while some others, 'the weak', eat only vegetables. Paul agrees with 'the strong' but in favour of peace and mutual support in the community he urges his hearers not to argue about food, but to leave it to the individual's own decision what one eats. The message is clear and unequivocal; for the Christian there is no ritually clean or unclean food. One should not cause dissension, however, or make a brother fall on the issue of food.[48] He urges his hearers to practise hospitality.[49] *Koinonia*, community, joint participation is his aim, in which food should serve for cohesion rather than exclusion or disruption.

Paul's Christianity was spread through social gatherings, and the first 'churches' met in private houses. Conviviality and hospitality were instrumental in the propagation of the gospel.[50] Anxiety and argument about what is served and what can be eaten on these occasions could seriously undermine group solidarity, and it is this fear that underlies Paul's attitude.

In 1 Corinthians, which seems to contain answers to actual questions put to Paul by the community, he reiterates his position that Christians are free from all dietary scruples: what they eat or do not eat will not commend them to God, as long as this liberty does not form a stumbling block to one's brother.[51] The 'strong' Christian may even eat with pagans, as long as he does not participate in a religious feast. One cannot participate in the Christian feast that commemorates the death of Christ and also take part in a feast celebrating demons.[52] The union with Christ is exclusive.[53] Paul's ambivalence to pagan gods, opposition to belief in their divinity, on the one hand, and, on the other, fear of their existence as demons whom the worshipper's sacrifice makes powerful would have appeared strange in the eyes of those who held traditional Jewish belief in the existence of only one God, despite the fact that some contemporary Jewish speculation did concern itself with supernatural beings, intermediaries between men and God. These angelologies, like Paul's demonology, may themselves be indications of the influence of the Hellenistic world on aspects of Judaism.

The Christian communal meal, at least in Corinth, fell short of Paul's ideal.[54] It appears that the rich stuffed themselves with food that they brought along, while the poor remained hungry.[55] Paul again emphasizes concern for the members of the Christian community and gives explicit instructions concerning the cultic significance of the breaking of bread and of the cup of wine, the body and blood of Christ, the partaking of which is the explicit sign of participation in the death of Christ.

The question of food reappears in some epistles whose Pauline authorship is in doubt.[56] References to the problem of food in these are occasioned by 'false teachers' or 'false teachings' that aimed to persuade Christians to abide by the Jewish food regulations or practise ascetical abstention.[57]

Who were the 'strong' and why would the 'weak' be made to fall by what one ate?[58] Instead of trying to advance specific proposals concerning the composition of the Roman community to whom the letter was addressed, since, according to his own words Paul himself did not know them personally at the writing of his letter,[59] or to add to the debate on the nature of factions in Corinth, it may be more profitable to regard the principles he set out in the letters as answers to problems that he encountered frequently in his groups, and consequently fully expected to be common also in a community of new Christians, whom he did not know personally.

Two problems must have been ever present in all early Christian groups: the first of these concerned itself with what was new in the new religion, with the meaning of the message; the second, and related one centred around the question of the relationship of the new creed to Judaism. Modern scholarly discussions of this question have generally been concerned with the 'Law', and Gentile versus Jewish-Christian factions have often been described with their various hypothetical leaders. The problem in early Christian groups may have been not only a theological question but also a practical one; and it may have been far more pervasive than any that may have been engendered by some representative of a 'circumcision party' sent from Jerusalem. The question must have arisen on all occasions when Christians met and read the Scriptures. Throughout the first hundred years of early Christianity, the recognized holy scripture was the Bible of Israel, in the Greek translation of the Septuagint.[60] How should a simple Christian understand his or her relationship to the whole of Judaism, not only the Law but the history of Israel, its prophets and its poets about whom he was taught at these gatherings? All new Christians knew that by joining the faith they had also acquired a long and distinguished history that ran its course from Adam to Jesus; they also acquired patriarchs, kings, prophetic writings, an ethical world-view and many common customs built on or around the 'Law'. How was the simple Christian to know what it meant to be 'liberated from the Law', and still identify with the history and keep the moral and ethical impulses embedded in the rest of the Judaic heritage? What must have attracted proselytes to ancient religions was more than a set of beliefs; pomp, ceremony, feast-days and other communal customs must have played their part. Even joining a philosophical school meant donning distinctive attire, undertaking to behave in particular ways characteristic of the school. Judaism provided ceremonies, communal feasts and fasts, holy days and New Moons, which according to many ancient writers attracted interest.[61] That not all new Christians found a religion without sabbaths and New Moons satisfying is attested by the fast development of Christian holidays, and the increasing appropriation and renaming of pagan and Jewish holidays by the church. In Paul's eschatological expectation, however, there was no need and no time for these; some of his hearers nevertheless were reluctant to do without religious ceremony. For those who came to Christianity through an interest first in Judaism, keeping some of these customs was the outward sign of belonging to a very special community. It is not surprising then that the question of Jewish customs should have caused discussion and controversy in early Christian groups, not only among the theologians but in all likelihood among the simple people too, whose desire was to behave in ways that are 'acceptable to God'.

Consequently the suggestion I am presenting here is that the 'weak' who only ate vegetables, as well as many of the other Christians to whom the apostle's polemic was directed, were gentile 'Judaizers' and not some pagan converts who still adhered to philosophical or ritual vegetarianism. This is supported by the fact that while Paul vigorously attacks Jewish beliefs and practices on every occasion that offers itself, nowhere in the letters is there even a hint that he is arguing against pagan religious or philosophical ideas that underpinned pagan vegetarian practices. Paul has nothing to say about the metempsychosis of the Pythagoreans, makes no reference to the ongoing arguments among Aristotelians, Stoics and others concerning 'rationality' in animals or of animal rights to justice.[62]

Paul endeavoured to dispel his hearers' perplexity concerning the relationship of the new faith to Judaism. The 'Law', he insisted, is irrelevant for those 'in Christ' and should be dispensed with. His conception of the Jewish Law that should be overthrown was rather narrow: his main attack is centred on circumcision, which should be done away with; the dietary laws need not be kept, for neither they nor the observance of Jewish feasts and fasts are of any use for the Christian. It is interesting to note that it is circumcision rather than the dietary regulations that invokes Paul's concentrated venom against the Jewish Law. With respect to food he is neutral; those who want to keep the rules of *kashrut* are 'weak' but should not be rebuked or alienated on account of food.

The rejection of all pagan and Jewish practices that Paul demanded of his converts may have left these in a state of insecurity. Paul, it is claimed,[63] well recognized the social and psychological vulnerability of new converts, and it is this recognition that evokes many of his ethical exhortations. A.J. Malherbe collected the evidence from ancient writers as diverse as Epictetus, Philo, Plutarch and others, to argue convincingly that conversion, whether to philosophy or to a new religion, was a disturbing and potentially disorientating experience. The social, intellectual, and behavioural transformation required of new converts often resulted in confusion, bewilderment and dejection. 'This distress was increased by the break with the ancestral religion and mores, with family, friends and associates and by public criticism.'[64]

In order to document Paul's understanding of this plight and his pastoral efforts to alleviate it, Malherbe points to Paul's extensive use of kinship terms. Christians are brothers, children of the same father, and so on, and he attributes this to a conscious effort on Paul's part to create and reinforce a sense of community in his readers. While Malherbe's work concentrates on the letter to the Thessalonians, his observation is relevant also to the rest of the Pauline corpus. Whether to counteract the alienation of new converts or to appropriate and make Christian a well-tried custom of pagan cult-associations, which set themselves up as brotherhoods with their benefactors as Father or Mother,[65] Paul emphasized at every opportunity the unity of the Christian community by likening it to one family. The apostle did not advise the 'strong' to relinquish meat and wine but cautions them not to attack, ridicule or in any way endanger a weak brother.[66] If eating or drinking cause disharmony and friction in the Christian brotherhood then it is better not to eat at all. The overstatement forces on the audience the extreme importance of peace in the community.

As all his letters testify, Paul had a very matter of fact attitude to food. Food was for everyday survival, needed until the Parousia. Food was sustenance, necessary for the living, and as such held no religious significance for him: 'Food is meant for the stomach and the stomach for food – and God will destroy both one and the other.'[67] The stomach, κοιλία, had a different status in Paul's mind from that of the body, σῶμα, and as a consequence, a different destiny. As his next sentence shows: 'The body is not meant for fornication, but for the Lord, and the Lord for the body.' The stomach does not seem to belong to that body which figures importantly in both salvation and damnation, it is only necessary and neutral machinery. The resurrected body will not have a stomach; on the other hand a fornicating body will not be resurrected!

Outside of mild warnings against drunkenness and greed, Paul perceived no great danger in eating. In this he is unusual among the moral preachers of his age.[68] His lack of concern with gluttony becomes even more striking in comparison with the repeatedly and stridently voiced anxiety shown on its account by another Hellenized Jew, his near contemporary, Philo of Alexandria. As noted earlier,[69] *opsophagia*, appetite for good food and a full stomach, were, in the eyes of the pious Alexandrian Jew, the road to lasciviousness and fornication, which in turn, led to all kinds of moral evil.[70] Sexual lust was even more abhorrent in the eyes of Paul, but nowhere in his letters is there any trace of the philosophic topos of 'subduing the passions' with respect to food, despite the fact that in his time this commonplace rolled easily off any pen or tongue even on the street corners. Philosophers of various schools lectured publicly, aiming to recruit followers who could be reformed and turned to the paths of rationality. Most of these connected gluttony with fornication and urged, some in less extreme tones than Philo, the control and restriction of both. In contrast, Paul's asceticism focused on sexuality, and his warnings against fornication did not flow from stoic clichés but were the outpouring of deep personal anxiety.[71] For the philosopher sexual passion was an impediment to rationality; for the health-conscious and worried among the Greeks it meant a potential danger leading to fatigue and the dissipation of precious bodily fluids;[72] for Paul it was the sin that excluded men and women from the Kingdom of God.[73] Gluttony did not tempt him and he makes no use of the age-old connection between it and fornication that was brandished with enthusiasm by many contemporary moral preachers.

CONCLUSION

Those who look for the roots of Christian abstinence from wine and meat or for advocacy of religious or ascetical fasting in the epistles of Paul will be disappointed. As will be seen in the following chapters, many later Christian writers who, for reasons of their own, advocated the need for fasting or for abstaining from meat and wine cited Paul, often quite freely and inaccurately, as supporting authority. Those who argue that Christian asceticism originated with Paul often assume that sexual asceticism necessarily implies food abstinence. Paul is the best proof that this is not the case. For Paul food is a necessity for everyday survival and as such is of no religious concern. Fasting for him is not a condition either for 'getting into' or for 'staying in' the religion or in the Christian community. Communal sharing of food should, in his view, contribute to the mutual upbuilding of the individual members and to the strengthening of the Christian community. The death of Christ is commemorated not by fasting but by communal sharing of bread and wine, and on that occasion, and only on that occasion, food and drink acquire religious meaning. Paul's asceticism is thus expressed only in sexual abstinence, which for him is not a philosophical quest for rational control, but derives from a deeply felt personal abhorrence of sexuality.

4

FOOD AND FASTING IN THE
ACTS OF THE APOSTLES

The gospels have no special message concerning food. The one New
Testament narrative in which attitudes to food are given central
importance is the Acts of the Apostles. Food and eating are mentioned
in Acts in three major contexts:

1 in descriptions of the communal meals of the followers of Jesus,
   who were praying, worshipping and giving thanks with 'breaking
   bread' in joyful spirit (Acts 2:42; 2:46; 16:34; 20:7; 27:33–6);
2 in food distribution or charity as this became institutionalized
   (6:1–3);
3 in the context of the problem that the Jewish food laws posed for
   the mission to the Gentiles (10:10–15; 11:2–3; 15:19–20).

Fasting is mentioned, with prayer, as preparation for the ceremony of
the 'laying on of hands' (13:2–3; 14:23). Fasting is also mentioned as
part of the Jews' conspiracy when bent upon murdering Paul (23:12).

Food as such, when mentioned in Acts, is generally regarded as
beneficial and strengthening, as an accompaniment to the apostles'
preaching and to rejoicing. Fasting among Christians is noted only
twice, and both times in the same ceremonial context.

ABOUT THE TEXT

In attempting to examine and put in historical perspective attitudes to
food and fasting expressed in the Acts of the Apostles, we are faced
with even more problems than those discussed in the previous chapter.
There is no scholarly agreement on whether this document represents
an attempt to write history or whether it is an early Christian travel
novel; there is no reliable knowledge about its author, nor about when,

where, for what audience and purpose he wrote the text. As an eminent commentator writes:

It would be easy to determine the place of the Lucan writings in early Christianity if we knew the author, especially if we could be sure that the Third Gospel and the book of Acts were written by Luke, the physician and companion of Paul (Col. 4:14). Then the time of composition could be limited to the years A.D. 60–80. The work would then be the most prominent document of the second generation, written in immediate contact with firsthand tradition.[1]

While some scholars still maintain the traditional attribution of authorship to Paul's companion, Luke the physician,[2] most others strongly contest this view. As Haenchen concludes:

The representation of Paul in Acts – not to mention the overall picture of missionary beginnings – shows that we have no collaborator of Paul telling the story, but someone of a later generation trying in his own way to give an account of things that can no longer be viewed in their true perspective.[3]

The dating of Acts by various scholars ranges from as early as AD 70,[4] to the mid-second century.[5] If Christian theology can be regarded as having a gradual development in time, from a 'primitive' to a more complex ideology of orthodox Catholicism, then Acts would fit with a less elaborate theology than what is expressed in the few extant mid-second-century 'catholic' writers like Justin or the 'Apostolic Fathers'. This seems to be the case not only with respect to the theology of Acts but also with respect to the organization of Christian groups, which in Acts appears to be less hierarchical than what other second-century witnesses would suggest. Conzelmann on these considerations puts the author in the 'third generation', and thinks that dating Acts somewhere between 80 and 100 'best fits all of the evidence'.[6] This kind of reasoning ignores the possibility that groups with varying theology and organizational structure, all considering themselves Christian, may have existed as the Christian message spread, that Luke's conception of what constituted Christianity and its 'history' may reflect only one of these competing views, and that he wrote it in order to defend his view against the competitors.[7]

It has been claimed that there are reminiscences of Acts in the Apostolic Fathers, but as Haenchen points out, it cannot be proven that the writings of any of these quote Acts; the often tenuous and vague resemblance is better attributed to the fact that all these writers were working with a stock of contemporary Christian formulas held largely in common,[8] and which was heavily dependent on the Septuagint. The first solid evidence for the existence of Luke-Acts comes from the second half of the second century.[9]

On the question of the value of Acts as history, the debate has been raging since the nineteenth century.[10] Even today opinions range widely. On the one side are those scholars who regard Acts as a historical work of considerable value, exemplified by F.F. Bruce and C.S.C. Williams, and more recently M. Hengel, who in his book, *Acts and the History of Earliest Christianity*, strongly argued that Luke 'is no less trustworthy than other historians of antiquity'.[11] On the opposite side a powerful array of scholars, utilizing methods of form-criticism and redaction-criticism, came to the conclusion that the author of Acts was primarily a theologian, working freely on various traditions available to him, or even creating his own 'traditions' in the service of his purpose of presenting an edifying account of the early church. M. Dibelius,[12] H. Conzelmann, E. Haenchen and J.C. Hurd represent this sceptical view concerning Luke's historical accuracy.[13] According to this view, the history 'Luke' writes is 'salvation history'; its form as a whole 'is stamped with the specific historical and theological views of the author'.[14] Historical reliability is not the concern of the work, which 'primarily intends to edify the churches and thereby contribute its part in spreading the Word of God farther and farther, even to the ends of the earth'.[15]

P.F. Esler goes even further in his sociological treatment of Acts, by claiming that 'Luke's theology has been largely motivated by social and political forces operating upon his community', which, he believes, consisted of some Jewish Christians and more 'Roman' Christians. Accordingly, Luke's purpose was to explain, to justify, to 'legitimate' Christianity to his Christian contemporaries. This 'legitimation' is a process that is carried out after a social institution has originated; it is a collection of ways in which an institution is explained and justified to its own members. The purpose of legitimation is to make 'objectively available and subjectively plausible' the meaning of a social institution, to create a 'symbolic universe' with a past, a present and a future, thus facilitating the integration of the life of the individual to the system.[16]

This short review of the uncertainties concerning the provenance of the document that we know as the Acts of the Apostles does not pretend to be exhaustive; in fact it hardly scratches the surface. The reason for including it here is to serve as a caveat. As stated earlier, the purpose of the present work is to examine a series of Christian texts concerned with food and fasting, in order to discover why particular Christians adopted the attitudes they did, and what factors may have influenced their outlook. For this task one would need to know who was the writer of the text, when he lived and where he wrote. In the case of the text under consideration here there are no reliable answers to any of these questions, only a great variety of more or less imaginative conjectures. Luke, if we may in truth call him by that name, would have had certain influences shaping his attitudes to food had he been an 'insider'[17] who had lived in Palestine. On the other hand he may have seen things quite differently had he been a Gentile Christian writing around year 100 in, say, Ephesus, and differently again if he lived and wrote in Rome sometime during the first half of the second century. Keeping this in mind we turn now to an examination of food and fasting in Acts.

COMMUNAL MEALS

The writer of Acts structures the story of the Church into distinguishable phases. The first phase, the apostolic, Jewish-Christian primitive church in Jerusalem is followed by the first conversion of Gentiles by Peter; next comes the model mission of Paul in the so-called 'first missionary journey' and the subsequent apostolic Council, which extends into a legitimated mission to the Gentiles without the Law, reaching all the way to Rome, to the centre of the Empire and of worldly power. Food has a role to play in all of these phases.

The narrative of Acts begins by describing the life of the disciples and followers of Jesus after the news of his resurrection. The disciples were 'men of Galilee', Jews who recently came up to Jerusalem with Jesus to celebrate Passover in a rented or borrowed 'upper room'. These disciples, in the narrative of Acts, become firmly based in Jerusalem, the theological and symbolic centre of Judaism. Acts 2:42–7 is a description of the life of this first community of Jewish Christians. The salient characteristics of this life were the communal sharing of all property, communal 'breaking of bread', devotion to the teaching of the apostles, attending the Temple and prayers, all of which activities were commonly shared signifiers of the ideal pious Jewish life.

Jewish groups, dedicated wholly to the study and observance of the Law, and living a pious, ascetic and communal life, were held up for admiration in antiquity not only by Jewish writers like Philo[18] and Josephus,[19] but even by Gentiles like the Roman Pliny the Elder.[20] The Jerusalem community described in the early part of Acts bears notable resemblance to these idealized groups. As more and more of the Dead Sea scrolls become available for scholars, comparisons between some aspects of the life of the Qumran communities and the earliest church have been attempted. A number of studies tried to relate the communal meals of Acts 2:42–7 to the religious common meal of the Dead Sea community described in *1QS* 6:4–5; *1QSa* 2:11–22.[21] But as Fitzmyer rightly points out, in reviewing the possible similarities between Qumran and the early Jewish-Christian community,[22] the notice of the Christian meal in Acts is so brief and contains so little detail that one cannot really make a valid comparison in this case. With respect to the similarity of Acts' description of the early Christian's *koinonia* and the community (*Yachad*) of Qumran, Fitzmyer is of the opinion that the Christians imitated for a time, with some modifications, these Qumran practices. Both groups, however, may have been following more widespread Jewish practices.

What does the author tell us of the Christian meal in this passage? The 'breaking of bread' is twice mentioned; the second time it is expanded with 'they partook of food with glad and generous heart'. The Greek words here suggest a full meal ($\mu\varepsilon\tau\varepsilon\lambda\acute{\alpha}\mu\beta\alpha\nu o\nu$ $\tau\rho o\phi\hat{\eta}\varsigma$). The interpretations of this passage generally fall into two categories; one sees in the breaking of bread a mere shorthand expression to denote the ordinary common meal,[23] while the other set of interpreters prefer to see in it a clear reference to the Eucharist, and insist that the passage as a whole depicts the original ritual of the Christian daily service.

With respect to the first of these, it is pointed out that while the expression is not found in classical Greek literature and is not usual in the Septuagint as a synonym for eating, in Hebrew and Aramaic the word 'to break' is used as the opening of the meal, sometimes without any word for bread, and often connected with the Hebrew word for blessing.[24] It is a common Jewish custom to start a festive meal with blessing, breaking and distributing the bread, and, similarly, blessing the wine and passing it around. It is difficult to know when this custom originated. The Bible commands: 'And you shall eat and be full and you shall bless the Lord, your God.'[25] Other biblical passages suggest that the people were not supposed to eat of the sacrificial meal until a blessing was pronounced over it.[26] The customary form of the blessing may have been based on a passage from Psalms: 'You cause . . . to bring forth food from the earth and wine to gladden the human heart . . . and bread to strengthen the human heart.'[27]

Extremely pious Jews, like the Essenes and Philo's Therapeutae, presumably would never have taken food without blessing the Lord for it. Since the obvious aim of Luke in Acts is to base Christianity firmly on its Judaic source and to prove that it is but the fulfilment of true Judaism, he represents the first Christian community as those pious Jews whose way of life would be admired by all – by good Jews and even by philosophically minded Gentiles.[28] Instead of searching in Acts for some actual splinter group of the Essenes, one should recognize that the idyllic description of the pious, all-sharing community joyfully eating together is a literary device that prepares for the confrontation to come, over precisely the issue of food and table fellowship, an issue, moreover, that is going to be central to the narrative.

As noted above, there are scholars who believe that instead of a community meal what is depicted here is the ritual of the Catholic daily service, but in such a fashion as to exclude the uninitiated. According to this view the description 'hints' at things in such a way that 'the non-Christian is not meant to understand what this is all about'.[29] It is claimed that the expression 'breaking of bread' is an entirely novel manner of speaking, denoting the Christian ritual meal, which, in the form known to us today, includes a sermon (then the instruction by the apostles), the contribution of offering, the Eucharist and prayers.

The text itself does not easily accommodate this interpretation. In striking contrast to the Lord's Supper of Paul's letter,[30] here only the bread is mentioned but not the cup. Interestingly, in the whole text of Acts, wine (or the cup) is never mentioned. The breaking of bread and sharing of food is coupled with 'praising God' and not with 'remembering the Lord's death until he comes'. Instead of hinting at things that only those with special knowledge would understand and thus excluding others, what the 'breaking of bread' passage does is to establish the Christian group from the earliest days of its history as a community without discord, an accepting community that shares food and table fellowship in gladness and peace and into which new converts are enfolded by the same act of sharing of food. This is repeatedly emphasized at various other places in the narrative.

Eating as a pleasant and sociable act that builds communities and includes and enfolds even strangers is further expressed in two other passages (16:34; 20:7–12), to which even the shipwreck story

(27:33–6) may be added. Some New Testament scholars like to see in all these passages the celebration of the Eucharist.[31] Against this speaks, as was argued above, the fact that there is no mention of the Eucharist as a sacrament anywhere in Acts. The 'breaking of bread' is never followed by any reference to the cup nor by any specific mention of Jesus or the Passion. The 'breaking of bread' stands generally for eating. Sometimes this expression stands for the beginning of a meal, at other times for the whole of it; whether one or the other, the breaking of bread is associated with a grateful blessing for the food.

This view is further supported by the episode of Acts 16:34, which brings to a happy conclusion one of Paul's many imprisonments with the conversion of his jailer in Philippi.[32] After his baptism the newly Christian jailer 'set food before them' and 'rejoiced' with all his household of new converts. Again, 'this is not a circumlocution for the *Eucharist* but is an act of kindness'.[33] The acceptance of food on the part of the apostle signifies the inclusion of a new convert into the community.

Acts 20:7–12 depicts another type of miracle, one that gives proof of an authority derived from divine forces: the power to raise the dead. In this episode the Christian group has gathered on Sunday evening (or maybe Saturday evening) 'to break bread', to have a meal together in the course of which they will also hear instructions from the apostle; Paul talks to them until midnight. A young lad falls asleep and tumbles down from an upper room window and is believed dead. Paul, with the rest of the horrified party on his heels, runs down to see what happened. Paul bends over the body of the youth, embraces him, and in a short while tells the frightened onlookers that 'his life is in him'. After which he returns to the upper room with the people following, breaks bread and eats.

The breaking of bread here, in all likelihood, may signify thanksgiving on the part of Paul, but the literary aim that the author manages to convey here is a tangible demonstration of relief from anxiety and the resumption of peaceful communal life after the near tragedy. The demonstration of Christian community and brotherhood as antidote to all privations and accidents of fate seems to be more in keeping with the author's motivation than any secret hinting at Christian arcane practices.[34]

In Acts 27:33–8, Paul urges the people on the storm-tossed ship to eat in order to gain strength, since they have taken nothing for fourteen days. Paul himself, according to his custom, broke bread while giving thanks to God in the presence of all, and ate. Thus encouraged they all took food. Against all those who would see in this the Eucharist or a 'prefiguration' of it, Haenchen argues that Luke describes only the blessing before the meal, which for Christians and Jews was a matter of course. Conzelmann agrees 'This is not a reference to the celebration of the Eucharist. The scene describes the way Christians customarily eat'.[35] Those who see the Eucharist in this episode too, as in all others where 'breaking of bread' is mentioned, would have to decide whether it is conceivable that Paul would perform a rite that the uninitiated were not allowed to witness, on the ship, in front of all the starved sailors, who most certainly were not Christians.

This concerted effort on the part of some New Testament scholars to see the Eucharist in most of the bread-breaking passages of Acts is due to the common difficulty they experience in facing the glaringly obvious fact that a writer who chose Paul as the hero of his work actually knew little about Pauline Christianity. The author of Acts liked to see shared meals as an integral part of Christian community life – because community life was important to him – but he wrote as if he had never heard of the *disciplina arcana*, '$\phi \acute{\alpha} \rho \mu \alpha \kappa o \nu$ $\acute{\alpha} \theta \alpha \nu \alpha \sigma \acute{\iota} \alpha \varsigma$', i.e. the formalized Eucharist. As was argued in the previous chapter, the Paul of the Epistles had little interest in arguing against Jewish food scruples, holding the view that those who felt safer by keeping these should do so, and should not be rebuked, and equally that those who felt strong enough without keeping them should not be troubled. In contrast to the Epistles, Acts presents food as the central issue.

Communal meals, as we have seen, were important aspects of group life in antiquity not only among Christians but also among Jews and Gentiles.[36] Sharing food cemented communities throughout the Roman Empire, as the evidence suggests for various cult associations, trade and burial societies. Archaeological and inscriptional evidence attests to *triclinia* attached to temples, shrines and synagogues in Greek cities.[37] Sociologists and anthropologists have emphasized the importance of food sharing for group formation and cohesion. Sharing food is known to alleviate anxiety, reduce hostility and friction within the group. The rules that determine with whom one may or may not eat largely determine whom one may or may not marry. Marrying may not have been much on the minds of the earliest Christians who expected at any moment to be transported bodily into the Kingdom of God. But when the hope of this did not materialize, and as life continued as it did on this earth, what would constitute proper Christian social life with all its possible interactions, including marrying, may have become a problem to address. This problem is dealt with in Acts in terms of the question of table fellowship. The answer that Acts provides to the question of whether the Christian group should or should not be exclusive is an emphatic negative; non-Christians should be lovingly included in table fellowship; inclusion will lead to conversion. As all the food passages in Acts testify, what one may eat or with whom one may share food was intended to become less and less of a problem with the relinquishing of Jewish customs, while eating itself never did pose a problem for the author. He saw it is a pleasant activity that binds the community in shared good will and joy.

CHARITY

Acts 6:1–7 introduces rather abruptly some new elements. The idyllic community is disturbed by 'murmurings'. Moreover the community is no longer homogeneous, but consists of 'Hellenists' and 'Hebrews'.[38] The Hellenists object to their widows[39] being neglected in the daily distribution. Since the apostles complain about having to wait on tables, the simplest conclusion may be that food distribution was meant.

Charity, the giving of food and support to the poor, to widows and orphans and to strangers was one the major commandments of God in the Old Testament, as noted earlier.[40] The notion of 'zedakah', an organized distribution system for the benefit of the needy based on self-taxation binding on all Jews, was later elaborated in the Talmud, but may go back to Second Temple period. There seem to have been two kinds of poor relief among the Jews, organized around synagogues, the 'soup-kitchens' or tamhui, where food was distributed daily, and the kupah, or weekly collection and distribution of money.[41] If the description is historically accurate, the early Christian groups may have taken over an established Jewish institution when they undertook to distribute food daily to the poor. Haenchen thinks that the fact that the Jerusalem Christians have developed their own poor relief system shows that they were no longer supported by the relief arrangements of the Jewish community, which presupposes a lengthy evolution and an estrangement from the synagogue.[42]

The narrative unit discussed here starts out, significantly, with: 'Now in these days when the disciples were increasing in number', then comes the statement of the problem, the short-changing of the widows in the daily distribution, then the solution of the problem that will ensure the equitable distribution, and the passage ends with: 'and the number of disciples multiplied greatly in Jerusalem ... '. The construction of the whole unit impresses on the reader the importance of charity, more specifically, the 'waiting on the tables' for the spreading of the mission.

There is, however, another possibility suggested by the passage. It is the following: a considerable amount of time has passed since the early idyllic communal days, and a significant number of 'Hellenists' have declared themselves followers of Jesus; but since, like Paul, they were not eyewitnesses, they were not represented in the leadership of the group. The 'murmuring' may have arisen from a power struggle at the outcome of which the 'Hellenists' succeeded to get seven of their representatives into some position of authority, and as a consequence brought in an increase in followers. As Conzelmann observes: 'The actual events which lie behind ... the selection of the seven can be perceived only vaguely, because Luke has radically reworked the material in order to avoid the impression of an internal crisis in the time of the apostles.'[43] In either case, the fact that the conflict surfaces over food distribution or charity may suggest the importance of this to the success of the mission.

Euergetism was an established institution in the Graeco-Roman world. Substantial numbers of the population of Rome and other urban centres depended heavily on the dole. Christians were not the first in realizing the possible political advantage inherent in feeding the people. Charity increases good will toward the giver, it obliges the receiver to listen to his benefactor; thus followers and proselytes may be gained. While the feeding of the poor was often a part of ancient euergetism which may have influenced early Christian practice through either Jewish or Greek examples, the particular picture that the passage in Acts conjures up resembles more the custom familiar from Talmudic sources of keeping a container for the collecting of food for the poor in the synagogue and then distributing its content daily to the needy.[44]

THE PROBLEM OF THE JEWISH FOOD LAWS

Acts 10:9–16 reports the vision of Peter, which is a part of the larger narrative unit that recounts the conversion of Cornelius, and this in turn inaugurates the mission to the Gentiles. The vision itself, as in all likelihood the whole story of the conversion, is a literary creation heavily dependent on the Septuagint. Peter is in Joppa, on the Mediterranean coast. At noontime, when most inhabitants of the Land of Israel would look for a cool and shaded place, he goes up to the roof of the house to pray. Luke's view of Jewish piety may have been based more on his reading in the Scripture that Daniel prayed morning, noon and at night,[45] than on close observation of pious Jews of Jerusalem or the Galilee of the first century, who seem to have found praying morning and evening satisfactory.[46] With Peter's noontime prayer the author again subtly emphasizes the apostle's strict Jewish piety and with it Christianity as the true growth of genuine Judaism.

Peter falls asleep or into a trance on the roof and sees the heavens open and descending from up high on a sheet all kinds of animals. Both the trance and the kinds of animals echo Genesis 15:12; 1:24. Peter is commanded to kill and eat. When he refuses, showing himself again as a strictly law-abiding Jew, the heavenly voice declares to him three times that what God has cleansed cannot be impure. God himself repeals the dietary law! This then prepares the way for Peter to go to Caesarea, but to do what? To baptize a Gentile? To enter a Gentile house? To eat meat with a Gentile? While it is universally acknowledged that the vision in the narrative opens the way to the mission to the Gentiles, opinions differ on how it does that. On the surface of it the vision undoubtedly gives Peter permission to eat all kinds of meat. But why did he need this permission now, on the way to Cornelius? Cornelius, described by the author of Acts as a centurion of the 'Italian Cohort',[47] was known as a devout God-fearer who, with all his household, was in the habit of praying constantly to God and giving alms liberally. He appears to be a man who, together with his household, was already following all the non-painful aspects of the law. What would have completed this picture of a pious proselyte was circumcision. But the vision is definitely not about circumcision but food. And it is pivotal to the whole of Acts, which is confirmed by the fact that the story is told again, in 11:4–10, and in addition it is summarized once more in 15:7–9. If, as is often claimed in explanation of the vision, Jews were prohibited from social intercourse with the uncircumcised, even to the point of entering their houses,[48] why did the vision deal with food and not, like Paul in his letters, directly with circumcision?

The first question one may ask is, did the Jews of antiquity indeed cut themselves off from social intercourse with Gentiles? To which, in all likelihood, the answer is no. Jews were *not* forbidden to interact with non-Jews, they were forbidden to eat non-kosher food and to indulge in idolatry. Peter's assertion that 'You know yourselves how unlawful it is for a Jew to associate with or to visit any one of another nation',[49] would not have been said by a person of Jewish background, nor would it have been accepted as true by a Jewish audience. It is more likely that this notion was based on some Greek writer's anti-Jewish and highly exaggerated charges, like that of atheism and misanthropy, for example, levelled against them by Apollonius of Molon.[50] But how did the Jews manage to interact with Gentiles if this involved eating together? E.P. Sanders suggests[51] three possible answers. One was to eat Jewish food. In the ancient literature he surveys, cooking vessels seem not to have caused problems, only the food itself. The Gentile host who entertained a Jewish friend would have had to buy wine and meat from a suitable source. It was not necessary to have a separate set of Jewish dishes and utensils. The second answer (given by Paul) is: do not enquire. Transgressions committed inadvertently are light, and, he says, it is probable that many people did not worry about them too much. The third possibility is given in the exemplary literature: bring your own food and wine, as did Judith[52] or eat vegetables and drink water, like Daniel.[53] Why then did Acts emphasize the rejection of the food laws, unlike Paul's letters, which pressed for the rejection of circumcision? These curious discrepancies in emphasis between the Epistles and Acts are attributed by some scholars to the passing of time, a distance of date and place of the writing of these documents, or a change in the nature of their intended audience. As noted above, information concerning date and place of the writing of Acts is lacking; one can only hazard guesses concerning its intended audience.[54] Despite the surface appearance, I do not think that it was written with a Jewish-Christian audience in mind. I would argue that Acts was written to a Gentile Christian church, with a substantial faction of enthusiastic Gentile Judaizers in it.

New Testament scholars tend to take the complete seclusiveness of the Jews for granted and regard the significance of the vision as being that it allows table fellowship between Jews and Gentiles. As Esler writes:

> the essential element of that story (the vision) was not the broad notion that God had authorized the mission to the Gentiles, but the far more particular idea that what had received divine endorsement was Jewish–Gentile table fellowship in the Christian communities.[55]

It is my view that one should disregard the surface of the narrative. The 'vision of Peter' may become clearer if we regard the purpose of the author to be the writing of a book in which he could explain to Christians – Gentile Christians that is – who they are and where they came from. In the author's own perception, Christianity was the only true outgrowth and indeed the fulfilment of Judaism. The Jewish Bible – in its Septuagintal form – he saw as Christianity's 'ancient and medieval history', while Jesus and the Apostles constituted for him the movement's 'modern history'. In his view, Christians are the real Jews, the true chosen people of God. Many Christians accepted this idea, but not a few accepted it all too well, by wanting to live like Jews and keep the food laws. The argument in Acts is addressed to Christians, against Christian Judaizers, not to accommodate the Gentiles but to separate from the 'circumcision party', i.e. from those who do not understand the new dispensation.[56] The passage concerning the objection of the 'circumcision party' to Peter's sharing food with Gentiles (11:2–3) again emphasizes the importance of eating together, conviviality, in the missionary activity of the early Christians. In addition to this it is the earliest sign of the opposition to Judaizers, to those Christians who believed literally the saying of Jesus that he came not to overthrow the law but to fulfil it, who as a consequence wanted to insist on the keeping of the Jewish food regulations, and possibly even circumcision.

It seems likely that the instruction to the Gentiles, the so-called Apostolic Decree (15:19–20, 29), is based upon Leviticus 17–18, which set the rules for non-Jews living in the Land of Israel.[57] Just as in the Old Testament these enabled Jews to interact with Gentiles, the Apostolic Decree sets down the basic requirements of social interactions. The Jews themselves may have given the lead by expecting God-fearers who wanted to attend their synagogues to keep these. For Luke this decree provides the continuity between the Old Testament's Israel and the church which was free of the law.[58]

FASTING IN ACTS

As a religious practice, as opposed to not eating for days on the stormy sea (27:32–6), or Paul's three-days' coma before his conversion (9:9), fasting is mentioned in Acts in the context of the ceremony of the 'laying on of hands'. There are three places in Acts where the appointment for some task is accomplished with the ceremony of the 'laying on of hands': once in Jerusalem, where the laying of hands follows prayer (6:6), then in Antioch where fasting is added to the prayer (13:2,3) and in the other cities of Asia Minor fasting and prayer accompany the laying on of hands (14:23).

The laying on of hands for transferring authority seems to have been a widespread practice in ancient cultures. For example, Egyptian kings are often depicted with the hands of a God or Goddess over their head. In the Old Testament the custom is spelled out in detail both for *semikha*, that is, the transfer of authority, and for blessing; laying of hands served even in the ritual for the transfer of guilt onto a scapegoat.[59] But neither the blessing nor the transfer of authority required fasting. On the contrary, Isaac had dinner served to him before he laid his hand in blessing on his firstborn.[60]

Fasting, when it came into Christianity, undoubtedly came from Jewish custom. As noted earlier,[61] pagans were little inclined to self-mortification by fasting, while the Jews were known, even notorious, in the ancient world for their fasts long before Jesus (who, as the Gospel tells, went against Pharisaic custom, and did not fast[62]). As we have seen in Chapter 1, the Jews found many occasions for fasting in addition to the one obligatory fast enjoined by the Torah. They fasted for the expiation of their sins, they fasted in commemoration of the many disasters of their nation's history; they fasted for rain; they fasted to implore their God for mercy. They may have fasted more often or more conspicuously in the Diaspora, possibly as substitute for sacrifice. Fasting, however, was not a part of the regular synagogal service, which consisted mostly of reading and expounding the law, which after the fall of the Temple, and in the Diaspora, may have also included prayer.

The closest Old Testament parallel to Acts 6:6 is Numbers 27:15–23 and Deuteronomy 34:9. Both passages deal with the appointment of Joshua as successor to Moses: 'And Joshua son of Nun was full of the spirit of Wisdom, for Moses had laid his hands upon him'.[63]

Acts 13:1–3 depicts the Antiochene congregation in the midst of service and fasting when the Holy Spirit instructs them to send Paul and Barnabas on its mission. Much has been made of the claim that, in antiquity, fasting was employed as a preparation for visions and revelation.[64] In this passage, however, there is no indication at all that the fast was for this purpose. The fasting mentioned is not emphasized nor is it praised or recommended in any way, here or anywhere else in Acts. It might just signify in both places where it occurs, here and in 14:23, that the events described took place in the early morning service, which, by the later part of the first century at least may have been conducted before dawn and so before eating.[65]

Some scholars would take Acts 9:9 ('and for three days he was without sight and neither ate nor drank'), a part of the narrative of Paul's conversion, and even the fourteen days the ship's company spent without food in chapter 27, as voluntary fasting. It is argued that Paul's fasting may denote penance or preparation for baptism.[66] This completely disregards, however, the author's literary aim, which was to make the entrance of his hero as gripping and memorable as possible. Paul's conversion from a persecutor into the 'chosen vessel' is accomplished after a shattering climax, a vision, that threw him into a blinding, paralysing, psychological crisis. The persecutor of Christians collapsed as if dead; three days later a Christian missionary rose in his place. There was nothing voluntary about it, as the author wants us to see; it was not Paul but the Lord who worked the miracle. To see Paul's not eating or drinking for three days as a voluntary penance on his part, as a pre-baptism fast, is again an attempt to read into Acts 'catholic' practices of which the document seems unaware. One may ask if indeed the three-days' fast was voluntary and symbolized the church's pre-baptismal procedures, was the accompanying three-days' blindness also voluntary, and what part of the liturgy did it signify?

Some Christian writers following Biblical examples, like the Jews, thought of fasting as an efficacious penitential act for sinners, and fasting was recommended before baptism by some second- and third-century sources.[67] Both of the above-mentioned instances of going without food in Acts, however, can be seen more reasonably as unintentional and, as such, dramatic devices used to underline the seriousness of events. The shock of encountering the 'Lord' struck Paul blind and unable to eat,[68] and sea-sickness may account for the scanty food intake of the ship's crew, who in any case, were not even Christians.[69]

CONCLUSION

Food and eating signify in Acts communal life and sharing; they accompany the apostles' preaching and are a part of the Christians' praying and rejoicing. Food is regarded by the author as a means of cementing the group in communal good cheer, as a means by which new converts are being included and made welcome in the fold and, finally, as physically strengthening. Fasting as a ritual coupled with prayer is mentioned twice in the narrative, without much emphasis. There is nowhere in Acts any exhortation to fast, just as there is none to virginity or any other ascetic practice. The most obvious influence on the text is that of the Old Testament in its Septuagintal form. The attitudes it expresses toward food do not show any discernible philosophical or medical views, outside of a religious simple piety that was held up for admiration among Jews, pagans and Christians alike.

5

CLEMENT OF ALEXANDRIA

As the imminence of the Second Coming, together with the 'end of the present world', receded into the unforeseeable future, Christian communities were left with an ever-greater need for detailed exposition of moral and ethical conduct that would suit their members in daily life. No writer gave this problem more painstaking attention than Clement of Alexandria. Among his surviving works there is a large treatise called *Paidagogos*, which may be seen as the first book of etiquette written for Christians. This book, as well as the rest of his extant works, are testimony to their author's deep commitment to the education of Christians. This, he thought, should commence with mastering the very basic skills, like how to wash behind the ears; then proceed to proper training in understanding of Scripture, and finally should even extend to the study of philosophy. Eager to take on the task of the educator, Clement comments extensively on all aspects of Christian conduct in his surviving works, which pay special attention to food, drink, and table manners; alongside these he gives instructions concerning exercise, bathing, clothing and marital intercourse.

In what follows I shall examine Clement's views concerning food and fasting in his two massive works, the *Paidagogos* and the *Stromateis*, and try to assess the experiences and some of the likely intellectual influences which may have helped to shape these, and also what they may reveal concerning the life and social milieu of the audience he was addressing.

THE AUTHOR

These tasks are made difficult by the same dearth of information concerning the author as faced us in the previous chapters. Nothing is known about Clement's life, save what may be surmised from his own writing; even less about Christian communities in Egypt up to his time. Lack of contemporary evidence about his life has, however, proved not to be a serious deterrent to a considerable amount of scholarly creativity.[1]

The only contemporary evidence of his existence is provided by a set of texts attributed to him. In these Clement reveals few details about his person; for the rest, even for the probable dates of his life, Eusebius, roughly a hundred years later, is the closest, if not a most reliable, source. Based on what is provided by his *Ecclesiastical History*,[2] the date of Clement's birth is estimated circa AD 150; his birthplace is generally thought to be Athens, but there are some who think that he was a native Alexandrian.[3] He, like his namesake Clement of Rome, is often assumed to be a descendant of someone in the household of T. Flavius Clemens, a relative of Domitian who was executed for 'asebeia'[4] under that emperor in AD 95, whom later Christians liked to claim as a convert to their faith.[5] The Alexandrian Clement's forbears, however, were pagans and he, as he briefly hinted in his writings,[6] a convert to Christianity. He recounts his travels in Syria, Palestine and southern Italy in search of teachers.[7] Among these men, whom he identifies only vaguely, modern scholars discern figures like Melito of Sardis,[8] Bardesanes[9] or Tatian,[10] the Jew Theophilus of Caesarea or Theodotus the Gnostic.[11] It is believed that he followed or found Pantaenus, his esteemed teacher, in Alexandria, where he settled around the year 180. According to the tradition transmitted by Eusebius,[12] Pantaenus, a convert well versed in Stoic philosophy, was the head of the catechetical school in Alexandria, an institution that prepared candidates for baptism. The same tradition holds that Clement took over this position on the death of Pantaenus around 190.[13] During a persecution that broke out in Alexandria in the time of Septimius Severus,[14] Clement is believed to have discreetly left the city. Since persecutions continued sporadically from 202 to 206,[15] the date of Clement's departure is uncertain. It is not known where he spent the rest of his life. Eusebius mentions two letters written by Alexander, bishop of Jerusalem, in which the name Clement appears. In one, the writer, who at the time seems to have been imprisoned in Cappadocia, recommends the carrier of his letter to the church in Antioch as 'the blessed presbyter'; in the other, written to Origen, Alexander mentions Clement and Pantaenus, both having departed from life at the time of the letter, as his teachers, not directly but through a kind of a chain of intellectual descent through Origen, whom the writer calls 'the best in all things, and my master and brother'.[16] These fragments in Eusebius reinforce the view that Clement was a teacher and give rise to the speculation that he may have been an ordained churchman,[17] for which there is little evidence in his own writing. Alexander's letters serve also to fix a probable date for Clement's death between 211 and 215.

Eusebius provides a listing of Clement's works, not all of which are extant today.[18] His surviving major works are the *Protrepticus* (*Exhortation to the Greeks*), *Paidagogos* (the *Tutor* or *Instructor*) and *Stromateis* (*Miscellanies*). There is also a short treatise entitled *Quis dives salvetur?* (*What rich man shall be saved?*[19]) in which the writer tries to accommodate wealth, used to good purpose, to the Christian ideal of poverty.[20]

The most commonly accepted 'fact' concerning the author of these tracts is that he is identified as an Alexandrian. He is called Alexandrian by most scholars not only to distinguish him from his namesake, Clement of Rome, but also because, as E.F. Osborn put it, 'his mental climate was that of Alexandria'.[21] He is seen to represent a Christian mentality that is peculiarly Alexandrian.[22] The 'fact' of Clement's Alexandrian nature may be less enlightening than it first appears. A lot is known about Ptolemaic and Roman Alexandria but almost nothing is known about Christianity in Alexandria until Clement himself.[23] The peculiarly 'Alexandrine' stamp that is often discerned in his work is thus defined largely from the characteristics of that very same work,[24] and the similarity it bears to that of the Alexandrian Philo, the Jewish Platonizer of Biblical exegesis. Clement, as has often been demonstrated,[25] and as will be shown again below, relied very heavily on the work of Philo in outlook, method and even the actual content of his writing. But just as the question is still open as to how 'Jewish' or how 'Alexandrian' was the 'mentality' of Philo, even more so remains that of the 'typical Alexandrian' nature of Clement's Christianity. Nevertheless, his use of symbolic or allegorical expression,[26] of Gnostic terminology, his insistence on an unwritten tradition handed down from father to son[27] and other features of his writing are often attributed to a specifically Alexandrian Christianity.

Alexandrian Christianity in turn has variously been depicted as dominated by Gnosticism,[28] as strong on Jewish-Christianity, and fighting against Gnosticism,[29] as strictly orthodox[30] or as characterized by an 'embryonic orthodoxy', not highly organized and somewhat indiscriminate in what it admitted, whether by way of Jewish practices or Gnosticism.[31] Against the background of such uncertainties it is no surprise that there is little agreement about Clement's own religious and philosophical affinities.

Clement's teaching is often seen as a reaction to the various heterodox Christian movements of his times. Some scholars believe that it was aimed to keep his flock uncontaminated by the ideas of various radical Christian groups, who were competing for followers in Alexandria.[32] Clement's own use of the term 'true Gnostic', for his ideal of the Christian sage, encourages the belief that he saw the various Gnostic systems as a threat, while the same may also testify to the attraction and popularity of some of the Gnostic trends in late second-century Alexandria.[33] Being a Gnostic, it appears, meant to possess special knowledge and as such not to be obliged to accept on blind faith any dogma promulgated by authority. The organizing orthodox church, which insisted that the only truth is the one handed down from the apostles to the church hierarchy, found the Gnostics a substantial threat to its authority. The intellectual stature of some Gnostics or the sheer intellectual effort they exerted in trying to understand the message of Jesus in their own way, however, must have made the Gnostic an attractive figure for Clement.[34]

How strongly Clement was influenced by Gnostic ideas is still being debated. He does not identify himself with the orthodox – these he sees as boorish rejecters of culture – neither does he refer anywhere in his writing to the Alexandrian church hierarchy. On the other hand, he does debate various tenets of heterodox sects. His pronouncements often oppose extreme dualism,

> Those then who run down created existence and vilify the body are wrong. . . . The soul of man is, confessedly, the better part of man, and the body is inferior. But neither is the soul good by nature nor is the body bad by nature.[35]

Writing against 'heretics' was already an established part of Christian propaganda in his days. Food practices and sexual behaviour were often singled out as a means of distancing the heretics from the true believers. Irenaeus, bishop of Lyons, wrote a long treatise, *Against Heresies*, towards the end of the second century, which Clement may have known. From among the many heretical groups described, Irenaeus singled out a number that, in addition to their dogmatic errors, were censured also for some peculiar food practices. Thus the followers of Saturninus, according to Irenaeus, held that 'marriage and generation are from Satan', they also abstained from animal food and 'drew away multitudes by a feigned temperance of this kind'.[36] On the other hand, the followers of Valentinus and those of Basilides attached 'no importance to meats offered to idols'.[37] The Ebionites practised the Jewish law, the Nicolaitanes 'lead lives of unrestrained indulgence ... and eat things sacrificed to idols',[38] while the Encratites 'preached against marriage, some also introduced abstinence from animal food'.[39] To attack an opponent not only on his views but also on his eating and mating habits, as noted before, was a part of ancient polemic.[40] Clement's attention to the same testifies that he was well aware of it.

Thus in religion Clement is seen variously as a Christian Gnostic or as a Christian affected by Gnostic speculations, a 'Christian liberal' fighting against Gnosticism and even as the exemplar of Christian orthodoxy.[41] He is often referred to as the first Christian philosopher,[42] variously a Platonist, Stoic or even an Aristotelian. As is clearly stated in his *Stromateis*, he saw himself as an eclectic and strongly argued for the eclectic approach to all worldly wisdom.[43]

The appraisal of his thought and style of writing also varies between opposing poles. Some regard him as a fairly educated Christian who was able to use contemporary anthologies and compendia of the best of Hellenic culture to impress his audience and convince Christians of the usefulness of Hellenic learning, and pagans of the superiority of the Christian way. Others extol his wide reading as evidenced by his ability to cite more than 348 authors. There are those who are impressed by his pure Attic style,[44] or, in contrast, by his 'command of literary language so perfect that he can afford to disregard the strict rules of Atticism';[45] while he himself admits that his style is not pure by classical standards.[46] There are scholars who judge Clement's style as restrained in comparison to his contemporaries, and think that content and meaning mattered more for him than form and elegance;[47] while others again are exasperated by his rambling presentation and unsystematic thought.[48]

CLEMENT ON FOOD AND FASTING

We now turn to the texts that convey Clement's views on the proper attitude to food both for the good everyday Christian and for the 'true Gnostic', the designation he uses for the educated, philosophical, 'knowing' Christian.[49]

The training provided by the *Paidagogos* (named after the slave whose task it was to care for and train the children of a wealthy household) lays only the necessary foundations upon which further education might produce the true Christian sage, the 'true Gnostic'. Some believe that Clement planned to write a sequel to the *Paidagogos* with the title *Didascalos* (the *Teacher*), others believe that his extant work, the *Stromateis*, serves this purpose of an advanced guide for the Christian sage.[50]

At the very outset of his educational project, in the first book of the *Paidagogos*, Clement, with breathtaking boldness, establishes his book's compelling authority by asserting that the educator, both as Tutor for the beginner and as Teacher for the more advanced, who speaks through the writer is no other than the Logos, Jesus Christ himself![51]

The Stoic concept of Logos, the rational principle active in the universe, had already been usefully appropriated by the Jewish Philo, as an explanatory device for the purpose of bridging the gap between Platonic and Old Testament conceptions of the deity. Philo saw the Logos of the Stoics as God's active, creative presence in the world. Philo, being both a pious Jew and a Platonist, had no need to personify it. For him the teacher who instructed humankind in God's mysteries was not the Logos but a human figure, Moses.[52] Clement equates Philo's Logos with the figure of Christ, whom he sees not only as God's creative presence in the world but also as tutor of respectable social skills, and as teacher and initiator into the higher mysteries. For him it is Christ the Logos who exhorts to conversion, who takes pains to instruct the beginner in some surprisingly basic rules of conduct, as we shall see, and finally reveals the true mystery to the Christian Gnostic.

The Jesus of the Gospels provided moral teaching and personal example, which his followers sought to emulate, but he himself did not provide systematic guidance on how to eat properly, how and when to wash or what clothes to wear. His message of Love did not include teaching on how to make love; an unfortunate omission that led to a considerable amount of perplexity and even mischief later. Clement, for his part, claimed to know exactly what sort of conduct in the minutiae of daily living was acceptable to Jesus the Logos. A large part of his efforts was directed to the writing of such guidance that would tell the simple Christian in simple language, and the more advanced Christian sage in more fitting philosophical terms, how to behave in all circumstances of everyday life.

Clement saw the Christian group as consisting of two tiers, beginners and advanced sages, that is to say, good and better Christians, a distinction innocent enough at the outset, but which looked forward to a long and unfortunate history. In keeping with this perception, Clement treated questions relating to food also on two different levels, first as instruction in the basic rules of conduct in the *Paidagogos*, and second as guidance to the advanced in the *Stromateis*.

Like a good Greek schoolmaster, he set out to teach first the basic skills upon which advancement in knowledge could be built. He seems to have had no doubts or hesitation about the kind of conduct he wanted to inculcate in his pupils. Respectability, the beacon towards which his Christians were urged to strive, was of the utmost importance for him. Next came frugality and temperance, the two virtues that in his view pave the way to respectability. Clement's image of the model Christian householder, his wife and children, owes little to the Jesus of the Gospels and much more to the precepts that contemporary moralists held up for well-to-do burgers who aspired to the philosophic 'good life' in the big cities of the empire. To convince his audience of the weightiness of his arguments, and not less to impress them with his erudition, he threw his net far and wide in search of witnesses and supportive authorities, a very large proportion of whom were pagan.[53] In both works he lavishly marshals pronouncements of ancient philosophers, aphorisms of physicians, quotations from poets and playwrights, and naturally, verses from Scripture. His exhortations are enriched with descriptions of admirable or deplorable habits of past times, faraway peoples and even some quaint animals. Clement's purpose was not to acquaint his audience with the works or the line of thought of his sources, but only to support his own argument with a well-chosen sentence of a known and respected authority. He knows that what he wants to say is right and the texts he cites simply prove it.[54] Few of his borrowings ever involve extended exposition, only a sentence or two to support the point in question. It is generally acknowledged that he used for this purpose various source books, compendia of famous sayings that were available and popular in his time.[55]

As noted above, Clement's aim was twofold: to teach respectable conduct to his charges, and, when they have achieved this, to teach them the proper philosophy. Why should a Christian learn philosophy? Because, he explains, philosophy is handmaiden to theology, a preparation for divine knowledge. The great virtue of philosophy, as Clement sees it, is that it:

'professes the control of the tongue and the belly and the parts below the belly', which in itself would be sufficient to recommend it, but it is even worthier of respect 'if cultivated for the love and knowledge of God'.[56]

Clement, and Philo from whom he borrowed this,[57] were not alone in viewing philosophy this way. Hellenistic philosophy long before their time had been turning away from the contemplation of the sensible world, concerning itself more and more with theology and ethics. As for his borrowing from others, Clement assures us that the eclectic philosophy paves the way to divine virtue: 'whatever has been well said by each óf those sects, which teach righteousness along with a science pervaded by piety – this eclectic whole I call philosophy'.[58]

The *Paidagogos* is, as was pointed out above, a handbook of Christian etiquette. Its major concern is practical and definitely 'this world' oriented. It elaborates in great detail on how Christians should conduct their daily lives, what to eat and how to eat, what to wear, how to use the bath, what exercises to do, how to conduct themselves in the marital bed; and so on. It is truly an 'education in the practical needs of life'.[59] The life in this case is not the afterlife. Even the rewards of the decorous and dignified conduct resulting from this training are reaped in this life by an increase in health, strength and, surprisingly, even beauty. Added to these are the not inconsiderable gains in economic wellbeing and the admiration of neighbours. The neighbours that Clement's pupils are meant to impress with their impeccable manners include, in addition to fellow Christians, well-bred pagans, products of the best of Greek *paideia*. Clement evidences a very high regard for Greek education. Where he denounces the pagans he denounces them for not living up to it.

The second book of the *Paidagogos* is devoted largely to eating, drinking and table manners. Some of the points raised here are also addressed and amplified in the *Stromateis*. The lesson starts with a strong echo of the well known and often discussed passage in Plato's Republic,[60] attributed to Socrates, which may have given rise also to the favourite commonplace of the Cynics:

> Other men live that they may eat, just like unreasoning beasts; for them life is only their belly – we eat only to live. Eating is not our main occupation, nor is pleasure our chief ambition. Food is permitted us simply because of our stay in this world.[61]

Clement's aim throughout the treatise is to inculcate the virtue of temperance. As was pointed out earlier,[62] in the second and third centuries there was still a great deal of popular interest in what the ancient philosophers of Greece had to say about 'the good life'. These were fondly remembered as sharing the conviction that health and strength are in some way importantly related to the 'good life'; health and strength were thought to depend upon or indeed, to be coextensive with the intellectual virtue of temperance.[63]

Health and strength are eagerly embraced by Clement as part of the Christian 'good life' too. It is important then to examine what in food is required for their maintenance: 'plain and ungarnished food, in keeping with the truth, suitable to children who are plain and unpretentious, adapted to maintaining life, not self-indulgence.' Any sort of food that 'aids digestion and restricts the weight of the body' will keep the Christian healthy and strong.[64] A Christian needs to be strong and healthy but he does not need the strength of athletes who live on a rich diet, and whom Clement, following a long and distinguished line of authorities, from Euripides to Galen, regarded as living in an unbalanced, unhealthy and miserable state.[65] Piety and prudery did not in themselves predispose to a hostile view of athletic training, as the example of Philo of Alexandria testifies. This may be a small but interesting point on which Clement clearly disagrees with Philo, to whose work in most other respects he is greatly indebted. Philo the pious Jew expressed considerable admiration for athletes, their training and even their diet.[66] Philo wrote about a century and a half before Clement, and tastes, even of pious sages, may have changed in time. Later philosophic pagans like Porphyry and certainly later Christian writers seem to have agreed with Clement's view that decorous philosophic conduct has nothing to gain from athletes or their diet.[67]

Excessive variety in food, he warns, should be avoided both on medical and moral grounds, 'for it gives rise to every kind of bad effect: indisposition of the body, upset stomach, perversion of taste . . .'.[68] This mistaken notion, which would lead to dietary deficiency diseases if acted upon, was, nevertheless, quite fashionable among moralizers. According to the Stoic Seneca,[69] Sextius believed that we should curtail the sources of our luxury; he was said to have argued that a varied diet was contrary to the laws of health and was unsuited to our constitution.[70] Sextius, in turn, is quoted by Clement's younger fellow Alexandrian, Origen, as someone whose sayings were familiar to Christians.[71] But at this point in the argument Clement does not appeal to Stoic ideas, but to medical opinion. No doubt because, just as today, so in Clement's times too medical opinion carried authority, he cites Antiphanes, a Delian physician, for the assertion that rich food is one of the causes of disease. This example of Clement's use of his 'sources' also points out the difficulty in which he put himself by claiming the divine Logos as the actual author of his work. Clement sees gluttony as moral evil which the Logos disapproves, but since he cannot find a God-given commandment concerning the subject, his Logos who, as noted above, is no less than Christ himself, is forced to rely upon anthologies of pagan writers for support! These, however, seldom have the force of authority and the general applicability of a divinely inspired command. So in order to back his view and to give force and generality to them he often quotes sayings out of context, presenting them as statements of a general physical law. So he adds the missing authority to back his own perception of the evil that, here for example, lurks in rich food.

The excesses of gluttony were frowned upon by all the ancient sages. The physicians, however, tended not to give general rules concerning food. As was discussed earlier,[72] food for the ancient physician was one of the most important therapeutic tools in his possession, an integral part of regimen that had to be carefully devised for each individual according to his or her state. Rich food could be bad for some but good for others. Physicians generally did not regard it to be in their professional interest to make simple sweeping general statements, like the one suggested by Clement.

Gluttony was an evil and a potential basis for all other evils, for many of the philosophers. As Plato wrote in the *Timaeus*:

> They who framed our kind knew what would be our incontinence in the matter of meat and drink, how greed would move us to consume much more than need and due measure call for.... They appointed the abdomen to be the receptacle for future surplus of meat and drink and made the guts wind and coil within it, lest quick transit of nutriment through them force the body to crave fresh nutriment too quickly, make it ravenous and so render the whole tribe of us, through gluttony, incapable of philosophy and music, deaf to the voice of our divinest part. [73]

Plato saw gluttony as a potential danger that would interfere with the more noble pursuits of the philosopher. For Plato's Jewish admirer in first-century Alexandria, Philo, who knew the *Timaeus*, gluttony becomes a veritable obsession, the stumbling block in the way to holiness, the direct source of lasciviousness and all other crimes.[74] Surprisingly, Clement is less anxious about gluttony's sure connection with lasciviousness and other crimes than is Philo. Instead he worries about gluttony as being unseemly, indecorous, uneconomical and, as a consequence, unbecoming of a respectable Christian. The difference in outlook is small, more a question of emphasis. Clement may not share completely Philo's sentiment concerning gluttony, but that does not prevent him from often borrowing phrases from his writings to express his own condemnation of it.

The glutton of comedy and satire had a very long history in Greek and Roman literature. As noted above, a connection between the type of food a man ate and his character was widely assumed. To characterize heroes or upright citizens as frugal eaters and villains as gorging themselves on 'luxurious food' (which more often than not led directly to sexual misconduct) became a convenient literary device.[75] Clement seems to try his hand at this type of satirical writing, relying heavily on topoi that were popular with Philo, Seneca and others.[76]

Greediness, in his eyes, can reach alarming proportions, even necessitating the importation of foodstuff from faraway places. Clement found the stimulation of a mercantile economy by people's needs and desires quite deplorable. Gluttons, as he writes,

> yearn for these fowl and dress them up with sweet sauces, ravenously providing themselves with whatever the land and the depth of the sea and the vast expanse of the sky produce as food. There is no limit to the gluttony that these men practise. Truly, in ever inventing a multitude of new sweets and ever seeking recipes of every description, they are shipwrecked on pastries and honeycakes and desserts.[77]

Lavish banquets were the targets of satire and moral denunciation, often by those who were not invited to partake. Clement singles out for special censure for their opulence and costliness, the Christian banquets given under the name of the *agape*, the religious communal meal,

> If anyone dares to mention the *agape* with shameless tongue as he indulges in a dinner exhaling the odour of steaming meats and sauces, then he profanes the holy *agape*, sublime and saving creation of the Lord, with his goblets and the serving of soup.[78]

The conflict about Christian conviviality goes back to the time of the apostles.[79] On the one hand it was a time-honoured custom to share food and provide hospitality, which may have also served as an effective tool in organizing the community and spreading the Word.

On the other hand these communal banquets often depended on the generosity of the wealthier members of the community, making obvious the social inequalities of the participants, as Paul's letter to the Corinthian community would testify. Like many pagan banquets, it appears that the Christian ones too, at least in Clement's view, provided opportunities for the ostentation of wealth, resulting in disruption instead of social cohesion. Clement does not object to the *agape*, if it is a feast 'permeated with love... an expression of mutual and generous good will.... Festive gatherings of themselves do contain some spark of love, from food taken at a common table we become accustomed to the food of eternity'. If the dinner is given in the name of love and friendly conviviality, if the food is 'plain and restrained ... free of a too rich variety',[80] then it will foster communal living, which Clement valued very highly for Christians.[81]

Clement returns to the topic of Christian conviviality and hospitality in his *Stromateis*, a work intended for the edification of the Christian sage, and reiterates that fellowship, love and hospitality belong together.[82] Community spirit, Clement believed, is enhanced by the two stoic virtues: self-sufficiency and frugality. Self-sufficiency, the ability to be independent of material things, in matters of eating meant for Clement that food should be limited to the proper amount, sustaining health but not pleasure.[83] Frugality in food both 'ministers to health of the body' and leaves enough of the resources to distribute to the needy. Thus both good health and Christian charity are served by frugality. But a diet that oversteps the limits of self-sufficiency carries with it all kinds of dangers: 'it harms man by dulling the mind and making the body susceptible to disease', it gives rise to a long list of undesirable character traits, like 'gluttony, squeamishness, gourmandizing, insatiability of appetite, voraciousness', and others all culled from the rich resources of Greek comedy and satire concerning parasites. Again, science is invoked to underpin the argument: 'It is a natural law that the body is not benefited by excessively rich food; quite the contrary, those who live on simpler foods are stronger and healthier and more alert'.[84]

That a rich diet dulls the mind was very satisfying to ancient moralizers; for those who cannot afford a rich diet it is comforting like the proverbial 'sour grapes'. The idea itself arose from a conception of the human body as a set of interconnecting containers, in which food and its by-products, the various excrements, compete for space with the spirit, a notion that goes back, as we have seen, to Plato's *Timaeus*; it will be greatly favoured by later Christian ascetics who will exhort the faithful to 'feed the soul instead of the body' with little evidence to prove that the two are mutually exclusive.

The Stoic philosopher's self-controlled and frugal approach to food is what the Christian should emulate under the guidance of the Logos. Clement, however, is aware of, and clearly follows, the apostolic message in stating that eating in itself has no religious significance for the Christian. As Clement sees it, 'the physical act of eating is indifferent'; one should only avoid food offered to idols, not for fear, since there is no power in them, but to 'show contempt to the devils': above all, Christians should not 'misuse the gifts of the Father by being spendthrifts like the rich son in the Gospel. . . . Surely we have been commanded to be master and lord not slave of food'.[85] The philosophic Christian does not even need to abstain completely from 'rich foods but should not be anxious for them'.[86] If they keep constantly in mind the danger of gluttony that ever lurks in conviviality, Christians do not have to avoid social occasions, but they must always behave with proper decorum:

> We must partake of what is set before us, as becomes a Christian, out of respect for him who has invited us and not to lessen or destroy the sociability of the gathering. We should consider the rich variety of dishes that are served as a matter of indifference, and despise delicacies as things that after a while will cease to be.

and one should offer thanksgiving, 'for he who always offers up thanks will not indulge excessively in pleasure'.[87] Clement here subtly infuses various New Testament pronouncements, like the acceptance of all food with thanksgiving, the distant echo of 1 Corinthians 6:13, that both food and the stomach are temporal things eventually destroyed by God, with the Stoic notion of food as being 'indifferent' and the need to avoid pleasure.

Clement worried also that lack of temperance and self-control in eating makes a man appear a fool. If a wealthy man eats without restraint he does wrong on two scores; he shows a boorish lack of the virtue of temperance, a most unphilosophical behaviour, and 'he adds to the burden of those who do not have'.[88] Clement saw his pupils as wealthy enough to afford lavish food and banquets but lacking breeding and refinement. With great seriousness therefore he turns to the task of advising on decorous table manners. One should eat politely, he says, keeping the hands as well as the chin and the couch clean, without twisting about or acting unmannerly while swallowing food. The hand should reach for food only discreetly; one should keep from speaking while eating, 'for speech is inarticulate and ill-mannered when the mouth is full'. Neither is it polite to eat and drink at the same time, because 'it indicates extreme intemperance to try to do two things together that need to be done separately',[89] and so he goes, churning out a seemingly interminable chain of petty pedantries.

After discussing how one should eat, Clement turns with equal seriousness to the question of what should be eaten. Concerning meat eating he was not of a single mind. Some philosophers, followers of Pythagoras foremost among them, rejected the eating of meat, mostly on religious and mystical grounds. Some Platonists, for reasons that may or may not have been different from those of the Pythagoreans, also followed a meatless diet. Clement greatly admired them.[90] On the other hand, he was fully aware that both the Old and New Testaments take meat eating for granted, but still proffered a mild plea against flesh food, both by misrepresenting the Pythagoreans' argument and by misquoting Paul's saying in his letter to the Romans.[91] The truncating of Paul's sentence and its use taken out of its proper context to support arguments against eating meat and drinking wine will have a long history in the writings of the Christian Fathers, some of whom found Peter's dispensation about animal food distasteful. Clement's reasons for abstaining from meat generally fit well with those given by pagan advocates of vegetarianism described by Seneca.[92] Thus he emphasizes that eating or not eating meat is not a religious concern, but it is an ethical consideration. If one eats meat one does not sin.[93] Just as Seneca who, under the influence of Stoic teachers, gave up oysters and mushrooms,[94] Clement too advises against appetizers, and for the same reason: for 'they lead us to eat when we are not hungry'.[95] Frugality should direct the Christian's choice of food. He would permit 'roots, olives, all sorts of green vegetables, milk, cheese, fruits and cooked vegetables of all sorts – but without sauces. And should there be need for meat, boiled or roasted, let it be given'.[96] Sauces represented in both comedy and moralizing literature the surest sign of luxury and decadence. They required the artistry of the professional cook, the use of rare and expensive ingredients, all for an act consuming time and resources with results most impermanent. While the banqueters greatly enjoyed these ephemeral artistic creations, others equally loudly harangued against the wicked sauces.[97]

Clement somewhat reluctantly allows the eating of meat, as seen above, for those who partake of it in moderation. It should be boiled or roasted. According to Greek literary clichés, roasting and boiling were considered the 'manly' way to prepare meat. Homer's heroes ate roasted or boiled meat, furthermore, they prepared it with their own hands. Any other way of preparing it was regarded as effeminate, luxurious, time consuming and requiring the artistry of a cook.[98]

In the *Stromateis* Clement enlarges on some of the problems involved in meat eating. Even though the Old Testament Law allows the eating of meat, still,

> if any one of the righteous does not burden his soul by the eating of flesh, he has the advantage of a rational reason. . . . Now Xenocrates . . . and Polemon . . . seem clearly to say that animal food is unwholesome, inasmuch as it has already been elaborated and assimilated to the souls of the irrational creatures. So also the Jews abstain from swine's flesh on the ground of this animal being unclean; since more than other animals it roots up, and destroys the productions of the ground.[99]

Clement was inconvenienced in his advocacy of vegetarianism by the Bible and by Stoic views, since both of these assigned animals to men for use. Granting this, he argues that not all of the animals were to be used for eating. Animals work for men and provide wool for clothing. Swine that is forbidden food by the Jewish Law, the Greeks regard as having no other use but to be eaten. Some people, says Clement,

> eat them as useless, others as destructive of fruits, and others do not eat them, because the animal has a strong propensity for sexual intercourse. So, then, the Law sacrifices not the goat, except in the sole case of the banishment of sins; since pleasure is the metropolis of vice. It is to the point also that it is said that the eating of goat flesh contributes to epilepsy. And they say that the greatest increase [in weight] is produced by swine's flesh. Wherefore it is beneficial to those who exercise the body; but to those who devote themselves to the development of the soul it is not so, on account of the habit that results from the eating of flesh. Perchance also some Gnostic will abstain from the eating of flesh for the sake of training, and in order that the flesh may not grow wanton in amorousness. 'For wine', says Androcydes, 'and gluttonous feeds of flesh make the body strong, but the soul more sluggish.' Accordingly such food, in order to clear understanding, is to be rejected.[100]

Clement is aware of the fact that some ascetic Christians refuse flesh food for ascetic reasons in order to reduce their sex drive, but he does not advocate it as absolutely necessary for the purpose.[101] Later Christians will take up the idea with great vigour.[102]

Clement advises that the best food is that which can be used immediately without being cooked, and next to this come inexpensive foods.[103] He cites the Acts of the Apostles[104] and the gospel[105] to reiterate that food for the Christian is not a religious concern, and that the only caution is not to eat meat sacrificed to idols. One suspects, however, that frugality came next to godliness in Clement's eyes: 'A middle course is good in all things, and no less so in serving a banquet. Extremes are, in fact, dangerous but the mean is good. Natural desires have a limit set to them by self-sufficiency'.[106] Aristotelian terminology comes in conveniently in arguing for Stoic self-restraint and Clementine frugality. As there is no sure way of judging when we have eaten enough to satisfy our body's actual physical needs, self-sufficiency is suggested as a safeguard. As the Cynics advised, eat what you can obtain cheaply and by the least amount of effort. Even the Jewish dietary laws, Clement argues, were given to safeguard frugality, and in that sense Clement regards them as very wise.[107]

Self-sufficiency and frugality guard against excesses and especially against pleasure, which Clement, following Philo, sees as the greatest danger facing the philosophic Christian. This, however, does not mean that Christians must give up sweetmeats, honey,[108] or even rich food, Clement reassures his disappointed flock, as long as they do not desire these. They should not eat for pleasure. For 'Among men, pleasure generally gives rise to some sense of loss and regret; overeating begets in the soul only pain and lethargy and shallow-mindedness'.[109]

To end his plea for moderation and frugality in eating Clement turns again to a 'scientific' or medical argument, one that is based on a very odd conception of bodily development, and is more in keeping with the convictions of Philo than with those of medical authorities:

It is said, too, the bodies of the young in the period of their physical maturing are able to grow because they are somewhat lacking in nourishment; the life principle which fosters growth is not encumbered – on the contrary, an excess of food would block the freedom of its course.[110]

It must be pointed out that nowhere in his lengthy discourse does Clement advocate fasting; he pleads only for moderation in food. It seems that the audience that he addressed was still concerned in some measure with the Jewish food laws, as he mentions foods 'disallowed to us', pig's meat and seafood which 'surpass other fishes in fleshiness and fatness'; these should be used, if at all, with caution and in moderation. The Law was wise, he stresses, to prohibit rich food, which, in addition to being unhealthy and fattening, engenders greed, is expensive, and absorbs attention and resources that are better spent elsewhere. Philo interpreted the Jewish dietary law both literally and symbolically. Following him, Clement sees great wisdom in the Law by which the Lord announced a long time ago that 'we are to exercise control over the belly, and what is below the belly' and which still teaches us 'patience and self restraint' by 'repressing our desires'. The Law is still useful for checking lust and condemning pleasure. Clement recommends to his philosophic Christians to avoid 'such articles of food as excite lust and dissolute licentiousness in the bed chamber and luxury'.[111]

Clement's Christians seem to have shown some concern with fasting on set days of the week, like pious Jews or, what is more likely, Judaizers, but the days designated were already different from those traditional among Jews.[112] Pious Jews could use the Second (Monday) or the Fifth day (Thursday) of the Jewish week for fasting in order not to interfere with the preparation and celebration of the Sabbath.[113] Christians who wanted to follow the practice, but wanted also to distinguish themselves from their Jewish neighbours, used the Fourth day and the day of Preparation. Interestingly, Clement uses the Jewish designation when referring to Wednesday and Friday, pointing out that the pagans name these for Hermes and Aphrodite, respectively. In the question of fasting too, Clement holds consistently to the apostolic view that food in itself is not a religious issue, and to the prophet Isaiah's warning[114] that decent conduct is what God wants from his people and not abstention from eating. His listeners may have pointed to Scriptural passages, like Tobit 12:8 advocating 'fasting with prayer', to which he replied: 'fasting signifies abstinence from all evils whatsoever, both in action and in words, and in thought itself'.[115] The significance of the fasting days, he says, is that the one has its name from Hermes the god of commerce and the other from Aphrodite, the goddess of love. A true Christian then fasts in all his life by abstaining from 'covetousness and voluptuousness from which all vices grow'. Clement clearly saw that it was not food but fornication that the Apostle warned against, which he explained as having three varieties, 'love of pleasure, love of money and idolatry. He [the Christian] fasts, then, according to the Law, abstaining from bad deeds, . . . and from evil thoughts'.[116]

Does Clement's attitude to Jewish Law indicate that his Alexandrian Christians were strongly influenced by Judaism,[117] or was he arguing against heretics, like the followers of Marcion, who would reject the Old Testament and deny the identity of its Creator God with the Father of Jesus?[118] He does not address the problem of Judaizers, or at least he does not see the keeping of Jewish food regulations as something that a Christian should reject – on the contrary, as we have seen; nor does he show any awareness of a need to defend the Old Testament as a part of Christian Scripture. His opposition to fasting, taken together with his arguments for the desirability of marriage for Christians, would seem to testify to his awareness and disapproval of radical Christians who may have advocated extreme asceticism. He has only scorn for the Encratites, comparing them with strange people, like the Hylobii, who

> neither inhabit cities, nor have roofs over them, but are clothed in the bark of trees, feed on nuts and drink water in their hands. Like those called Encratites in the present day, they know not marriage nor begetting of children.[119]

He brings Scriptural evidence to reject those heresies that objected to wine on religious grounds and employed only bread and water in the Eucharist, a practice that Clement deplores as clearly not in accord with the rule of the church.[120] The Encratites, followers of Tatian, in the decade after 170 formed this group in their leader's native Syria as a reaction against the increasing acceptance of Hellenistic culture by Christians. The Encratites rejected marriage as sinful and renounced the use of meat and wine in any form. The reference to water-drinking heretics may concern the Jewish-Christian sect of the Ebionites who believed that Jesus the man was elevated to the rank of Messiah, and insisted on keeping the Law from which all bloody sacrifice was eliminated. Sacrifices were replaced by a life of poverty and sharing of all property by the community. The Ebionites purified themselves by daily washing, and participated in a ritual meal of bread and water.[121]

Much more than in the case of food, when it comes to the question of drinking, Clement's advice becomes deeply coloured by sexual anxiety. Sharing with Philo the conviction that wine is a 'drug of madness',[122] he expresses admiration for those who drink water, the 'nourishment of sobriety'. Boys and girls should, as a general rule, be kept from drinking wine, 'the most inflammable of all liquids', which, when poured into 'flaming youth' stimulates their 'wild impulses and festering lusts'.[123] It is imperative to attempt to extinguish the beginnings of passion in the young, as far as possible, 'by excluding them from all that will inflame them – Bacchus and his threat'. For wine, he believes, even causes the sexual organs to mature before their time, 'as the wine takes effect, the youths begin to grow heated from passion, without inhibition, and the breasts and sexual organs swell as harbinger and image of the act of fornication'.[124]

Even adults should not drink wine before the evening. Clement advises them to have no liquids at all with their lunch (in the climate of Alexandria!), so that the dangerous moistness of their body would dry up. Heated and moist bodies were generally believed by the ancients – physicians and laymen alike – to be prone to sexual lust.[125] Wine, having the power of both heating and moistening the body, was viewed as highly dangerous, especially for the young whose bodies were 'by nature' hot and moist. Clement seems to regard even water as dangerous. Sexual prudery combines with frugality in Clement as the motive force of his teaching. Drinking too much fluid, even water, he assures his reader, is also uneconomical, since it simply wastes the food by washing it away. True frugality and prudence dictate that the food should be carefully masticated so that most of it would be digested and as little as possible wasted. Spiritual Christians, just like spiritual pagans, were wishing for the smallest quantities of excrement possible.[126] Excrement, in addition to being an unsavoury reminder of the earthbound nature of our body, had a more sinister aspect in the mind of Clement and, following him, in the minds of other Christian Fathers. Excrement, he asserts, when it accumulates around the 'organs of generation' arouses lust![127] This piece of wisdom is embedded in a discussion of exercise and digestion, but it is more indebted to the vivid picture that Philo paints of the dependence of lust on gluttony[128] than to medical theories.

Clement does not forbid wine completely. The mature person, less susceptible to sexual lusts, may have wine towards evening, when the temperature has cooled, and the day's work has been accomplished, in order to 'stimulate the failing natural heat of the body with a little artificial warmth. . . . Those who have already passed the prime of life may be permitted more readily to enjoy their cup'.[129] Wine was believed to be good for health by many and diverse authorities. Consciously following the writer of the *Epistle* who urged Timothy to take some wine for the sake of his stomach,[130] Clement recommends that wine should be used for the sake of health: 'Just as food is permitted to relieve hunger, so drink is to ease thirst, provided the greatest caution is taken against any abuse, for tasting wine is fraught with danger'. The danger is sexual arousal in the young as we have seen, but when the old man is overcome by wine, Clement warns, he becomes pugnacious and 'returns every offense of a drunken neighbour'.[131]

In drinking too the Christian should be careful to behave with proper decorum. He should not drink fast and show greed, and should not slurp noisily.[132] Women, as customary, are reproached more severely for undignified behaviour, since they are, or should be 'especially trained in good manners',[133] they should not open their mouths wide in a disgusting fashion nor expose their necks while drinking, they should not belch like men, but most importantly they should not be sexually enticing! Women's behaviour should be strictly controlled, lest they make both men and women fall 'by attracting the eyes of men to themselves'.[134] The favourite exhortation, familiar from Philo, appears again:

> We must keep firm control over the pleasures of the stomach, and an absolutely uncompromising control over the organs beneath the stomach. If, as the Stoics teach, we should not move even a finger on mere impulse, how much more necessary is it that they who seek wisdom control the organ of intercourse?[135]

Can Clement's writings be taken as evidence for the social class or background of Alexandrian Christians at whom they presumably were directed? Unfortunately there is no evidence to show whether his writings were read at all by his contemporaries. There is no mention of Clement in the extant writings of his fellow Alexandrian and supposed follower in the catechetical school, Origen. This fact is well-nigh inconceivable to some modern scholars, who generally believe that Clement must have been Origen's teacher, and see support for this in the fact that Origen entitled an early work *Stromateis*, after Clement's book of the same title.[136] This work is now lost, leaving Origen's acquaintance with Clement hypothetical in the extreme.

Having no access to contemporary comments on Clement makes any statement concerning his social milieu somewhat uncertain. It may also be argued that his writing could only be taken as evidence of his own and his audience's social background if we knew that we could hear in it his own voice – that is, if the text was his own creation. The fact is, as we have seen, that a substantial part of it is snipped out and pasted together from earlier literature, and that his work as a whole is most consistently and heavily indebted to that of Philo.

A comparison between the aims of Philo and those of Clement may provide some clarification. When writing about fleshly nature, Philo also had in Greek literature a rich vein to mine for gold nuggets to use in denouncing gluttony, which he saw as the symbol of sensuality and a serious moral failing. It was far from Philo's mind, however, to write a book of etiquette with instructions for everyday conduct; his interest was not in inculcating refined manners, but in extolling the superiority of pure intellect over the attractions of sense perception. Philo's approach is strictly moral-philosophical. Clement's emphasis is very different, in its concern with the etiquette and niceties of everyday life. He borrowed the denunciation of the glutton not merely as contrast to the praise of self-control; he went much further, giving detailed and painstaking advice on how to safeguard oneself from becoming gluttonous. Neither did he parade all the old literary commonplaces concerning gluttony only in order to show his erudition,[137] but, it seems, he actually meant his pedantic instructions to be followed. The advice he gives, which carefully pays attention even to such problems as how the well-mannered Christian should burp,[138] reflects a social milieu that was obviously not that of a wealthy, highly educated class of converts, as is often suggested.[139] Members of a secure aristocracy, or people born into an established upper class, do not want lessons on comportment; their behaviour is assumed to be the measure of the prevailing manners. It is usually new money, or those aspiring to move upwards on the social scale, who are most concerned with 'proper' manners. It is quite likely that many in Clement's audience were Christians who had acquired enough wealth to enable them to have the good things in life, like servants, good food, furnishings and ornaments, and now they were keen on acquiring respectability. Clement sought to provide them with this by teaching them good manners of Greek *paideia*. Whether Clement wrote about table manners in response to an expressed request by his flock, which felt a need for respectability, or whether he himself had a need to make his fellow Christians behave with what he regarded as respectable manners, and thus more acceptable in polite company, cannot be decided without external evidence. Instead of being his actual audience, it is more likely that an 'educated upper class' was, both for him and for his audience, what sociologists call a 'reference group', that is the group which they perceive as desirable and to which they would like to belong. If the audience of the Roman Stoic Seneca can be characterized as 'insecure yet upwardly mobile readers', as it was, on good grounds, by Habinek,[140] then Clement's Alexandrian Christians would be even more so. If H. Chadwick is right in assuring us that

'Clement belongs to the world he is addressing',[141] his writings suggest that this world consists of an economically well-to-do but socially insecure group, whose members would like to come in from the margins of society and be accepted as refined and cultured burgers. The Christians Clement was speaking to were married people. As Peter Brown envisages it, 'Clement's church, like the community addressed by Hermas in Rome, had remained a loose confederation of believing households'.[142] Indeed, the whole tenor of his work conjures up for the modern reader pictures of a community similar to those Paul visited in the course of his travels in Acts, communities consisting of married, economically secure households of traders and artisans, who aspired to godliness. A very similar group now in Clement's Alexandria seems to aspire not only to godliness but also to bourgeois respectability. At least that is how Clement perceives them, and what he offers them is a Christian *paideia*. He teaches them that a Christian should choose a life that is well balanced and temperate. In complete agreement with Philo and the Stoics, Clement argues that concentration upon pleasures of the senses is alien to a divine nature.[143] Self-control in drinking and moderation in eating are natural ways of producing both health and beauty.[144] Clement's guidelines stress temperance, decorum and, most of all, frugality. The love of money and vanity are even greater evils than gluttony.[145]

As we have seen, Clement's attitude to food and his negative attitude to fasting may have been reinforced by the distaste he shows to the extreme asceticism of Encratites or others, whom he may have encountered in Alexandria or read about. Where he clearly addresses ascetical Gnostics is in his treatment of marriage. Clement does not oppose marriage. On the contrary, he makes a strong plea for it. Marriage and the management of a household he sees as important aspects of the education of the Christian man and, like Paul, as a safeguard against sin.[146] Countering various radical Christian positions, Clement is set against the rejection of sexual intercourse that is motivated by hatred of the body. Sexual intercourse should be practised by Christians only in marriage and only for the procreation of children, which according to Clement should be accomplished with little or, if possible, no pleasure at all. How a dutiful Christian husband could impregnate his wife without experiencing sexual excitement remains a mystery, despite Clement's celebrated frankness in matters pertaining to marital relations.[147] As Chadwick pointed out, nothing could be more mistaken than to think of Clement as a comfortable and worldly figure.[148] His own inclination is probably best expressed in his words, 'Food is a necessity, sex strains the nerves, spreads a mist over the senses and tires the muscles'.[149]

Clement, like many of the condemned Gnostics, envisaged two kinds of Christians. The simple Christian, represented by his flock, for whom he wrote the *Paidagogos*, whose behaviour should reflect '*metriopatheia*', temperance and frugality; and the other, the superior Christian sage. The most salient attribute of the true Christian sage or, as he likes to call him, the true Gnostic, is *apatheia*, or complete suppression of bodily impulses. The true Gnostic is 'free of all perturbations of the soul.... He is subject only to affections that exist for the maintenance of the body, such as hunger, thirst and the like'.[150] Then, expounding a Platonism familiar from Philo, he himself comes very close to a dualist position;

> Now the sacrifice which is acceptable to God is unswerving abstraction from the body and its passions. This is really the true piety.... For he who neither employs his eyes in the exercise of thought, nor draws aught from his other senses, but with pure mind itself applies to objects, practises true philosophy.[151]

The Platonist extolled a way of life for the elite few, the philosophers, while Philo preached apatheia for the man who retired from the active life, after having fulfilled his duties, in order to devote his life to piety and philosophical contemplation. Clement holds up this as the ideal of Christian perfection:

> The struggle for freedom, then, is waged not alone by the athletes of battles in wars, but also in banquets, and in bed, and in the tribunals, by those who are anointed by the Logos, who are ashamed to become the captives of pleasures.[152]

Eating, drinking and marrying are necessary and therefore permitted to Clement's Christians as long as they do not enjoy any of it! How can, he asks, 'what relates to meat and drink and amorous pleasure, be agreeable to such a one? Since he [the Christian sage] views with suspicion even a word that produces pleasure, and a pleasurable movement and act of the mind'.[153]

To conclude this survey of Clement's attitudes to eating and fasting we can say that Clement seems to hold fast to the apostolic tradition, which did not regard food as a *religious issue* and did not advocate fasting. What makes Clement important for future development of Christian ethics and attitudes to the body is his insistence that the etiquette he presented to his flock, which went into even the most intimate aspects of private life, was inspired by Christ. It was Christ who instructed his follower what kind of food to eat, and even how to prepare it. It was Christ who watched over the married couple's bedroom, making sure that they do not embrace in the wrong position or for the wrong reason. The result of this unfortunate appeal to the highest possible authority for the support of Clement's own prejudices, which St Paul himself did not risk to make when giving his views on marriage, was to open up the most intimate part of an individual's life to ecclesiastical scrutiny.

6

FOOD AND FASTING IN THE WORKS OF TERTULLIAN

The question of food as a religious issue in Christian life was raised forcefully in the late second or early third century. A writer who provided ammunition for debates that continued centuries after his death, and whose brilliant expressions and highly arbitrary biblical exegeses were borrowed and even blatantly plagiarized by later Latin Christians, was Tertullian. This 'gifted and magnificently articulate' Christian writer, the 'inimitable master of Latin rhetoric',[1] is again somewhat of an elusive figure. He wrote both in Greek and Latin, but is remembered as the first great Latin Christian writer, indeed, as the most brilliant Latin stylist in early Christian literature.

THE WRITER

Little is known about his life. Apparently born in Carthage, he converted to Christianity in adult life and lived his adult years in the time of the Severan dynasty. His extant writings are dated to the brief period between AD 196 and 212;[2] his famous Christian contemporaries in the East included Clement of Alexandria and Origen. Eusebius, the first surviving source that mentions him almost a century later, takes him for a lawyer.[3] Jerome, at the end of the fourth century, gave him a Roman centurion for father, made him a priest in the church of Carthage and claimed that he left the church, 'impelled by the envy and insults of the Roman clergy', lapsing into the Montanist heresy in his middle years, and that he lived to a ripe old age.[4] His legal training, his sojourn and fame in Rome as a lawyer, his priesthood, have often been repeated by subsequent commentators,[5] until finally T.D. Barnes in his thoroughgoing study almost completely erased this picture. Barnes argues that it is a trivialization of Tertullian's religious attitudes to assume that his conception of the life of faith as the 'militia Christi' resulted from being the son of a soldier and, similarly, denies that Tertullian's legalistic approach to Christianity reflects professional expertise in jurisprudence.[6] Instead of a priesthood in the Carthaginian church, Barnes crowns him as the great Christian orator, a true Christian representative of the Second Sophistic.[7]

He wrote against the Jews and the pagans, attacked vigorously and refuted heresies within the Christian fold. His theological analyses expressed principles that were then considered, or later developed, as orthodox dogma. Thus he defended the position that God created from nothing (*Adversus Hermogenem*); that the soul is corporeal and is created with the body (*De Anima*); that Christ was incarnated into a real body, not as the Docetist heresy claimed, into a spiritual one (*De Carne Christi*); he argued for bodily resurrection against those who denied its possibility (*De Resurrectione Carnis*), and for the unity of 'nature' but distinction of 'persons' within the Trinity (*Adversus Praxeam*), which in the next century would form the basis for the orthodox position in the great Christological debates of the church.

In addition to apologetical and anti-heretical treatises, Tertullian also wrote a number of works concerning Christian conduct. These include views on attending the circus or theatres (*De Spectaculis*), on professional activities fitting or unfitting for Christians (*De Idololatria*), on sexual and marital practices (*Ad Uxorem, De Exhortatione Castitatis, De Monogamia*), and on the comportment and dress of women (*De Virginibus Velandis, De Cultu Feminarum*), and others.

His 'orthodox' conception of the faith did not protect him from being regarded by some as a heretic.[8] Some of his writings witness a disillusionment with what he saw as 'laxities' of the church. It is a generally accepted view that with time he became increasingly more strict and demanding towards Christian conduct, and that for this reason he was attracted by the rigorous practices of the Montanists. The Montanists seem to have initiated an ascetic movement motivated by a renewed belief in the imminent eschaton, and by the ecstatic experiences of their leaders, interpreted by them as prophecies revealing the continued guidance of the Holy Spirit, the Paraclete. The movement, led by Montanus and two women, Priscilla and Maximilla, spread quickly, since by the end of the second century it was hotly debated in far-flung areas of the empire, from Rome to Gaul and Tertullian's Africa.[9] The Montanists were soon declared heretics by Asian bishops, while others seem to have acknowledged the fact, at least for a time, that they were orthodox in all matters of Christian doctrine.[10] Whether he left the orthodox church to join the Montanist in mid-life,[11] as Jerome tells us, or whether he was from the time of his conversion to Christianity a member of a strict rigorist group, which was at some point during his life drummed out of the Carthaginian church as Montanist heretics, is a matter of conjecture. In any case Tertullian appears to have been the movement's most distinguished convert.

FOOD AND FASTING IN TERTULLIAN'S WORK

Significant views concerning Christian eating habits or fasting are expressed in the *Apologeticus*, *De Spectaculis*, *De Patientia*, *De Poenitentia*, with the most extensive treatment of the problem in the treatise on fasting, *De Ieiunio*.[12] This last is an explicitly Montanist treatise, while the other four contain no mention of the 'New Prophecy', and are judged by most commentators as dating from Tertullian's so called pre-Montanist period.[13]

The *Apologeticus* (*c.* AD 197) was addressed to the magistrates of Carthage in defence of the Christians of the city who, harassed by the mob, were tried in the courts unjustly and by inappropriate procedures and were condemned without being allowed adequate defence. Tertullian's aim was to provide this. The defence was put in the form of a virtuoso public oration. Clearly intended for the ears of the educated classes, it contains references to over thirty literary authorities, both Greek and Latin,[14] for the overawing and, at the same time, for the delectation of a learned audience. Whether it ever reached its intended target cannot be ascertained. Just like earlier Greek apologists, Tertullian in this work wished to defend the Christians against pagan accusations of immorality and bad citizenship. His brilliant innovation consisted in turning the apology into scathing attacks on most aspects of the life and customs of polytheistic society. He scoured the literature from Herodotus to Aulus Gellius for evidence of outrage and moral degradation and at every turn endeavoured by comparison to make self-evident the moral superiority of the Christians.

Communal food practices of the Christians were viewed with suspicion by non-Christians; nasty rumours often circulated about their banquets, not stopping short of lurid accusations of cannibalism and incestuous orgies as being their main attraction. Tertullian turns the accusation back on the accusers. He deplores the luxury and wastefulness of contemporary eating habits. Since philosophers and orators from Plato to Seneca preached temperance, self-restraint and self-sufficiency, Tertullian's intended audience would, of course, be thoroughly familiar with the figure of the rich banquet as the conventional sign of contemporary decadence. They all would have heard from the mouth of any aspiring social critic about a long-past, frugal golden age 'before Lucullus introduced luxury to the Romans'; and that this luxury with fancy banquets prepared by professional cooks brought with it nothing but effeminacy and all kinds of corruption.[15] Following this tradition, Tertullian too contrasts present-day decadence with the moral fortitude of a legendary past by appealing to the great days of the Roman past when sumptuary legislation, like the Lex Fannia, promulgated before the third Punic War, prevented excess.[16] 'Mos maiorum' and the ancient Roman frugality embodied in it were a favourite rhetorical gambit:

> Where have those laws gone that limit luxury? The laws that
> forbade more than hundred *asses* to be allowed for a banquet or
> more than one fowl to be set on the table and that fowl not
> fattened either.... Now not only senators but freedmen and
> slaves give 'centenary' banquets [costing a hundred thousand
> sesterces].[17]

Meanwhile pagan festivals make the city look worse than a tavern and the celebrants care for nothing but 'to make mud with wine, to rush about in droves for outrage, impudence and the incitements of lust' – all under the pretext of religion, which becomes 'an occasion for indulgence'.[18]

Is this a description of actual events in Carthage, an outdoor banquet in celebration, for example, of the victory of Severus or, as is more likely, a literary allusion, a borrowing from Tacitus[19] or another writer? Tertullian, like his contemporaries, orators and writers of the Second Sophistic, enjoyed writing literature on literature. The well-worn characters and situations of classical Greek and Roman writing, familiar to the audience from childhood through a shared education, appeared more 'real' to them than real life. They preferred the clever use of a well-known topos to drastic novelties. Ostentatious and expensive banquets together with the nostalgic comparisons with an earlier age of frugal self-control were used by Tertullian, for the same purpose that these served for many other, non-Christian orators of antiquity: Trimalchio and his guests, who were familiar to all, could be made to blush with shame under the stern gaze of an ancient Cato, who was equally well known and respected by all. But Tertullian's aim was not simply to deplore the useless luxury of his contemporaries. He had a more important task, to prove the innocence and moral superiority of Christian customs by once and for all clearing his fellow Christians from accusations of secret orgies, cannibalism and infanticide. Here again the best defence he thought was attack. As was his custom, he ransacked the literature for cases of human blood-drinking and conveniently found various instances of it in Herodotus, Sallust, Pliny the Elder and others. Armed with these 'facts' as evidence for the prevailing customs of his contemporaries, he confronted the enemies of the Christians.[20] How could those who themselves are in the habit of drinking human blood accuse Christians of killing and eating children, when:

> we do not include even animal's blood in our natural diet. We abstain on that account from things strangled or that die of themselves, that we may not in any way be polluted by blood, even if it is buried in the meat.[21]

In order to put to rest all the rumours circulating about the communal meal of the Christians and to prove its superiority to the sorry spectacle of luxurious and immoral pagan banqueting, Tertullian reveals to the outsiders the nature and conduct of the Christian banquet, the *agape*. This, he writes is worth whatever it costs since the money is:

> spent in piety's name for with that refreshment we help the needy. No, not as among you, the parasites who aspire for the glory of selling their freedom, authorised by their belly to fatten themselves at the cost of an insult; . . . we do not take our places at table until we have first tasted prayer to God. Only so much is eaten as satisfies hunger; only so much drunk as meets the needs of the modest. They satisfy themselves only so far as man will who recall that even during the night they must worship God. . . . After water for the hands come the lights . . . from Holy Scriptures or to sing from heart to God before the rest; so that is a test of how much he has drunk. Prayer in the like manner ends the banquet. Then we break up; but not to form groups for violence . . . nor outbursts of lust; but to pursue the same care for self control and chastity, as men who have dined not so much on dinner as on discipline.[22]

Communal meals were shared by the earliest Christian communities according to Paul's letters and the Acts of the Apostles, and the *agape*, the festive Christian banquet, is often mentioned in other early

Christian sources. It seems that this solemn prayerful communal sharing of food was still practised in Carthage at the time, just as it was, as we have seen, in Clement's Alexandria.[23] Here Tertullian's description is more likely to be based on his own actual experience rather than on literary examples. It may also be the case, as Barnes suggests, that many of Tertullian's own treatises originated as lay sermons or after-dinner speeches at these Christian banquets.[24]

The shape of the meal, its sequence of blessings, food, drink, hand-washing and further prayer, all bear strong resemblance to Jewish festive meals of families or religious communities, the *chavuroth*.[25] Whether this resemblance was reinforced by contemporary Jewish influences on Carthaginian Christians or dates back to the origins of Christianity is difficult to decide. There are no traces of African Christianity that can be dated before the second half of the second century. The origins of the church in Carthage are obscure. Christianity may have come to Carthage through the Jewish colonies in Tripolitania and elsewhere in North Africa or it may have arrived directly from Rome.[26] Neither of these routes would necessarily exclude Jewish influences. Christians, like the Jews, devoted a day in the week to resting and sharing communal meals, and Tertullian reminds his reader that this custom was taken over even by those who knew almost nothing of Judaism.[27] Barnes, in his *Tertullian*, argues very strongly against any direct influence of contemporary Judaism on Tertullian or his community in Carthage:

> For Tertullian (as for many later Christians) Judaism was an unchanging fossilized faith, not to be taken seriously or deserving proper attention. Any similarity which he displays to contemporary Judaism does not originate in direct deriva-tion. Two monotheistic faiths with so much in common and both placed in the same alien environment could hardly avoid adopting closely similar attitudes. Nothing indicates, therefore, that the Jewish community of the city or its teachers exerted much influence on the development of Christianity in Carthage or on Tertullian.[28]

As I shall try to show in the following, this statement is not quite tenable at least as far as religious *practice*, as distinguished from religious dogma, is concerned, and it is especially questionable with respect to practices of food and fasting.

According to Barnes, all the Judaic colour that can be sensed in Tertullian's work comes from his reading of the Old Testament. The *agape*, however, follows more in its details Jewish customs described not in the Old Testament but by later Jewish sources, like Philo and the Mishnaic tractate *Berakhoth*. And as I shall argue below, there is other evidence in Tertullian's attitude to food – and especially to fasting – that indicates Jewish influences, despite his admittedly strong hostility to the Jews.

In the *Apologeticus*, Tertullian's argument is not aimed at the Jews but at polytheistic society and its powerful institutions confronting the Christians. What worries him concerning the *agape*, and what he sets out to deny, is not its similarity to Jewish feasts, but its similarity to pagan communal meals, banquets provided often by wealthy pagan benefactors. His aim was to stress the superiority of the Christian way by exaggerating differences and to contrast, in what may easily have appeared as similar customs, the giving of banquets for a good cause. Sodalities and professional organizations shared communal meals, which were often subsidized by rich pagans. Wealthy benefactors, not only the emperors, on occasion provided food for the populace in the course of exercising patronage.[29] When they provided banquets for the people on various festive occasions, non-Christian benefactors practised euergetism, a custom that was long part of Hellenistic city life and its system of political patronage.[30] The motivation for it is hard to assess, but it is claimed by some scholars today, especially by those who would like to draw a sharp distinction between pagan benefaction and Christian charity, to have been simply the wish of the *euergetai* to please themselves.[31] The aim of these banquets or the distributions of food, drink or money as the *'sportula'*, was not the relief of poverty but rather the glorification of the donors, who were no doubt well aware of the political persuasiveness of the gesture. Nevertheless all classes of the free population may have benefited from them.[32] The pagan host of the second century, unlike his Christian counterpart, had no explicit ideology to spread and no universal church to organize. The benefactor may have expected admiration, gratitude, entertainment and, possibly, various personal services from the guest, in return for the hospitality. The *agape* is seen by Tertullian as a form of alms-giving, and what the Christian host expected from the recipient in return for this charity was the confession of the faith and participation in the service to the Christian God.

Even if granted that the difference in motivation of Christian and non-Christian benefactors was substantial,[33] the apparent similarity of actual banquets was not lost on Tertullian and that is why he felt the need to deny it. To do this he turns again to commonplaces from literature. The parasite, the poor penniless fellow, driven by constant hunger, who was willing to do just about anything to please his host who fed him, was of course a favourite and well-worn figure, familiar from the Greek comic writers and Roman satirists.[34] But, as becomes clear from his description of the banquet, the Christian guest just like the parasite had to sing for his supper.[35]

Having forcefully shown the innocence of the *agape* and its moral superiority to pagan debauchery, Tertullian turns to refute the basic complaint levelled against Christians, that is their uselessness as citizens, whose life and work do not benefit their cities. What he says in refutation of this claim is of interest to the historian, for it throws some light on the daily life and habits of his community. The Christians, he insists, live alongside their pagan neighbours, use the same meat markets, baths, shops, inns and market days, 'and the rest of the life of buying and selling', and if they do not recline to eat in public at the *Liberalia*,[36] they still do their part for the benefit of the whole community:

> In case the rains don't come pagans sacrifice ram offering. We, parched with fasting, pinched with every austerity, abstaining from all food that sustains life, wallowing in sackcloth and ashes, importune heaven with reproach, we touch God; and then, when we have wrung mercy from Him – Jupiter has all the glory![37]

This rare description of a communal supplication for rain involving fasting with self-humiliation bears an uncannily close resemblance to the Mishnaic description of the Jewish communal fast for rain.[38] North Africa was similarly dependent on meagre yearly rainfall, and the Jews of Carthage may also have turned to the same custom of fasting for rainfall that their co-religionists used in the Land of Israel. The close resemblance of the Jewish and Christian practices here again would cast some doubt on Barnes's assertion that Tertullian was unaware of contemporary Jewish ideas or customs.[39]

Little is known about the Jewish community of Carthage or its teachers in Tertullian's time. Direct personal connection between them and Tertullian cannot be shown. He may have received his inspiration from personal contact with Jews or, what is more likely, he may have been accepted, upon his conversion, into a Christian community of Judaizers, those in favour of following certain Jewish traditions, and learned it from them. In any case, the fasting described here is like Jewish fasting, offered for the expiation of sins. It is clearly not ascetic fasting, nor is it aimed at the rejection of the body.

In the *Apologeticus*, Tertullian presents a Christian community worthy of the highest praises, a community with which the writer identifies himself without reservation. As far as daily life was concerned these Christians were meat eaters, who used the city's meat markets and inns just like any of the other inhabitants. Moreover, they did not seem to scruple about buying meat that may have been sacrificial offering. From the restrictions imposed by the Apostolic decree in Acts 15:20, 29, which enjoins Christians not to eat meat that had been sacrificed to idols or meat with blood in it, Tertullian's Christians retained only the part that came from Leviticus, the injunction against eating blood, an injunction that informed Jewish slaughtering practices and eating habits.[40] Obtaining meat free from the taint of sacrifice may not have been a problem in Carthage but eating meat with blood in it was still as abhorrent for this community as it was for the Jews.

The Christians, like the Jews, did not take part in sacrifices and public celebrations because of the idolatry, wastefulness or what they considered to be immorality of these. They kept every seventh day for rest, again similar to Jewish practice. Their communal feast, the *agape*, was organized with blessings, prayer and hand-washing, like Jewish festival meals. Finally, the only fast attested in the *Apologeticus* is a fast for rain, the only parallel for which is the Jewish practice attested in the Mishnah.

It has been argued that African Christianity was grafted onto a pre-existent, Semitic pagan religion centring upon the cult of Saturn, the ritual observance of which may have resembled that of the Hebrew Tabernacle.[41] But these supposed Saturn-worshipping pagan contemporaries of Tertullian did not fast for rain. When he compares Carthaginian pagan supplication for rain to that of the Christians, he does not say that 'our fasting is better than yours'; on the contrary, he explicitly states that the pagans of Carthage sacrificed a ram to Jupiter in case the rains did not arrive, while the Christians fasted. The Christian fasting that he describes does not seem to originate in any such pagan practice but, in all probability, comes from the Jewish fasts that it resembles. His treatise on fasting also seems to support this view, for in it he clearly states that many ancient peoples conducted various solemnities in order to induce the gods to send rain. It was, however, the Jews who combined fasting, ashes and mourning attire with day-long penitential prayer: 'A Jewish fast . . . is universally celebrated . . . throughout all the shore, in every open place they continue long to send prayer up to heaven.'[42]

The treatise *De Spectaculis* was composed with a different audience in mind; it was written not for a polytheist elite but for his own Christian co-religionists. In clear contradiction to the *Apologeticus*, where he insisted on the Christian's good citizenship in sharing and contributing to the life of the city, here he exhorts them to live their life separated from their pagan neighbours, to despise their theatres, circuses and other public festivities. With respect to food here he recalls the apostolic injunction against sacrificial meat when he writes:

> we do not eat what is offered in sacrificial or funeral rite, because 'we cannot eat of the Lord's supper and the supper of demons'. If then we try to keep our gullet and belly free from defilement, how much more our nobler parts, our eyes and ears, do we guard from the pleasures of idol sacrifice and the sacrifice for the dead – pleasures not of the gut and digestion, but of spirit, soul and suggestion – and it is purity of these far more than that of the intestines, that God has a right to claim of us.[43]

Significantly, he quotes not Acts 15:20 but Paul's first letter to the Corinthians 10:21, where it is not the food in itself that is of importance but the incompatibility of worshipping God and taking part in polytheistic rituals. The pomp and pageantry of these often attracted even those who were not adherents of the cults. It is not what goes into the Christian's stomach that worries Tertullian here. As an educated man of his time he assumes here the philosophic stance, common to many of the schools, of distinguishing between the nobler and inferior parts of the human being.[44] The mind or intellect and the soul fall in the first, the belly and the organs below it fall in the second of these categories. Tertullian's purpose in the whole treatise was to convince his Christian audience to keep the 'nobler' parts of their body, their eyes and ears, these gates to the mind, pure from the allurements of pagan spectacles. He singles out funerary banquets[45] and insists that Christians should not partake in funerary rites; he also urges them to shun the theatres and circuses. Tertullian's protest against funeral banquets is interesting in the light of the well-attested later custom of Christians to build shrines to saints and martyrs where, just as at the graves of the pagan dead, votive offerings were brought together with food and drink, and banquets were held in their honour, often even with the slaughter of animals.[46] Some of the later Christian authorities disapproved of the custom. Augustine in the *Confessions* tells how Ambrose, bishop of Milan, prevented Monica from taking food and wine to a shrine there, which she was accustomed to do in her home town in North Africa.[47]

In *De Spectaculis*, Tertullian does not ask his fellow Christians to give up the pleasure of eating, he only urges them to give up pagan entertainment. In exchange he offers them the hope of the greatest future pleasure imaginable, that of seeing all their pagan neighbours roast in everlasting hell; 'what laughter, what joy and exultation!'[48] The humble self-sacrificing piety, the need for suffering and martyrdom for the love of God is coupled in Tertullian's writings with the most lurid, sadistic expressions of hatred and hostility towards those he saw as the enemy – whether pagans, Jews, heretics, or Christians whose conception of the faith differed from his own.

Fasting is given much more space in Tertullian's writing than joyous communal meals. He is the first Christian propagandist for fasting whose writings survive. In his treatise *De Patientia*, he extols the Christian virtue of patience, admitting candidly that it is a virtue that he himself sorely lacks. The bodily manifestation of patience, he says, is 'the mortification of the flesh as a sacrifice acceptable to the Lord'. It is interesting to recall that for his Alexandrian contemporary, Clement, the 'sacrifice most acceptable to the Lord' was a philosophic 'apatheia', a complete disregard for the passions of the flesh. For Tertullian the sacrifice required active mortification of the flesh. As he elaborated on it further, this self-humiliation consists of wearing 'mourning dress along with meagre rations . . . plain food and a drink of clear water . . . persevering in sackcloth and ashes'.[49] All of these will enhance the value of prayer.[50]

The aim of fasting, which Tertullian urges on Christians, here and in his other works, is clearly the atonement for sins, the same aim for which Jews fasted from the time when it was first enjoined upon Israel in Leviticus. As discussed earlier,[51] among the Jews the purpose of fasting was to express remorse, and to expiate sins. In addition to the Day of Atonement, individuals or communities often used fasting as self-punishment, in the hope of averting greater punishment from God. It was also suggested above that after the destruction of the Temple in Jerusalem pious Jews may have conceived of fasting as a possible substitute for the sacrifice that could not be carried out any more. By the time of the Mishnah (*c.* AD 200), fasting of graded duration and severity was developed among pious Jews, the most severe fast being the one where abstinence from food was accompanied by abstention from bathing, from marital relations and from wearing shoes. Sackcloth and ashes were put on the body to signify mourning and extreme self-abasement. Compare this with the practice urged by Tertullian for the expiation of sins in *De Poenitentia*:

> With regard also to the very dress and food of the penitent this discipline enjoins him to go about in sackcloth and ashes, to cover his body in squalor of mourning, to cast down his spirit with grief, to exchange his sins for harsh treatment of himself; to have no acquaintance with any food or drink but the plainest, and this not for his stomach's sake but his soul's.[52]

The only substantial difference between Tertullian's penitential practice and the Jewish one is that the Jewish fast generally meant going without any food and drink for a specified duration of time, while Tertullian only urges living on bread and water.

Tertullian's major pronouncement on the need for Christian fasting is contained in a tract entitled *De Ieiunio adversus Psychicos*, which is devoted exclusively to the development of a rationale for it. This treatise, by a Tertullian who clearly identifies himself in it as a Montanist, was written after he had joined the Montanist sect, or after he and his rigorist Christian group were rejected by the majority of Christians in Carthage as Montanist heretics. According to Barnes, in writing it Tertullian 'no longer harboured any real hope of persuading those who rejected the New Prophecy. He was writing rather to justify, to vindicate and to encourage the Montanists alone.'[53] The treatise, however, is addressed throughout its length to the orthodox Christians who, led by their bishops, accused Tertullian and his fellow Christians of being Montanist heretics and innovators.

Montanist practices, advocated by Tertullian, emphasized communal compulsory fasts, which were an undoubted innovation: they urged the prolongation of the '*stationes*' (individual voluntary fasts lasting a few hours or a half day) into the evening, added two weeks of xerophagy (the eating of dry food, with no meat, gravy, moist vegetables or wine), and abstaining from washing for the same duration.[54] These were the reasons for a charge of heresy or false prophecy, which may have led, despite Tertullian's doctrinal adherence to orthodoxy, to the pronouncement of an anathema.[55]

The tone of the treatise clearly suggests that Tertullian's 'Pneumatic' or spiritual Christians were a small beleaguered group facing the majority of Carthaginian Christians. The whole treatise is written for the purpose of denouncing this majority. The cardinal sins of the opposition, in Tertullian's eyes, consisted in not forbidding second marriages, not imposing compulsory fasts and not being sufficiently eager for martyrdom. Since he dealt with the question of monogamy and martyrdom in other places, *De Ieiunio* is devoted entirely to the argument for fasting.

At the outset, Tertullian distinguishes two classes of Christians. We have already encountered a similar attempt in Clement of Alexandria, who drew a class distinction between 'simple' Christians and the Christian 'Gnostic'. Clement, who fashioned himself as a 'Gnostic', or a Christian philosopher, naturally saw greater virtue in the advanced 'knowing' Christian; however he showed no hostility, only condescension, towards the second-class 'simple' Christians. The same cannot be said of Tertullian, who aimed a substantial portion of his strongest invectives against those whom he regarded as second-class Christians. These he called Psychics, who never rose above the level of 'animal faith', and whom he accused again and again of caring for nothing but 'the flesh', of which they 'wholly consist', being 'as prone to manifold feeding as to manifold marrying'. Clearly superior to these, Tertullian's first-class Christians, whom he called 'spirituals' or Pneumatics, discipline themselves by 'imposing . . . reins upon the appetite, through taking sometimes no meals or late meals or dry meals, just as upon lust, through allowing but one marriage'.[56]

To underpin the 'natural' connection between proneness to 'manifold feeding' and 'manifold marrying', he calls upon the familiar and worn-out cliché, much beloved by satirists and moralizers, that the two vices, 'gula' and 'libido', gluttony and lust, are inseparable.[57] This piece of shared wisdom, repeated endlessly by all self-appointed guardians of public morality, with the aid of Philo, Clement of Alexandria and Tertullian, will be assured a long history in later Christian rhetoric too. Later Christians like Jerome will enjoy repeating or paraphrasing Tertullian on gluttony and lust:

> these two are so united and concrete, that, had there been any
> possibility of disjoining them, the pudenda would not have been
> affixed to the belly itself . . . the order of vices is proportionate to
> the arrangement of the members.[58]

Surprisingly, however, Tertullian does not proceed by developing the implications of this interdependence. He does not propose fasting as a *remedy* for lust. Like Philo or Clement of Alexandria, Tertullian too sees gluttony and sexual lust as the greatest enemies of religious piety. Like these, he too believes that if one gives into one of these pleasures one will surely be conquered by the other. The fact is concretely manifested, in his view, by his enemies the Psychics, who do not fast and do not oppose second marriages! All the more interesting is the fact that in the rest of the treatise he keeps the accusation of gluttony and lust as more or less two separate and parallel whips with which to lash his opponents. Fasting throughout the work is urged for its own sake and not as a means for guarding against sexual desire.

To answer the objections of the Psychics against fasting, which he knows they base on some selected sentences from Scripture (Matthew 15:10–21; Mark 2:18–20; 7:15; 1 Corinthians 8:8), he undertakes to trace the principle of fasting through both the Old and the New Testaments back to its earliest source, to the first man, Adam.

The primordial sin of man is disobedience, which was caused by his gluttony. This is the sin that is transmitted to all humans;

> I hold, therefore, that from the very beginning the murderous gullet was to be punished with the torments and penalties of hunger. Even if God had enjoined no preceptive fasts . . . unbidden, I would, in such ways and at such times as I might have been able, have habitually accounted food as poison, and taken the antidote, hunger, through which to purge the primordial cause of death, a cause transmitted to me also, concurrently with my very generation.[59]

The first and foremost aim of fasting for him is penance for disobedience to God, which manifested itself not in sexual transgression but in eating. Reading closely the Old Testament he argues that God himself demands fasting as 'sacrifice'.[60] The rationale for fasting is simply this:

> that by a renewed interdiction of food and observation of precept the primordial sin might now be expiated, in order that man may make God satisfaction through the same cause through which he has offended, that is, through interdiction of food . . . hunger might rekindle, just as satiety had extinguished salvation.[61]

Like many other ancient thinkers going back to Hesiod, Tertullian also assumes that in the primordial 'golden age' human beings were vegetarians. He reads in his Bible that before the flood humans were grass eaters and only after the flood was permission granted to eat all meat but without the blood in it.[62] Since the passage in Genesis 1:28, 'and have dominion over the fish of the sea and over the birds of the air and over every living thing that moves upon the earth', does not expressly state what 'dominion' actually meant, and since, furthermore, Genesis 1:29 mentions food only with respect to plants and the fruit of trees, Tertullian assumes that meat eating started after the flood, when in Genesis 9:3 it is explicitly stated: 'Every moving thing that lives shall be food for you; and as I gave you the green plants, I give you everything'.[63] Tertullian does not advocate general abstention from meat. 'Why then was the limit of lawful food extended after the flood?' he asks, and goes on to explain that

> it was not suitable for man to be burdened with any further special law of abstinence, who so recently showed himself unable to tolerate so light an interdiction – of one single fruit – having had the rein relaxed, he was to be strengthened by his very liberty.[64]

Continuing the survey of the Old Testament he shows that appetite was as conspicuous among the sins of Israel as it was for Adam, and that for this very reason the Levitical laws were introduced. 'When God began to choose for himself a people . . . certain things being prohibited as unclean, in order that man, by observing a perpetual abstinence in certain particulars, might at least the more easily tolerate absolute fasts', and since Israel preferred the fleshpots of Egypt, 'from men so ungrateful all that was more pleasing and appetizing was withdrawn, for the sake at once of punishing gluttony and exercising continence, that the former might be condemned, the latter practically learned'.[65] The Psychics, those Christians who opposed the fasting practices he recommended, were in his eyes the obvious contemporary counterparts of the fleshpot-loving Israelites of the Bible.

He turns next to consider the advantages of fasting, both for mind and body. He claims that before eating,

> by nature the mind (is) much more vigorous, the heart much more alive, than when that whole habitation of our interior man stuffed with meats, inundated with wines, fermenting for the purpose of excremental secretion, is already being turned into an obsession with the lavatory, where, plainly, nothing follows so near but the savouring of lust.[66]

The idea that feeding the body dulls the mind recurs in many ancient moralizers. It is often repeated by Philo and we have seen it expressed in Clement's writings. Since Tertullian here appeals to 'nature', one might expect him to marshal medical or scientific authority to support his claim, but instead he again chooses the Bible: 'The people did eat and drink and they arose to play'.[67] The 'play', he says, was immodest. And echoing the sentiment of Philo, whose writing displayed an exaggerated dread of gluttony,[68] he declares that 'Food destroys or damages all discipline'.[69]

Another advantage that he sees in fasting is that it elevates man to the presence of God. Moses fasted forty days and he saw and heard God, and so did the other prophets:

> Abstention from food makes God tent-fellow with man – peer, in truth, with peer! For if the eternal God will not hunger, as He testifies through Isaiah, this will be the time for man to be equal with God, when he lives without food.[70]

The aspiration to become 'equal' to God appears inconsistent with the humility and self-abasement demanded by Christian piety. The idea of imitation of God was present in Judaism and also in Stoic and Platonic philosophy, but it meant different things to Jews and pagans. The commandment the Jew received: 'Be holy because I am holy', meant that man should keep the law in order to be pure and sinless in the eyes of his God, but not to compete with him. 'To be the slave of God is the highest boast of man', said Philo,[71] who knew the philosophic aspiration to 'godlikeness' but himself was a pious Jew. Tertullian's religious aspiration was also to be a servant of God as is expressed in the whole tenor of this work except for the particular statement quoted above. Aspiring to equality with God seems to be a most impious idea for both Jews and Christians, who liked to regard themselves as children of God. The aim to become godlike by denying the passions is an idea more suited to the motivation of Stoic philosophy, which left strong marks on Tertullian's thought despite his attempts to reject it. Seneca, the Roman Stoic, was admired and accepted by him as 'almost a Christian'.[72] The aspiration to become 'God's tent-fellow' may reflect reminiscences of the writings of Seneca:

> Learn to be content with little, and cry out with courage and with greatness of soul: 'We have water, we have porridge; let us compete in happiness with Jupiter himself!... you must crave nothing, if you would vie with Jupiter; for Jupiter craves nothing'.[73]

The similarity of Tertullian's thought and feeling to the Stoic ideal is very strong, but he does not pursue it any further, possibly realizing its un-Christian nature. Instead he returns to the evidence proving the power and efficacy of fasting in protecting one from the anger of God.

All the individual and communal fasts found in the Old Testament are brought out to prove that God delights in the fasts of his people. Similarly, Old Testament examples are produced to prove that fasting is the proper accompaniment of prayer, especially in perilous times and in mourning, when one naturally would not think of food. That this type of fasting was still practised among Jews in post-biblical times is evidenced by the efforts of some rabbis to prohibit it in cases where fasting would weaken the mourner, who is already weak and suffering.[74]

In addition to the obliteration of sins and the averting of perils, fasts will merit visions and mysteries. Moses fasted and saw God, so did Elijah and, says Tertullian, God wrought miracles for the fast of Daniel.[75]

From the ancient proofs Tertullian turns to 'modern' ones, to examples of fasting from the New Testament. This document, however, did not provide him with easy support for claiming a 'God-given law of fasting'. True, he finds here the prophetess Anna, 'who both recognised the infant Lord, and preached many things about Him to such as were expecting the redemption of Israel'.[76] Anna for Tertullian embodied the essence of the true 'spiritual' Christian, she was a once-married widow, who remained a widow and spent her life, according to the gospel, in fasting and prayer. She exemplified Tertullian's message: that only those who fast and who marry only once are able to understand God and Christ.[77] But he never claims that Anna stayed a chaste widow *because* she fasted.

Christ himself, he continues, fasted at his own baptism: 'he was initiating the "new man" into "a severe handling" of "the old", to show the devil that the new man is too strong for the whole power of hunger'.[78] In the Gospels of Matthew and Luke, Jesus's forty-days fasting sojourn in the wilderness, which establishes him in the line of the holy prophets of Israel, following Moses and Elijah, is narrated following the story of his baptism at the hands of John. All attempts to attribute significance to the connection of the two episodes, Jesus's baptism and his fasting, came from later exegeses. These had to struggle with the problem that Jesus fasted not before but after his baptism. Christian baptism celebrates joyful resurrection with Christ, thus making fasting after the immersion quite inappropriate. Fasting and prayer for the forgiveness of sins as preparation for and, as such, preceding baptism were mentioned in some early Christian literature that Tertullian knew. Justin Martyr[79] describes fasting before baptism as do some other early documents too, like the *Didache*, whose dating is uncertain.[80] Pre-baptismal abstention from food strongly resembles Jewish penitential fasting. The fact that Christian writers in the fourth and fifth centuries still find it necessary to urge and promote fasting before baptism suggests that it was not a generally shared practice.[81]

In his attempts to call these gospel narratives as witnesses for this 'law', Tertullian exhibits his remarkable talent for quibbling and for twisting the meaning of a text to suit his purposes. He smoothly avoids the issue of the timing of Jesus's fast by stating that 'the Lord Himself consecrated His own baptism . . . by fasts', and, despite the fact that He had the power of turning stones into bread and the Jordan river into wine, He preferred fasting as a way of initiation of 'the new man' by a 'severe handling' of 'the old'. And if this argument is not very rigorous, since it is the post-baptismal 'new man' who receives the 'severe handling', another well-tried one is reiterated: the Devil tempts by means of food, so Jesus fasted in order to show the Devil that 'the new man' is too strong for the power of hunger.[82] Tertullian's argument misleadingly presupposes that Jesus and the apostles were habitual fasters, claiming that Jesus even *added* a law to fasting, i.e. that it should be done 'without sadness', for why should what is salutary be sad?[83]

Having amassed all the evidence from Scripture to support his claim that fasting is a religious act required by and pleasing to God, Tertullian then turns from total fasts to argue for the efficacy of dietary restrictions. In his eyes, abstention from certain kinds of food is a partial fast. Here he has to tread with caution. Rejecting the Jewish abstention from certain kinds of food was a crucial step in Christian self-definition and separation from Judaism. Little wonder then that orthodox Christians looked at Montanist partial fasts, the so-called *xerophagiae*, with considerable suspicion. Tertullian again turns to the Old Testament first for examples of similar practices in the 'most ancient and efficacious religion'.[84] The story of Daniel is recalled again to argue against the doubters and those who would worry about the effects of xerophagy on the body: eating vegetables and drinking water made Daniel and his companions 'more handsome' and 'spiritually cultured'.[85] Daniel's three weeks of mourning with restricted food or xerophagy signified self-humiliation, which God rewarded by sending an angel to him. An angel was sent also to Elijah and offered him bread and water and not meat! This proves to Tertullian that the practices of xerophagy 'expel fear, and attract the ears of God and make men masters of secrets. In time of pressure and persecution and whatsoever difficulty, we must live on xerophagies'.[86] Similar restriction of the diet to dry foods is a necessary accompaniment of the confession of one's sins, 'with such food did David express his own confession of sin; eating ashes indeed as it were bread, that is, bread dry and foul like ashes: mingling moreover his drink with weeping – of course, instead of wine'.[87] Samuel and Aaron of the Old Testament are called upon to support the God-pleasing character of abstinence from wine. The question whether the apostle Paul had known the practice of xerophagy is skilfully side-stepped by pointing out how many privations he had undergone, and how he warned against drunkenness. How indeed could a man like him oppose xerophagy? He only advised Timothy to drink a little wine as medicine for his ailing stomach: 'by this very fact he has advised abstinence from wine as worthy of God, which on a ground of necessity, he has dissuaded'.[88]

Another objection that the orthodox raised against Montanists and that Tertullian wanted to demolish was against their twice weekly compulsory fasts, the *stationes*. Among some pious Christians, just as among some pious Jews, certain days of the week were traditionally singled out for special observance, when those who felt the need for it could fast for a number of hours, or keep a vigil with prayers.[89] We have seen how Clement of Alexandria explained fasting as abstaining not from food but from covetousness and lasciviousness.[90] It seems likely then that Tertullian may have been accurate in reporting the orthodox attitude concerning the *stationes*, when he claims that they did not regard them as apostolic institutions but a matter of individual choice and piety. To refute those who accused the Montanists of capricious innovation in turning the *stationes* into obligatory fasts, Tertullian again turns to the Scripture, this time however not with great success. There are no fasts like these in the Old Testament. The Monday and Thursday exercises of pious Jews appear only in post-biblical literature. The fact that there is no instruction either concerning the keeping of *stationes* in the New Testament does not seem to dampen his zeal; he urges that in this, as in any other case of perplexity or doubt, the continuing instructions of the Spirit should be followed. For this he, quite justifiably, cites as authority the apostle Paul: 'And if . . . there are matters which you are ignorant about, the Lord will reveal to you' (Philippians 3:15). The Paraclete, the Spirit, the continuing guide of the Montanists, reports Tertullian, made clear to its followers the significance of the *stationes* as remembrance of the crucifixion. The reason for the prolongation of the fast beyond the ninth hour, he says, is 'that we are to fast to a late hour, awaiting the time . . . when Joseph took down and entombed the body . . . Thence it is even irreligious for the flesh of the servants to take refreshment before their Lord did'.[91]

After having produced all the evidence from both Testaments for the 'advantages which the dutiful observances of abstinence from, or curtailment or deferment of food confer',[92] Tertullian is ready both to defend Montanist practices from accusations of innovation or, even worse, of heresy, and to attack the orthodox in return as lax, self-indulgent, gluttonous 'Psychics', who only care for the flesh. How can Montanist fasting practices be inspired by the Devil, as the 'Psychics' insinuate; for would the Devil insist on the carrying out of God's commands? Fasting is a duty towards God and not the Devil, but the Paraclete directs Christians to fulfil this duty in the name of Christ.[93] But the orthodox do not believe that the Holy Spirit speaks through the Montanist prophetesses; they all seem to be reassuring themselves that true prophecy ceased with John. The reason for this is their love of comfort and hatred of discipline. Even if the command to fast did not come from the Paraclete, Tertullian argues, true Christians would, by their own initiative, humble and abase themselves not only for averting God's anger and not just 'to obtain his protection or grace' but also to prepare for martyrdom, the aim and crowning glory of Christian life: ' . . . the prison must be familiarized to us, and hunger and thirst practised', so that, when the final conflict comes, 'the tortures may not even have material to work on', since the Christian is nothing but skin and bones.[94] While the soul of the true Christian, by frequent fasting, gains 'the most intimate knowledge of death', the Psychics 'furnish cookshops in the prisons to untrustworthy martyrs' who, being drunk at their trial, can only belch in place of confession![95]

Like a prosecutor in a court of law, Tertullian proceeds to pierce the inconsistencies of the opponents' case. He knows that even the Psychics fast sometimes on occasions that are not explicitly ordered by Scripture, like on the Pascal-day, or that some keep short *stationes* for some individual need. Do they not themselves then indulge in the practice of 'novelties'? Moreover, whole communities fast occasionally when the bishops issue mandates for fasts to the church communities. But, he accuses, these fasts are proclaimed most often for the purpose of collecting contributions of alms in 'beggarly fashion'.[96] And if they practise this kind of communal self-abasement on the command of a 'mere human', the bishop, how can they brand as heresy the communal fasts and xerophagies and long *stationes* of the Montanists that are inspired by the Paraclete?[97] 'Look at the Jewish calendar, and you will find it nothing novel that all succeeding posterity guards with hereditary scrupulousness the precepts given to the fathers'.[98] Tradition has to be adhered to, but as he points out, Christian councils are held all over the provinces of Greece,[99] where the deeper questions of Christian identity and behaviour are handled and sometimes new things admitted for the common benefit. Some of these, Tertullian knew, were not entirely hostile to the Montanists.

The 'Psychics' accuse the Montanists of novelty and at the very same time they taunt them with keeping to antiquated, Judaizing forms.[100] To answer the charge of 'Galaticism',[101] Tertullian accepts the charge that the Montanists are observers of 'seasons, days and months and years'. But, he claims, that they would only be 'Galaticizing' if they kept these in Jewish fashion, that is to say, as *legal* ceremonies. But instead of pursuing further what even to him must have been a rather feeble defence, he goes on to point out that Christians themselves observe days that are Jewish in origin.

Tertullian's 'Psychic' opponents apparently defended their position by pointing to the pastoral epistle warning against those who 'bid to abstain from meat'.[102] Tertullian rejects this as irrelevant to the practices of his 'Pneumatic' fellow-Christians. The apostle had indeed warned against the future appearance of pretentious liars in whom he foresaw those heretics, 'who would enjoin perpetual abstinence to the extent of destroying and despising the works of the Creator: Marcion, Tatian, or Jupiter the Pythagorean heretic'.[103] The Montanists do not belong with these. For after all the lengthy and vehement arguments he marshalled in favour of fasting, it turns out that the Montanists 'interdiction of meat' is limited to 'two weeks of xerophagia in the year, and not the whole of these – sabbaths and the Lord's day being exempted, we offer to God abstaining from things which we do not *reject but defer*'.[104] In order to fortify his own position, he calls on the apostle Paul for witness, cleverly and quite dishonestly distorting the key sentences in Paul until they turn completely against the plain meaning of the text.[105] By selective citations and misleading juxtapositions of food-related sentences from the Pauline Epistles, he argues that Paul only chided those who abstained from food because of contempt and not from duty! He quotes, out of its context, the truncated sentence: 'It is good not to eat flesh and not to drink wine', and promptly continues it with 'for he who in these points does service, is pleasing and propitiable to God'.[106] Taking biblical quotations out of context had a long history even before Tertullian, as Robin Lane Fox points out;[107] however, later advocates of fasting will all follow Tertullian's way of regrouping and reinterpreting Paul's pronouncements concerning food, to the point where his original intention will have been totally lost and a contrary 'apostolic' message supporting food and fasting as religious concern will have been fabricated.

To reinforce his argument that even if God preferred the works of righteousness he still requires sacrifice, 'which is a soul afflicted with fasts',[108] Tertullian now turns to a long list of instances from the Bible where divine wrath was brought down upon the self-indulgent. The horrible punishments meted out by God should be a warning, he says, both to the people and to their leaders the bishops, even Pneumatic ones, in case they may ever have been guilty of incontinence of appetite. Fasting is service to God, he asserts again and again. Moses and all the prophets ordered this service.[109] Even the idol-worshippers show various forms of self-abasement as service to their idols. As in the *Apologeticus*, here again he describes cultic customs in case the rains do not come in time. There are barefoot public processions, the magistrates go without their purple finery, reverse the fasces, utter prayer and offer a victim.[110] In some colonies, he writes, there is an annual rite when in sackcloth and ashes the suppliants beg their idols, while baths and shops are closed till the ninth hour, like the self-abasement of the people of Nineveh.[111] And of course there is the Jewish fast, which he says, 'is universally celebrated'. All these people do service to their deity by some form of self-abasement, and still the Psychics heap abuse on the Pneumatics for their xerophagies. The Psychics are worse than the idol-worshippers:

> For to you your belly is god, and your lungs a temple, and your paunch a sacrificial altar, and your cook the priest, and your fragrant smell the Holy Spirit, and your condiments spiritual gifts, and your belching prophecy.[112]

In the conclusion of this treatise Tertullian attacks his opponents the Psychics without mercy, flinging at them all the prurient accusations that the pagans were in the habit of using against the Christians, of gluttony, drunkenness, and even incest: 'with you "love" shows its fervour in sauce-pans, "faith" its warmth in kitchens, "hope" its anchorage in waiters; but of greater account is "love" because that is the means whereby your young men sleep with their sisters!'[113] As in the *Apologeticus*, Tertullian here too felt attack to be the best defence. In this case he aimed the attack against his fellow Christians, against the orthodox propaganda, which by this time regarded Montanism as heresy, and as was customary when faced with non-conformists, accused them of gluttony, lasciviousness, avarice, exploiting orphans and widows, usury, robbery, avoiding martyrdom and even of ritual murder.[114]

The pleasure-loving Psychics, Tertullian thundered, are driven by appetite and its 'appendages . . . lasciviousness and luxury'; as opposed to them his own Pneumatic Christians are the only ones who heed what the apostle said, that 'they who are in the flesh cannot please God':

> Emaciation does not displease us; for it is not by weight that God bestows flesh any more than He does the Spirit by measure. More easily through the 'straight gate' of salvation will slender flesh enter; more speedily will lighter flesh rise; longer in the sepulchre will drier flesh retain its firmness.

Olympic athletes and boxers should stuff themselves with food for they need muscles – he continues – but the Christian martyr's contest is not against flesh and blood, it is against the powers of evil,

> Against these it is not by robustness of flesh and blood, but of faith and spirit that behoves us to make our antagonistic stand . . . an overfed Christian will be more necessary to bears and lions than to God. Even to encounter beasts, it will be his duty to practice emaciation.[115]

As noted above, the *De Ieiunio* is probably the first and certainly the most extensive Christian tract on fasting to come down to us from the early church. Its battling tone and defensive advocacy of the practice indicate that in Tertullian's time fasting as a religious practice was not generally favoured by the urban, bishop-led Christian communities and certainly not by the church in Carthage. As his writings suggest, most Christians of Carthage in the early third century ate a diet that was similar to that of the pagans; it included meat, which most of them were reluctant to give up even for two weeks of xerophagy. Conviviality of shared festive meals was an important part of communal life. It appears that some Christians, having taken over the Jewish practice of keeping certain days of the week for voluntary individual pieties, kept half-day fasts, the so-called *stationes*. The bishops also recommended fasts on occasions, often for the purpose of fund-raising for alms. As Tertullian testifies, however, neither food nor fasting practices were at this time a part of the 'pattern of religion'[116] among the majority of Carthaginian Christians. Instead of being integral to 'getting in' or 'staying in' the Christian church, habitual fasting and self-mortification in Tertullian's time was still regarded by most orthodox Christians as 'innovation' and the hallmark of heresy.

It was pointed out earlier that Tertullian's understanding of the nature of Christianity, as it is revealed in tract after tract of his surviving work, was consistent with what probably was and definitely later became the 'orthodox' dogma. He was rejected as a 'heretic', not on account of his theology but mostly because of the harsh practices he advocated. A comparison of what he says about supplication for rains in the early tract, the *Apologeticus*, and the late *De Ieiunio* is instructive not only for what it reveals about Christian customs, but for its implications for Tertullian's biography. As may be recalled, in the *Apologeticus* he writes that in case the rains fail to come 'we Christians' fast in sackcloth and ashes; in *De Ieiunio* he accuses Christians of doing nothing on these occasions when even the pagans humble themselves in front of their idols to beg for rain. Unless one argues the unlikely proposition that the orthodox Christians of Carthage fasted for rain in the 190s but gave up the practice by 210, the discrepancy in his statements about these fasts supports the possibility that, from his very conversion to Christianity, Tertullian belonged to a rigorist Christian group that practised some Jewish pieties. Just like Tertullian himself, his group always regarded itself as orthodox Christian, but more strict in its practices than others, demanding of its members fasting, the seeking of martyrdom and opposition to second marriages; and it was not Tertullian and his group that left to join the Montanists, but the orthodox who found their demands excessive and threw them out of the fold.[117]

Nothing is known about Tertullian's life and personality outside of what his writing suggests. The personality reflected in these does not seem to change. Indeed, if these were all written within the span of fifteen years or so, in his forties and fifties, one would not expect substantial personality changes to be reflected in them. Most of his works reveal a deeply felt despair at human sinfulness and personal guilt. The way of salvation for him lay in martyrdom. Admiration for the courage of martyrs may have influenced his conversion. His ideal of the church was a company of saints, an elite avant-garde. He wanted to belong to this 'militia Christi'; even more, he wanted to lead it. The religious act of utmost importance for him was sacrifice. The acceptance of Jesus's self-sacrifice and the identification with this through baptism was not sufficient for him. As a Christian, he saw the aim of life as self-sacrifice through martyrdom. The God of the early Hebrews who was pleased and appeased by sacrifice appealed strongly to his overwhelming sense of guilt. He was among those Christians who, having been freed from the Jewish law and its daily observance, missed 'the daily contest where merit and failure were clearly marked'.[118] The Jews themselves, who rejected Christ, were abhorrent to him, but he found some Jewish practices worthy of continuation. Jewish fasting – the practice itself and the rationale for it – he found worthy of acceptance by the true, spiritual Christian. Like the Jews, Tertullian saw fasting as self-punishment for sins, as a sign of self-abasement and humility in the sight of God, as an expression of mourning and contrition. He believed, like the Jews, that fasting is pleasing to God, that prayer accompanied by fasting is more certain to reach the ears of God, and, again like some pious Jews, thought that the diminution of one's fat and blood by fasting is a pleasing substitute for the sacrificial victim of olden times.[119] Tertullian's conception of sin was unlike that of the Jews, but his approach to its expiation was modelled on Jewish practice. Jewish concern centred around living according to the Torah; rather than any 'original sin', the Jews worried about many potential sins arising from failure to keep God's commandments. While deeply regretting Adam's fall, few Jewish thinkers shared Tertullian's faith that an individual could make restitution to God for Adam's transgression by starving himself.

Fasting for Tertullian meant a cultic activity that in itself was pleasing to God. He may or may not have been, as Peter Brown claims, a 'voracious reader of medical literature';[120] all one can say is that his tract on fasting shows absolutely no evidence of any medical influence. His graphic linking of overeating, excrement and lust,[121] popular with moralizers like Philo and Clement of Alexandria, and effective as a rhetorical device in attaching the disgust aroused by the image of excrement to both overeating and lust, is not a view for which any medical knowledge would be required.

Many of Tertullian's works reveal an intense personal revulsion from sexuality, from the 'commingling of the flesh'. Sexual continence, he advised, will buy sanctity for the Christian.[122] His deep commitment to the Bible prevented him from outright rejection of marriage. Even for married couples he urged continence and, as we have seen, strongly opposed second marriages. It is the more striking that in light of his attitude to sexual continence, fasting is never suggested by him principally as a means to reduce sexual appetite. Like most ancient moralizers and satirists, he too connected gluttony with lust, but, as noted earlier, he does not recommend fasting as a safeguard of chastity.

In addition to being a religious act of self-humiliation pleasing to God, fasting appears to be of the utmost importance for Tertullian as a means for the distinguishing of a Christian elite, the Spirituals, from second-class Christians, or mere Psychics. The most outstanding of this elite were the martyrs. But martyrdom did not come to everyone or came too slowly. In the meantime fasting provided not just a training for martyrdom but a convenient way of distinguishing the truly committed Christians from the lax opportunists.

Tertullian's stringent elitist demands went against the ideology that aimed to save all sinners. They also opposed the political needs of a growing church for an increasing power base, which ever greater numbers of decent but un-heroic members could provide. He and his Montanists were excluded as heretics from the church. His conception of fasting as penitence was later taken up by the church faced with the problems of sinners, of those who 'lapsed' during the persecutions.[123] A way had to be found through which the repentant could be readmitted into the church. The Jewish practice of expiatory fasting, made Christian by Tertullian, was later accepted for this purpose.

7

FOOD AND FASTING IN ORIGEN AND EUSEBIUS

Origen, the prolific Biblical scholar, whose views fuelled controversy and often furious clashes among Christians for centuries, is another Alexandrian whose writings may provide insight into Christian attitudes to food and fasting in the early third century. More than that, his figure, as it emerges from the pen of his biographer, may also point to important changes in these attitudes that were taking place in the following century. As in the case of Clement or Tertullian, so too in Origen's, contemporary evidence concerning his life is minimal. Outside of the meagre information that can be gained from his extant works concerning his personal history, most of what is known about his life and personality comes from a biography written more than fifty years after his death, in the early fourth century, by an enthusiastic admirer, Eusebius, bishop of Caesarea, who devoted Book VI of his *Ecclesiastical History* to Origen's life.[1] Considering that Eusebius was born probably more than a decade after Origen died, and that he had relatively little information at his disposal about Origen's life, most modern scholars tend to agree that Eusebius's account of Origen's life is not always reliable. It is often noted that he seems to have accepted gossip and rejected or suppressed evidence that did not accord with the ideal of an orthodox saint of his own time and taste. Some critics see the Life as belonging more in the genre of hagiography than history.[2] The historians often differ among themselves as to which detail or aspect of Eusebius's biography they accept or reject. Strangely, however, they all seem to believe Eusebius when it comes to Origen's extreme asceticism, to which point I shall return later. My purpose here is not to add to the attempts to discern the 'real Origen', since I agree with Patricia Cox[3] that on the basis of the information available today it is impossible to write a true life of Origen.

In what follows I shall examine Origen's own pronouncements

about Christian food practices, supporting it, as far as this kind of evidence permits, with the testimony provided by his student, Gregory Thaumaturgos, in order to focus on some glaring inconsistencies concerning the form of asceticism he is believed to have practised, inconsistencies that may throw some light on differences between third-century Christian ascetic ideals and those of the fourth and later centuries. I shall argue that it is not the Origen who lived in the late second and early third century in Alexandria and Caesarea in Palestine, but the Origen created by Eusebius in the early fourth century, who, as a literary hero, is the first in a long and woeful line of orthodox Christian 'holy' men and women who will starve, abuse and mutilate their physical bodies in search of salvation.

ORIGEN THE PERSON

Concerning his life and work, the following bare outlines may be surmised on the basis of his own writing without reference to Eusebius: Origen (c. 185–c. 253) was born and brought up in Alexandria, where he acquired both pagan and Christian education. Throughout his life he devoted his energies to Biblical exegesis and textual criticism, and to teaching and preaching to Christians. In all his work he insisted that the Scriptures are divinely inspired and unerring. Their true meaning, however, could be apprehended not by a literal reading of the texts, but by strenuous intellectual search after the divine message hidden behind the words. Following Philo, the Jewish biblical exegete Origen, like Clement, adopted the allegorizing method to bring out the moral and spiritual essence of the Bible. Even more than his predecessors, Origen accommodates everything to the 'spiritual' meaning of the scriptural passages, often without distinguishing between metaphorical and literal contexts. Like Clement, he combined with this allegorizing a 'typology' – a way of explaining certain personages or events in the Old Testament by claiming them as 'types' of the New Testament, that is to say, as prefigurations, or promises of the fulfilment to come with Jesus and the rise of the church. Allegorizing and the use of typology enabled him to interpret any passage he wished 'as enshrining a spiritual truth which he had in fact derived from a source other than the biblical text'.[4] His overwhelming aim was to squeeze out of the Jewish Bible a supporting structure for Christian doctrine, morality and ecclesiastical practice.[5] Scripture for him was the self-revelation of God, for the doctrines in Scripture disclose, each in a partial and sequential way, the nature of the Logos who is fully disclosed in his incarnation. Origen's interest centred on the spiritual doctrine and not the flesh, the actual words.[6] Some aspects of his speculations earned him the hostility of his fellow Christians who suspected heresies in these. His christology, the view of Christ as a second God,[7] eternally generated by the first one, differed from the trinitarian definition which later became the accepted orthodox dogma. This, together with his belief in the pre-existence of soul,[8] in the spiritual nature of the resurrected body,[9] in the educational aim of the punishment meted out by God and his insistence that salvation is possible for all,[10] constituted what Henry Chadwick describes as 'a stone of stumbling for many in the three hundred years following his death'.[11] They also led to his official condemnation as a heretic by the General Council of 553 under the emperor Justinian.

ORIGEN ON FOOD AND FASTING

In his mature years, c. 245,[12] on the urging of his patron, Ambrose, Origen undertook the writing of an extensive defence of Christianity against the attacks heaped upon the faith by Celsus, a philosophic pagan, whom Origen himself did not know and who, in all likelihood, was long dead at the time when Origen wrote to refute his charges.[13] Origen's own views on the place of food in Christian life are expressed in this work. These views, as we shall see, differ very little from those expressed by his elder fellow Alexandrian, Clement.

The setting for the first mention of food in *Contra Celsum* is a discussion of Jewish and Egyptian custom. Origen seems to be arguing against Celsus's unfavourable comparison of Christian food practices, or possibly the lack of clear-cut regulations concerning eating, with the more fastidious Jewish avoidance of pork and the even more admirable custom of Egyptian priests and Pythagoreans who are wholly vegetarians. Quoting Acts 10:14–15, Matthew 15:11:17 and 1 Corinthians 8:8, all of which are unanimous in saying that 'meat does not commend us to God', Origen explains that

> we do not set great store on refraining from eating, nor yet are we induced to eat from a gluttonous appetite (οὐ μέγα φρονοῦομεν μὴ ἐσθίοντες οὐδ ἀπὸ γαστριμαργίας ἥκομεν ἐπὶ τὸ ἐσθίειν). And therefore, so far as we are concerned, the followers of Pythagoras who abstain from all things that contain life, may do as they please.[14]

Origen understood clearly that both the Egyptian priests and the Pythagoreans abstained from animal flesh for religious or mystical reasons. As opposed to these, he declares clearly and unambiguously and in strict adherence to the Pauline teaching, that for Christians eating or fasting has no religious significance. Gluttony is rejected as unbecoming to Christians, just as it was rejected by Paul, Philo, Clement or, for that matter, by any pagan commentator on morals. If some Christians abstain from meat eating, they have a different reason for it than the Pythagoreans, who abstain on account of the fable about the transmigration of souls,

> We, however, when we abstain, do so because 'we keep under our body, and bring it into subjection' [1 Corinthians 9:27] and desire 'to mortify our members that are upon the earth, fornication, uncleanness, inordinate affection, evil concupiscence' [Colossians 3:5] and we use every effort to 'mortify the deeds of the flesh' [Romans 8:13].[15]

As Origen understood it, whether the Christian ate or abstained was of no concern to God. A virtuous life and sexual purity were, in his eyes, the essential demands facing those who wished to approach the divine. He expressed great pride in the fact that even the simplest uneducated Christian kept himself far from any sexual immorality or licentiousness, and that many have turned away completely from all sexual experience. These, he claimed, unlike some of the pagan ascetics, were able to maintain their chastity without the use of drugs or external force, 'for them not hemlock but a word is sufficient to drive out all lust from their mind as they worship God with prayer'.[16] Apparently those for whom a word was not sufficient to drive out all lust from their mind tried to do it by employing a vegetarian diet. Clement of Alexandria, as will be recalled, believed that rich food, especially the meat of pigs, may lead to amorousness. Clement also suggested that some 'Gnostics' refuse the eating of meat for the sake of self-discipline. He was, however, rather vague about the purpose of this self-discipline. To my knowledge, the sentence of Origen quoted above is the earliest explicit statement to the effect that dietary restriction, in this case a vegetarian diet, was actually used by some Christians for the express purpose of suppressing sexual desires. It should be noted that Origen does not advocate the practice but only reports it as a possible reason for a Christian's vegetarianism.

Abstaining from meat was one of the practices of which heretics were often accused by their detractors who liked to call it 'feigned temperance'.[17] Origen himself fought against the ideas of Marcion, Saturninus and other Gnostics with all his might.[18] It would not be surprising if he was wary of advocating their food practices. Concerning food he never departs from the message of the Pauline Epistles.

Just as in his attitudes to food, Origen's views concerning sexuality and marriage also closely resemble that of the apostle Paul: 'God has allowed us to marry wives, because not everybody is capable of the superior condition which is to be entirely pure'.[19] Going even further perhaps than Paul, Origen expresses a deep personal revulsion against the human sexual nature; in his mind 'works of generation and lust are chastised by the torments of Gehenna',[20] a view more radical than any expressed by the apostle, and one that comes dangerously close to the views of Saturninus and his followers who, according to the testimony of heresy hunters, believed that marriage and generation were the work of Satan.[21] As far as food is concerned, however, Origen's pronouncements are based on the guidelines expressed in Acts, and on the gospel of Matthew. Moreover, he follows the apostle Paul faithfully, often quoting from the Epistles precisely; or when paraphrasing he does it accurately. Jesus liberated his followers from the burdensome food laws of the Jews, for 'it is not what goes into the mouth that defiles a person, but it is what comes out of the mouth' (Matthew 15:11). The Christian is not judged on whether he eats or does not eat (1 Corinthians 8:8). His religious duty is to avoid 'evil intentions, murder, adultery, fornication, theft, false witness, slander' (Matthew15:17–19). Christians are only forbidden to eat meat that was sacrificed to idols, was strangled or had blood in it (Acts 15:28–9). Origen's explanation of these prohibitions, however, is a curious one that ignores the Jewish or Old Testament meaning that equates blood with life. According to him, eating of blood is forbidden to both Jews and Christians because blood is the 'food of demons who are nourished by the vapours rising from it', and since from a strangled animal the blood cannot escape, there is the danger that by partaking of its meat one would inadvertently share a demon's dinner, which is forbidden to Christians, for 'people who are devoted to the supreme God ought not to feast with demons'.[22]

Next, Origen turns to Celsus's objection to the futility of the apostolic prohibition. Celsus had argued that since the demons were given charge, presumably by the supreme deity, of providing humans with food, drink and even the air they breathe, in order to remain consistent the Christian should refuse to partake all of these, otherwise he could not help but associate with demons. In response, Origen insists that only food and wine used in polytheistic sacrifice is prohibited to Christians.

Pagan and Christian thinking was curiously similar when it came to populating the void that divides the world from the realm of the supreme god. Origen believes that not demons but benevolent angels oversee the produce of the earth, while pagan demons are 'responsible for famines, barren vines and fruit-trees, and droughts, and also for the pollution of the air, causing . . . death of animals and plague among men'. He hastens to add that the demons can only do their damage by 'divine appointment', the purpose of which is to convert humanity from doing evil. But those who do everything in the name of God and in accordance with Christian principles,

> when they eat and drink, they are feasting not with any demons, but with divine angels.[23]

In all of Origen's discussion of Christian food practices there is no mention of fasting. Food and wine are God-given blessings that should be used for the maintenance and health of the body. One should abstain from gluttony and not eat for the sake of pleasure. Shunning gluttony, as we have seen repeatedly, was not a peculiarly Christian stricture; most upright pagans and Jews embraced it. Clement, as we have seen, introduced into Christian thinking a fear and distrust of the simple enjoyment that generally accompanies the satisfaction of bodily needs. Origen's Christians similarly shun pleasure for its own sake. Clement's comments concerned with eating and drinking reflect this fear of pleasure more clearly and sharply than those of Origen. As pointed out above, Origen states unequivocally that his religion leaves the Christian free to eat any meat unless it was sacrificed to idols or contained blood. He, like Seneca and Clement, knows the popular aphorism attributed to the shadowy Sextus, who may have been a Stoic philosopher with vegetarian leanings, that said: 'The eating of animals is a matter of indifference; but to abstain from them is more agreeable to reason'.[24] In Origen's eyes, however, it is much more vital for the Christian to abstain from all vice and wickedness than to abstain from the flesh of animals. Unlike Clement, who tried to make the apostle Paul into a vegetarian teetotaller, Origen quotes fully and interprets correctly the relevant passages of Paul's letters: 'we are indeed to abstain not only from the flesh of animals, but from all other kinds of food, if we cannot partake of them without incurring evil, and the consequences of evil'.[25] He emphazises repeatedly that those Christians who abstain at times from eating the flesh of animals do it not for religious scruple and not for the same reason as Pythagoras; they do not believe that souls may descend so low as to enter the bodies of the brutes.[26] Christians honour only the rational soul, and pay honour to the body as the dwelling place of the rational soul. It seems that Origen's Christian abstainers from meat did not use the Platonist argument attributing rationality to animals[27] in order to justify their custom, neither were they deterred from eating meat by the cruelty or injustice to the animal this custom entailed. They, and Origen, had the Bible as testimony that only human beings were created in the image of God with rational souls, and that the animals were created for the use of humans.

Origen does not deny Christians the right to satisfy their bodily needs for food and drink and he does not advocate abstinence from meat and wine. On the other hand, in his work on Christian doctrine, *De Principiis*, he treats with considerable contempt those Christians who hope for the resurrection of their earthly bodies, and think

> that the fulfilment of the promises of the future is to be looked for in bodily pleasure and luxury; and therefore they especially desire to have again, after the resurrection, such flesh as may never be without the power of eating and drinking and performing all the functions of flesh and blood, not following the opinion of the apostle Paul regarding the resurrection of a spiritual body. And consequently they say, that after the resurrection there will be marriages and the begetting of children.[28]

Food, drink and the begetting of children all pertain to 'this life' and they are needed for the maintenance of the earthly body and the continuation of humankind. Scripture promises for the resurrected spiritual body: 'the bread of life, which may nourish the soul with the food of truth and wisdom and enlighten the mind, and cause it to drink from the cup of divine wisdom according to the declaration of Holy Scripture'.[29] Like his fellow Alexandrians Philo and Clement, Origen also considers the overpowering passions among the evils that affect and destroy people and endanger their hope for salvation. Origen, however, is worried about much more complex human failings than gluttony or the indecorous guzzling of wine. He believes that salvation is threatened:

> when a soul is consumed by the fire of love, or wasted away by

zeal or envy, or when the passion of anger is kindled, or one is consumed by the greatness of his madness or his sorrow; on which occasions some, finding the excess of these evils unbearable, have deemed it more tolerable to submit to death than to endure perpetually torture of such a kind.[30]

In his main surviving work Origen evidences little or no concern about food. The Scriptural passages dealing with food, just like all other passages, he allegorizes also in his homilies and understands the New Testament sayings as being opposed to fasting.[31] As noted above, his views regarding food reflect attitudes similar to those of the apostle Paul and of the writer of Acts. This is hardly surprising in a man who devoted his life to the study of the Bible and for whom the centre of truth and the final authority was vested in the Christian Scriptures. Neither is it surprising to find an indifferent, matter-of-fact attitude towards food, similar to what the Stoics professed, in a philosophically minded religious teacher, who saw as the highest attainment of a Christian's life the total absorption in intellectual and spiritual contemplation of the deity. It is true that he regarded the spiritual advance toward this aim as 'the progressive suppression of the mind's responsiveness to the pull of the flesh'.[32] The prime symbol for the 'pull of the flesh' for Origen, as for Paul, was sexuality,[33] not food.

Evidence suggesting that he, just like Clement, regarded food, exercise, rest and sleep as necessary for the health and well-being of the body is given also in a fragment of a letter written by him, in which he complains about the pressure that Ambrose, his patron and employer, put upon him 'by his own zeal for work and passion for sacred studies'. Clearly, the demands of Ambrose, and not the natural ascetic inclinations of Origen, led to the daily routine described here:

for neither when we are engaged in collating can we take our meals, nor when we have taken them walk and rest our bodies. Nay, even at times set apart for those things we are constrained to discourse learnedly and to correct our manuscripts. Neither can we sleep at night for the good of our bodies, since our learned discourse extends far into the evening.[34]

This fragment complaining about hurried meals and loss of sleep and a too demanding employer gives a glimpse of the personal attitude of the man to the necessities of life, an attitude that, as we saw, is consistent with what he taught and preached.

147

Origen's own writings give us no basis to believe that he ever fasted. Like Clement, his elder contemporary, he too was both attracted and repelled by various Gnostic attempts to combine faith with intellectual theorizing, which in the Alexandria of their time was valued highly among pagans, Jews[35] and Christians alike. Some Christians went too far in their search for knowledge, mixing their faith with dualistic speculations. Rejecting matter as evil, some of these groups may have introduced practices that they believed to be consistent with their spiritual insight. Some of them were known to preach against marriage and to enjoin abstention from meat and wine. There seem to have flourished many variants of the faith. Some, as we have seen, were reported as conspicuous for the food practices they advocated. There were also Judaizing Christians who preferred to keep Jewish food laws and fasts, not necessarily as extreme as the Ebionites,[36] who seem to have celebrated the Eucharist with bread and water. Most of these variants, whether intellectual or ritualistic in content, were regarded with suspicion and hostility by others who thought of themselves as 'orthodox' Christians. Those who wanted to distance themselves from the Gnostics and other 'heretics' condemned also their ascetic practices as feigned piety and pretended temperance. Both Clement and Origen considered themselves true orthodox Christians; equally, both men put high value on an individual, intellectual search for God. Both were careful not to be identified as heretics. Clement, as we have seen, approved of marriage and sexual intercourse for the sake of procreation, if it was accomplished without pleasure. He favoured abstention from meat, but was careful of what he preached, lest he should be classed with the heretics. Food was needed for the health and strength of the body. He interpreted fasting allegorically, as abstaining from covetousness and lasciviousness.

Origen clearly advocated sexual asceticism more strongly than Clement, but he also stopped short of rejecting marriage, which would have identified him as a heretic. His life's work centred on a spiritual and intellectual reworking of the text of the Bible. More systematically than Clement, he allegorized the Scriptures, leaving very little of their literal meaning unturned. Even the bread and wine of the Eucharist acquired in his interpretation a symbolic complexity, with levels of tangible and spiritual significance in place of the traditional view of these as the body and blood of Christ. His explanation of the Eucharist in his *Commentary on Matthew* does not suggest an ascetic rejection of food and wine. Here the high-flying symbolism is made clear by basing it on the commonly shared conviction that food and wine are both good and necessary for health and good cheer. As he explains, bread sustains us and enables us to work. The Eucharistic bread therefore symbolizes Christ as the word of righteousness, manifested in action. Wine gladdens the heart, which in the Bible is the seat of intellect. The Eucharistic wine, therefore, symbolizes Christ as the Word of truth, manifested in contemplation.[37]

Origen sees action and contemplation as two aspects of the Christian life, and both as avenues in which the Christian may pursue perfection. There is nothing in his writing that would suggest hostility to the living body to the point of refusing to feed it. It is sin that he is fighting. Sin is in actions and thoughts. Even when he writes about Christian penitence, in place of Jewish sin-offering sacrifice he suggests repentance of sins, alms-giving, forgiving the sins of others, abounding love and martyrdom, but he does not advocate self-punishment by fasting.[38]

This view of Origen's attitude to food and fasting is not contradicted by the testimony of Gregory Thaumaturgos, a one-time pupil and devotee of Origen who later became bishop of Neocaesarea. In his *Panegyric* on Origen, Gregory describes in glowing superlatives the great teacher who, from their first meeting, so profoundly influenced the rest of his life. There is nothing in this work directly concerning food. The asceticism of Origen that Gregory describes in the ninth chapter of the *Panegyric* is that of the perfect Stoic sage. Origen, we are told, inculcated in his pupils, both by teaching and personal example, the virtues of prudence, temperance, fortitude and justice, as 'proof against grief and disquietude under the pressure of all ills'.[39] Gregory himself, writing later in his *Canonical Epistle*,[40] cites 1 Corinthians 6:13 and Matthew 15:11, as did his teacher, to argue that Christians need not worry about what goes into their mouths. The purpose of the epistle was to denounce covetousness among Christians, who, it appears, used the confusion of barbarian (Gothic) raids to enrich themselves. In it the bishop prescribes the procedures for the penitent before he can again participate in worship with the community.[41] There is not a word about fasting. Of course, Gregory's lack of interest in fasting, no matter how suggestive it is, cannot be taken as evidence for the attitude of his teacher. But had he been the devoted pupil of a fasting, self-mortifying saint, one would be justified in expecting some trace of this, either in his remembrance of his teacher or in his own practical pastoral work. The lack of it adds support to the view, argued above on the basis of Origen's own words, that he held a Stoic's attitude that food was necessary for life, but should not be pursued for pleasure.

Origen's matter-of-fact attitudes to food and to the needs of the body do not fit at all well with the image of the Christian holy man created by Eusebius. His mild pronouncements would be quite surprising and incongruous had they been expressed by one who was famous for his harsh ascetic practices, who mortified his flesh by fasting, by abstaining from wine, who walked all his life without shoes and who slept little, never in bed but on the hard ground. This is the Origen whose personality and life history are handed down to posterity in the sixth book of Eusebius's *Ecclesiastical History*. We have to turn now to this biography, which may have had a more lasting influence on the shaping of Christian ascetic ideals and attitudes to food than the actual writings of Origen himself.

ORIGEN AS THE HERO OF EUSEBIUS

Origen, the hero created by Eusebius, was born a Christian to a pious and devout Christian father, who educated his son in both Christian and Hellenic knowledge. The son was distinguished by Christian piety of the orthodox kind from his earliest childhood. As an adolescent, he encouraged enthusiastically his father's martyrdom. His great capacity for intellectual work was recognized early, enabling him to support himself after his father's death by teaching secular subjects.[42] Persecutions made the life of Christians difficult in Alexandria at the time, so much so that there was no one left in charge of teaching Christian doctrine at the catechetical school in Alexandria. Origen, as his biographer claims, was appointed by the bishop to this task at the age of eighteen. He saw as his duty in this post not only to expound the Scriptures, but also, as it appears, actively to encourage his pupils to seek martyrdom. Eusebius tells us that he made quite a name for himself and became celebrated among the leaders of the faith for the great number of martyrs his exhortations produced, 'For not only was he with them while in bonds, and until their final condemnation, but when the holy martyrs were led to death, he was very bold and went with them into danger'.[43] It was only the direct intervention of the hand of God that saved him from sharing with his pupils the martyrdom he so fervently advocated and so courageously courted.

Eusebius believes that Origen's miraculous ability to produce so many martyrs for the church was due to his 'admirable conduct according to the practice of genuine philosophy. For they saw that his manner of life was as his doctrine, and his doctrine as his life'.[44] This 'admirable conduct' consisted of the following in Eusebius's words:

> Through the entire day he endured no small amount of discipline; and for the greater part of the night he gave himself to the study of the Divine Scriptures. He restrained himself as much as possible by a most philosophic life; sometimes by the discipline of fasting, again by limited time for sleep. And in his zeal he never lay upon a bed, but upon the ground. Most of all, he thought that the word of the Saviour in the Gospel should be observed, in which he exhorts not to have two coats nor to use shoes, nor to occupy oneself with cares for the future.

He treated himself so harshly 'that he was in danger of breaking down and destroying his constitution.'[45] As the final and crowning touch on this portrait of the 'philosophic life' of endurance of 'cold and nakedness', of going without shoes, and abstaining from wine and all but the most frugal amount of food, Eusebius reveals Origen's 'daring deed' of self-castration. This deed in Eusebius's view 'evidenced an immature and youthful mind, but at the same time gave the highest proof of faith and continence'.[46]

Eusebius testifies further concerning his hero's success and fame as a teacher who attracted many pupils, not only from his own city but from far and distant places, who,

> drawn by the fame of Origen's learning, which resounded everywhere, came to him to make trial of his skill in sacred literature. And a great many heretics, and not a few of the most distinguished philosophers, studied under him diligently, receiving instruction from him not only in divine things, but also in secular philosophy.[47]

Having been invited by leaders in the church to settle doctrinal disputes, or by secular dignitaries, among whom there was no less than an empress, who wanted to meet the famous sage in person, he travelled widely. He visited Rome, Arabia, Palestine and Athens. Constant study, including an effort to acquire proficiency in the Hebrew language as a necessary research tool for the investigation of the Bible, teaching and preaching day and night and frequent long distance travels did not seem to exhaust his amazing store of energy, a fact to which his phenomenal literary output stands as testimony.

As a result of mounting tension arising from the hostility shown to him by the leaders of the church, Origen left Alexandria around AD 230. He settled in Caesarea in Palestine, where on an earlier visit he was ordained presbyter. Here he continued his energetic, active and productive life. Apparently his generous but demanding patron Ambrose followed him to Caesarea and continued with great enthusiasm to provide material support in the form of books, secretaries, copyists and all that was needed for the continued output of biblical commentaries.

His long and active life ended sometime after the Decian persecution of AD 250, during which he came near to martyrdom. Eusebius writes that Origen was imprisoned and severely tortured. No torture could break his resolve. He was, however, not granted the crown of martyrdom; for some evil reason the interrogating judge refused to execute the old man.[48] He lived to write a letter about his suffering in prison, the letter that presumably served as Eusebius's source.

This is the portrait of Origen and the outline of his life created by Eusebius. Patricia Cox in her book, *Biography in Late Antiquity*, makes a perceptive and thoroughgoing analysis of this portrait. She regards Book VI of the *Ecclesiastical History* as an attempt by Eusebius to create a Christian 'holy man', and demonstrates how this fits into a long tradition of Greek biography, sharing with the genre the common characteristics of panegyrical exaggeration of the hero's achievements, the interest in highly idealized types of individuals, and especially in the lives of philosophers. Typically these biographies put forth the lives of various philosophical masters 'not only as models for the perpetuation of particular philosophical schools but also as polemics to be employed in furthering one tradition at the expense of others'.[49] The historical bits of information in these biographies of 'holy men' were used to support an ideal portrait against a realistic background, and often 'sources were cited to create the guise of history'.[50] These citations, however, did not make the biographies more historically reliable. This fashion persisted into late antiquity, when indeed her best examples of the genre were written.

Eusebius's biography conforms to the pattern described above in all details. Its polemical aims, as Cox argues, were directed at two different communities. In the Christian community the polemic was aimed against those who doubted Origen's orthodoxy, and in the pagan community against those who questioned his philosophical integrity. These divergent polemical directions forced Eusebius to try to fuse the 'type' of the ideal Christian churchman with the well-worn image of the wise and highly virtuous philosopher. In addition to these Janus-faced polemical aims, Eusebius had an apologetic purpose and used the figure of Origen to promote unity among Christians and, in addition, a proselytizing one in presenting to pagans a Christian 'saint' who combines in himself the highest philosophical virtues with Christian piety.[51]

To what extent, if any, do the attitudes expressed by the surviving works of Origen conform to Eusebius's picture? As we have seen above, what he had to say about food in no way suggests a fasting ascetic. His writings, however, do provide ample evidence for his distaste for sex and for his unfavourable views on marriage, despite the rather grudging admission of its acceptability for the sole purpose of procreation. If he practised what he wrote, as in all likelihood he did, then he must have lived a sexually abstinent life. Did he castrate himself, as Eusebius claims? There is nothing in his own words that would suggest that he approved of such drastic means for the securing of chastity. On the contrary, as we have seen above, in his arguments against Celsus he proudly pointed to simple Christians who lived in lifelong chastity, fortified only by their conviction and using no drugs or force. He expressed disapproval of self-castration also in his *Commentary on Matthew*.[52] Of course, he may have committed his 'daring deed' in a despondent moment in his youth, as Eusebius claims, and regretted it later. If the story is true, it again brings into question the habitual abstinence from food and wine that is so fondly attributed to him by Eusebius. As we have seen earlier, Origen was of the opinion that the only possible reason for a Christian for abstaining from meat may be to control the sexual urge, a view based most probably on the widely shared belief that a meat diet and the liberal use of wine heat and moisten the body and make it sexually more responsive.[53] If he had taken care of the problem of sexual temptation once and for all in his early youth, why, we may ask, would he feel the need for habitual fasting? And equally well one may go on to ask how a man who mortified his flesh with fasting, who walked barefoot and had little sleep, could carry on such a phenomenally active and productive life of teaching, travelling and writing. His scholarly output is ranked with the Roman encyclopaedist Varro and Augustine of Hippo as one of the most prolific in antiquity.[54] Historians who accept Eusebius's picture of Origen as a self-mortifying fasting ascetic should consider that most of the famous acrobats of fasting were *written about*; they themselves wrote nothing. This is not surprising, since scholarly output requires work and energy, which is provided by food.

Why did Eusebius pick Origen as his hero and why did he dress him in the clothes of a stereotyped figure, who by his time was somewhat worn out, and who was often ridiculed by some of the educated and looked upon with suspicious disapproval even by some of the pious among them?[55]

That Eusebius had a special need for this kind of a figure is suggested by the fact that the creation of the figure of Origen was not Eusebius's first attempt to use the genre. The formative influence for it was undoubtedly the *Therapeutae*, the community of pious Jews that Philo, writing in the first century AD, used to embody the ideal, both as principle and practice, of the contemplative life. Eusebius, in the fourth century, accepted the description as reality and chose to believe that Philo reported on the life of Christian holy men.[56] The frugal diet of these holy philosophers, who lived on bread and water, ate only after sunset, and were so completely devoted to pious study that they often forgot to eat for two, three or even six days, so impressed Eusebius that he used the same regimen to characterize the first of his *Martyrs of Palestine*. Procopius, who according to Eusebius, was martyred in the first year of the persecution of Diocletian (303–4):

had dedicated his life to philosophy and from a child embraced chastity of conduct and a most rigorous mode of living and he buffeted his body [1 Corinthians 9:27], lived on bread and water every two or three days and often he passed even a whole week without food.[57]

This characterization contains all the important features of the Eusebian holy man: philosophy, chastity, phenomenal frugality in food and martyrdom. It comes as no surprise then that Eusebius clothes his hero, the most important Christian intellectual of his own city, with these very same features. Origen had settled in Caesarea and the city remained for over two decades the centre of his activities, where his renown as a great teacher and Christian intellectual attracted many admiring students, as the thanksgiving oration of Gregory Thaumaturgos testifies. For Eusebius, Origen was not only a highly regarded Christian sage, but also his own city's local hero.

Eusebius's own life was strongly intertwined with the city of Caesarea. He was probably born there in the 260s, a decade or more after Origen's death; he worked there with Pamphilus, who, after studying in Alexandria, settled in Caesarea, and together they collected a substantial library that contained many of Origen's works. Around 313 he became bishop of the city, a post he retained until his death in 339 or 340.[58] Caesarea was a cosmopolitan city with a large, mixed population of various ethnic groups and creeds, among them a growing Christian community. By about 190 the community had a bishop, but Christian scholarship in Caesarea gained a reputation only in the third century, with the arrival of Origen.[59] Eusebius, like his mentor Pamphilus, regarded himself as intellectual heir to Origen,[60] and it is easy to see how important it became for the Christian scholar and later bishop of the city to make his city's first Christian intellectual into its local hero and saint. Origen's fame and stature may have helped to enhance the importance of the church of Caesarea, in comparison with that of neighbouring Jerusalem, whose bishop traditionally enjoyed great prestige as the occupant of an apostolic see.[61]

There seems to have been a growing need for heroes and drama in some Christian circles, especially felt after the cessation of the persecutions. Origen himself, long before the 'peace of the church', expressed a nostalgia 'for the old days when under persecution one could be sure of the authenticity and integrity of the believers', in view of the complacency and quarrels in the community that was facing him.[62] With nothing to revive the hopes of an imminent End, Christians were at risk to boredom, that powerful enemy of religious commitment.[63] That Eusebius was deeply anxious about complacency born of security is shown in his perception of it as the cause that brought on the great persecution. Following Origen, he believed that too much freedom brought on pride and sloth, envy and in-fighting, hypocrisy and pretence, and many other evils that eventually brought divine judgement on the Christians in the shape of the persecutions.[64] Thus he keenly felt the need to keep martyrdom in the centre of Christian consciousness, as is shown by the voluminous writings he devoted to the lives of martyrs both in the *Ecclesiastical History* and also in a separate work, the *Martyrs of Palestine*. When persecution was no longer threatening, a substitute for martyrdom had to be found. The Origen of Eusebius, the thoroughly 'orthodox' intellectual, who with his own hands put an end to his sexual nature, who fasted and wore no shoes, who lived in poverty and slept on the ground, was created to provide a model for those Christians who found the lifting of external oppression regrettable and the life of the now state-supported church morally weak and dreary. Christianity, many wanted to believe, brought something new, but with the power of the empire buying into it, it was increasingly difficult to discern what the new thing was.[65] There were Christian groups long before the conversion of

Constantine who believed that the 'new thing' that Christ's message brought was an end to marriage and sexual life and that true commitment demanded the strictest asceticism of all baptized Christians. Most advocates of these ideas were branded as Gnostic 'heretics' and, together with the radically dualistic Manichees, were excluded by the orthodox church. Many of those who rejected the religious or philosophical justification for it still found the self-mortifying asceticism of these sects awe-inspiring.[66] The 'heretical' claim that true Christianity meant a radical asceticism became increasingly attractive with the passing of the heroic age of persecution. By adopting ascetic practices such as those of Eusebius's hero, the truly committed Christian could attain a kind of bloodless martyrdom, with much of the admiration and hero-worship that real martyrdom entailed.

Very soon the literary image caught on. In the 350s a book about the life of Antony, the desert hermit, appeared, which dropped the emphasis on intellectual aspects by choosing as its hero an illiterate Egyptian peasant, but which followed and highly exaggerated the self-mortifications outlined by Eusebius.[67] The book was an enormous success, and with it a new ideal of Christian perfection became firmly established. This ideal, it seems to me, was a far cry from the philosophic self-restraint held in high esteem by the two Alexandrian Christian intellectuals. The following two chapters will examine attitudes to food and fasting in ascetic propaganda and in ascetic practice.

8

JEROME AND ASCETIC PROPAGANDA

Jerome – Eusebius Sophronius Hieronymus – was born in the thirties or forties of the fourth century,[1] in an empire that was ruled by Christian emperors, either Constantine himself or his sons. He came into a world in which Christianity 'was rapidly consolidating its ascendancy, but in which Christians were becoming more and more divided into those whose commitment was deep-rooted and the much greater number whose Christianity was conventional, superficial, sometimes opportunist'.[2] With Christianity becoming the accepted and favoured religion of the empire, the divisions among Christians became increasingly apparent, not only along the dimension of commitment but also on the very nature and meaning of the faith, with its implications both for theological discourse and political power. Not having to fear the power of the State, having even a stake in it, enabled Christians to focus increasingly on their differences; they soon intensified their conflicts and fought each other for both spiritual and worldly power with vigorous ferocity. Christian asceticism, put forward by its promoters as the spiritual basis for authority, became an integral part of this struggle. Christian attitudes to food and fasting from this period will be influenced by the ascetic ideology to such an extent as to make impossible their discussion independent of this propaganda. The present chapter will treat therefore attitudes to food and fasting in ascetic propaganda, while the next and last chapter will discuss them in monastic practice.

Jerome, whose writings provide the focus in this chapter, was one of the most erudite and energetic champions in this war. Much more is known about his personality than about our previously discussed writers. In contrast to them, he was not reticent about himself; indeed, he fervently hoped that posterity would know him as he wanted to be known. The events of his life elucidate his writings, and these, in turn,

157

provide insight into his character. A provincial with obscure lineage, Jerome names Stridon (in Dalmatia or Pannonia) as his birthplace.[3] His parents were Christian[4] of modest means[5] who, nevertheless, provided him with the best of Latin education that a young man of the age preparing for a career in imperial administration could wish for. His extant works evidence no gratitude and show no attachment to his parents.[6] The education he received, at first probably in his home town then in Rome under the famous teacher Aelius Donatus, was saturated with the classical heritage that 'impregnated his mind too deeply ever to be obliterated'.[7] This education, in Hagendahl's words,

> made him an antique rhetor with all the merits and faults, mental and literary, which rhetorical training implies: the brilliancy and fluency of style, the power of invention, the subtlety of mind, the ready wit and recklessness of a thorough controversialist, the tendency to superficial ostentation and selfconceited overbearingness.[8]

A love for the well-turned phrase, a prodigious memory and an equally phenomenal ambition for fame,[9] and a need to dominate others formed the substrate of a personality upon which the rhetorical training worked its finishing touches.

Jerome's life is known mostly from what he cares to tell about it, none of which can be taken either as particularly introspective nor as objective. He was attracted early both to power and to asceticism. Early, too, he may have realized that the latter may lead to the former; ascetics were attracting attention.[10] He had a series of friendships with men,[11] towards whom he was intensely loving and fiercely possessive. Each of these friendships broke up in 'a sudden storm'.[12] He is silent on the causes, but the pattern repeats. Neither his friends, who shared his background and interests, nor later the monks of Chalcis[13] nor the Roman clergy would accept him as he wanted to be accepted. The life of a hermit, even one well provided with a library, secretaries and language tutor, was, however, not for him.[14] Jerome returned to city life, to Antioch, Constantinople and Rome, centres of wealth and both secular and ecclesiastical power. In Rome he found a patron, a cause, and a group which, it seems, was willing to accept his domination.[15] The patron was no lesser a personage than Damasus the pope; the cause which he undertook, apparently with the support of Damasus, was to induce wealthy Roman Christians to follow the ascetic life.[16] The intimate friendly circle that accepted his guidance consisted not of men this time but a group of wealthy ladies. The enjoyment he gained from the meek submission of a group of women to the imposition of his will may well have been enhanced by the fact that the women were his social superiors. The wealth and social position of the women compensated for the 'weakness of their sex'.[17] After three years spent as their spiritual guide and basking in the pious ladies' admiration, the idyll ended abruptly. In 385 a council of the Roman clergy summoned Jerome before them and told him to leave the city.[18] A short time later he settled in Bethlehem where he was followed by his most faithful disciples, Paula and her daughter. The two women devoted the rest of their lives and all their financial resources to minister to his needs and to those of their double monastery in Bethlehem. Here, until his death on 20 September 420,[19] he continued with prodigious energy the great work of biblical translation and commentary, and through vigorous correspondence and various polemical treatises he maintained also the unceasing battle for the ascetic life, against those whom he considered enemies of orthodoxy and against all those who disagreed with him. From the 390s he was involved in many of the famous Christian controversies and quarrelled bitterly with a number of people. The Origenist debate, which engaged his energies for several years and resulted in the final rift between him and his one-time friend Rufinus, and the quarrels with Jovinian, Vigilantius and the Pelagian 'heresy' gave Jerome renewed opportunities to attack without mercy any opposition to his conception of Christian asceticism.

The most substantial pronouncements of Jerome concerning food are found in his letters and polemical treatises written in the defence of virginity, Christian asceticism, and in the promotion of his own particular monastic ideal.[20] The prototypes for this ideal are laid down in writings that constitute Jerome's excursions into the field of holy biography. Inspired by the phenomenal social success of the *Life of Antony*,[21] Jerome also tried his hand at writing biographies of hermits, who competed in holiness, if not in popularity, with the sainted Antony.[22] These 'lives' appear as new, Christian shoots on an old and popular literary tree, the biography of the divine sage. Jerome's 'biographies', like others of this genre, reflect their author's own personal concerns and convictions more than those of his 'heroes',[23] just as the 'orthodox' teaching of Antony presented in his *Life* is believed to characterize the views of the author rather than those of the hermit.[24] Ancient biographers of holy men, pagan or Christian, had little regard for the actual facts of their subjects' lives. Their aim instead was to defend and to affirm an ideal embodied in the hero.

Ancient biographies of holy men should not be read with an expectation of finding in them any sustained historical veracity, as if they represented some subgenre of history. The genre itself helped to create and to promote the myth of the holy man, both Christian and pagan.[25]

There are some uniform traits that characterize these men, such as wisdom, unshakeable devotion to the divine and asceticism, which by late antiquity 'connotes not mere "training" but a renunciation of worldly values',[26] which in Christian writing turns into severe bodily deprivation and often actual abuse. An obligatory part and parcel of the Christian stories was the heroic fast, with insistence on the miraculously meagre amounts of food on which the holy men were able to survive. Jerome, in the *Life of Paul, the First Hermit*, writes:

> I call as witnesses Jesus and his angels that . . . I saw monks: one lived as a recluse for thirty years on coarse barley bread and muddy water; another subsisted on five dried figs a day... [27]
> These things will seem unbelievable to those who do not believe that all things are possible for those who believe.[28]

The impossible feat of living without adequate food became the sure sign that the Christian hero had achieved '*caelestis vita*' on earth.[29] Since starvation is universally dreaded, the spectacle of self-imposed starvation usually strikes the beholder with awe. This fact was well recognized and exploited by the tellers of these miraculous tales, as it is still recognized by those who resort to hunger strikes as political weapon.

It would appear also that the more unbelievable the privations depicted, the more satisfying these stories became for the well-fed urban readership for whose edification they were composed.[30] Jerome's own 'autobiographical' sketch depicting his suffering in the Syrian desert, in his famous *Letter to Eustochium* (22:7), belongs to this same genre, with himself, in this case, the fasting hero. The purpose for which these stories were written and circulated is clearly stated in the letter. After describing with blazing colours the temptations of the flesh he suffered in the desert even after weeks of starvation and self-torture that gave him small relief from his vivid sexual fantasies, Jerome brings home forcefully the inevitable comparison: 'If such are the temptations of men whose bodies are emaciated with fasting so that they have only evil thoughts to withstand, how must it fare with a girl who clings to the enjoyment of luxuries?'[31]

The literature on the desert heroes was created and propagated for the purpose of making the wealthy Christian upper class embarrassed.[32] To hold up an image of the desert-dwelling solitary who had no needs, not even for the most basic sustenance, was to warn against private greed and avarice. Jerome addresses the reader of his *Vita Pauli*, whom he expects to be a wealthy person:

> let me ask those ... who clothe their homes with marble, who string on a single thread the cost of villas, what did this destitute old man ever lack? ... But paradise awaits that poor wretch, while hell will seize as its own you golden people.[33]

In the classical tradition, avarice was deplored as a betrayal of the needs of the city; Christian thought reinterpreted this anxiety as a betrayal of the needs of the Church.[34]

Survival on meagre food rations is, of course, not the only feature of these *Vitae* that demands serious effort in suspending disbelief. Jerome's claims for his own privation in the desert of Chalcis,[35] just like his tales of monks who survived on five figs a day, have to be accorded the same credit and reality as the loaf of bread brought to the monks by an obliging raven,[36] or the grave dug for Paul by a pair of grieving lions;[37] 'all things are possible for those who believe'![38]

The monk's life, as promoted by Jerome in his biographies, had a number of visible distinguishing characteristics. The holy men fasted, did not wash, wore rough clothes and slept on the ground. These signifiers of holiness were not invented by Jerome, but were increasingly praised and admired by Christian writers, many of whom, like Eusebius, as we have seen earlier, saw these as the manifestation of the ideal comportment for the 'philosophic' Christian, and as signs of true piety. Jerome's Eastern contemporary and fellow propagandist for the virginal life, John Chrysostom, also recommends fasting, vigils, sleeping on the ground and other self-imposed hardships for Christian virgins.[39] He is not alone in his praise of monasteries as peaceful havens: 'there we will find sackcloth and ashes ... fasting and sleeping on the ground'.[40]

These four external signs of ostentatious rejection of the amenities of civilized life were not even a Christian invention. The Cynic sage who lived frugally on what he could find, who drank only water, had one garment, used no oil, and slept on the ground, was a figure well known in Classical Greek literature. Whatever form their particular ascesis took, the aim seemed to be total freedom from social constraints; by rejecting the amenities of civilized life they felt in a good position to criticize and upbraid the foibles of urban society.[41] The fact that they took nothing from society enabled them to hurl abuse at its shortcomings, its greed and avarice. The popularity of the figure is attested by the fact that as late as the Augustan age 'Cynic epistles' still circulated, written by unknown authors under the names of philosophers of the fifth and fourth centuries BC. The letter by Pseudo-Crates, for example, declares that needing little is nearest to God while the opposite is farthest away. The writer advises a would-be disciple to become accustomed to drinking water, 'to eating by the sweat of your brow, to wearing a coarse cloak, to being worn out (by sleeping) on the ground'.[42]

Not all the philosophically inclined pious found this approach to God attractive. As discussed earlier, in connection with Jewish piety,[43] Philo of Alexandria adamantly rejected the idea that the refusal of food and drink, of the use of bath and oil, carelessness about one's clothing and sleeping on the ground, were in any sense expressions of self-control or piety.[44]

Christian asceticism's expressed aim was 'to take up the cross and follow Christ'; the writings of Jerome amply testify, however, that assuming the persona of the holy man with its fourfold signs provided authority, while the 'desert' gave him the platform from which to criticize and often hurl insults, very much in the fashion of the Cynics, at Christian society. Nothing expresses it better than Jerome's own words: 'from the caves which serve us for cells we monks of the desert condemn the world. Rolling in sackcloth and ashes we pass sentence on bishops'.[45]

As an ascetic monk Jerome reserved the right to himself to point a finger at all the shortcomings and vice in Christian society and even to demonstrate, by writing a history of the Church, how the 'Bride of Christ' lost virtue while gaining wealth and power.[46] The promised history was never written, but no opportunity offering itself in treatises or correspondence was missed for the documentation of this lost virtue and the exposition of the hypocrisy of the clergy, the greed and gluttony of monks who 'visited virgins', the lewdness of nuns and the total corruption that he perceived in every corner of Christian society.

Before I turn to Jerome's writings that are addressed directly to the question of food, another problem needs some attention, his attitude to women. Despite the increasingly large literature on the subject, some discussion of it is required here in order to appreciate the dietary rules he proposes. A number of his letters written for the purpose of guiding the recipient toward the ascetic life contain dietary advice. The advice Jerome gives, as will be shown, is highly coloured by sexual anxieties, and due to his peculiar views on female nature and sexuality his admonitions are often dependent on the gender of their recipient.

Jerome's most vigorous ascetic propaganda was directed toward women.[47] This was not, as is often claimed, because of his warm affection for women. Many modern commentators, faced with the unrelenting hostility expressed in the whole corpus of Jerome's writings, appeal to his so-called loving friendship with a large coterie of Roman women in order to add weight to their interpretation of the tone of his writing as due to the influence on him of the misogynistic tradition of Graeco-Roman literature. All the information about Jerome's celebrated friendships with women of 'the Roman aristocracy' comes from his own writings. While the veracity of his writings in other matters is often questioned,[48] his large and devoted female following is often accepted, used as reliable evidence for the Christianization of Rome, for the role of 'aristocratic women' in this process[49] and for the history of fourth-century women's life and asceticism.[50]

The large number of women friends, on closer scrutiny, boils down to only two households, that of Marcella[51] and that of Paula. The letters he wrote, moreover, were not intended as intimate communication but, as missiles in a propaganda campaign, in self-promotion and in public debate, were meant for wide circulation. Jerome consciously intended his treatises written in letter form to be widely circulated, and in all probability to remain for posterity as a neatly arranged public document of his life.[52] Whether the addressees indeed asked for them and whatever they made of the contents when they read them will never be known. Not one letter from the women survives.[53]

Sexual continence was central to Jerome's conception of Christian asceticism,[54] which in turn served as the foundation of spiritual authority for him. Sexual continence was a difficult condition to maintain. The blame for this he projected in large measure on women. Making use of the abundant storehouse of misogynistic material in classical, Jewish and Christian traditions just referred to, he projects his own obsessive sexual fantasies and anxieties onto the female sex.[55] Women are by nature sensuous, lewd, and corrupt. Christian women too are worldly, most of them gluttons, drunkards and false pretenders.[56] Even consecrated virgins cannot escape his scorn, they only pretend to fast, they sleep in the same bed with men, and abort or kill the proof of their sin.[57]

The only way to protect the faithful from women's sensuous and lewd nature and the temptation to sin that they embody is to guide them forcefully into an ascetic life of seclusion and self-mortification. His ideal Christian woman was:

> one who mourned and fasted, who was squalid with dirt, almost blinded by weeping. . . . The psalms were her music, the Gospels her conversation, continence her luxury, her life a fast. No other could give me pleasure but one whom I never saw eating food.[58]

This picture of his friend and lifelong follower and supporter, Paula, is often dismissed by modern commentators as a ridiculous exaggeration.[59] The praise for the self-mortifying, praying and fasting woman as the only acceptable female figure is, however, consonant with Jerome's contempt for marriage and the loathing and extreme hostility he voices toward women, *mulierculae*, as he often refers to female-gendered human beings. Fasting for Jerome becomes a weapon to fight this evil of sexual enticement and a method for isolating its source behind bars. In letter after letter addressed to women, he urges them not to share the pleasures of the table, to keep secluded and to fast for the sole purpose of cooling their 'hot little bodies'.

Jerome has read Tertullian, who collected countless examples[60] from Scriptures of divine condemnation of gluttony and divine approval of simple food. Jerome paraphrases, half-heartedly and without giving credit, Tertullian's major aim for fasting: 'we must take all care that abstinence may bring back to Paradise those whom repletion once drove out'.[61] But that is not the true motivation for Jerome. Fasting, he believed, was essential, for it was the best antidote to sexual urges. Tertullian, as will be remembered, believed and preached fervently that fasting was a religious duty, for God required it as sacrifice.[62] Jerome, quite on the contrary, asserts:

> Not that God, the Lord and Creator of the universe, takes any delight in the rumblings of our intestines or the emptiness of our stomach or the inflammation of our lungs; *but because this is the only way of preserving chastity.*[63]

Among all the possible reasons that Christian writers may have had for urging their followers to fast, Jerome's concern with fasting is only as an antidote to sex, as a method for bloodless castration. While he himself confessed that he found giving up delicious food harder even than leaving 'home, parents, sister, relations',[64] still he preached a cruel regimen of near starvation for young women and female children. Fasting, as the surest weapon against the demon of fornication, was urged by Jerome on all who would be celibate; but, as will be seen, somewhat different dietary advice was given by him to men and to women.

Jerome saw the human body as heated by food. The richer, the better-tasting the food was, the more heat it provided. The heat provided by food he conceived not as energy but as particularly sexual fuel. Heated bodies are sexually charged, the greater the body heat the more irresistible the sexual urge. To support his own views, Jerome often claims the opinions of medical writers, especially Galen.[65] He may have read Galen but his understanding of the connection between food and sex is much less nuanced and complex than Galen would have it. Jerome writes:

> Physicians and those who have written on the nature of the human frame, especially Galen in his treatise *On Health*, say that the bodies of young men and full-grown men and women glow with an innate warmth, and that for persons of these ages all food is harmful which tend to increase that heat, while it is conducive to health for them to eat and drink anything that is cold.[66]

In writing this, he reads into Galen something to which the physician would have had reason to object. The Galenian theory, as we have seen,[67] was based on the four humours and the four 'qualities': the 'hot', the 'cold', the 'moist' and the 'dry'. Health was a balance between these, and disease was the contrary, a state of the body that was out of balance. Despite the need for balance, heat was somewhat privileged among the 'qualities', for it was needed for all the important functions of the body, including the 'coction' or digestion of food. Children were born with innate heat and were moist; as they grew older they got gradually drier and cooler. Old men became both cold and dry. The sexual urge was dependent on both the 'hot' and the 'moist', adequately present in the young and adult; with ageing 'hot' and 'moist' gradually turned to 'cold' and 'dry', with the corresponding dwindling of the urge, or, what is more likely, the performance. Jerome, in contrast, was not quite certain that even the cooling of old age would result in a corresponding evaporation of the urge for fornication.[68]

The physician saw his task as helping to keep the bodily machine functioning; unlike the Christian ascetic, medical science generally did not aim to change human nature. The bodily machinery functioned well when basic needs could be satisfied without incurring pain or discomfort. Physicians, unlike the moralist, tended not to generalizations but tried to find solutions to individual problems. In prescribing food, the followers of the Hippocratic school believed that 'nourishment occurs when the nourishing food is assimilated to the nourished body' and since like is assimilated by like, i.e. food that is warm or dry is taken up easily by bodies that are dry or warm respectively, 'in those who have a harmonious constitution, the pleasanter the food is, the more nourishing it proves'.[69] They tended to advocate treatment 'of opposites by opposites' only for unbalanced, diseased states. On the other hand, pious moralizers like Philo, Clement or Tertullian enjoy repeating the age-old commonplace favoured by the guardians of public decency, namely that luxury in food and drink will lead to debauchery and all sorts of excess. Jerome, like these, may call on physicians to lend the support of professional prestige to his own views on diet, which in turn are shaped by his ascetic purposes and express his own anxieties. The supporting 'evidence' from the physicians is often dragged in by the hair, its meaning twisted beyond recognition.

The dangerous connection between food and sexuality, between the 'pleasures of the belly' and the pleasures of 'what is below the belly',[70] was a well-worn Hellenistic commonplace, familiar to all both from moralizing literature and from comedy; for the adaptation of this topos in aid of religious piety Jerome had as predecessors, as we have seen, Philo, Clement and Tertullian. Gluttony, according to Philo, even if it does not lead to eating forbidden food, will lead to insatiable sexual desire, in some cases even for one's own wife! The blame for this, as he sees it, rests on the body:

> which contains a great amount of fire and moisture; the fire as it consumes the food, quickly demands more; and the moisture is drawn as a stream through the genital organs, and creates in them irritation, itchings, and titillation without ceasing.[71]

The unbreakable link between food, body heat and sexual desire became an extremely important fixture in the world of ideas shared among Christian advocates of virginity in Jerome's age. As Ambrose, bishop of Milan, writes:

> An external fire is extinguished by pouring on water... inward heat of the body is cooled by draughts from the stream, for flame is fed or fails according to the fuel... in like manner then the heat of the body is supported or lessened by food. Luxury then is the mother of lust.[72]

Jerome knew Ambrose's writing on virginity and fasting and shared his ideas, even appealing to the bishop's authority for the support of his own argument for virginity.[73] Later on several occasions Jerome likened Ambrose to an ugly crow who decks himself out with other birds' feathers.[74] Another enthusiastic friendship gone sour!

The problem of the young woman trying to maintain her chastity while 'her body is all on fire with rich food'[75] engaged Jerome in a number of his writings.[76] In his letter to Furia, a young widow, he spells out explicitly the dietary regimen she should follow in order to maintain herself in virginal widowhood. In the first place, he advises her not to drink wine but to live on water, which cools the natural heat of the body.

> Secondly, in the way of food avoid all heating dishes. I do not speak of meat only ... but with vegetables also anything that creates wind or lies heavy on the stomach should be rejected. You should know that nothing is so good for young Christians as a diet of herbs .... By cold food the heat of the body should be tempered .... This is the reason why some of those who aspire to a life of chastity fall midway on the road. They think that they need merely abstain from meat, and they load their stomach with vegetables which are only harmless when taken sparingly and in moderation. To give you my real opinion, I think that nothing so inflames the body and titillates the organs of generation as undigested food and convulsive belching .... Regard as poison anything that has within it the seeds of sensual pleasure. *A frugal diet which leaves you always hungry is* to be preferred to a three days' fast, and *it is much better to go short every day than occasionally to satisfy your appetite to the full.*[77]

Women, in order to extinguish their sexual urges, should avoid wine 'as poison'.[78] They should not eat meat. And to support this he appeals to the Apostle Paul. He repeatedly[79] cites a truncated sentence from Paul's epistle to the Romans (14:21) out of context: 'It is good for a man neither to drink wine nor to eat flesh.'[80] This is a falsification of the intent of the apostle who – as was argued earlier – taught that food should not be a religious issue, and who urged his flock to tolerate each other's food preferences. Peter Brown believes that Jerome contributed more heavily than did any other contemporary Latin writer to the definitive sexualization of Paul's notion of the *flesh*.[81] As was argued earlier,[82] the texts of Paul's letters may indeed lend themselves to this sexual interpretation; however, to make the apostle into an advocate of vegetarianism goes against all his teaching on the question of food. Jerome here summons the authority of the apostle Paul and using his own prestige as interpreter of scripture, blatantly falsifies Paul's message in order to impose his obsessive caution on the women. Jerome's opposition to meat eating was motivated by the same fear as his opposition to wine: meat overheats the body and leads to sexual lust. As we shall see later, it was not Paul who inspired this belief but a Neoplatonic philosopher and enemy of Christianity, whose ideas he plucked to deck himself out like the proverbial 'ugly crow'.

Not only were wine and meat banned from the diet of women who were intent on a chaste life, but even heavy vegetables that create wind. Excrement in Jerome's mind was linked with the sexual urge. Here again one can sense echoes of Tertullian and Clement of Alexandria, both claiming that excremental secretions stimulate sexual lust: 'Lusts are aroused when the excrement gathers around the organs of generation'.[83] This view may have been based, as Aline Rousselle writes, on medical speculations that regarded sperm as consisting of an excess of 'humours' that results from absorbing too much food.[84] It is difficult, however, to attribute to Jerome or the others adherence to any one of the various and often conflicting medical theories concerning the origin of sperm.[85] As was discussed earlier, philosophers, moralizers and doctors all made some connection between food and excrement, food and sex, and sex and excrement. Some of these often disputed bits of ancient biology were picked up by ancient polemicists when they came in handy for an argument. Few of the Church Fathers evidence any serious interest in medicine or science. Jerome himself is noteworthy in his frequent sharp declamations against physicians and natural philosophers.[86] The naturalistic sounding description of excrement and its connection with the sexual act had two advantages to recommend them for Jerome, as for the others. First, they had a ring of medical expertise that may have given these views added authority, and second, by connecting the mental image of excrement with sexual desire, they hoped for a transfer of the conjured feeling of disgust from one to the other.

As eating was asserted to lead to lust, so fasting was to promote continence. Not only were pious women encouraged never to satisfy their hunger, they were also enjoined to separate themselves from society, where many women 'are intemperate as to the amount of food they take'[87] and where 'women care for nothing but their belly and its adjacent members'.[88] The virgin is advised to keep to herself and if possible never to leave her room, to 'mortify and enslave her body', 'to blush at herself and be unable to look at her own nakedness', 'to quench the flame of lust and to check the hot desires of youth by cold chastity'.[89]

Jerome wrote two letters in which he gave advice on the education of young children. Both children were committed to a lifelong virginity, 'offered to God', by the parents. Both were girls. There is no evidence in the sources of any male child of well-to-do urban Christians being vowed to a life of celibacy by his parents. But some parents seem to have listened to Ambrose's advice:

> You have heard, O parents, in what virtues and pursuits you ought to train your daughters, that you may possess those by whose merits your faults may be redeemed. The virgin is an offering for her mother, by whose daily sacrifice the divine power is appeased. A virgin is an inseparable pledge of her parents, who neither *troubles them for a dowry*, nor forsakes them, nor injures them in word or deed.[90]

Jerome on the one hand seems to disapprove of the parental oblation of deformed or otherwise unwanted daughters,[91] on the other he writes manuals of instruction of how to bring up the girl who was consecrated to eternal virginity already in her mother's womb. These instructions, which include total seclusion of the girl from her own age-mates, both boys and girls, confinement to her cell, study of Scripture, excluding any secular material, meagre food and drab clothing, make sure that she will not stray from the path, simply because she will not be able to. She will not know any other life, any other taste or any other possibility. The method of education Jerome proposes for these unfortunate girls is seen by Hagendahl as a 'terrible scheme bearing the impress of ascetic fanaticism, regardless of a child's nature, aimed at suppressing even the most innocent joy of life.'[92]

> She should not take her food in public, that is, at her parents' guest-table; for she may there see dishes that she will crave for. And though some people think it shows the higher virtue to despise a pleasure ready to your hand, I for my part judge it part of the surer self-restraint to remain ignorant of what you would like.... Let her food be vegetables and wheaten bread and occasionally a little fish ... let her meals always leave her hungry.... I disapprove altogether of baths in the case of a full-grown virgin. She ought to blush at herself and be unable to look at her own nakedness. If she mortifies and enslaves her body

by vigils and fasting, if she desires to quench the flame of lust and to check the hot desires of youth by a cold chastity, if she hastens to spoil her natural beauty by a deliberate squalor, why should she rouse a sleeping fire by the incentive of baths?[93]

Jerome's instructions to women concerning methods for the preservation of virginity bear a more than chance resemblance to the conditions that give rise to and are involved in anorexia nervosa. The diagnosis of this disease – which is generally regarded today as a psychologically induced physical illness – is based on the following manifestations. The first is a self-induced weight loss of serious proportions, which would surely follow from living on bread and water and a meagre amount of vegetables and never satisfying one's hunger. Second are obsessional ideas about the body, about perfection and guilt and fear of eating, which provide the motivation for, and maintain the behaviour of, self-starvation. The texts described above would have provided ample food for these obsessional thoughts. The third manifestation of anorexia comes as the result of the excessive weight loss, and this is indeed the loss of sexual interest together with loss of menstruation. Anorectics today give various reasons for curtailing their food intake; most often they express a loathing for their own body, fear and guilt about eating, fear of losing control, obsessional aspirations to 'perfection' and an equally obsessional concern with the ugliness of fat. All of these were – as we have shown – eagerly fostered by Jerome.

Just as today not all those who identify with the cultural norms that equate thinness of body with beauty, health and power, become anorectic, so in the time of Jerome too, not all those who equated emaciation with holiness became emaciated, and died in it; but some did. The story of Blaesilla, if told today, could easily enter medical textbooks as an example of that 25 per cent of cases of anorexia that end in death.

We learn about Blaesilla, the older daughter of Jerome's patroness and friend Paula, from Jerome's letters,[94] which aim to defend their writer from accusations of being responsible for the death of the young woman, or, possibly, to defend him from his own guilt. What emerges is the following. Blaesilla, a happy, worldly young woman of about twenty, suddenly lost her husband after a short marriage. Jerome, her mother's spiritual mentor, probably in collaboration with Paula, instituted a vigorous campaign to oppose a possible second marriage for her, which was customary in wealthy Roman families but was frowned upon by Christian ascetics. The tragedy of her husband's death may have left her weak and vulnerable to disease, or maybe she succumbed to the same illness that killed her husband: we do not know. What is known is that she suffered from fever for nearly thirty days, during which time, it seems, her mother and self-appointed 'spiritual father' did all in their power to convince the young woman that all her suffering 'has been sent to teach her to renounce her overgreat attention to that body which the worms must shortly devour',[95] and that she should 'mourn the loss of her virginity more than the death of her husband',[96] and so on. When she was finally on the way to recovery from her illness, she was encouraged to exchange her involuntary abstinence from food that was due to fever for voluntary fasting, in order 'not to stimulate desire by bestowing care upon the flesh'.[97] Jerome's efforts were crowned with success. 'Her steps tottered with weakness, her face was pale and quivering, her slender neck scarcely upheld her head', wrote her satisfied mentor;[98] Blaesilla was turned into a fasting, weeping, praying nun and in less than three months after her conversion she was dead. The mother was so prostrated with guilt and grief that she was carried out fainting from the funeral procession while the assembled mourners murmured that Blaesilla was killed with fasting and pointed accusing fingers at Jerome.

In contrast to his exhortation to fasting written for women, the instructions Jerome proffers to male ascetics are more moderate in substance and less shrill in tone, even if the basic purpose remains the same: 'by abstinence to subjugate our refractory flesh eager to follow the allurements of lust'.[99] In a letter advising Nepotian[100] on how to be a good priest, he attacks those who practise exotic and ostentatious fasts. What seems to be singled out here for objection is the periodic xerophagy, so eagerly advocated by Tertullian around AD 200. As will be recalled,[101] Tertullian and the Montanists deplored the laxity of bishops and their flocks with regard to fasting. They believed that fasting was a sacrifice pleasing to God, and for that reason they offered a period of xerophagy, lasting two weeks, during which only dry food was eaten, no oil, no wine, and no juice of any kind used. Montanists were still around in Jerome's time,[102] and from various other remarks of Jerome one may gain the impression that some ascetics experimented with xerophagic diets.[103] Of this Jerome disapproved:

> Impose upon yourself such fasting as you are able to bear. Let your fasts be pure, chaste, simple, moderate, and free from

superstition. What good it is to abstain from oil and then to seek after food that is troublesome to prepare and difficult to get, dried figs, pepper, nuts, dates, wheaten flour, honey, pistachios? All the resources of the garden are laid under contribution to avoid eating ordinary bread. I have heard that some people outrage nature, and neither drink water nor eat bread, but imbibe fancy decoctions of pounded herbs and beet juice, using a shell to drink from, in place of a cup. Shame on us! We do not blush at such silliness and we feel no disgust at such superstition. Moreover, by such fancifulness we seek a reputation for abstinence. *The strictest fast is bread and water:* but as that brings no glory with it and bread and water are our usual food, it is reckoned not a fast but an ordinary and common matter.[104]

Similarly in the letter to Rusticus on the good and bad monk he states explicitly:

your aim is to quench the heat of the body by the help of chilling fasts. But let your fasts be moderate, since if they are carried to excess they weaken the stomach, and by making more food necessary to make up for it lead to indigestion, which is the parent of lust.[105]

In his letter to Eustochium, he describes the various forms of monastic life that he claims to have observed in Egypt and points to what he considers as the best of these. His choice for the ideal life for the monk is within a communal, coenobitic organization.[106] He extols the superiority of the coenobitic life, with its hierarchical structure, organized work and absolute obedience, also in other letters.[107] The idealized picture he paints of the Egyptian coenobites bears a strong resemblance to Philo's and Josephus' descriptions of Jewish ascetics. The diet on which these monks were said to live is frugal but adequate for the sustenance of life and work: 'The fare consists of bread, pulse and greens, and salt and oil is their only condiment. The old men alone receive wine.'[108]

It is a curious fact that while Jerome, the great popularizer of the hermit's life, endeavoured to base his own reputation and authority on his experience as a 'desert hermit' and came as a monk to Rome, this same Jerome found almost all monks, especially the solitaries, objectionable. When occasion for it arose, he deplored monks who competed with one another in fasting, accusing them of doing everything for effect. He denounced monks for visiting virgins, for disparaging the clergy and for gorging themselves with food on feast days.[109] Jerome, veteran of the scorching desert, teller of tales of heroic fights with the demons of fornication, visitor and intimate of virgins and widows, and merciless critic of the shortcomings of the clergy, certainly did not like competition in these fields! The only monkish lifestyle that he valued was the one that he himself never tried: that is, the life of the coenobite who would accept meekly the rule of his superiors. The 'biographer' of Paul, the first hermit, and Hilarion thoroughly disapproved of the solitary life:

> In solitude pride quickly creeps in, and when a man has fasted for a little while and has seen no one, he thinks himself a person of some account ... he stretches out his hand for anything that his gullet craves; he does what he pleases and sleeps as long as he pleases; he fears no one, he thinks all men his inferiors, spends more time in cities than in his cell ... among the brethren he makes a pretence of modesty, in the crowded squares he contends with the best.[110]

Some – he claims – also have skills 'in inventing monstrous stories of their struggles with demons, tales invented to excite the admiration of the ignorant mob and to extract money from their pockets'.[111] The issue of food, or rather the rejection of it, was a part of Jerome's rhetoric used in the campaign for celibacy. The early church ordained married men and elected as bishops the most substantial members of Christian communities, 'those who appeared to be outstanding in eloquence, birth and other distinguished qualities'.[112] The fourth century witnessed increasing efforts to promote the ascetic ideal, which eventually resulted in the legal enforcement of celibacy among the Western clergy.[113] The devaluation, even denigration of marriage, the concomitant elevation of virginity as the highest Christian virtue 'was designed to clear a place for ascetics, and especially celibates, in the Christian clergy, challenging the consensus that had built up over the centuries around the leadership of a married clergy whose probity as householders served to index their sobriety and fitness for Christian authority'.[114] The traditional authority was based on civic excellence, towards which most who so wished were able to strive; this new authority, based on strict asceticism, aimed to impress by qualities that most found for themselves impossible to follow. Renunciation of sexuality and excruciating self-mortifications gave its professors ascendancy over their social superiors. The propaganda for celibacy became a tool with which the authority of men who were unwilling or unable to embrace it could be undermined. As Kate Cooper describes it in her study,[115] the competition raged between two groups of late Roman men: married men in positions of civic or cultural importance, and celibate men, usually of a lesser rank, who wished to advise and control the married. Jerome fits into the latter category. His bitterness and disappointment following his failure and consequent retreat from Rome is witness to his aspirations, which, it seems, even included the papacy.[116]

Traditional civic values and the married state apparently did not lack defenders among Roman Christians. Jerome's lengthiest and most elaborate statement of the proper Christian attitude to food and fasting is contained in his treatise, *Adversus Jovinianum*,[117] written in 393 in his retreat in Bethlehem after a period of seven years of cease-fire in his polemical battles. As he claims in the opening lines of the treatise, he wrote it in response to the request of some of the Roman brethren who asked him to refute the dangerous teaching of Jovinian directed against extreme asceticism.[118] As far as can be deduced from the arguments marshalled against him by his various opponents[119] the main tenets of Jovinian's teaching were as follows:

1 That a virgin is no better as such than a wife in the sight of God.
2 Abstinence is no better than a thankful partaking of food.
3 A person baptized with the spirit cannot sin.
4 All sins are equal.
5 There is but one grade of punishment and one reward in the future state.
6 Jesus was born by true parturition.

The first two of these hit close to Jerome's heart. An ageing monk, known as the champion of virginity, he could not have let the enemy raise his head without giving fight. Responding to the welcome request of his friends – if indeed there was any such request – by writing a rebuttal of Jovinian, at the time when the man was already excommunicated by both Pope Siricius (Rome, 390) and Ambrose (Milan, 391)[120] may also have given him the chance to call himself once again to the attention of the Roman Christian establishment and the clergy whom he deeply resented and in whose eyes he remained an outcast.[121] The enthusiasm with which he set out to annihilate Jovinian would certainly suggest this.

In what follows I shall only discuss Jerome's rebuttal of Jovinian with respect to the need to fast.

Jerome's arguments for the proper Christian attitude to food in this work are appropriated, ironically, from the writings of a Montanist 'heretic' and a pagan enemy of the faith, Tertullian and Porphyry, without giving these the slightest credit. Jerome's unscrupulous use of Porphyry has been recognized a long time ago, writes Hagendahl, who calls Jerome a 'skilful mosaic artist' who intersperses between the borrowings from Porphyry excerpts from other pagan authors, as well as quotations from Christian writers and the Bible. As to the other non-Christian authors, 'all that Jerome reports – names, book titles and data – are to be found in Porphyry'.[122]

Porphyry's treatise, *On Abstinence from Animal Food* was the major text Jerome used, adding to it from Tertullian's treatise *On Fasting*. Porphyry summarizes the ancient arguments for vegetarianism.[123] First, he argues for the philosopher's need for tranquillity of the soul, which is hindered by overloading the stomach with rich food; next, he appeals to history, showing that animal sacrifice brought degradation on the people, leading to human sacrifice and warfare; third, he urges the recognition of human kinship with animals as rational beings, and that the killing and eating of rational beings is unjust; and finally, he holds up the example of wise nations and ancient sects who abstained. Jerome will borrow generous amounts of all these, with the exception of the third line of argument. As a Christian biblical exegete, he would not contradict the Old Testament, where God gave man dominion over all the beasts. It was difficult enough to disregard Peter's vision[124] and to twist Paul's teachings[125] on food in the effort to justify his urging vegetarianism on Christians.

It seems that Jovinian appealed to the epistles of Paul as witness to his claim that food is not a religious issue for Christians, and that all food is allowed as long as it is received with thanksgiving. To counter this Jerome writes a history of food from the world's beginning. Both Porphyry and Tertullian believed that, in the beginning, in the golden age or paradise, people were vegetarian. Jerome writes:

the eating of flesh was unknown until the deluge. But after the deluge, like the quails given in the desert to the murmuring people, the poison of flesh-meat was offered to our teeth. But after the deluge, together with the giving of the Law which no one could fulfil, flesh was given for food, and divorce was allowed to hard-hearted men, and the knife of circumcision was applied, as though the hand of God had fashioned us with something superfluous. But once Christ has come in the end of time, and Omega passed into Alpha and turned the end into the beginning, we are no longer allowed divorce, nor are we circumcised, nor do we eat flesh, for the Apostle says 'It is good not to eat flesh, nor to drink wine.' For wine as well as flesh was consecrated after the deluge.[126]

In this 'developmental' sequence, Jerome traces Christianity's origins in Judaism, showing that Christianity is a further development that makes Judaism obsolete. Divorce and circumcision, salient characteristics of Judaism, are to be rejected, but instead of the customary gentile attack on the Jewish dietary laws, he introduces here a novelty, the rejection of meat and wine. And of course the apostle Paul is cited again for support.[127]

Pigs and wild boars and stags and the rest of living creatures were created, that soldiers, athletes, sailors, rhetoricians, miners, and other slaves of hard toil, who need physical strength, might have food.... Our religion does not train boxers, athletes, sailors, soldiers or ditch diggers, but followers of wisdom, who devote themselves to the worship of God, and know why they were created and are in the world from which they are impatient to depart.[128]

This does not seem to make much sense. Could Jerome, at the end of the fourth century, really mean that an active life or heavy physical labour disqualified one from becoming a Christian? Probably not; he lifted the above argument from Porphyry, in whose line of thought this paragraph fits meaningfully, for there it refers to philosophers who, having 'abundant leisure', engaged in the quiet contemplative life and not in heavy physical work, do not need to eat meat to keep up their strength and superfluous weight. It is interesting to note that while Porphyry's philosophy concerned itself with the soul's approach to the divinity through a determined neglect of all but the most necessary life-sustaining needs of the body, among his arguments for the philosophic vegetarian diet he also considers the question of health. He knows that most people eat meat, and that doctors and philosophers recommend meat eating for reasons of health. 'Abstinence from meat eating is not simply recommended to all men, but to philosophers', for whom, because of their inactivity, a vegetarian diet is healthier and easier to digest.[129]

Following Porphyry closely, Jerome then argues that those who wish to be perfect (a substitution for Porphyry's philosophers) should not eat flesh or drink wine, for it is better to enrich the mind than to stuff the body. A discourse follows, still along the pattern of Porphyry, on the different eating habits of different peoples. Jerome claims to have seen savages at their horrid banquets, and he recounts how the Attacotti of Britain eat human flesh.[130] Other meat eaters like the Scots have no wives of their own but like beasts they indulge their lust to their hearts' content, and so on; while the Christians abstain from meat to 'subjugate' the flesh, for they know that 'The eating of flesh and drinking of wine and fullness of stomach is the seed-plot of lust'.[131]

All the arguments marshalled from the Bible, from history, philosophy and medicine for Jerome boil down to one main reason for fasting, the same as it always was for him, a method for the desexing of the body. Unlike Tertullian, Jerome was not interested in Jewish fasting for the atonement of sins, nor in fasting for good causes like alms-giving, for gaining visions, or in mourning. Fasting for him was the only way to keep one's chastity.

As his attacks on Manichaeans indicate,[132] he was well aware that his shrill advocacy of fasting and virginity differed little, if at all, from Manichaean asceticism. Even his distinction between virgins and worldlings, first-class and second-class Christians, parallels that between the Manichaean elect and hearer. Jovinian, as probably other Christians, warned that the rejection of this world and denial and mortification of the body reflects a radical dualist impulse present in Manichaeism.[133] Ascetic living was a cornerstone of the Manichaean faith. The identifying sentence of a Manichaean elect, found in both Eastern and Western sources is: 'We do not eat meat, or drink wine and we abstain from women.' A Manichaean document preserved in Coptic, the Kephalaia of the Teacher says:

> the first righteousness which a man will do to become truly righteous is this: He will practice celibacy and purity . . . That he purify his mouth from all flesh and blood, and not taste anything which is called wine or intoxicant.[134]

The document also states that 'The first work of the Catechumenate which he accomplishes is fasting-praying-and-alms',[135] and that 'the holy man punishes his body through fasting',[136]

The great debate on asceticism in the fourth century had grave implications not only for clerical celibacy and the nature of authority within the church; it raged over the relative valuation of marriage against virginity in the hierarchy of merit in Christian life, and in the course of it the most intimate aspect of personal existence was opened up for public scrutiny. The church increasingly asserted its right to control the core of an individual's private life, with the psychological, social and economic consequences that such control entailed. The debate aroused strong passions. All the major Christian figures of the time in both East and West had contributed to it.[137] The surviving literature, however, is overwhelmingly one-sided. The battling tone of the champions of virginity suggests strong opposition. Mysteriously, almost nothing survived from the writings of the other camp, only a few names and the outlines of arguments reflected in the potentially distorting mirror of their vehement refutations written by those who emerged the victors in the debate. These were elevated to sainthood by a grateful posterity. The propaganda campaign was successful, virginity became both an ideal for all and a reality, a way of life, for some; while sexuality, in all but its most curtailed and functional aspect, became Sin, *par excellence*, in Christian thought for centuries to come. Jerome played an important part in this propaganda campaign. As radical asceticism gained ground in the Church, orthodox Christianity tried to distance itself from accusations of dualism, but despite sophistic arguments claiming that it was not the material body that was to be rejected but only sin that works in it, and despite the belief in bodily resurrection, the fact remains that by the fourth century strong voices, Jerome's foremost among them, demanded that the unresurrected living body, especially the female body, was to be hated and mortified. While most of his fellow propagandists extolled virginity and deplored fornication, Jerome was obsessed with sex, his impulses ranging from titillation to deep revulsion. Marriage for him had no power to ennoble the sexual union of men and women. Men he saw in constant danger from the temptation of women, whether young or old. Since castration was forbidden, the only method for making one a 'eunuch for the Kingdom of Heaven' was fasting; it was not a foolproof method, but he saw no better one. Men should live in each other's company and carefully calibrate their food intake; eat enough to live and work but not to 'overheat their blood'. Ascetic women, however, should keep to their cells, live on 'herbs', not even sharing the table of the family. In Jerome's eyes even dedicated virgins are safe only if they are secluded, closed out of even the most basic network of human exchanges: the family meal. Such was the ascetic propaganda. There is little reliable evidence dating to these times on the basis of which one could describe objectively the actual ascetic practice, no detailed descriptions of monastic diets which would allow an appraisal of daily food intake. In an attempt to give a more balanced account of Christian attitudes, in the following short chapter I shall examine some texts that address the problem of food and fasting in ascetic practice.

9

AUGUSTINE AND ASCETIC PRACTICE

Augustine (354–430) wrote his *Confessions* not before the year 397, a time when he could look back on his conversions from Manichaeism to Platonic philosophy and then to sexual continence until finally, fulfilling his mother's fervent wish, he was baptized into orthodox Christianity. More than that, he wrote it when he was already the Catholic bishop of Hippo and also the head of a monastic community. The work, a brilliant Catholic theological propaganda tract, is written as an autobiography, or more precisely, as a self-revelatory soliloquy addressed to the ears of God. It covers the period of Augustine's life from birth at Thagaste in 354 to the death of his mother on their return to Africa from Italy after his own acceptance of baptism in 387, depicting the man's long journey from his mother's womb to the womb of his mother's church.

It has been noted that this autobiography has a pointedly didactic aim. Its intended audience was not God alone: 'I desire to act in truth, making my confession both in my heart before you and in this book before the many who will read it.'[1] Some see a connection between the pattern of the *Confessions* and Augustine's method for the instruction of catechumens,[2] others believe that the work was addressed to Catholic ascetics in order to explicate the writer's views on the nature of asceticism.[3] Whatever audience it was aimed for, the *Confessions* invite the reader to follow the progress of 'a great sinner' on his way to becoming a 'great saint',[4] or at least an ascetic, first-class Christian. In the last parts of the book after the biographical details, Augustine examines in depth his own inner life; this self-analysis proffers a kind of blueprint for the proper or desirable way of relating to God and to the world on the part of the Christian.

The problems of food and drink in Augustine's own ascetic life are discussed in Book X of the *Confessions*, where he reviews the various bodily senses and the dangers of temptation arising from each of them. Unlike Jerome and many of his fellow-Christian ascetic propagandists, Augustine does not lump together but clearly distinguishes the need and desire for food and those for sex. Food is a necessity, 'for we repair the daily wastage of our bodies by eating and drinking', until the time comes, he says, echoing the apostle Paul,[5] when God will bring both food and our animal nature to an end, and exchange 'this corruptible nature of ours with incorruptible life'. In the present life, he admits, he finds pleasure in food. Pleasure, even of the most innocent kind, was suspect, not only in the eyes of Christian ascetics but to some extent in the eyes of all those aspiring to philosophy, whether Jews, Christians or pagans, as we have had repeated occasions to see. The commonly shared trope was that pleasure was enticing; once experienced it was increasingly hard to resist and unresisted it turned man's mind from contemplation of higher things. Augustine, deeply impressed by the Neoplatonist idea that the soul's approach to the divine is through detachment from the material world and freedom from passion, naturally accepted this trope. As a consequence, he displays the requisite amount of philosophical trepidation on contemplating the pleasure he experiences in eating; the danger of becoming its captive – he protests – arouses his anxieties:

> Every day I wage war upon it by fasting. Time and again I force my body to obey me, but the pain which this causes me is cancelled by the pleasure of eating and drinking. For of course hunger and thirst are painful. Like a fever they parch and kill unless they are relieved by remedies of food and drink. . . . I look upon food as medicine. But the snare of concupiscence awaits me in the very process of passing from the discomfort of hunger to the contentment which comes when it is satisfied. For the process itself is a pleasure and there is no other means of satisfying hunger except the one which we are obliged to take. And although the purpose of eating and drinking is to preserve health, in its train there follows an ominous kind of enjoyment, which often tries to outstrip it, so that it is really for the sake of pleasure that I do what I claim to do and mean to do for the sake of my health.[6]

It is of significance for the understanding of Augustine's conception of earthly life that he uses the metaphor of sickness often when he deals with the biological needs and impulses of the human body. Hunger is like *fever*, food is *medicine*. Medicine is, more often than not, bitter and unpleasant. The body's needs are allowed to be ministered to as a physician would minister to the sick. The purpose is to keep the body alive. What is pleasant passes the limits of strict medicinal use and becomes, in his eyes, dangerous. If the need for food and drink was like fever, much more so was sexual desire.[7] As will be seen below, Augustine considered sexual desire, even that of the married Christian couple, as a sickness for which intercourse was allowed as medicine, just as food and drink were medicines for the infirmity of hunger and thirst. Only the weak, as he saw it, succumbed to sexual desires; strong and weak alike, however, were ill with hunger and thirst, and without food and drink, the proper 'medicine', they all would die.[8] Food and drink he recognized as necessities of life, and also, like all things that satisfy the basic survival needs of the body, as a source of pleasure. As Augustine well perceived, there is no way one can give up pleasure when it comes to food and drink. To give up food and drink means death. Hunger and thirst are powerful and potentially painful goads to action. Man, like most animals, has to expand energy in search of sustenance, the successful result of which is highly rewarding; the relief from hunger and thirst is pleasure. Actually, the highly valued Christian practice of fasting, instead of eliminating pleasure, may even maximize it when finally food is taken.

The acceptance of food and drink, even as necessary medicine, is not without its problems. Admittedly, one needs to eat and drink for the sake of health, but how much, and what? Augustine is deeply exercised by the concerns of the Stoic who intended to live 'according to nature'. How much is sufficient according to nature, and at what point does it become superfluous? Just like Seneca, the Stoic sage, Augustine too deplores the inability of humans to judge precisely what should be the measure of food and drink to have, or to estimate precisely the point when they have eaten just enough for the maintenance of health. Like Seneca, Augustine too suspects that some of his cravings for food are not only for the sake of health but for enjoyment:

> for what is sufficient for health is not enough for enjoyment, and it is often hard to tell whether the body, which must be cared for, requires further nourishment, or whether we are being deceived by the allurements of greed demanding to be gratified.[9]

Augustine, who is, ostensibly, writing a contrite confession to the ears of his God alone, is, in this instance, a little more candid than Seneca, who, assuming the persona of the old experienced sage, writes to instruct a young novice about the philosophic life. While Seneca blames his father's anxiety, and his own duties in public life for his relinquishing the extremely frugal philosophic diet of his youthful enthusiasm, Augustine admits that his soul is

> glad that the proper requirements of health are in doubt, so that under the pretence of caring for health it may disguise the pursuit of pleasure... Drunkenness is far from me. By your grace may you prevent it from coming near! But there have been times when overeating has stolen upon your servant.[10]

Next he confronts the question of what kinds of foods are allowed for the Christian. Not so much to justify his own practice, but rather to set the record straight, Augustine stresses that God created the earth, water and air, and all that these contain for sustenance for man, for man is weak, and he quotes the apostle and the gospels as witnesses to the fact that eating and drinking are indifferent in the eyes of God.[11] In sharp contrast to Jerome, he reads his Bible, at least those passages in it that deal with food, absolutely straight. As would be expected, he also cites the verses from Scripture which caution against gluttony and drunkenness, because as he says: 'It is the uncleanness of gluttony I fear, not unclean meat'.[12] Christians, he reminds himself, were given permission to eat all meat that was suitable for food, and again by quoting examples from both the Old and New Testament he emphatically shows that a vegetarian diet in itself is not more conducive to holiness than one containing meat. While 'Esau was defrauded by his greed for a dish of lentils', the prophet Elijah was fed on meat and 'John the Baptist, remarkable ascetic though he was, was not polluted by the flesh of living creatures, the locusts that were granted him as food.'[13]

What is the meaning of this long and carefully constructed discussion on food? Its didactic aim seems to be no more than the teaching of the need for temperance in food. This is supported by carefully chosen scriptural passages, all of which reinforce the Pauline message that food is of no religious concern, and that vegetarianism or other extreme food practices are not in themselves part of the requirements for 'being in' the Christian religion; they are not demanded even of the ascetics.[14] One can be a most dedicated 'first class' Christian and still eat meat.[15]

Food and drink in and of themselves, and both in moderation, did not seem to cause grave problems of conscience for Augustine. This view of Augustine's attitude to food is supported by the lack of emphasis on fasting in his other works; there are no treatises or sermons in which he would enjoin strenuous fasts or abstention from meat and wine for the sake of mortification of the flesh.

Nevertheless, there are scholars who view Augustine's attitude to food and the chapter dealing with food in the *Confessions*, differently. L. Ferrari in his article 'The gustatory Augustin',[16] regards the *Confessions* and also this part of Book X as literally autobiographical, revealing an Augustine sorely tempted by the demons of gluttony. He then proceeds to search the whole work for other evidence to support his view of Augustine as a man who in all his life suffered inordinately from the allurements of the sin of gluttony. He attributes, as a source of Augustine's idea of original sin, his observation of gluttonous greediness in new-born infants, described in the first book of the *Confessions*.[17] A more attentive reading of this passage reveals, however, that what horrified Augustine was not the infant's wanting food – which was available in abundance – but the violence of anger and jealousy exhibited by the child on seeing another infant being fed. Ferrari goes even so far as to take Augustine's words literally, when he says that he could give up sexual intercourse but food he cannot give up,[18] and comes to the conclusion, which even he himself finds somewhat surprising, that Augustine's major inner conflict was with his gluttonous rather than with his sexual nature.[19] Be that as it may, the effort he expanded in attempting to suppress sexuality in himself and others is immeasurably more substantial in his writing than the attention he gave to suppressing gluttony – a fact that is somewhat surprising in light of the ascetic propaganda in which, as noted earlier, fasting was the 'only way to preserve chastity'.

Augustine was well versed in ascetic propaganda, and, as his self-disclosures in the *Confessions* testify, he was attracted by the ideal of celibate asceticism long before his conversion. Among his contemporaries, Catholic Christians were not the only advocates of chastity and fasting. In all his writing concerning food, it seems that Augustine is careful not to give an opportunity to those of his detractors who would be tempted to use his well-known Manichaean past as ammunition against him in his many controversies. It was no secret that he spent nine years as Manichaean hearer or catechumen before finally accepting Catholic baptism.

Manichaeism energetically competed with Catholic Christianity, presenting itself as the true religion of Jesus. Mani, the movement's founder, saw himself as the 'apostle of Jesus Christ', and challenged the church by insisting that 'the religion of Jesus was ascetic as the majority of baptised Christians were not'.[20] The Manichaean community consisted of a two-class system, with the Elect being celibate and strict vegetarians who did not touch wine. The most ascetic among them refused the use of baths and sleeping in bed, thus taking on all the behavioural signifiers of the 'holy man'. The religion of the Manichaeans was probably one of the strongest influences on the development of monastic asceticism. The sexual and alimentary self-restraint with which the followers of Mani confronted the competing religions filled some followers of these with great admiration for their fortitude and ethical standards. How close the figure of the Manichaean Elect came to that of the revered Desert Father is clearly demonstrated by the insistence of the author of the *Vita Antonii* that the originator of self-mortifying desert monasticism was a strictly Catholic Christian, and not a Manichaean.[21]

The asceticism of the Manichaeans that forbade the eating of meat, the drinking of wine, and sexual intercourse was firmly based on a dualism of good and evil and on the eternal struggle between light and darkness, spirit and matter. Divine Light, according to Mani, has become mixed with and entrapped in the Darkness of the material world. The religion involved an elaborate system of worship, education and ascetic practice that promised the practitioner self-knowledge, gnosis of the soul, and the gradual liberation of particles of light from matter. The recurring self-identification of the Manichaeans, as discussed earlier, was: 'We do not eat meat, or drink wine and we abstain from women'.[22] Fasting was believed to be particularly meritorious for it subdues the sinful flesh and enhances the divine soul. Not all could live according to these strict rules. The sect accepted a frank 'double standard' of behaviour.[23] For the Manichaean Elect absolute chastity, a strict vegetarian diet and poverty were essential requirements of 'being in' the religion, the *sine qua non* of full salvation, while the second-class Manichaean, the Hearer, who could recognize but not correct the evil that was part of his existence, by accepting the new 'Gospel of Light' and by supporting the Elect with food and alms 'could assist the release of the particles of goodness that were trapped within him'[24] and hope for a higher existence in the next life.

S.N.C. Lieu discusses in his work on Manichaeism the various intellectual, social, even aesthetic ways in which Manichaeism may have appealed to Augustine. The high ascetic standards of the sect contributed to this, for as Lieu argues, Augustine was early on attracted to the ascetic ideal, but these conflicted with his worldly ambitions and lifestyle. The Manichaean sect's division into two classes 'offered an escape-route to his conscience as it allowed him to live according to his acquired habits and at the same time through his service to the Elect he was assured of a part of the cosmic redemptive process through their pure living'.[25]

After he left the Manichaeans and converted, Augustine turned on them, and using the issue of their food customs, especially their vegetarianism, he attempted to expose and ridicule the speciousness of their beliefs in the transmigration of souls, the entrapment of pieces of God in vegetation, and the like.[26] Long after he parted company with Manichaeism, his Manichaean past was often held against him,[27] a fact due most likely to his darkly hostile and pessimistic views concerning human sexuality. The inescapable sin, the 'Original Sin', which the great saint implanted into Christian consciousness for the ages to come, was inseparably linked to human sexuality.

Sexuality, as Augustine clearly articulated it, was the 'sharply delineated symptom of Adam's fall' that signified a break in the hitherto undivided person,[28] the vanishing of the total rational control that, as he imagined it, characterized man in the Garden of Eden. Sexuality for Augustine was the ever-present sign of man's falling away from God, which brought with it as its consequence death. He looked with deep pessimism on short-lived earthly existence, and taught that 'the Christian's eye must always be trained on eternal life. The more he loves what is immortal, the more vehemently he will hate what is transitory'.[29]

Concupiscence or lust, the inseparable aspect of fallen sexuality, he thought to be deeply deplorable even in marriage.[30] Like Ambrose, Jerome and other advocates of Christian asceticism of the fourth century, Augustine also saw the Christian flock as ranked in two classes, the celibate and virginal constituting the first-class avant-garde, with the married but preferably continent as the inferior second class. Marriage itself he allowed for the procreation of children,[31] but the pleasure that accompanies the act of procreation he viewed as a sickness, as vice of nature, and as an evil.[32]

Augustine's tone when writing about marriage may have been somewhat less offensive and contemptuous than that of his elder contemporary and fellow advocate of monastic asceticism, Jerome, but as the most influential early Latin theologian and shaper of Catholic orthodoxy, he was 'the man who fused Christianity together with hatred of sex and pleasure into a systematic unity'.[33]

While accepting as his own the Manichaean ascetic fervour,

Augustine, as a Catholic and a bishop, meticulously avoided appearing as a Manichee.[34] Nowhere is this more evident than in Book X of the *Confessions*, where he argues painstakingly that what is evil is not the life of the senses but the tension that arises when the appetites arising from the senses clash with the will directed by reason. The only appetite that seemed to Augustine 'to clash inevitably and permanently with reason was sexual desire',[35] and not the need for food and drink. In choosing what to keep and what could be thrown over from Manichaean ascetic practice, without hesitation he chose celibacy and turned against vegetarianism. However, even after he repudiated his Manichaean past and attacked and fought against Manichaean theology, Augustine retained their dark pessimism concerning the material world and the emotional force of their attitude to sexuality. This was recognized by his opponents.[36] Thus, even if he had felt the need for ascetic self-restraint in eating, he could not have advocated a strict vegetarianism or extreme fasting, lest this should be held as another proof of his Manichaeanism. He could have argued, of course, for a Christian vegetarian diet and protested, like Jerome, that it meant not a rejection of God's gifts or belief in the evil nature of all that is begotten by coition as held the Manichees, but that the Christian vegetarian only 'kept his body down' by his diet. The fact is that Augustine did not advocate a meatless diet.

In addition to his need to distance himself from his Manichaean past, there could be other reasons for Augustine's moderate attitudes to food and fasting. Augustine's ascetic ideal was strongly coloured by his deeply felt need for male companionship.[37] He was not a hermit but an eminently social being. He was a bishop with responsibilities for a sizeable, and apparently rather unruly, flock, and he also gathered around him a monastic community. In both of his capacities, he faced the problems arising from the daily life of communities, of people living and working together. His pronouncements concerning food may profitably be compared with those of other monastic leaders, who, instead of or in addition to ascetic propaganda, had to provide instructions and rules, for the actual daily life of groups of people living together as communities. Ascetic exhortations and propaganda aside, these men who took upon themselves the task of directing groups of religious enthusiasts had to face the practical problems involved in keeping their flocks together, working and praying in peace and obedience. The extremes of self-denial in food and drink and the highly individualistic and inventive mortifications of the flesh, which were popularized by the fabulous literature about desert hermits and provided inspiration for ascetic living to many Christians, were not conducive to community living. As both leaders of city congregations and fathers of monastic communities must have found out from bitter experience, these self-imposed privations often led to irritability, lethargy, depression, forgetfulness and, most importantly, an inability to work.[38] The advice given to monks by men like Basil of Caesarea and Augustine, and by others who wrote the early monastic Rules, all seem to reflect this recognition.[39] The Christian, according to this consensus, should not be a slave of meat and wine, and should not desire food and drink beyond what is necessary for health. Extravagance should be avoided in eating, drinking and personal possessions. The monastic individual should be obedient and should carry out the work that his superior assigned to him without complaint. This is the kind of advice the Greek Father, Basil of Caesarea, gave to monastics around AD 364.[40] He also states explicitly that temperance does not mean drastic avoidance of food, which would result in the violent dissolution of the body, 'but a denial of the pleasant things, ordained, out of a motive of piety, towards the purification of the tendencies of the flesh'.[41]

In similar fashion, Augustine's message to his ascetics is that one should struggle daily against greed for food and drink – but eating is not like sex, an evil that the Christian can decide 'once and for all to repudiate and never to embrace again'. Instead one must hold back the appetite for food and drink 'with neither too firm nor too slack a rein'.[42] Since human beings are weak, God will not take it amiss if they are, on occasion, enticed a little beyond the strict limits of need.

Augustine returns again to a discussion of food in his treatise on *The Usefulness of Fasting*, which is clearly addressed as advice to his own monks concerning food and fasting. In it he explains how the mortal body, the seat of the appetites, should be restrained and treated like a servant or beast of burden: 'Let the one placed over you rule you so that the one placed under you may be guided by you. Your flesh is below you; above you is your God'.[43] In this view, in which the Platonic distinction is carried to its extreme conclusion, the human personality is split, the body is made into an object or at best a slave, it becomes divorced from and external to the person, who is to work upon it, shape it, restrain and mortify it, until it becomes almost like a piece of inanimate clay. The 'true' or 'real' inner person who rules this object with cold dispassion is in turn ruled by an invisible force 'above', whose commands and wishes the true person is expected to know and carry out. This breaking up of the human personality cast a very long shadow over Western mentality; the annals of psychiatry up to our days testify to the efforts that have gone into trying to put the pieces together again. It is not a coincidence that Freudian theory conceptualizes personality as a threefold process, with the Superego, the conscience or an ideal self, sitting in judgement over the Ego, the acting, coping and more or less rational self, which in turn is both energized and goaded by the Id, the raw, uncivilized needs and impulses rising from the body.[44] Freud's aim was to heal the split and to empower the Ego to function effectively by consciously recognizing and integrating into itself the various components of the personality.

The dangers implicit in the self-management taught by Augustine, along his threefold division and hierarchical control of personal conduct, are strikingly illustrated today in the illness of anorexia nervosa; in this life-threatening condition, an ideal 'above' commands the person to treat her or his body[45] as a slave, as an object 'below' her, and, with iron determination, to shape it into something else.[46] The bad servant is starved into submission – often even to the point of death.

To be fair, Augustine was more charitable than many of the famous athletes of asceticism, and did caution his monks against a too severe mortification of their bodies by extreme fasting. Rather, he suggested, the body, as a slave, should be restrained but its legitimate needs should be attended to, within limits; and again like a slave, it should be trained to be satisfied with what it gets. Fasting does *not* mean giving up food, but only food that one likes. He warns the brethren, 'Your fasting would be rejected if you were immoderately severe toward your servant.' Eating and drinking are *licit pleasures*, that is they are permitted by the one ruling 'above'; but there is always the danger that enjoying them may lead to yielding to *illicit* joys: 'He who restrains himself in no ways from permitted satisfactions is dangerously near those which are not permitted.' When he urged upon his Christian flock in Hippo self-restraint in eating, Augustine certainly did not mean days without food and water, nor the giving up of meat and wine. What he meant by fasting was the avoidance of enjoyment, the shunning of pleasure. This is how he defines fasting: 'I do not ask from what food you abstain, but what food you choose. Tell what food you prefer so that I may approve your abstaining from that food'.[47]

Augustine, following the path marked out by Philo and Clement, saw grave danger in 'pleasure', even the simple pleasure gained from the satisfaction of hunger. Like his predecessors, he too deeply distrusted his fellow humans and belittled the power of even the most committed Christians sanely to moderate their own behaviour. Nevertheless, concessions had to be made in the face of human 'weakness'. The severe regimen of the ideal embodied in figures of holy hermits and virgins was held up for admiration, but the Christian morality preached for the benefit of the multitudes, as reflected in bishops' sermons and various canons of church councils of the period, prescribed much less heroic measures. Moderation and frugality in food and drink were urged.[48] Fasting, under the guidance of the church, meant only giving up meat and wine for a time, and for the more devout, living on bread and water during Lent. The main thrust of the bishops' exhortations was aimed against gluttony and drunkenness rather than against eating and drinking in themselves. The bishop of Hippo instructed his people that, if they were not able to keep a fast, at least they should partake of food with moderation.[49] In similar vein, the Eastern bishop John Chrysostom, a staunch advocate of asceticism, when addressing his city flock knows what he can realistically demand of them: 'Enjoy your baths, your good table, your meat, your wine in moderation – enjoy everything in fact, but keep away from sin!'[50]

The rhetoric for self-mortification was toned down. The discrepancy between the ideal created by the propaganda for the 'angelic life on earth', without bodily needs and wants, and the sheer inability of the biological organism to approach this ideal, seems to have been appreciated by Augustine, and by others who were faced with problems of daily life in Christian communities. The ideal continued to be held up, but more for inspiration than for emulation. The fabulous accounts of superhuman privations willingly undergone by faraway heroes of the desert were to inspire Christians to live modestly and to eat and drink in moderation. This is supported by what little evidence there is for the actual daily life in early monastic establishments, suggesting that even the monks ate an adequate daily diet. As fifth- and sixth-century accounts of Pachomian monasteries indicate, these had vegetable gardens in which they grew all the necessary vegetables; they had orchards with fruit trees and date palms, which the monks cultivated with great care; they worked in the fields growing wheat; they even had vineyards. The coenobia had also shepherds and cattle drivers. The evidence suggests that the monks used in their kitchen cheese and even small amounts of meat.[51] In practice they ate a diet that could sustain health and strength.

CONCLUSION

The present work has surveyed attitudes to food expressed in early Christian literature and attempted to assess the various cultural and social influences that affected their formation and development. As we have seen, the texts reveal a variety of views concerning life's sustenance. The sharing of bread and wine was seen as an essential aspect of the life of the Christian community from the earliest texts. It became formalized as the celebration of the Eucharist central to Catholic dogma, thereby adding sublime meaning to food as sustenance of both body and soul. The realization then comes upon the reader of these texts as an unexpected surprise, that food, life's basic requirement, and the source of the most simple, direct, biologically determined pleasure in life, was never in itself valued positively in this literature. At best, food and eating were tolerated as necessary for life, and as potentially valuable as symbolic gestures of fellowship and confirmation of mutual social support, that helped to cement communities; at worst, they were seen as the devil's snare, leading to greed, social division and disruption and, most dangerously, to sexual temptation. Present to some extent even in Paul, we have seen that the danger of pleasure in eating is increasingly emphasized by third and fourth century writers.

As a corollary, fasting, whether viewed favourably or not, receives a progressively larger share of the writers' attention. Attitudes to fasting ranged widely. Some, deprecating it as a Jewish custom, useful only for the ostentation of piety, held that the practice was irrelevant and unnecessary for those 'living in Christ'; while others, finding the penitential fasting practices of the Jews efficacious also for the expiation of Christian sins and, as such, an act pleasing to God, urged the acceptance of the practice on all who would be truly religious. Fasting as an expression of grief and mourning, common among

191

pagans and Jews in bereavement, was felt by many to be a natural part of the Easter vigil for Christians. Finally, we have seen writers who urged severe fasting on Christians, not because they thought that self-starvation was pleasing to God, who, in their view, cared not for the state of the stomach, but because it was essential in the struggle against the 'demons of fornication', the only method for the suppression of the natural sexual urges of the body.

As this survey suggests, there is a kind of chronological sequence in the attitudes expressed by these texts. The early texts, the New Testament and writings that mirror attitudes to food expressed in the Pauline Epistles and Acts (also in the Apostolic Fathers, not included in the survey), show a natural, matter-of-fact acceptance of food and eating and emphasize the social importance of food in conviviality, in enhancing the feeling of brotherhood and as a gesture conveying mutual acceptance into the Christian group. The writers of these texts saw the repudiation of the Jewish Law, the opening of the gates of Christianity to the gentiles and the gaining of 'souls' as of utmost importance. Consequently, they insisted that Christians are unlike the Jews; for them food has no religious significance, and neither eating or nor fasting will earn for anyone merit with God. Food, they realized, was of social significance, for it could either promote or disrupt the Christian brotherhood. There are no exhortations to fasting in these texts.

Fasting, if mentioned occasionally in some early texts, is presented to emphasize piety, as accompaniment of prayer, and as a sign of self-abasement in the sight of God. These texts, like the *Didache* and the *Shepherd of Hermas*,[1] are generally believed to have been heavily influenced by Jewish-Christianity; indeed, one of the reasons proffered as evidence for this view is the typically Jewish use of fasting they describe.

The first surviving propaganda tracts urging all Christians to fast originated at the very end of the second or in the early third century. They may be considered in light of the persecution and martyrdom of Christians. Whether there were many confessors who gave up their lives for the faith or only a few, those who were not called to martyrdom, or who did not have the fortitude to stand up to it, could find in fasting a way to relieve their guilt and shame for their own weakness. To bear witness to Christ, even with one's life, could conceivably be regarded as a duty of a Christian, whose God sacrificed his own son's life for the salvation of humankind; the New Testament itself, however, did not lend easy support for the contention that fasting is a pleasing 'sacrifice for God' and as such a religious duty, as Tertullian, the first vocal advocate of Christian fasting, claimed. As the Christian movement filled its ranks with growing numbers of converts, sadly it may have encountered a corresponding increase in the number of sinners. Penitence for sins was a religious duty for Christians, just as it was for the Jews, and this may have led to the reinvention of fasting, now as a Christian religious act, and to the increasing appreciation of its value in penitential practice, until by the Middle Ages fasting became a part of all the penitential rules. By that time, however, it was forgotten that the practice originated in Judaism.

In Tertullian's time, penitential fasting in the Jewish fashion seems to have been favoured only by rigorists who wanted to preserve Christianity as a creed for a select group of committed people. The heterogeneity of actual Christian society appeared to these as a cause for alarm, and they saw in the sheer ordinariness of its daily life a betrayal of the true vocation of the Christian. The rigorists called on the truly committed to close their ranks and show their mettle by the strictest abstemious practices. In the words of Mary Douglas, they expressed their sense of social disorder by the powerfully efficacious symbols of impurity and danger,[2] which they hoped to combat with fasting and strict monogamy. Others, who were more intent on seeing Christian society live in peace and internal harmony, and who aimed at gaining souls by including converts, did not seem to favour practices that were difficult to bear and socially disruptive. Writers like Clement of Alexandria and Origen, committed Christians as they were, seem to have had no great interest in self-starvation; they held that it is not food but vice that the Christian should abstain from. Following the example of Philo, the Alexandrian Jew, who attempted to fuse Judaism with Hellenistic philosophy, these Alexandrian Christians tried to explain Christianity to Christians and pagans alike as being the most noble of philosophies and the best way of life. In their enterprise they necessarily introduced the concepts and language of Hellenistic philosophy and literature. Through their efforts, if not through their intentions, the Platonists' overvaluation of the soul at the expense of the body and the Stoics' opposition to the passions, with the concomitant distrust of bodily pleasures, entered the language of Christianity. In matters relating to everyday conduct, this meant for Clement and Origen an emphasis on moderation and frugality in eating and drinking. Temperance and resistance to the lure of pleasure were pagan moral precepts welcomed into Christianity by these

Alexandrians. They did not advocate fasting. Later Christians went much further than the philosophers, among whom even the most ascetic of Platonists maintained that one should take care of one's body as a musician takes care of his instrument, a view shared by both Clement and Origen.

What the Christians added to the Stoic conception of lofty, philosophic comportment was the Jewish Philo's ever-watchful God. To the ethical principles that the philosophers could only recommend to their followers, the Christians added powerful forces of motivation with the promise of heavenly reward and the terror of everlasting punishment in the burning fires of hell!

The most vigorous propaganda for fasting and the mortification of the flesh came with Christianity's rise to power. With the increase in opportunities and positions of power that opened up for Christians, under Constantine and his successors there came an influx of converts, some of whose motivation may have derived more from worldly interests and expediency than religious fervour. Increasing imperial favour shown to church authorities tended to blur the boundaries between political power and religious leadership. A new kind of authority was sought by many Christians, an authority based not on wealth or birth but on some peculiarly Christian virtue, on some clear signs of 'holiness'. These signs of holiness had to be such that all would marvel at them, many would aspire to them but, due to the great personal cost they exacted, few could acquire them. Celibacy, the complete rejection of the sexual nature of the body, came to be regarded as the symbol of holiness and, as such, as the basis for entering the Christian 'avant-garde'. The biological organism, however, is not built for celibacy; it is not 'according to nature' 'to keep the body down', as most of the propagandists of virginity soon realized. The recalcitrant body had to be forced into submission by actively denying its other needs too. Those aspiring to be first-class Christians by lifelong celibacy soon found a new use for fasting. While self-starvation in itself was not believed to be of any interest to God, it was, however, the only way to keep one's virginity and this, according to this view, was most pleasing to God.

It is difficult to recognize in the writings of Jerome or of his fellow apostles of virginity and propagandists for the mortification of the flesh any remnants of the views of Hellenistic philosophy's or medicine's regard for the health and strength of the human body. Indeed, the ascetic mode of life as reinterpreted by its Christian promoters, the likes of Eusebius, Athanasius and Jerome, rejected all the rules and recommendations of Hippocratic hygiene.[3] Even Augustine, who as a bishop and leader of a monastic community was less prone to the exaggerated fervour of ascetic propaganda, saw the normal needs of the human body for food and drink as illness, and allowed as medicine for it only what was necessary to sustain daily existence.

Modern commentators are still at a loss in trying to explain this Christian propaganda that so violently rejected the healthy human body with its basic biological needs. While it is true that Christians were promised a bodily resurrection, and also that the remnants of the dead bodies of holy martyrs were fought over and highly venerated, all of which may show a certain type of concern for the body, it is equally true that this concern puts high value on the dead body and not on a living, healthy, strong and beautiful one. To say that the self-mortification urged in these texts constituted Christian 'overachievement' or perfectionism[4] does not explain why in particular the self-inflicted torture of starvation was seen by Christian ascetics, just as by anorectics today, as 'perfection'.

As a result, in large measure, of the influential work of sociologists and anthropologists like Mary Douglas, it has become widely held that human symbols – and especially body symbols – reflect in some ways perceptions of society and of the relationship between society and its constituent individuals. Historians too have been paying increasing attention to the possible interactions between views of the human body and the peculiarities of a given society. If indeed the anthropologists like Douglas and Soler are right,[5] and there is a strong link between a group's dietary habits and its perception of the world, then the promoters of early Christian asceticism saw around them a world that must have appeared to them as highly complex and threatening – a world in which alien elements came together and commingled, diluting the pristine purity of the ideal Christian society. They felt the Body of the Church, the Bride of Christ, as being invaded by unworthy, even downright poisonous elements. Such weighty social anxiety, if translated itself into simpler body symbols, would make increasingly urgent the guarding of the individual Christian's body, and with it the Body of the Church, from pollution, by closing up of all its orifices. For obvious anatomical reasons the female body would lend itself more easily to this transfer of symbols, and as we have seen the propaganda for virginity and fasting was indeed directed more heavily toward women.

As noted above, it would be tempting to see these texts as witnesses to the history of the development of 'asceticism' in Christianity. This, however, would be quite misleading, not merely because of the general difficulty of 'reading off' the actual culture of a society from literary texts of a highly artificial and formal character. Apart from this general difficulty, there is the question of selection. The texts that survived reflect the views of writers whom later Christians liked to see as the founders and representatives of their church. From their own writing it is, however, evident that at no time did they represent the only view of what it meant to be a follower of Christ. The writings of the others were not saved by posterity. Despite the dearth of written evidence from those who followed Jesus on different paths, it is clear that from the beginning there were many interpretations of his message. As early as the so-called *Pastoral Epistles*, there were those among Christians who believed that the 'new thing' brought by Jesus was the abolition of marriage, while others advocated poverty and a meatless and wineless diet; there were also Christians who lived according to Jewish customs and believed in the expiatory power of fasting, and many others. We see them reflected in the surviving texts as if 'through a glass darkly', but they definitely were there and in not insignificant numbers, probably long before fasting and the mortification of the flesh became of interest for the Fathers of later orthodoxy.

Before the 'peace of the church', it seems that hostile pagans or Jews constituted the major perceived danger for orthodox Christians; dissenters, that is Christians with different interpretations of the creed, were perceived with increasing animosity as the external threat to the Christian community diminished. As shared food habits and attitudes play an important part in social life, influencing mate selection and group cohesion,[6] so too accusations of unacceptable eating and mating practices have always been among the methods used by social groups to distance those whom they perceived as threatening. Slander, gossip and ridicule, the age-old weapons of social exclusion, most often concern themselves with the food habits and sexual customs of their targets. In the same time-honoured fashion as accusations of peculiar sexual and food practices played their part in distancing Christians from pagans and Jews, those too who fought against 'heretical' Christians found gossip and slanderous allegations concerning food and sex practices useful in the propaganda war waged for their exclusion from the Church.

These 'heretic' groups, including the Manichees, all considered themselves true Christians and followers of Jesus. The ascetic practices of some of these attracted awe and admiration. Those who saw themselves as 'orthodox' Christians were faced with a conflict: many of them found these 'heretic' practices useful for themselves when the need arose for establishing 'holiness' and 'spiritual' authority. The conflict was not solved. Fasting, vegetarian practices and the following of Jewish food strictures continued to be used as signs by which to detect heretics, outsiders, and various enemies of orthodoxy. On the other hand, within the orthodox Church, celibacy and ascetic fasting became firmly established as the highly respected outward signs of holiness, denoting members of a small and select group of first-class Christians. But even among the orthodox the propaganda for asceticism succeeded in the face of vigorous opposition, again only seen 'through a glass darkly' in the polemical literature directed against those who tried to save orthodox Christianity from setting unachievable standards of behaviour, standards that wilfully turned against the basic biological nature of humankind, and would even season the pleasure of good food with guilt and fear of damnation.

NOTES

INTRODUCTION

1 *The New Oxford Annotated Bible*, edited by B.M. Metzger and R.E. Murphy, 1991.

2 Translated by F.A. Wright in *Select Letters of St. Jerome*, LCL, p. 183.

3 Concerning the dating of the Acts of the Apostles, see Chapter 4 of this volume, p. 75; Jerome's letter, *Ad Asellam* was written at Ostia in August, AD 385.

4 Only seventy-eight years, about the span of a long human life, separated the 'edict of Milan', in 313, which proclaimed the toleration of Christianity, from the constitution of Theodosius, in 391, forbidding the public celebration of pagan cults.

5 Georg Misch, *A History of Autobiography in Antiquity*, 2 vols, trans. E.W. Dickes, 1951, vol. 1, p. 17.

6 Louis Dumont, 'A modified view of our origins: the Christian beginnings of modern individualism', in Michael Carrithers *et al.* (eds), *The Category of the Person*, 1985, pp. 93–122, quoted in Judith Perkins, 'The "self" as sufferer', *HThR* 85, 1992, 245–72.

7 Michel Foucault, 'Technologies of the self', in *Technologies of the Self: A Seminar with Michel Foucault*, ed. Luther H. Martin, Huck Gutman and Patrick H. Hutton, 1988, pp. 16–49. For an opposing view see Gedaliahu G. Stroumsa, 'Caro Salutis Cardo: shaping the person in early Christian thought', *HR* 30, 1990, 25–50, who would disregard the extreme ascetic practices as mere aberrations, while claiming the Christian doctrine of soul and body and the merging of the Greek and Jewish philosophies as the sources for the modern self.

8 Quoted in S.J. Korchin, *Modern Clinical Psychology*, 1976, p. 62.

9 As the titles of these ground-breaking works indicate: Michel Foucault, *The History of Sexuality*, trans. R. Hurley, 3 vols, 1978–88; Peter Brown, *The Body and Society: Men, Women, and Sexual Renunciation in Early Christianity*, 1988; Paul Veyne (ed.), *A History of Private Life*, vol. 1, trans. A. Goldhammer, 1987. This last mentioned work attempts to cover a much larger topic than sexuality, which, however, still figures significantly in what its editor calls the dramatic story of the transition

from 'civic man' to 'inward man' when the 'acid of Christianity' was poured on the 'Roman reagent' (ibid. p. 1).

10 Reay Tannahil, *Food in History*, 1973, repr. 1988, p. 3.

11 Jean Soler, 'The semiotics of food in the Bible', in R. Forster and O. Ranum (eds), *Food and Drink in History, Selections from the* Annales: *Economies, Societies, Civilisations*, vol. 5, 1979, pp. 126–38, at p. 126.

12 Paul Fieldhouse, *Food and Nutrition: Customs and Culture*, 1986.

13 W. Robertson Smith, *The Religion of the Semites: The Fundamental Institution*, 1957, p. 269.

14 E. Diehl, *Pompeianische Wandinschriften und Verwandtes*, 1910, p. 641. Sociologists and social anthropologists have recognized the symbolic importance of food in group formation and cohesion; see, for example, Jack Goody, *Cooking, Cuisine and Class*, 1982; P. Farb and G. Armelagos, *The Anthropology of Eating*, 1980; F.J. Simoons, *Eat Not This Flesh*, 1961.

15 E.H. Erikson, 'Identity and the life cycle', *Psychological Issues* 1, 1959, 18–164.

16 Hilde Bruch, *Eating Disorders. Obesity, Anorexia Nervosa and the Person Within*, 1974.

17 See, for example, Patricia Cox Miller, 'Desert asceticism and "the body from nowhere"', *Journal of Early Christian Studies* 2, 1994, 137–53.

18 Mara Selvini Palazzoli, *Self-starvation: From the Intrapsychic to the Transpersonal Approach to Anorexia Nervosa*, 1974; quoted in Sheila MacLeod, *The Art of Starvation*, 1981, p. 19.

19 Peter Brown, *The Body and Society*, p. 32.

20 The list is based on research reported in M.A. Bass, L.M. Wakefield and K.M. Kolasa, *Community Nutrition and Individual Food Behaviour*, 1979.

21 M. Detienne and J.-P. Vernant, *The Cuisine of Sacrifice Among the Greeks*, trans. Paula Wissing, 1989; O. Murray, 'The Greek symposium in history', in E. Gabba (ed.), *Tria Corda: Scritti in onore di A. Momigliano*, 1983, pp. 257–73; W.J. Slater (ed.), *Dining in a Classical Context*, 1991; Emily Gowers, *The Loaded Table: Representations of Food in Roman Literature*, 1993; J. d'Arms, 'Control, companionship and clientela: some social functions of the Roman communal meal', *Echos du Monde Classique, Classical Views* 28 NS 3, 1984, Special Issue 327–48.

22 Caroline Walker Bynum, *Holy Feast and Holy Fast: The Religious Significance of Food to Medieval Women*, 1987.

23 Plutarch, *Cato Maior* 4:2.

24 Rudolph Arbesmann, *Das Fasten bei den Griechen und Römern*, 1929; 'Fasting and prophecy in Pagan and Christian antiquity', *Traditio* 7, 1949–51, 1–71.

25 Arbesmann, 'Fasting and prophecy', p. 1.

26 Ibid., p. 5.

27 Ibid., pp. 2–3.

28 Ibid., pp. 4, 6.

29 Ibid., pp. 8–9.

30 Ibid., p. 31.

31 Ibid., p. 50.

32 Ibid., pp. 52–71.

33 Herbert Musurillo, 'The problem of ascetical fasting in the Greek patristic writers', *Traditio* 12, 1956, 1–64. The evidence for the alleged importance of fasting in religious development comes from J.S. Black, 'Fasting', *Encyclopedia Britannica*, 13th edn, vol. 10, 1926, pp. 193–8 and the similar entry in the *Encyclopedia of Religion and Ethics* 6, 1951, pp. 759–71, by J.A. MacCullogh and A.J. Maclean. Both encyclopedia entries rely heavily on anthropological reports of religious practices of pre-literate peoples. The relevance of these findings to highly complex and literate societies has not been proven.

34 Musurillo, op. cit., p. 63.

35 Witness to this are publications like V.L. Wimbush, (ed.) *Ascetic Behavior in Greco-Roman Antiquity: A Sourcebook*, 1990; the collection of essays edited by A. Green, *Jewish Spirituality: From the Bible through the Middle Ages*, 1985; and an ever-growing number of articles in learned journals.

36 E.R. Dodds, *Pagan and Christian in an Age of Anxiety*, 1965, p. 29 n. 1; Carl A. Mounteer, 'Guilt, Martyrdom and Monasticism', *The Journal of Psychohistory* 9, 1981, 145–71.

37 Marilyn Nagy, 'Translocation of parental images in fourth-century ascetic texts: motifs and techniques of identity', *Semeia* 58, 1992, 3–23.

38 For examples of this approach see Benedicta Ward, *Harlots of the Desert: A Study of Repentance in Early Monastic Sources*, 1987; Philip Rousseau, *Ascetics, Authority, and the Church in the Age of Jerome and Cassian*, 1978.

39 E.P. Sanders, *Paul and Palestinian Judaism: A Comparison of Patterns of Religion*, 1977, develops the concept of 'a pattern of religion' as a useful tool for the comparison of religions. A pattern of religion is the description of how a religion is perceived by its adherents to function; 'the way in which a religion is understood to admit and retain members is considered the way it functions' (ibid. p. 17).

40 Or from even farther fields, e.g. 'object relations theory' and 'anthropological culture theory' employed by Marilyn Nagy, op. cit. (n. 37 above); 'construction of visual perception theory' and 'theories of performative rituals in contemporary art' by Patricia Cox Miller, op. cit. (n. 17 above).

41 Any good textbook of human physiology or nutrition may be consulted for more extensive details. The purpose here is to provide the reader in brief with some basic principles of the physiology of nutrition necessary for the appraisal of some of the claims of the texts. The following discussion is based on R. Smith and W.P.T. James, 'Nutrition', in D.J. Weatherall, J.G.G. Ledingham and D.J. Warrell (eds), *Oxford Textbook of Medicine*, 2nd edn, 1987; V.R. Young and N.S. Scrimshaw, 'The physiology of starvation', *Scientific American*, 225(4), 1971, 14–21; W.A.R. Thomson, *Black's Medical Dictionary*, 1974; A. Keys, J. Brozek, A. Henshel, O. Mickelsen and H.L. Taylor (eds), *The Biology of Human Starvation*, 2 vols, 1950; G.F.M. Russell, 'Anorexia nervosa', *Oxford Textbook of Medicine*, 1987.

42 An average female body would utilize somewhat less, since the female body contains a larger proportion of body fat that is metabolically inert.

The basal metabolism per unit of lean body mass, however, is the same in both sexes.

43 *The Body and Society*, pp. 446–7.

CHAPTER 1

1 Geza Vermes, in his brilliant and influential study, *Jesus the Jew*, 1973, places Jesus firmly in the environment of first-century Galilee.

2 As Schürer writes, 'Jewish communities of greater or lesser extent and significance had settled in almost every part of the civilized world, and remaining on the one hand in lasting relation with the motherland and, on the other, in active contact with the non-Jewish world, they were of great importance to the internal development of Judaism as well as to its influence on the rest of the civilized world.' E. Schürer, *The History of the Jewish People in the Age of Jesus Christ, 175 B.C.–A.D. 135* (a new English version revised and edited by G. Vermes, F. Millar and M. Goodman 1986), Vol. III, Chapter 1, p. 3.

3 Whether one follows Neusner in seeing ancient Jewish religion as a set of separate or varied trends before the emergence of rabbinic Judaism (J. Neusner, 'Varieties of Judaism in the formative age', in A. Green (ed.), *Jewish Spirituality: From the Bible through the Middle Ages*, 1985, pp. 171–97), or agrees with Morton Smith and E.P. Sanders, who discern the existence of a 'normative Judaism' long before the fall of the Temple (Morton Smith, 'Palestinian Judaism in the first century', in H.A. Fishel (ed.), *Essays in Graeco-Roman and Related Talmudic Literature*, 1977, pp. 199–214; E.P. Sanders, *Judaism, Practice and Belief 63 BCE–66 CE*, 1992, p. 47), the importance of the Pentateuch for Jewish life and self-definition can hardly be denied.

4 Jewish apologists of the first century, Philo and Josephus, writing for a Hellenized Jewish or Gentile readership, describe Moses as the Lawgiver. In the Pentateuch, however, it is explicit that it is God who gives the Torah, repeatedly instructing Moses, 'Speak to the people of Israel and say to them . . .', followed by detailed commands.

5 Alan F. Segal, *Rebecca's Children: Judaism and Christianity in the Roman World*, 1986, p. 4. Most scholars realize that the covenant idea was central to all forms of Judaism (Sanders, *Judaism* (see n. 3 above), p. 524, n. 38).

6 Genesis 17:12–15; Leviticus 12:3.

7 David Sperling sees as one of the crucial differences between the religion of Israel and that of its neighbours the emphasis on this historical role of Yahweh ('Israel's religion in the ancient near east', in A. Green (ed.) *Jewish Spirituality: From the Bible through the Middle Ages*, 1985, vol. 1, pp. 5–32).

8 'In terms of day-in and day-out Jewish practice, both in Palestine and in the Diaspora, the food laws stood out, along with the observance of the sabbath, as being a central and defining aspect of Judaism' (E.P. Sanders, *Jewish Law from Jesus to the Mishnah: Five Studies*, 1990, p. 27).

9 Leviticus 11; Deuteronomy 14.

10 Leviticus 3:17.

11 Exodus 23:19; 34:26; Deuteronomy 14:21.

12 R.J. Forbes, *Studies in Ancient Technology*, 2nd edn, 6 vols, 1964, vol. 3, p. 86; G. Hamel, *Poverty and Charity in Roman Palestine, First Three Centuries C.E.*, 1989, pp. 25, 27–34. Similarly for Greek society see Marcel Detienne and Jean-Pierre Vernant, *The Cuisine of Sacrifice Among the Greeks*, trans. Paula Wissing, 1989, pp. 3, 5, 11.

13 Deuteronomy 14:5; Deuteronomy 12:15 clearly indicates that the eating of non-sacrificial meat was taken for granted.

14 Leviticus 11:22.

15 On the basis of these texts alone it is impossible even to hazard guesses as to how much meat was available, how often it was eaten and by what classes of people. Meat regulation, however, is the central issue of the dietary laws. There is no law concerning vegetables. This observation may not be trivial in light of the fact that there were other ancient cults that forbade the eating of certain vegetables, e.g. garlic (cult of the Magna Mater) or beans (the Pythagoreans), etc.

16 Mary Douglas, *Purity and Danger*, 1966. Developing the idea of separation further, Jean Soler writes, 'The Mosaic logic is remarkable for its rigor, indeed its rigidity.... It is self-evident that the very inflexibility of this order was a powerful factor for unification and conservation in a people that wanted to "dwell alone"' (J. Soler, 'The semiotics of food in the Bible', in R. Forster and O. Ranum (eds), *Food and Drink in History, Selections from the* Annales: *Economies, Societies, Civilisations*, vol. 5, 1979, p. 137).

17 Deuteronomy 12:15.

18 In Daniel 1:8–18, the hero and his companions decide to live on vegetables, not because of any objection to a meat diet but in order to keep from defiling themselves with non-kosher Gentile food in the court of the king. Daniel 10:2–4 describes a temporary (three weeks) mourning, during which Daniel ate no meat and drank no wine. Daniel was granted visions. The meatless diet, however, is not advocated as superior or more religious than meat eating. Josephus writes of Jewish priests who lived on figs and nuts while imprisoned in Rome (*Vita* 13–14), outdoing Daniel by not even accepting vegetables cooked by Gentiles. The priests' food choice seems to be dictated again by the constraints of the situation rather than by a religious valorization of vegetarianism.

19 Modern scholars still disagree as to how far the demands for food purity were extended. For a perceptive treatment of the topic with a comprehensive review of the various scholarly positions, see E.P. Sanders, 'Did the Pharisees eat ordinary food in purity?', in *Jewish Law* (see n. 8 above), pp. 97–131.

20 Josephus, *Antiquities* 18:12. This may only have been an attempt on the part of the historian, who was proud to have been a Pharisee himself, to claim for them the fashionable Stoic restraint and moral fortitude. He explicitly likens the Pharisees to the Stoic school of Greek philosophy. As we will see in the following chapters, Stoic philosophy generally

held that animals were for human use, and did not advocate vegetarianism.

21 *Antiquities* 18:14–15, also *Jewish Wars* 1:110: 'a body of Jews with the reputation of excelling the rest of the nation in the observances of religion, and as exact exponents of the laws ...'. On the nature of the Pharisees and Pharisaism there is extensive scholarly literature now, stimulated in no small degree by Christian views that saw the Pharisees as the major opponents of Jesus and Pharisaism as the epitome of dry legalism that supposedly characterized Judaism in contrast to Christianity, a religion of faith, love and charity. Jacob Neusner in a large number of publications describes the Pharisees as indeed being concerned with matters pertaining to rite, with keeping the ritual purity laws outside the Temple as well as inside. See, for example, *From Politics to Piety*, 1972; 'Varieties of Judaism'. For a summary of current research on the Pharisees and for a more complex and finely nuanced view of their positions and historical role, see Sanders, *Jewish Law*, pp. 97–242; *Judaism*, pp. 380–452.

22 Josephus, in *Jewish Wars* 2:132–3, describes their food habits as involving two daily communal meals where the baker (σιτοποιός) places the bread and the cook or butcher (μάγειρος) places the meal in front of them. Josephus also mentions among their occupations the tanning of animal hides. It may be assumed, in the face of no contrary evidence, that the meat of some of these animals was consumed by the community. Archaeological finds of animal bone deposits around the Qumran camp provide additional support for the accepted view that the Dead Sea community ate meat (R. de Vaux, *Archaeology and the Dead Sea Scrolls*, 1973, pp. 12–13). For the Essenes and the Qumran community see Schürer, op. cit. (n. 2 above), vol. 2, Appendix B. On food and purity concerns of the Essenes, see Sanders, *Judaism*, pp. 352–61.

23 Sanders, *Judaism*, p. 195.

24 Ibid., p. 252.

25 Psalms 24:4–5.

26 Sanders, *Jewish Law*, p. 161. For an excellent discussion and summary of Biblical purity laws, see pp. 134–52.

27 Leviticus 19:2; 20:7, and other places.

28 Ibid. 22.

29 Ibid. 18:22.

30 Ibid. 19:29.

31 For the sacrificial cult see Leviticus. For an evocative description of the life in and around the Temple in first-century Judaism, see Sanders, *Judaism*, pp. 103–18 and pp. 125–45 for sacrifices and festivals.

32 Deuteronomy 14:23–7.

33 *Spec. Leg.* 1:221.

34 Ibid. 1:70. In other places Philo attributes various other meanings to the sacrificial cult. In *Deus* 7–9, for example, he concentrates on the allegorical meaning of the purity demanded from the sacrificers; in *Ebr.* 87, he distinguishes between the blood sacrifice, necessary for the multitudes, and the sacrifice of the high priest at the inner altar that is 'bloodless and is born of reason'.

35 Sanders is of the opinion that 'Philo had visited the temple, and some of his statements about it . . . seem to be based on personal knowledge' (*Judaism*, p. 104).

36 *Antiquities*, 4:203.

37 Sanders, *Judaism*, p. 256.

38 Deuteronomy 14:28–9; 26:12; and many other places.

39 Proverbs 1:19; 2:16; 7:1–27; 10:3; 15:27; 19:15; 23:1–8; 29–35; 31:2–8; Ecclesiasticus 31:12–31 and many other places.

40 Ecclesiasticus 31:23–4.

41 *1QS* (Serekh: the *Community Rule from Qumran*) 6:24–7:25; 8:16–9:2 in Geza Vermes, *The Dead Sea Scrolls in English*, 3rd edn, revised and augmented, 1987.

42 Deuteronomy 6:3; also 5:33; 6:18 and many other places.

43 *Antiquities* 1:14.

44 Deuteronomy 7:13.

45 Ibid. 8:8–11.

46 Leviticus 26:3–13.

47 Ibid. 26:14–45.

48 The Law expressly forbade self-laceration as something that the idol-worshippers practise in mourning, Leviticus 19:28; 21:5 and Deuteronomy 14:1.

49 Leviticus 23:26–33; Numbers 29:7–11.

50 See Isaiah 58:3–6, where both expressions (*tzom* and *inui nephesh*) are used for arguing that God was more interested in his people's soul-searching and repentance of wickedness than in their refraining from food.

51 The Bible recognizes also some voluntary 'self-affliction'. As Numbers 30 attests, individuals could take a vow to 'afflict themselves' for a given time. The Law here specifies how a woman's vows can be annulled by her father or husband.

52 Exodus 34:28; Deuteronomy 9:9.

53 *Encyclopaedia Judaica*, 'Fasting and Fast Days'; Rudolph Arbesmann, 'Fasting and prophecy in Pagan and Christian antiquity', *Traditio* 7, 1949–51, pp. 1–71. For an opposing view see S. Lowy, 'The motivation of fasting in Talmudic literature', *JJS* 9, 1958, p. 20, n. 11. Contrary to the persistent opinion that long-term fasts produce visions, evidence seems to indicate that long-term fasting causes lethargy and apathy during which even dreams disappear (A. Keys, J. Brozek, A. Henshel, O. Mickelsen and H.L. Taylor (eds), *The Biology of Human Starvation*, 2 vols, 1950).

54 Elijah's fast in 1 Kings 19:8 belongs to the same type; the presence of God, here as a Messenger, sustains the prophet in a superhuman condition. With these passages the forty-days fast became a signifier of the true man of God.

55 Deuteronomy 9:18.

56 2 Samuel 1:11–13.

57 Ibid. 3:31–6.

58 Ibid. 12:16–20. Fasting and mourning for a sick friend are attested also in Psalms 35:13.

59 1 Kings 21:27; fasting to avert disaster also in 1 Samuel 7:5–7; Jeremiah 36:3–11; Esther 4:1–4, 4:16; Joel 1:14–17, 2:11–12, 2:15; and other places. Nehemiah 9 describes a public fast of all Israelites who confess their own sins and the transgressions of all their ancestors and beg forgiveness and liberation from oppressive foreign rule.

60 Judges 20:26–8; 1 Samuel 7:5–13.

61 Ezra 10:1–6.

62 1 Samuel 28:8–22.

63 1 Kings 21:8–15. There are interesting echoes of this passage in Josephus and in the Acts of the Apostles, showing that both authors read their Bible and recognized a good story when they saw one. Josephus describes how a 'depraved and mischievous man named Ananias proposed . . . that a public fast should be announced. . . . they should reassemble . . . without arms. . . . This he said, not from motives of piety, but in order to catch me and my friends in this defenceless condition' (Vita 290). The author of the Acts relates how the Jews bound themselves with an oath neither to drink nor eat in order to kill Paul (Acts 23:12–16).

64 Zechariah 7:2–6; 8:18–20; Sanders, Jewish Law, pp. 81–3.

65 In the Gospel of Luke, the Pharisee boasts of fasting twice a week (Luke 18:12). According to the Didache, an early Christian work that reflects Jewish ideas and practices on the one hand, and attempts to distance Christians from the Jews on the other, the 'hypocrites' (i.e. the Jews) fasted on Mondays and Thursdays; the Christians should not imitate them but should fast on Wednesday and Friday. It is not clear from either source whether the twice a week fasting was a regular or occasional practice (Sanders, Jewish Law, p. 82). The days may have been specified as those appropriate if and when one felt the need for fasting.

66 Judith mourned for her husband and 'wore sackcloth around her waist and dressed in widow's weeds. She fasted every day of her widowhood except the Sabbath Eve and the Sabbath itself, the Eve of New Moon, the feast of New Moon and the festival days of the House of Israel' (Judith 8:6). The community fast described in Judith 4:9–13 (as also in 1 Maccabees 3:47–51 and 2 Maccabees 13:12) is not ascetic practice but an accompaniment of supplication to God in time of disaster.

67 The prophetess Anna never left the Temple, serving God night and day with fasting and prayer, in the Gospel of Luke (2:36–8).

68 4 Maccabees 1, 2 is a lecture on the mastery of passions by reason, embodied in Jewish religious Law. Ascetic fasting for the control of sexual passions is seen in Testament Patr. Joseph 3:4; 4:8; 10:1–2.

69 S.D. Fraade, 'Ascetical aspects of ancient Judaism', in A. Green (ed.) Jewish Spirituality: From the Bible through the Middle Ages, 1985, vol. 1, pp. 253–88, at p. 262. Sanders sees Jewish ideas of dualism and belief in the resurrection of the soul as originating in aspects of Persian religion that penetrated the West and influenced Judaism in particular (Judaism, p. 249). Later these rather vague dualistic notions received reinforcement by Platonic or Pythagorean theories. Feldman points to Gnostic doctrines that influenced certain first-century Jewish groups, especially

the Essenes. These 'Gnostic-like' doctrines, in his view, are the dichotomy of body and soul, a disdain for the material world, a notion of esoteric knowledge and an intense interest in angels and in problems of creation (Louis H. Feldman, 'Palestinian and Diaspora Judaism in the first century', in Hershel Shanks (ed.), *Christianity and Rabbinic Judaism: A Parallel History of their Origins and Early Development*, 1993, pp. 1–39).

70 In 4 Ezra, fasts lasting seven days separate the visions (5:20 and 6:35) while food is limited to plants for other seven-day periods preceding the divine messages (9:26 and 12:51). Similarly the visionary in 2 Baruch 20:5–6 fasts for seven days.

71 Michael Edward Stone, *Fourth Ezra*, 1990, pp. 118–19.

72 Emero Stiegman, 'Rabbinic anthropology', *ANRW* II.19.2, 1979, 487–579.

73 H.L. Strack and G. Stemberger, *Introduction to the Talmud and Midrash*, trans. M. Bockmuehl, 1991, p. 6.

74 Lowy, op. cit. (n. 53 above), p. 21. Mourning for the dead is meant here, since fasting as a sign of mourning for the Temple or other national disasters was never discouraged.

75 The Mishnah is extended by its companion, the Tosefta (redacted between AD 200 and 400); organized along the same division of tractates, it often clarifies, complements or extends Mishnaic principles (J. Neusner, *The Mishnah: A New Translation*, 1988, Introduction, p. xxii).

76 The ninth tractate of the second division of the Mishnah (Seder Moed).

77 *Taanith* 1:4–7.

78 Tosefta *Taanith* 1:8.

79 *Taanith* 2:2–5. This pious man is experienced, presumedly in the Torah and prayer, a father of children, and he is poor, his 'cupboard is empty'.

80 Jeremiah 39:2; 52:12–13.

81 *Taanith* 4:6.

82 Thought to belong to the third generation of Babylonian Amoraim, *circa* later third century. On the problems of the biographies and dating of the rabbis see Strack and Stemberger, op. cit., pp. 62–110.

83 Babylonian Talmud (BT hence), *Berakhoth* 17a.

84 *Taanith* 4:3. Even the starting of a fast for rain on a Thursday was problematical for the rabbis in the Mishnah for this may prevent actions necessary for the honour owing to the sabbath; *Taanith* 2:6.

85 *Taanith* 2:10.

86 Tosefta *Taanith* 2:12.

87 'Any matter of doubt as to danger to life overrides the prohibitions of the Sabbath', *Yoma* 8:4–6; Tosefta *Taanith* 3:2.

88 S. Lowy, op. cit. (n. 53 above) p. 22.

89 One of the second generation of Tannaim (c. 90–130), contemporary of Rabban Gamaliel II, whose position for the leadership he seems to have challenged for a time (Strack and Stemberger, p. 76).

90 Jerusalem Talmud (JT hence) *Shabbath* 3:4.7c.

91 He may have been the same Joshua mentioned by Jerome as a follower of Hillel around the time of the destruction of Jerusalem (Strack and Stemberger, p. 72).

92 BT *Hagigah* 22b.
93 He may be Shimon ben Yohai, a third generation Tanna (c. 130–60).
    But, as Strack and Stemberger caution (p. 64–5), often several rabbis
    have the same name, which, especially where the name of the father is
    omitted, makes correct identification difficult or impossible.
94 BT *Nazir* 52b.
95 For further examples of rabbinic fasting for minor offences see S. Lowy,
    op. cit. (n. 53 above), p. 22.
96 If he was the son of the honoured Rav Ashi who was reported to have led
    the academy at Sura for fifty-two years and who died in 427, then the
    story told about the life of Rav Hiyya may be located in the late fifth
    century, when the self-denying, chaste 'holy man' was highly regarded
    by both Christians and philosophical pagans. Celibacy was not valued
    similarly by Jewish tradition. The divine command, 'Be fruitful and
    multiply' (Genesis 1:28; 9:7) was taken seriously. R. Eliezer ben
    Hyrcanus, at the end of the first century, would equate abstinence from
    marital sexual intercourse with shedding human blood (BT *Yebam.*
    636).
97 BT *Kiddushin* 81b.
98 There are some voices in early rabbinic Judaism that seem to promote
    abstinence as an ideal, but whether a significant number of these
    promote it as an ideal to which all of Israel should aspire is questionable.
    Steven D. Fraade, op. cit. (n. 69 above), argues for an 'ascetical tension'
    in rabbinic Judaism, a tension between individual piety and concern for
    the whole community. He argues strongly against those who see
    Judaism as antithetical to 'asceticism'. The article is valuable in that
    it shows how many ways one can stretch the notion of asceticism. The
    stricter definitions some use would leave Judaism somewhat bereft of
    ascetic spirituality, a concept that is presently enjoying increasing
    popularity even in scholarly circles. If defined in the widest sense one
    could then agree with Josephus, who saw Torah study as ascesis
    (*Antiquities* 20:265).
99 BT *Taanith* 11a, attributed to Samuel, a Babylonian first generation
    Amora.
100 BT *Taanith* 11b, 14b 22b. Tosefta *Taanith* 2:12.
101 JT *Sotah* 3:4,12a; Tosefta *Taanith* 2:12; 3:7b BT *Taanith* 11a–b, 13a,
    13b.
102 Tosefta *Sotah* 15:10–12; BT *Baba Batra* 60b, the sayings are attributed
    to a third-generation Tanna (after the revolt of Bar Cochvah), Rabban
    Simeon ben Gamaliel II (or his associate R. Ishmael), who refers to the
    views of R. Joshua, who saw the destruction of the Temple.
103 *Spec. Leg.* 1:186.
104 *Taanith* 1:6; Sanders, *Jewish Law*, pp. 13, 20.
105 *Historiae* 5:1–13.
106 *Divus Augustus* 76:2.
107 *Epistulae ad M. Caes.* II:9.
108 *Geographica* 16:2:34–46. In addition to fasting Strabo claims that the
    Jews abstained from meat and practised both circumcision and excision
    (of females). For neither of these claims is there any evidence.

109 For an extensive collection of ancient authors' views on Jews and Jewish practices see Menachem Stern, *Greek and Latin Authors on Jews and Judaism*, 3 vols, 1974–84.

110 *Epigrams* 4:4.

111 Tacitus, *Historiae* 5:1–13; Juvenal, *Saturae* 14:105–6; Seneca, *Epistulae morales* 108, and others. Most of these authors, representing the opinions of the leisured classes, considered the sabbath as a poor excuse for indolence, idleness and sloth.

112 The literature on both proselytism and on the nature of God-fearers is enormous. For the argument for proselytism with an extensive review of both the ancient sources and their modern treatment, see Louis H. Feldman, *Jew and Gentile in the Ancient World*, 1993; for the opposing view and a different perception of Jewish–Gentile relations in antiquity, see Martin Goodman, *Mission and Conversion: Proselytizing in the Religious History of the Roman Empire*, 1994.

113 The literature on Philo is extensive. A good introduction to Philo is the chapter of Henry Chadwick, 'Philo and the beginnings of Christian thought', in A.H. Armstrong (ed.), *The Cambridge History of Later Greek and Early Medieval Philosophy*, 1967, repr. 1991, pp. 137–95.

114 And in the course of this effort he succeeded in destroying the Old Testament's narrative integrity by pressing a pious moralizing message into which he tried to fit the historical content.

115 'The history of Christian philosophy begins not with a Christian but with a Jew, Philo of Alexandria, elder contemporary of St. Paul', so starts H. Chadwick in his appraisal of Philo; op. cit. p. 137. Philo was important enough for the church historian Eusebius to claim him to be a quasi-Christian; according to him, Philo conversed with St Peter in Rome! Eusebius listed a large number of his works (*Ecclesiastical History*, 2:4; 2:17; 2:18).

116 *Gig.* 29–33.

117 *Her.* 68, 85, 273; *Som.* 1:139; *Deus* 111–15; *Ebr.* 101; *Abr.* 9. and other places. There are many works on Philo's philosophy. The present discussion is indebted to the chapter on Philo in John Dillon, *The Middle Platonists: 80 B.C. to A.D. 200*, 1977, to David Winston, 'Philo and the contemplative life', in *Jewish Spirituality*, pp. 198–231, and most substantially to Chadwick op. cit. (n. 113 above).

118 *Conf.* 177.

119 *Leg. Alleg.* II.27–30; Chadwick, 'Philo', p. 146.

120 *Cher.* 107.

121 See Chapter 2 below for discussion of this matter.

122 For examples see *Spec.Leg.* I.148; II.50, 193–6; III.9–11; *Op.* 158–9; *Det.* 101–3, 135–7, 156–9; *Cont.* 74 and countless other places.

123 *Op.* 158.

124 *Det.* 19.

125 *Cont.* 34–5. Eusebius the Church historian was convinced that the Therapeutae whom Philo describes here were early Christians. This is most unlikely. But his tale of fabulous endurance in fasting may have been the forerunner of many similarly fabulous Christian stories.

126 *Ep.* 11, in A.J. Malherbe (ed.), *The Cynic Epistles*, 1977.

127 *Gig.* 34–5; see also *Leg. Alleg.* II:29 where he urges his reader to 'banish folly and take food soberly'.

128 *Fug.* 33–6, 38; *Praem.* 51.

129 E.P. Sanders, *Paul and Palestinian Judaism: A Comparison of Patterns of Religion*, 1977, p. 17.

130 As Lowy emphasized, on occasion of a public fast for rain or for averting disasters, ordinary people noted for their piety often led the prayer, occasionally even the prayer of an ass driver was held to have brought rain; op. cit. (n. 53 above), p. 27.

131 Numbers 30:3–26; Mishnah, *Nedarim* 10.

132 Philo's Therapeutae are reported to dream, presumably as a consequence of their frugal life, 'of loveliness of divine excellences and powers' *(Cont.* 26).

133 An exception is Saul compelling the woman at Endor to call up the spirit of Samuel in 1 Samuel 28:20.

134 Fear of demonic possession through food, together with fasting for inducing visions and for increasing magical powers, figure importantly in Arbesmann's treatment of the motivation for fasting in antiquity, which he bases on the claims of anthropologists who worked with pre-literate societies. It seems that in this respect there is an unbridgeable gap between these societies and the 'people of the Book'.

CHAPTER 2

1 On variety even among the eating habits of Greeks themselves, among whom the Spartans were known to be abstemious, the Boeotians coarse and given to gluttony, the Thessalians gourmets, etc., see B.A. Sparkes, 'The Greek kitchen', *JHS* 82, 1962, 121–37.

2 Charles Robert Phillips, 'The sociology of religious knowledge in the Roman Empire to A.D. 284', *ANRW* 2.16.3, 1986, 2677–773.

3 The term 'pagan' is unfortunate because it is uninformative. If it has a meaning at all, then it describes all the peoples of the Empire and beyond who were neither Christian nor Jewish. Most modern attempts to describe 'paganism' as adhering to cults or even as an 'ism' reveal a view of the ancient world heavily conditioned by Christian categories (Robin Lane Fox, *Pagans and Christians*, 1986, pp. 31–2). I have considered substituting for 'pagan' the term 'polytheist', which is increasingly employed by some modern authors who want to distance themselves from the Christian bias (see, for instance, Garth Fowden, 'The last days of Constantine: oppositional versions and their influence', *JRS* 84, 1994, 146–71). But this term would not describe fairly those who were philosophical theists or those who were devotees of just one god or goddess. For the sake of brevity and convenience, in the following I shall use the term 'pagan' with the only meaning that the referent is not Christian or Jewish.

4 There were numerous instances of proscriptions of religious cults, but these arose from perceptions of particular anti-social practices on the part of the cult and not from any philosophical rationale of heresy. Any

cult was free until some aspect of its activity ran contrary to prevailing community standards (Phillips, op. cit. (n. 2 above), p. 2746; Fergus Millar, 'The imperial cult and the persecutions' in *Le Culte des souverains dans l'empire romain*, Fondation Hardt, Entretiens sur l'antiquité classique 19, 1973).

5 Walter Burkert, *Homo Necans: The Anthropology of Ancient Greek Sacrificial Ritual and Myth*, trans. Peter Bing, 1983, pp. 22–82. It may be safe to assume that the practice of sacrifice is older than the oldest of our literary sources. No one knows what gave rise to the practice, or when, what the first victims were, whether animal, vegetable, or that most titillating of all sacrificial fantasies, the human virgin. There are various highly speculative accounts of its origins. Burkert's reconstruction is based on much anthropological research and is indebted to Freudian psychoanalytic views.

6 Ibid., p. 296.

7 Henri Hubert and Marcel Mauss, *Sacrifice: Its Nature and Function*, trans. W.D. Halls, 1964; H.H. Scullard, *Festivals and Ceremonies of the Roman Republic*, 1981, p. 25; Lane Fox, *Pagans and Christians*, pp. 115–18.

8 Walter Burkert, *Greek Religion*, trans. John Raffan, 1985, pp. 73–4.

9 Cicero, *Laws* (2:8–12).

10 Xenophon distinguishes between '*thuomena*' and '*thereomena*' (*Anabasis* 5:3:9). S. Dow and D.H. Gill, 'The Greek cult table', *AJA* 69, 1965, 103.

11 Lucian, *De Sacrificiis* 12.

12 Burkert, *Greek Religion*, pp. 242–6; H.S. Versnel, 'The Festival of Bona Dea and the Thesmophoria', *Greece and Rome* 39, 1992, 31–55.

13 Cato, *De Agricultura* 83, 132, 134, 139, 141.

14 For descriptions of the act of the sacrifice and the various actors see Burkert, *Greek Religion*, pp. 55–9; R.M. Ogilvie, *The Romans and their Gods*, 1969, pp. 41–52; G.J. Szemler, *The Priests of the Roman Republic: A Study of Interactions Between Priesthoods and Magistracies*, Coll. Lat. 127, 1972; Scullard, op. cit. (n. 7 above), pp. 22–7.

15 Quoted in Athenaeus, IV 146.

16 T. Mommsen, *The History of Rome*, trans. William Purdie Dickinson 1894, vol. 4, p. 208.

17 Lane Fox, *Pagans and Christians*, p. 70.

18 Burkert, *Greek Religion*, p. 107.

19 J. Scheid, 'Sacrifice et Banquet à Rome', *MEFRA* 97, 1985, 193–206.

20 Paul Veyne, *Bread and Circuses: Historical Sociology and Political Pluralism*, trans. Brian Pearce, 1990, p. 268, quoting Mommsen, *Staatsrecht*, vol. II, p. xii.

21 Veyne, *Bread and Circuses*, p. 220.

22 Richard Gordon, in 'Religion in the Roman Empire: the civic compromise and its limits', in Mary Beard and John North (eds), *Pagan Priests: Religion and Power in the Ancient World*, 1990, pp. 235–55, argues that sacrificial euergetism could be an effective religious method by which the ruling elite accumulated symbolic capital as long as the Empire was stable enough. In his view, 'by appropriating sacrifice, the elite announced its protection of the social rules implicit in sacrifice –

sex roles, family structure, rules for food, in short "our way of life" ' (p. 252).

23 Veyne, *Bread and Circuses*, p. 220.

24 It is known, for example, that the ancient Feriae Latinae were organized on the principle of representatives. One person from each of the Latin communities claimed a portion of the meat at the sacrifice (Livy 32:1:9). This could have provided a model. Rome was divided early on into thirty curiae, each with its own flamen and curio, each had its own assembly hall where members met to feast together on holidays (Dionysius Halicarnassensis 2:23; Ovid, *Fasti* 2:525–30). Under Augustus the city was again divided into over 200 *vici* or neighbourhoods for purposes of religious and community functions, each with its *vicomagister* (Suetonius, *Divus Augustus* 30). This could have provided the system for distribution or some form of real or symbolic inclusion in the feast. And finally, there was the army. There can be no doubt that a large part of the army feasted on sacrificial meat. There are memorable records of this in Josephus (*Jewish War* 7:16–17) and Ammianus (22:12:6). J.H.W.G. Liebeschuetz, *Continuity and Change in Roman Religion*, 1979, pp. 81–2, lists additional sources for sacrificial banquets and food distributions.

25 Virgil, *Aeneid* 5.77–9, 95–9.

26 Ovid, *Fasti* II 535–40.

27 Veyne, *Bread and Circuses*, pp. 220–1. Veyne sees the custom of leaving instructions in wills for the arrangements for the funeral, which included pleasures for the people on that occasion, not as religious piety or euergetism but as an opportunistic gesture to curry favour with the plebs and to encourage electoral corruption.

28 Lucian's *De Luctu* was written to ridicule the common Greek customs of mourning.

29 Lane Fox, *Pagans and Christians*, p. 61.

30 Ibid., p. 84. A.D. Nock, 'The historical importance of cult associations', *Classical Review* 38, 1924, 105–9, pointed out that these cult associations were like a family; the benefactor was usually referred to as *Pater* or *Mater*, while the members often called each other *fratres*, *adelphoi* – that is, brothers. The shared banquets and the possession of a common place of burial made this conception of a family more real.

31 Lane Fox, *Pagans and Christians*, p. 83.

32 D.G. Orr, 'Roman domestic religion: the evidence of household shrines', *ANRW* 2 16.2, 1978, 1557–91.

33 J.S. Black, 'Fasting', *Encyclopaedia Britannica*, 13th edn, vol. 10, 1926, pp. 193–8; J.A. MacCullogh and A.J. Maclean, 'Fasting', *Hasting's Encyclopedia of Religion and Ethics*, 1951, vol. 6, 759–71; Rudolph Arbesmann, 'Fasting and prophecy in Pagan and Christian antiquity', *Traditio* 7, 1949–51, 1–71.

34 Clifford Herschel More, 'Greek and Roman ascetic tendencies', in H.W. Smyth (ed.), *Harvard Essays on Classical Subjects*, 1912, 97–140. Even Arbesmann, who believes in the universality of fasting as a religious practice, had to admit that νηστεία in the strict sense of the word as

abstention from food and drink for a fixed period is very rare indeed in Greek and Roman religion ('Fasting and prophecy', p. 8, nn. 24–6).

35 *Theological Dictionary of the New Testament*, ed. Gerhard Kittel, trans. G.W. Bromeley, 1964–76, vol. 4, Behm, 'νῆστις νηστεύω, νηστεία', 925–35.

36 Athenaeus, VII 308. Aristotle (*Historia Animalium* 591 b2) wrote: 'this fish is a scavenger, eating carrion, and is poor food except when it is empty'.

37 See Chapter 1 of this volume, pp. 21, 32.

38 Alciphron, *Letters* 2:37:2; Athenaeus, VII 307; Rudolph Arbesmann, *Das Fasten bei den Griechen und Römern*, 1929, pp. 90–4.

39 Cornutus, *Theologiae Graecae compendium* 28 (ed. C. Lang) 1881, p. 55, cited in Arbesmann, 'Fasting and prophecy', p. 3.

40 Philo, *Vita Mosis* 2:23–4.

41 Arbesmann, *Das Fasten*, p. 94.

42 Jerome, *Letters* 107:10.

43 Herodotus (2:40) describes as a strange and unusual custom the fasts that Egyptian priests observed before entering the sanctuary for sacrifices.

44 Arbesmann, 'Fasting and prophecy', p. 5.

45 See Chapter 1 of this volume, pp. 21–2, 24.

46 F. Cumont, *Oriental Religions in Roman Paganism*, English trans. 1911, repr. 1956, pp. 40–1, and *The Mysteries of Mithra*, English trans. 1903, repr. 1956, pp. 141, 160; Arbesmann, *Das Fasten*, p. 83. This may be the reason why some Christian scholars (e.g. Cumont, *Oriental Religions*, pp. 3–19) regard these as 'true' pagan religion as opposed to 'empty' cult. On religion and cult, and on their endurance into the late Empire, see Lane Fox, *Pagans and Christians*, pp. 64–101 and pp. 580–1 respectively. R. Gordon sees the difference between the ruling cults of the empire and the 'oriental' cults in that ascetic practices 'were options within the context of the oriental cults' (*Pagan Priests* (n. 22 above) p. 248).

47 Walter Burkert speculates: 'Puberty initiation, agrarian magic and sexuality in the great experience of life overcoming death' (*Greek Religion* (n. 8 above), p. 277).

48 Juvenal, *Saturae* 6:511–45, 13:93; Persius, 5:185.

49 'Pagan authors never went beyond circumspect allusions, and the Christian writers who strove to tear off the veil of secrecy were seldom able to produce more than vague insinuations' (Burkert, *Greek Religion*, p. 276).

50 Phillips, op. cit. (n. 2 above), p. 2699.

51 Roman poets often complained about the periods of sexual abstinence the Goddess imposed on her devotees, the poets' lovers, during the days of her festivals, e.g. Tibullus, 1:3:23–7; Propertius, 2:33.

52 'Frequent sacred repasts maintained a spirit of fellowship among the mystics of Cybele, Mithra, or the Baals', Cumont, *Oriental Religions*, p. 41. John E. Stambaugh, 'The function of Roman temples', *ANRW* 2.16.1, 1978, 554–608, describes, among others, temples of various

oriental cults. In most of these there seem to have been spaces provided for the shared meals.

53 Apuleius, *Metamorphoses*, Book 8.

54 Ibid., 8:29.

55 Burkert, *Greek Religion*, p. 277.

56 Arbesmann, 'Fasting and prophecy', pp. 9–11, citing Iamblichus, a rather late source.

57 Plutarch, *De Iside et Osiride* 2:352, trans. J.G. Griffith, 1970, p. 121.

58 Cato, *De Agricultura* 70.

59 Ovid, *Fasti* 4:657.

60 For a Latin example see Cato, *De Agricultura* 141; for a Greek one see the paean to Hygieia, written by Ariphon in the fourth century BC, which was still remembered about six hundred years later by Athenaeus, who brings his philological feast, the *Deipnosophistae*, to a conclusion with it.

61 Juvenal, *Saturae* 10:356.

62 For modern treatments of plagues and epidemics described in ancient sources (Hippocratic corpus, Thucydides, Lucretius, Diodorus Siculus, Celsus, Pliny the Elder, Galen, Cyprian, Procopius, etc.), see A. Patrick, 'Ancient Greece and Rome', in D. Brothwell and A.T. Sandison, *Diseases in Antiquity*, 1967; M.D. Grmek, *Diseases in the Ancient Greek World*, trans. Mireille and Leonard Muellner, 1983. R. Jackson in *Doctors and Diseases in the Roman Empire*, 1988, pp. 53–4, emphasizes that even in the Rome of aqueducts, baths and latrines people lacked understanding of the importance of the most basic hygienic measures. So the baths and latrines often contributed to the spread of disease, intestinal parasites, diarrhoea and dysentery that were so frequently mentioned by medical writers. E.G. Ellis, *Ancient Anodynes: Primitive Anaesthesia and Allied Conditions*, 1946, shows that ancient writers were aware of the pain reducing qualities of certain plant extracts, notably that of the white poppy (*Papaver somniferum*), which is opium. However surgeons failed to make use of them. Wine seems to be the most widely used anodyne.

63 Graham Anderson, *The Second Sophistic*, 1993, p. 17. Writing about the orators, writers and teachers of the empire he shows how much their conceptual world was dominated by classical Greece, from its philosophies to its comedies.

64 Diogenes Laertius, *Lives of Eminent Philosophers* III 78, LCL.

65 Ibid. III 80.

66 Ibid. VI 70.

67 Ibid. VII 90.

68 Ibid. VII 106; 107; 109.

69 Ibid. X 128.

70 Ibid. VIII 9; 13; 23; 28; in agreement with Athenaeus, IV 157.

71 With the possible exception of Epicurus, who is said to have held that health is in some cases a good and in others a thing of indifference (Diogenes Laertius, *Lives of Eminent Philosophers* X 120); and pleasure, the search for which he advocated, he defined as the absence of pain in the body and trouble in the mind (ibid. X 131).

72 Hippocrates, *On Ancient Medicine* III 40.

73 Hippocrates, *Regimen in Health* I 2.

74 Euripides, Xenophanes of Colophon, Achaeus of Eritrea, and others are quoted by Athenaeus (X 413–14), as objecting to athletes for being victims of their belly, and thus not being able to acquire wealth to increase that of the family. The public is being berated by these critics for admiring athletes with 'their loins bare, their sleek arms swelling with youthful power... strong shoulders glistening in youthful bloom', and for preferring their contests to those of moral teachers.

75 'How many men train their bodies, how few their minds!', 'It is foolish and quite unfitting for an educated man to spend all his time on acquiring bulging muscles, a thick neck and mighty lungs...' Seneca had low opinion of athletes or men who tried to emulate them, while as a good Stoic he believed that one should take good care of one's body, and that regular exercise was a part of the 'good life' (*Epistulae morales* 80:2; 15:2).

76 Hippocrates, *On Ancient Medicine* IV 6.

77 H.A. Harris, *Greek Athletics and the Jews*, 1976, shows that Philo may have gone through the typical education of a Greek boy.

78 See Chapter 1 of this volume, pp. 29–31.

79 Philo, *Som.* I 251.

80 Philo, *Spec.Leg.* II 230.

81 Harris, *Greek Athletics*, p. 73.

82 Philo, *Som.* II 9.

83 Philo, *Leg.All.* I 98.

84 Charles Burton Gulick in his introduction to the English translation of Athenaeus's *Deipnosophistae*, LCL 1927: repr. 1969.

85 Athenaeus I 4–6; III 112–13; IV 164 on cookbook writers. Some philosophers deplored the phenomenon: Musonius Rufus, the Roman Stoic of Nero's time complained that 'as some people have written books on music and medicine, so some have even written books on cooking which aim to increase the pleasure of the palate, but ruin the health' (Cora E. Lutz, 'Musonius Rufus "The Roman Socrates"', *Yale Classical Studies* 10, 1947, 3–151, at p. 115).

86 Athenaeus, III 102–3; IX 378.

87 Ibid., III 102.

88 Apicius, XXVII; John Edwards, *The Roman Cookery of Apicius*, 1984, p. 11.

89 This common experience gave rise to various literary topoi, and also to one of the popular metaphors for society and class struggle: for example, the story of Menenius Agrippa and the Roman plebs.

90 Asclepiades of Bithynia, who had a highly successful practice in Rome in the first century BC, is thought to have been an atomist. He and some of his followers held that the body is composed of tiny elements, *onkoi*, with invisible pores between these. For a thorough exposition of what can be known of Asclepiades, see J.T. Vallance, *The Lost Theory of Asclepiades of Bithynia*, 1990.

91 The idea of the four basic elements, of which everything in the universe is made, is attributed to Empedocles: Plato, *Timaeus* 8:2.

92 Vallance, op. cit., p. 93.

93 This notion of health as equilibrium between the four elements is attributed to Alcmaeon of Croton. Alcmaeon's notion of equilibrium can be traced back to Anaximander. See James Longrigg, *Greek Rational Medicine, Philosophy and Medicine from Alcmeon to the Alexandrians*, 1993, p. 90. In Hippocratic medicine, especially as it was propagated by Galen, the element of heat is given special importance. According to Galen's elaborations, there are two kinds of 'heat', ordinary heat that burns, and innate heat, which is involved in all of the important functions of the body. Innate heat comes to the embryo through the semen and it is moderated in the body by respiration.

94 Hippocrates, *On the Nature of Man* IV.

95 Since the focus of interest here is food, I shall not discuss speculations concerning the role of respiration in digestion and beliefs in respiration through the skin (cf. Longrigg, op. cit., pp. 140–1).

96 Hippocrates, *On the Nature of Man* IV.

97 Hippocrates, *On Ancient Medicine* IX.

98 Galen too describes in great detail the evils that follow prolonged fasting: exhausted strength, bilious humours, severe heartburn, nausea and constipation – even epileptic fits! (Peter Brain, *Galen on Bloodletting*, 1986; C.G. Kühn, *Claudii Galeni Opera Omnia*, 20 vols, repr. 1964, vol. XI, pp. 186, 199, 241).

99 Galen, *De Alimentarum Facultatibus I*; Kühn, op. cit., vol. VI, pp. 468–71.

100 This list is made up on the basis of Celsus, *De Medicina*, the Hippocratic *Regimen in Health* and Galen, *De Alimentarum Facultatibus*; Kühn, op. cit., vol. VI. The range of edible animals and birds is quite a lot wider than the typical European diet uses today.

101 Longrigg, op. cit., pp. 79–80. There were other, slightly variant views concerning the nature of the semen, which do not concern us here. All theories regarded it as a precious bodily fluid, and worried about its depletion.

102 Athenaeus, I 12; VI 274–5; XII 543; Musonius Rufus, 18A and 18B (in C.E. Lutz, op. cit. (n. 85 above), pp.112–15, 116–21.

103 Celsus, *De Medicina*, I.1.

104 Ibid. In *Porneia: On Desire and the Body in Antiquity*, trans. Felicia Pheasant, 1988, Aline Rousselle argued that ancient medical writings reflect deep sexual anxieties harboured by the culture of the empire. We shall not consider here the question of how wide a generalization one can draw from medical fragments. (For a discussion of this see the review of the book by Mary Beard in *JRS* 81, 1991, 180.) Sexual anxieties may have been stimulated by philosophical-medical views, described above, that regarded sperm as the final distillate of the 'best blood' produced by the body's 'vital heat', mixed with pneuma, the 'vital spirit'.

105 Celsus, *De Medicina*, I.2,5.

106 Some characteristic pieces of advice: 'He can tell his body is sound if his morning urine is whitish, later reddish; the former indicates that digestion is going on, the latter that digestion is complete. If digested well the man may rise, if not he should stay in bed' (I.2,4). With respect

to food, 'a surfeit is never of service, excessive abstinence is often unserviceable, if any intemperance is committed, it is safer in drinking[!] than in eating. Secunda mensa does no harm to a good stomach, in a weak one it turns sour' (I.2, 8–10).

107 As Wesley D. Smith argues in his book, *The Hippocratic Tradition*, 1979, the theory of temperaments, qualities, composition of the body, and the effect of food, etc., has its roots far back in the Greek view of how the body works and of the relation of environment to health and disease. What Galen calls Hippocratic medicine, however, is more or less his interpretation and comes most directly from the pneumatic school of medicine, which, under Stoic influence, worked out the four-element, four-humour theory of disease and health, and worked also on equivalence of seasons to temperaments and on the temperaments of food. In Galen's writings the assorted medical treatises written at various periods become the writing of Hippocrates the originator of logical or dogmatic medicine, the direct predecessor and teacher of Galen. All other schools of medicine, or all those with whom Galen chose to disagree, are accused of misunderstanding, misrepresenting or falsifying Hippocrates.

108 Galen was a syncretist; his principal acknowledged philosophical debt is to Plato. As regards the proper conception of science he is more of an Aristotelian than a Platonist (R.J. Hankinson in his Introduction to *Galen on the Therapeutic Method, Books I and II*, 1991, p. xxiv).

109 The food ingested was thought to undergo further 'cooking' in the stomach by the heat of the body; the 'warmer' the person's nature the easier his or her digestion was expected to be.

110 As W.H.S. Jones remarks in his introduction to his translation of Hippocrates, the acceptance of various philosophical ideas on the part of physicians was just as opposed to the progress of scientific medicine as were beliefs in the divine origin of disease that they replaced. For a contrary opinion see Longrigg, op. cit. (n. 93 above), Introduction. There were physicians who rejected the use of philosophic systems, wanting to base their method only on experience, the Empiricists (Celsus, *De Medicina*, Proem.); these were not better, since they also lacked knowledge of anatomy and physiology.

111 Galen, *On the Therapeutic Method*, I.5.4; I.5.6, trans. R.J. Hankinson, p. 22.

112 Robert Montraville Green, *A Translation of Galen's Hygiene*, 1952, Ch. 7. As will be recalled, Celsus left ample room for occasional overindulgence in food and drink and overexertion in physical activity for the healthy.

113 Howard C. Kee, commenting on the pragmatic common-sense of Celsus in *Medicine, Miracle and Magic in New Testament Times*, 1986: 'Thus our best-preserved source for knowledge of Roman medicine in the early first century of our era fits well with the picture one gains from the historical sources of the political rulers: deferential to tradition, at least for public relations purposes, but dedicated chiefly to what produces results' (p. 41).

114 Plato, *Republic* III 406 C.

115 I.M. Lonie, 'A structural pattern in Greek dietetics and the early history of Greek medicine', *Medical History* 21, 1977, 235–60. The attribution of diseases to faulty diet empowered the physician in the ancient world, just as it does today, to shift the blame for the disease whose true cause is unknown to the sufferer who ate the wrong diet. As the true cause of a disease is discovered the attribution of it to diet disappears.

116 R. Jackson, op. cit. (n. 62 above), p. 9.

117 Glen W. Bowersock, *Greek Sophists in the Roman Empire*, 1969, pp. 69–71. It seems that public debates on medical issues were popular in Rome and other cities even in earlier times: see, for example, the rather hostile account Pliny gives of Asclepiades of Bithynia, who gained wealth and fame in Rome by his eloquent lecturing at the end of the second century BC (*Natural History* 26:12–20).

118 Musonius, 14 (see n. 85 above).

119 About Galen's fights against competitors and his consequent success in Rome, see some of his own treatises: *On Venesection* (Kühn, op. cit., vol. XI, pp. 147–249); *Prognosis to Epigenes* (Kühn, vol. XIV, pp. 599–673); see also W.D. Smith, op. cit. (n. 107 above), pp. 77–83. Bowersock, op. cit. (n. 117 above), pp. 89–100, gives a general description of public professional quarrels in Galen's time.

120 Galen wrote his treatise *On Hygiene* expressly for those who do not have to work!

121 Dio Chrysostom, *Third Discourse*, 124–7 LCL.

122 L.R. Lind, 'The tradition of Roman moral conservatism', in C. Deroux (ed.), *Studies in Latin Literature and Roman History* I, Collection Latomus 164, 1979, pp. 7–57.

123 Thomas N. Habinek, 'An aristocracy of virtue: Seneca on the beginnings of wisdom', *Yale Classical Studies* 29, 1992, 187–203.

124 Musonius, *Discourse* VI.

125 Ibid. XIV.

126 Ibid. XVIIIB. An alarmist attitude against sweet-tasting food seems to go back a long time before the introduction of refined sugars. One may wonder how much of present-day warnings about the dangers of sweet food are motivated by similar moral anxieties instead of rational considerations. The unequal distribution of food at Roman banquets was deplored by many: Juvenal, *Saturae* 5; Martial, *Epigrams* 3:60; 3:49; 2:43; 4:85; 6:11; Pliny the Elder, *Epistulae* 2:6. For a modern treatment of the inequality of the Roman banquet see John D'Arms, 'Control, companionship and clientela: some social functions of the Roman communal meal', *Echos du Monde Classique, Classical Views* 28 NS 3, 1984, Special Issue, 327–48.

127 A saying attributed to Socrates or to Diogenes, e.g. Aulus Gellius, *Noctes Atticae* 19:2,7; Diogenes Laertius, *Lives of Eminent Philosophers* II:34; Musonius, *Discourse* XVIIIB. What Plato said in the *Republic* 559a is often quoted, that the desire of eating to the point of health and fit condition – that is the desire for just food and a relish – is a necessary desire; it must be satisfied or one dies. See also Athenaeus, *Deipnosophistae* X 413.

128 For the error of this view, see the Introduction to this volume, p. 12.

129 Seneca, *Epistulae morales* 108:18.

130 Of all the philosophies floating around in Rome, Mommsen favoured the Cynics, for the Cynic system 'was confined to the having no system at all and sneering at all systems and all systematizers' (op. cit. (n. 16 above), vol. 5, p. 444).

131 Some Cynics had an extremely pessimistic view of mankind, which earned them the charge of misanthropy; others claimed to be physicians out to cure mankind of folly. Abraham J. Malherbe, 'Self-definition among Epicureans and Cynics', in B.F. Meyer and E.P. Sanders (eds), *Jewish and Christian Self-definition*, vol. 3, 1982, pp. 46–59.

132 Aristophanes, *The Clouds*; Juvenal, *Saturae* 2:1–28; Athenaeus, *Deipnosophistae*, Alciphron, *Letters* (parasites, 19); Lucian, *Icaromenippus*; and many others.

133 See now the interesting treatment of this in Emily Gowers, *The Loaded Table: Representations of Food in Roman Literature*, 1993.

134 Plutarch, *Moralia* 1094C; 686C–D. A disdainful attitude to dining pleasures is not a peculiar characteristic of ancient moralizers. Mommsen shows his own when he writes: 'But no sort of luxury flourished so much as the *coarsest* of all – the luxury of the table' (op. cit. (n. 16 above), vol. 5, p. 387).

135 Diogenes Laertius, *Lives of Eminent Philosophers* IX 3–6.

136 Ibid. VII 167; IX 43; Athenaeus, *Deipnosophistae* II 46.

137 Ibid. VI 234.

138 Cassius Dio, *Roman History* lviii:21.

139 Garth Fowden, 'The Platonist philosopher and his circle in late antiquity' *FILOSOFIA* 7, Yearbook of the Research Center for Greek Philosophy at the Academy of Athens, 1977.

140 John M. Dillon, 'Self-definition in later Platonism', in B.F. Meyer and E.P. Sanders (eds), *Jewish and Christian Self-definition*, vol. 3, 1982, pp. 60–75.

141 But not even this type of 'askesis' went as far as self-mortification. D.A. Dombrowski, 'Asceticism as athletic training in Plotinus', *ANRW* II.36.1, 1987, 701–12, argues convincingly for distinguishing Plotinus's ascetic practices from penitential self-mortification.

142 For example, Philostratus's 'biography' of the first century sage Apollonius of Tyana, the various lives of Pythagoras and other highly idealized biographies of philosophers.

143 Richard Sorabji, *Animal Minds and Human Morals: The Origins of the Western Debate*, 1993, p. 183. The book provides a thorough review of the various positions in the ancient debate concerning men's use and exploitation of animals. See also J. Hansleiter, *Der Vegetarismus in Antike*, 1935; Damianos Tsekourakis, 'Pythagoreanism or Platonism and ancient medicine? The reason for vegetarianism in Plutarch's Moralia', *ANRW* II.36.1, 1987, 366–93.

144 Empedocles, c. 495–c. 435 BC, emphasized kinship with animals. He believed in reincarnation even into plant forms. Meat eating he saw as people devouring each other (Sorabji, op. cit., p. 175).

145 Pythagoras was probably born after 530 BC. There is no contemporary documentary evidence about him, but many later attempts to reinvent

him. According to some tradition he organized a communal daily life for his followers, based on equal sharing of resources, favoured equality of the sexes, diapproved of homosexuality and extramarital intercourse, but encouraged marriage and sex within marriage; believed in reincarnation and opposed animal sacrifice and eating of flesh. There is no unanimous agreement, however, in the sources about his vegetarianism. Some tradition ascribes to him the development of diet for athletes (Sorabji, op. cit. p. 172–4; W. Burkert, 'Craft versus sect: the problem of Orphics and Pythagoreans', in B.F. Meyer and E.P. Sanders (eds), *Jewish and Christian Self-definition*, vol. 3, 1982, pp. 1–22).

146 Tsekourakis, op. cit. (n. 143 above).

147 In Plutarch, *De esu carn.*; *De sanit. tuend.*

148 Porphyry writes that most of the common folk eat meat because they believe that it is healthy, so do the physicians, who even use meat to treat disease. Most of the philosophers belonging to the Peripathetic, Epicurean and Stoic persuasions also eat meat (*De Abstinentia* 1:1–27).

149 Ibid. 1:27.

CHAPTER 3

1 Helmut Koester, in his article 'Writings and the spirit: authority and politics in ancient Christianity', *HThR* 84, 1991, 353–72, follows the developing importance of written documents in early Christianity and shows how letters that in their origin were political instruments, written in the secular and administrative genre of epistolary literature, by the end of the second or beginning of the third century became regarded as inspired bearers of religious truths and the infallible source for religious doctrine. As a result of this process, as Peter Brown acknowledges, 'Paul left a fatal legacy to future ages', which shaped Christian attitudes to sexuality (*The Body and Society: Men, Women, and Sexual Renunciation in Early Christianity*, 1988, p. 55). As will be seen in the following chapters, later Christian writers often quoted and misquoted Paul not only in respect of sexuality but also in order to further their own arguments for ascetic food abstentions.

2 The only exception to this is 1 Corinthians 7:5, which in the King James version, for example, says: 'defraud ye not one the other except it be with consent for a time that ye may give yourselves to fasting and prayer and come together again', or, in another version: 'Do not deprive one another except perhaps by agreement for a set time, to devote yourselves to prayer, and then come together again, so that Satan may not tempt you because of your lack of self-control' (*NRSV*).

Both the *Greek New Testament* (eds K. Aland, M. Black, C.M. Martini, B.M. Metzger and A. Wikgren 1990) and *NRSV The New Oxford Annotated Bible* (eds B.M. Metzger and R.E. Murphy 1991) use the second version of the text above without 'fasting'. The editors of the *Greek New Testament* indicate in the apparatus criticus their virtual certainty that 'fasting' is an interpolation from later insecure sources. A similar insertion of the word 'fasting' occurs in Mark 9:29, where it is equally relegated to a footnote by the editors of both the Greek and English texts. However, the existence of these variant versions seems to indicate that Christian writers or copiers from the fourth and fifth centuries on tended to make a strong mental link between prayer and fasting.

3 The dating of the various components of the New Testament is extremely problematic. The Gospel of Mark is thought to have been compiled around the time of the destruction of Jerusalem, A D 70; the Gospel of Matthew around A D 80–100; dates ranging from the end of the decade of the 60s to 135 have been suggested for the Gospel of Luke, and 90–100 for that of John. The letters of Paul, if genuine, must have originated in the period between 50 and the early 60s. For a survey of scholarly opinion concerning the dating of the components of the New Testament, see Werner Georg Kümmel, *Introduction to the New Testament*, revised edn, trans. H.C. Kee, 1975.

4 John Coolidge Hurd, Jr., *The Origin of 1 Corinthians*, 1965, Introduction, p. xv.

5 2 Corinthians 10:10.

6 In recent studies concerned with the occasion and motivation of Paul's letters, much more ink has been spilled on external factors, like the situation in which some of the communities addressed by Paul found themselves, than on any attempt to look at the writer and his personal motives (J.C. Hurd, op. cit. (n. 4 above)). This would be quite a surprising state of affairs if one was dealing with a secular letter writer! Add to this the fact that outside of Paul's letters there is no shred of evidence about his communities, while we do have a pack of his letters, giving his views, feelings and reactions. Almost all studies of Paul are products of theological interest, and this, focusing on the message, tends to disregard the nature of the 'chosen vessel'.

7 Geza Vermes, *Jesus and the World of Judaism*, 1983, p. 54.

8 Very little is known about the collection, editing or transmission of the Epistles. Marcion (c. A D 140) knew them. The writer known as Clement of Rome (c. 100) knew Romans and 1 Corinthians, and Ignatius of Antioch (c. 107) mentions a collection of Pauline letters (2 Ephesians). Similarly, the Second Epistle of Peter, which scholarly consensus today dates to the second century, writes about a collection of Paul's letters as if they were already regarded as equal to the 'other scriptures' (3:15–17); and Polycarp (d. 155) mentions Paul and his letters in his *Epistle to the Philippians* (3:2).

9 For a discussion of the Acts of the Apostles as history see below, Chapter 4. It has often been pointed out that the dating and suggested sequence of Paul's letters on the basis of information provided in Acts is unsound (J.C. Hurd, op. cit. (n. 4 above), p. 42). For an opposing view to the one expressed here, see Thomas H. Campbell, 'Paul's missionary journeys as reflected in his letters', *JBL* 74, 1955, 80–7, where it is argued that the sequence of Paul's activities that can be inferred from his own letters is remarkably compatible with the information in Acts. However, even among scholars who believe that Acts contains important and reliable historical details, there is increasing recognition of its overarching

theological aim, and that in the service of this aim the writer may have shaded Paul's reactions, character and even his biography, in order to bring him and the other apostles closer and to offer a picture of basic unity among the early Christians. Helmut Koester (*History and Literature of Early Christianity*, 1982, ch. 9) advises caution in the acceptance of most of the details of Paul's biography provided by Acts – including his purported Roman citizenship. H.C. Kee points out that Paul's conciliatory image as drawn by Acts 'does not fit well with evidence of disagreement among the first generation of Christians that is apparent in Paul's letters and other first generation Christian writings' ('After the crucifixion – Christianity through Paul', in H. Shanks (ed.), *Christianity and Rabbinic Judaism*, 1993, p. 83). Most of the discussion in the present chapter, therefore, will focus on the Paul of the Epistles.

10 The best recent example of the large number of scholarly efforts to try to force some agreement between Acts and the Epistles in order to write a biography of Paul is by Martin Hengel, *Acts and the History of Earliest Christianity*, trans. J. Bowden 1979. Another example is Robin Lane Fox, *The Unauthorized Version: Truth and Fiction in the Bible*, 1991, p. 209.

11 Compare, for example, Josephus's repeated appeal to his family background in order to authenticate his role as a writer of Jewish history (*Jewish Wars* 1–3), or as an interpreter of Judaism and Jewish Law (*Apion* 1:54; *Vita* 1–8). He gives not only his own full name but also his father's and mother's genealogies, the number of his brothers, and the name and education of his one full brother.

12 Edwin A. Judge, in 'St Paul and classical society', *JAC* 15, 1972, 19–36, an article that mostly lists the imponderables concerning Paul's place in his society, remarks that Paul 'has been too much at home in modern times for us to appreciate how acute his alienation from his own may have been'.

13 Saul of Tarsus, his supposed Jewish name and birthplace, comes from Acts; Paul himself mentions neither. The city which, according to his own letters, appears to be his residence, or at least an important location for his activities before his missionary journeys, is Damascus.

14 Romans 11:1; Philippians 3:5.

15 In opposition to Kee, op. cit. (n. 9 above) p. 97, I do not believe that 'a Hebrew born of Hebrews' in its context (Philippians 3:5) would necessarily mean that he was raised in a Hebrew-speaking family; it is perfectly compatible with his being from a Jewish family of a Greek city. As Koester (*History and Literature*, p. 97) points out, 'it is (also) evident from his letters that Paul was a Hellenistic Jew who grew up in an environment in which Greek was the everyday language'.

16 Romans 7:9. This passage has caused a number of exegetical problems. See for example Ernst Käsemann's *Commentary on Romans*, trans. G.W. Bromiley, 1980, where he argues that the use of the first person singular pronoun in the whole of chapter 7 does not mean that Paul is referring to his own experiences but to that of the human race. Since Paul claims that he was 'circumcised on the eighth day, of the people of Israel, of the

tribe of Benjamin, a Hebrew born of Hebrews' (Philippians 3:5), how could he have ever been 'alive apart from the Law'? It is quite conceivable however, indeed it is a matter of common sense, that some circumcised Jews, even those born in Jerusalem, would live lives in the Graeco-Roman Diaspora that would be considered 'apart from the Law'. Take, for example, Martial's friends in Rome, Menophilus, the Jewish actor, who tried to hide the sign of his Jewishness under an enormous penis brace (*Epigrams* VII.82), and the Jewish poet, born in Jerusalem, who seems to have competed with Martial in more fields than just poetry (*Epigrams* XI.94), and others, all indicating that there may have been many Jewish families living in the Diaspora which, outside of circumcision, adhered very loosely to the Law. Thus in this case we should accept what Paul actually says as autobiographical.

17 Adolescent search for the 'good life' and conversion to philosophic or religious life is not a modern phenomenon, but is frequently described in ancient literature too. Josephus in his autobiography describes his adolescent search for the right doctrine; from the age of sixteen he submitted himself to 'hard training and laborious exercises' of each one of the three dominant 'sects', in succession, after which he spent three years in the wilderness with a hermit. At the age of nineteen he returned to the city and settled to a life of the Pharisees (*Vita*, 2:7–12: as a simple reckoning would suggest, he may have learned a lot of philosophy but not much arithmetic!). Philosophers of all schools exhorted their listeners to convert to the philosophic life (Seneca, *Epistulae morales* 53). The followers of wandering philosophers bent on changing their way of life are familiar figures in pagan literature; see the caricatures that Lucian draws of them in works like *Philosophies for Sale* and others.

18 Galatians 1:14.

19 Romans 7:15–21.

20 Ibid., 7:7.

21 Ibid., 7:22–5.

22 Ibid., 7:8.

23 Galatians 2:20.

24 See Chapter 1 of this volume, p. 20.

25 E.P. Sanders, *Paul and Palestinian Judaism: A Comparison of Patterns of Religion*, 1977, pp. 547–8.

26 Few scholars face this fact as squarely as G.E.M. de Ste Croix, who writes in *The Class Struggle in the Ancient Greek World*, 1981, p. 104, 'the most powerful influence exerted upon early Christianity toward disparaging sex and even marriage was the seventh chapter of St Paul's First Epistle to the Corinthians. . . . Indeed Paul suffered from an aversion to sex as such'.

27 Elaine Pagels, for example, argues with the observation of a non-theological commentator's view: 'George Bernard Shaw was wrong when he accused Paul of inventing religious celibacy, which Shaw called "this monstrous imposition upon Jesus"; and Shaw was also wrong to attribute Paul's celibacy to his "terror of sex and terror of life". For Jesus and Paul, as for the Essenes, such drastic measures were not a reflection of sexual revulsion but a necessity to prepare for the end of the world,

and to free oneself for the "age to come"' (*Adam, Eve, and the Serpent*, 1988, p. 17). This, however, begs a number of questions, such as: on what basis may one assume that the celibacy of Jesus – if he was indeed celibate – or that of the Essenes was based on the kind of attitude toward the flesh that Paul's letters express; and, the more fundamental psychological question, if not 'terror of sex and terror of life' then what made him want to see the end of this world?

28 Hans Conzelmann, *I Corinthians: A Commentary on the First Epistle to the Corinthians*, trans. J.W. Leitch, 1975 p. 95.

29 As was pointed out by G.E.M. de Ste Croix in a riveting seminar given in Oxford in 1992.

30 Käsemann, *Commentary on Romans*, pp. 193–200.

31 Rudolph Bultmann, *Theology of the New Testament*, trans. Kendrick Grobel, 2 vols, 1959, vol. 1, p. 188.

32 In addition to the question of his views on sex and marriage the debate ranges over such problems as whether he was for or against the equality of women, was he for or against slavery, was he a liberator or an advocate of 'love-patriarchy' (a strange term coined by Gerd Thiessen, *The Social Setting of Pauline Christianity: Essays on Corinth*, ed. and trans. J.H. Schütz, 1982).

33 Sanders, *Paul and Palestinian Judaism*, p. 523.

34 Ibid., p. 522.

35 Vermes, op. cit. (n. 7 above), p. 56.

36 Sanders, *Paul and Palestinian Judaism*, p. 441–7; Conzelmann, op. cit. (n. 28 above), Introduction, p. 9.

37 Romans 1:24–8; 7:7–14, 15–25; 1 Corinthians 6:9,12; Galatians 5:19, etc.

38 1 Corinthians 6:15.

39 Ibid., 10:16–23.

40 Not only is there contradiction with respect to Paul's attitudes to Judaism between his epistles and the picture painted by Acts, a picture long suspected to be the invention of 'Luke' the writer, but also, as J. Ziesler points out, Paul's own statements about the Law 'are problematic and difficult to reconcile with one another.... we may be forgiven for suspecting that Paul had not managed to sort the whole matter out for himself'. Nevertheless he sees Paul as rejecting the Torah 'both as a means of salvation, and also as the definitive guide to life under God' (*Paul's Letter to the Romans*, 1989, p. 50). U. Wilkens in a similar vein asserts that there is in Romans a conception of the Law as curse from which the crucified Christ gives redemption (*Die Brief an die Römer*, 1978–82, vol. 2, pp. 84, 86, 121–3). E.P. Sanders argues that Paul's rejection of the Law was not only a theological view but that it was bound up with his conviction on which he staked his life and career, namely, that he was apostle to the Gentiles. 'The salvation of the Gentiles is essential to Paul's preaching; and with it falls the Law; for as Paul says simply, Gentiles cannot live by the Law (Galatians 2:14)... It is the Gentile question and the exclusivism of Paul's soteriology which dethrone the Law, not a misunderstanding of it or a view predetermined by his background' (*Paul and Palestinian Judaism*, p. 497).

41 Ibid., pp. 447–500.
42 See the Introduction to this volume, p. 8.
43 Sanders, *Paul and Palestinian Judaism*, pp. 17–18.
44 See Chapter 1 of this volume, pp. 14–15.
45 H. Koester, op. cit. (n. 1 above), p. 357. Conzelman, along similar lines but emphasizing less the political nature of the letters, sees Paul as practising 'applied theology' (op. cit. (n. 28 above), p. 8).
46 That there is no scholarly consensus concerning these is shown by the short survey of views concerning Paul's opponents provided by J.L. Sumney: 'W. Schmithals finds Gnostics in most of Paul's letters, while F.C. Baur finds Judaizers in the same letters. In the case of *Galatians*, some interpreters – including Baur, Lightfoot, and Burton – find Judaizers, while Ropes detects antinomian Pneumatics and Schmithals sees Gnostics. As for *II Cor.* Gunther catalogues no fewer than thirteen different proposals for the identity of the opponents, while E.P. Sanders states that he had found fourteen different hypotheses about them. Again, Gunther cites no fewer than eighteen different proposals for the identity of the opponents in view in *Philippians* 3' (*Identifying Paul's Opponents: The Question of Method in 2 Corinthians*, 1990, p. 9).
47 Romans 14:17.
48 Ibid., 14:17–23.
49 Ibid., 12:13.
50 Ziesler, op. cit. (n. 40 above), p. 351.
51 1 Corinthians 8:8–10; 10:23–32.
52 It is to be noted that in all the discussions of food in this epistle or in any of the others there is no mention of the 'Apostolic decree' (Acts 15:19–20, 29; 21:25). Paul may have ignored it purposely or may have been unaware of it. Conzelmann suggests that neither Paul nor the community of Corinth had any knowledge of it (op. cit., pp.137–8). The fact that he also passes over it in silence in Romans may be a further element that casts doubts on the historical veracity of Acts.
53 1 Corinthians 10:1–22.
54 Ibid. 11:20–9.
55 Kümmel, op. cit. (n. 3 above), p. 272. This seems to be the simplest explanation of the passage. Many more complicated explanations are suggested depending upon each interpreter's own picture of the nature of the Corinthian community. Those who see them as Gnostics believe that they despised any sacrament; those who vote for them being 'pneumatic enthusiasts' believe that they each celebrate their own sacrament instead of a communion. Conzelmann, op. cit. (n. 28 above), pp. 195–201, reviews the various positions, as well as the discussion concerning the shape of the Eucharist in Paul's time. Whether the community meal in the early church before Paul was a continuation of the table fellowship of Jesus with his disciples or a commemoration of the Last Supper cannot be decided, since the first actual reference to the Lord's Supper is this one in Paul's letter.
56 Ephesians and Colossians are thought to have been written by some collaborator or disciple of Paul. The authorship of Colossians is still debated both on linguistic and theological grounds. A good review of

the problem is in Kümmel, op. cit. (n. 3 above), p. 340–6: after weighing the arguments on both sides he accepts Paul's authorship. The so-called Pastoral epistles, 1 and 2 Timothy and Titus, however, are regarded by the majority of scholars as the product of a later generation for they reflect new organizational patterns developing in the churches. With respect to attitudes expressed to food, eating and fasting, the deutero-Pauline letters and the Pastorals keep close to those of the Pauline epistles. Some writers, however, believe all of the letters to be of Paul or his close companions, claiming that the institutional developments go back to the first generation of the apostles (Kee, op. cit. (n. 9 above), pp. 115–16).

57 Colossians 2:16–17, 20–3; 1 Timothy 4:1–5.

58 In addition to the intriguing but hitherto unresolved problem of composition of the Roman Christian community, and the equally elusive question of who its founder was, there is also the puzzle of the 'weak' who eat 'only vegetables'. Suggestions put forward include Christians worried about meat sacrificed to idols, poor Gentile Christians who only ever saw meat in a cultic context and so turned vegetarians to avoid pagan cultic associations (Ziesler, op. cit., p. 327). Käsemann rules out Jewish orthodoxy, since, he says, general abstinence from meat and wine did not prevail among the Jews, not even among the Essenes, who could not dispense with wine on sabbaths at least, and whose members who worked agriculturally 'could hardly do without meat'. After discarding sectarian Jews this way as the possible 'weak' ones, he finally decided that 'the ironical exaggeration which has the weak eating only vegetables shows that it is not a matter of meat offered to idols, it is a matter of fundamental vegetarianism, with which abstinence relative to wine appears to be linked in verse 21' (Romans, p. 367).

59 For an additional list of the various attempts to discover the nature of Paul's Roman opponents see Kümmel, op. cit. (n. 3 above), pp. 313–14. Kümmel finds these attempts unconvincing and believes that the letter's importance lies in setting forth the Pauline message in the ongoing debate with Jewish teaching.

60 Koester, op. cit. (n. 1 above), p. 364.

61 For example, Philo, *Vita Mosis* 2:4:23–5; Josephus, *Apion* 2:281; *Jewish War*, 7:45; Louis H. Feldman, 'Palestinian and Diaspora Judaism in the first century', in H. Shanks (ed.), *Christianity and Rabbinic Judaism: A Parallel History of their Origins and Early Development*, 1993, pp. 30–6.

62 It is true that neither vegetarianism nor abstinence from wine was normal in Jewish circles (see Chapter 1 of this volume). Jews, however, most certainly would have refused un-kosher meat, meat sacrificed to idols, and often wine or oil produced by gentiles. Ziesler is possibly correct in his view that it is more likely that abstinence from meat was only on particular occasions, as when a group of Christians met for a meal and some of them were uncertain about the provenance of the meat provided by the host. He further speculates that Christians who had scruples about eating meat sacrificed to idols may have been, in practice, vegetarians (op. cit. (n. 40 above), p. 328). This is predicated

on the widely shared but questionable notion that all meat in antiquity was sacrificial meat. There is considerable evidence against this view. Varro, *Res Rusticae* II.5:11 indicates that in Rome livestock was sold either for sacrifice or for the meat markets and the procedure for the sale in each case was different. See also the very relevant article of Justin J. Meggitt, 'Meat consumption and social conflict in Corinth', *JThS*, NS 45, 1994, 137–41; and Chapter 2 of this volume, on ancient vegetarianism, pp. 58–9.

63 A.J. Malherbe, *Paul and the Thessalonians: The Philosophic Tradition of Pastoral Care*, 1987.

64 Ibid., p. 47.

65 A.D. Nock, 'The historical importance of cult associations', *Classical Review* 38, 1924, 105–9.

66 Ziesler, op. cit. (n. 40 above), p. 334.

67 1 Corinthians 6:13.

68 In marked contrast to many guardians of public decency, philosophers and orators of the Graeco-Roman world who, as we have seen (Chapter 2 of this volume, pp. 55–6), were unanimous in warning against the dangers of gluttony.

69 See Chapter 1 of this volume, pp. 30–1.

70 Philo, *Op.* 156; *Det.* 101–3, 135–7, 156–9; *Spec. Leg.* 32:193; *Cont.* 9:74 and countless other places.

71 Against H.C. Kee and others who refer to Paul's moral norms as a blend of Jewish tradition and Hellenistic stoic philosophy (Kee, op. cit. (n. 9 above), p.123). The attempt to see Paul as a Stoic philosopher goes back to antiquity. There existed even a spurious correspondence between him and the Roman Stoic, Seneca. It is doubtful if either man ever even heard of the other. It may be pointed out, however, that Paul's matter-of-fact acceptance of eating shows no traces of Seneca's self-conscious worrying about his appetite, e.g. *Epistulae morales* 59:13; 108:17–23; 110:18.

72 Aline Rousselle, in *Porneia: On Desire and the Body in Antiquity*, trans. Felicia Pheasant, 1988, p. 17, perhaps somewhat overstates her case for sexual anxiety on evidence from medical writing.

73 Uta Ranke-Heinemann, in *Eunuchs for the Kingdom of Heaven: the Catholic Church and Sexuality*, trans. Peter Heinegg, 1990, argues that Christianity has preserved to this day antiquity's legacy of hostility to pleasure and the body. Sexual pessimism in antiquity derived mainly from philosophical aspirations and medical caution and not as in Christianity from the curse of sin and punishment for it. She assigns the responsibility for later Christian attitudes to sexuality to Augustine. The views on sexuality expressed in the Pauline Epistles attracted personalities with strongly negative attitudes to sex, such as Jerome and Augustine, and provided scriptural justification for their views.

CHAPTER 4

1 Hans Conzelmann, 'Luke's place in the development of early Christianity', in L. Keck and L.J. Martyn (eds), *Studies in Luke-Acts*, 1980, pp. 298–316.

2 In a review of J.C. O'Neill's book, *The Theology of Acts in its Historical Setting*, 1963, by H.F.D. Sparks, in *JThS* NS 14, 1963, 457. More recently Robin Lane Fox, *The Unauthorized Version: Truth and Fiction in the Bible*, 1991, p. 129. On the evidence for the writer of Acts being a physician see n. 69 below.

3 Ernst Haenchen, *The Acts of the Apostles: A Commentary*, trans. B. Noble and G. Shinn under the supervision of H. Anderson, revised and brought up to date by R. McL. Wilson, 1971, p. 116 (*Commentary* hence).

4 F.F. Bruce, *The Acts of the Apostles: The Greek Text and Introduction with Commentary*, 3rd edn, 1990, on the basis of the latest event alluded to in the book itself: the completion of the two years Paul spent in Rome, which he puts at AD 60–1. Another example of early dating is C.S.C. Williams, 'The date of Luke-Acts', *Expository Times* 64, 1953, 283–4, who puts the writing of Acts to AD 66–70, to before the appearance of the Third Gospel in its present form. The arguments for early dating are generally based on the absence of any account of Paul's death and the absence of any mention of, or indeed any hint of familiarity on the part of the author with, the *Pauline Epistles*.

5 Most scholars tend to agree that Luke's Gospel is earlier than Acts, and that this Gospel was composed after the destruction of Jerusalem in AD 70. J.C. O'Neill puts the composition of Acts somewhere between 115 and 130, close to the time of Justin Martyr.

6 H. Conzelmann, *Acts of the Apostles: A Commentary*, trans. J. Lindburgh, A.T. Kraabel and D.H. Juel, ed. E. Epp with C.R. Matthews, 1987, p. xxxiii, and op. cit. (n. 1 above).

7 Some scholars see an expressly anti-gnostic tendency in Luke, e.g. C.H. Talbert, *Luke and the Gnostics: An Examination of the Lucan Purpose*, 1966. Haenchen considers Luke's teaching as one of the many variants of Gentile Christian theology that grew up alongside the theology of Paul (*Commentary*, pp. 91–110).

8 'The edificatory language of the subapostolic period was familiar to the writer of *Acts* and readily employed by him. *Acts* breathes the very spirit of the age' (Haenchen, *Commentary*, p. 9).

9 The martyrdom of the men of Lugdunum (177–8) cites Acts 7:60 (Eusebius, *Ecclesiastical History* 5:2,5), Irenaeus in *Against Heresies* (c.180) found Acts useful in his struggle against gnosticism; from it he could demonstrate the unity of the apostolic message. We are here even presented with statements, eagerly repeated in years to come, about the author as 'sectator Pauli', who 'wrote into a book the gospel Paul preached' (*Against Heresies* 3:1:1; 3:10:1; 3:14:2). The tradition about Luke that Irenaeus outlined contains nothing that he could not have read out of the author's two-volume work. There is no trace of any knowledge of Luke from independent sources (Haenchen, *Commentary*,

p. 9). The *Muratorian Canon*, a document most commonly dated at the end of the second century (I.H. Marshall, *The Acts of the Apostles: An Introduction and Commentary*, 1980, p. 44), refers explicitly to Luke as the author, a physician and companion of Paul (lines 2–7; 34–9). After the late second century, the earliest subsequent mention is found in Eusebius, *Ecclesiastical History* 3:4:6 (Conzelmann, *Commentary*, p. xxxiii).

10 For a review of this debate see W.W. Gasque, *A History of the Criticism of the Acts of the Apostles*, 1975.

11 M. Hengel, *Acts and the History of Earliest Christianity*, trans. J. Bowden, 1979, p. 60.

12 M. Dibelius, *Studies in the Acts of the Apostles*, trans. H. Greeven, 1956.

13 J.C. Hurd writes that the author of Acts appears to have had incomplete knowledge of the events he recounted and, on the other hand, that he had a number of literary and theological motivations that controlled the presentation of his materials (*The Origin of 1 Corinthians*, 1965, p. 42).

14 Conzelmann, *Commentary*, p. xli.

15 Ernst Haenchen, 'The Book of Acts as source material for the history of early Christianity', in L. Keck and L.J. Martyn (eds), *Studies in Luke-Acts*, 1980, p. 278.

16 P.F. Esler, *Community and Gospel in Luke Acts*, 1987. This is a sociological analysis in which he takes the concepts of legitimation, symbolic universe, etc., as these were developed by P.L. Berger and T. Luckmann's work, *The Social Construction of Reality*, 1966.

17 Marilyn Salmon, 'Insider or outsider? Luke's relationship with Judaism', in J.B. Tyson (ed.), *Luke-Acts and the Jewish People: Eight Critical Perspectives*, 1988, pp. 76–82.

18 Philo, *Prob.* 72–91; *Hypoth.* 11:1–18; *Cont.* 1–90.

19 Josephus, *Jewish Wars* 1:3:78–80; 2:7:111–13; 2:8:119–61; 2:20:566–8. *Antiquities* 13:59:171–2; 18:15:18–22.

20 Pliny the Elder, *Natural History* 5:17:4.

21 K.H. Kuhn, 'The Lord's Supper and the communal meal at Qumran', in K. Stendahl (ed.), *The Scrolls and the New Testament*, 1958, pp. 65–93; J. van der Ploeg, 'The meals of the Essenes', *JSS* 2, 1957, pp. 163–75; E.F. Sutcliffe, 'Sacred meals at Qumran?', *Heythrop Journal* 1, 1960, pp. 48–65.

22 J.A. Fitzmyer, 'Jewish Christianity in Acts in light of the Qumran Scrolls', in L. Keck and L.J. Martyn (eds), *Studies in Luke-Acts*, 1980, pp. 233–57.

23 Conzelmann, *Commentary* (n. 6 above) and Haenchen, *Commentary* (n. 3 above); K. Lake and H.J. Cadbury, *The Acts of the Apostles*, English translation and commentary in F.J. Foakes-Jackson and K. Lake (eds), *The Beginnings of Christianity*, 1933, p. 28.

24 Lake and Cadbury, op. cit., p. 28.

25 Deuteronomy 8:10.

26 1 Samuel 9:13.

27 Psalms 104:14–15.

28 Fellowship and sharing were held in high regard by Plato, *Republic* 4:424a; 5:449c; Aristotle, *Nichomachean Ethics* 8:9, 1159b 31; Cicero *De Officiis* 1:16:51.

29 Bauernfiend quoted in Haenchen's *Commentary* (n. 3 above). Haenchen himself strongly disagrees with him, and sees no traces of the *'disciplina arcana'* in this passage, which, he thinks, depicts communal meals (p. 94). J. Jeremias, *The Eucharistic Words of Jesus*, trans. A. Erhardt, 3rd edn, 1966, pp. 118–21, is among those who see in this a specifically Christian Eucharist. He writes, 'The constantly repeated assertion that "breaking the bread" is an expression used in Jewish sources meaning "to have a meal" is an error that it seems to be impossible to eradicate' (ibid., n. 1, p. 120). See also J. Jeremias, *Jerusalem in the Time of Jesus: An Investigation into Economic and Social Conditions During the New Testament Period*, trans. F.H. and C.H. Cave, 1969: breaking of bread, he asserts here, is the *'disciplina arcana'* (n. 21). A kind of compromise is struck by the *Commentary* of F.F. Bruce, op. cit. (n. 4 above), who points out that the Hebrew *paras* and Aramaic *peras* ('break') were used absolutely in the special sense of breaking bread at the beginning of a meal and saying grace while doing so. In this passage, however, the Lord's supper is probably intended: while this was celebrated in the course of a fellowship meal, the emphasis on the act of breaking the bread suggests that this circumstance, wholly trivial in itself, was the significant element of the celebration. But it could only be significant when it was a *'signum'* of Christ's being broken in death.

30 1 Corinthians 11:23–7.

31 J. Jeremias, *Eucharistic Words*, 1966; Philip H. Menoud, 'The Acts of the Apostles and the Eucharist', in *Jesus Christ and the Faith, a Collection of Studies by P. Menoud*, trans. Eunice M. Paul, 1978, pp. 84–106; Bo Reicke, 'Die Mahlzeit mit Paulus auf den Wellen des Mittelmeers Act. 27,33–38', *ThZ* 4, 1948, 401–10, and others.

32 Another miraculous escape from prison, a literary genre of which there are at least three examples in Acts. Many scholars (starting with Celsus, *apud* Origen, *Contra Celsum* 2:34) have remarked on the similarity of these to Greek literary convention, as expressed, for example, in the *Bacchae* of Euripides (see a discussion of this with an attempt to distinguish between Christian 'religion' and pagan 'magic', in Lake and Cadbury, op. cit. (n. 23 above), vol. 4, pp. 196–7).

33 Conzelmann, arguing against Menoud (*Commentary*, p. 133).

34 Marshall, *Commentary* (n. 9 above), pp. 326–7. Lake and Cadbury cannot settle the question whether in v. 7 the breaking of bread means 'having supper' or of celebrating the Eucharist. 'The former seems the more probable, but there is no real evidence to enable the question to be settled', they conclude (pp. 255–6).

35 Haenchen, *Commentary* (n. 3 above). In his discussion of this voyage and the shipwreck, Haenchen shows convincingly that if things progressed as Luke claims, then instead of being the rescuer, Paul would have been responsible for the shipwreck! See also his article in *Studies in Luke-Acts* (n. 1 above), p. 277.

36 See Chapters 1 and 2 of this volume.

37 M.H. Williams, 'The Jews and Godfearers Inscription from Aphrodi-
    sias: a case of patriarchal interference in early 3rd century Caria?',
    Historia 41, 1992, 297–310.

38 There have been various attempts to clarify the meaning of the term
    'Hellenist' as it is used here (see Lake and Cadbury, op. cit. (n. 23 above),
    p. 64; Bruce, op. cit. (n. 4 above)). The general consensus of scholars
    today, in agreement with John Chrysostom (*Hom.* 14 on Acts 6:1), is
    that these were Greek-speaking Jews. This much is agreed, since the
    point where they appear in the narrative sequence is before the
    conversion of the first pagan. They are indeed the Jews who will lead
    to the spreading of the mission out of Jerusalem and eventually to the
    Gentiles. There are some fancy speculations about the differences in
    political outlook between Hellenists and Hebrews. O. Cullmann, for
    example, regards them as Jews of 'syncretistic tendency' forming a
    bridge between Qumran and the primitive church (cf. J. Daniélou, *Les
    Manuscrits de la Mer Mort et les origines du Christianisme*, 1957, p. 61).
    Conzelmann (*Commentary* (n. 6 above), p. 45) makes inferences about
    their conduct on the basis that they were the first to be attacked. 'They
    must have come into conflict with observance of the law in Judaism,
    that is, they may have continued Jesus's line more clearly than the
    Twelve did.'

39 A skilful literary allusion to Exodus 22:21–4?

40 See Chapter 1 of this volume, p. 19, n. 38.

41 Mishnah, *Peah* 7:7. A slightly different system is described by Jeremias,
    Jerusalem in the Time of Jesus (n. 29 above), pp. 131–3.

42 Haenchen, *Commentary* (n. 3 above).

43 Conzelmann, *Commentary*, p. 44. Haenchen also detects in this narrative
    much more than meets the eye. He points out that the writer of Acts,
    intending to blunt the contrast between the factions, presents a story
    full of contradictions. Hellenists and Hebrews must have had mutual
    grievances, which must have led to the short-changing of the widows.
    The split between the two groups, he thinks, may represent 'the first
    confessional schism in church history' (his article in *Studies in Luke-Acts*
    (note 15 above), pp. 263–4).

44 Mishnah, *Peah* 7:7; see also Jeremias, *Jerusalem in the Time of Jesus*, pp.
    131–3.

45 Daniel 6:10; the same is expressed in Psalms 55:16–17.

46 E.P. Sanders, *Jewish Law from Jesus to the Mishnah: Five Studies*, 1990, pp.
    74–5.

47 During the years of the administration of Agrippa I there were no
    Roman troops stationed in the city. There is evidence for a '*cohors II
    Italica civium Romanorum . . . exercitus Syriaci*' from the time of about AD
    69 on into the second century; Conzelmann, *Commentary* (n. 6 above), p.
    81, Haenchen, *Commentary* (n. 3 above), p. 346, Marshall, *Commentary*
    (n. 9 above), tried to get around the problem by placing the Cornelius
    incident before AD 41.

48 Cf. Acts 10:28.

49 Ibid.

50 Menachem Stern, *Greek and Latin Authors on Jews and Judaism*, 3 vols, 1974–84, has quite a collection of other, similar accusations. Pagan writers' criticism of the Jews centred around the exclusivity of their food customs, the barbarousness of circumcision and their idleness on the Sabbath. But as E.P. Sanders points out, such statements were generally not calm, unbiased social observation, but aspects of exaggerated or completely fabricated charges that were often on a level with the later accusation that Christians were cannibals (*Jewish Law*, p. 282).
51 Ibid.
52 Judith 10:5.
53 Daniel 1:12. Sanders, *Jewish Law*, p. 282.
54 About the only assertion that can be made concerning the audience for which it was written is that its diet included a substantial amount of meat. For if they had lived almost exclusively on a vegetarian diet and had a very negligible meat intake, sharing food would not have been such a problem, and the question of acceptable or unacceptable animal meat would have been of much less relevance. Looking at it another way, the making of all kinds of animal meat 'kosher', that is, clean for food, would indicate that the mission to the Gentiles was aimed at a social layer that could afford meat and did eat meat habitually.
55 Esler, op. cit. (n. 16 above), p. 99. He even goes so far to assert that table fellowship between Jews and Gentiles threatened the whole of Jewish 'ethnic identity' (p. 103); 'from the Jewish point of view, Jews ate with Gentiles only at a price of denying their ethnos and their faith' (p. 105).
56 A similar conclusion is reached from a different angle, both about the substantial incompatibility between the Paul of the Epistles and the Lucan Paul, and about the absence of Jews among those for whom Acts was written, in Michael J. Cook, 'The mission to the Jews in Acts: unraveling Luke's "Myth of the 'Myriads' " ' , in J.B. Tyson (ed.), *Luke-Acts and the Jewish People: Eight Critical Perspectives*, pp. 102–23. Cook writes, 'the Lucan Paul's repeated resumption of overtures to the Jews now appears a device by which Luke can assign responsibility for the underrepresentation of Jews, in Christian ranks, to Jewish intransigence'.
57 The burden of the law from which the Gentiles living among the Israelites were to be relieved comprised first and foremost circumcision, then the many other legal prescriptions and prohibitions. The 'pollution of idols' may have included eating meat sacrificed in pagan rites. 'Fornication' referred to marriage in prohibited degrees of relationship (Leviticus 18:6–18), 'what is strangled' to animals slaughtered other than ritually (Genesis 9:4). Leviticus 3:17 forbids the eating of blood. The prohibitions are also found in Leviticus 17:10–14; 19:26; Deuteronomy 12:16; 23; 15:23.
58 Conzelmann, *Commentary* (n. 6 above), p. 119. Dibelius, op. cit. (n. 12 above), pp. 93–101 suggests that Luke had shaped the account as a whole to fit his purpose, while Conzelmann suggests that Luke may have fashioned scenes from reports about the council, and has inserted the decree into such reports for his own reasons (*Commentary*, p. 121). The speech given to Peter (15:7–11), for example, is neither Jewish nor

Pauline. Neither a Jew nor the Paul of the Epistles would call the law an intolerable yoke. As Haenchen observes (*Commentary*, p. 446), this reflects 'the law seen through Hellenistic Gentile Christian eyes, as a mass of commandments and prohibitions which no man can fulfil. Luke here is obviously speaking for himself and transmitting the views of his age and milieu'. As to verses 16–18, 'nearly every commentator concedes that the Jewish Christian James would not in Jerusalem have used a LXX text (Amos 9) differing from the Hebrew original as scriptural proof. It is not James but Luke who is speaking here'(ibid.).

59 Leviticus 1:4; 16:21; Exodus 29:19; Numbers 8:10–14; 27:18–23; Genesis 48:14; Deuteronomy 34:9.

60 Genesis 27:18.

61 See Chapters 1 and 2 of this volume.

62 Mark 2:18–22.

63 Deuteronomy 34:9.

64 Rudolph Arbesmann, 'Fasting and prophecy in Pagan and Christian antiquity', *Traditio* 7, 1949–51, 1–71. An example of this in early Christian literature is *The Shepherd of Hermas*, 2:2:1; 3:1:2; 3:10:6. This mid-second century document is believed to show strong Jewish influence (H. Koester, *History and Literature of Early Christianity*, pp. 257–61).

65 Pliny the Younger, *Letter to Trajan* 10:96:7: 'They had met regularly before dawn on a fixed day to chant verses alternately among themselves in honour of Christ as if to a god and also to bind themselves by oath.... After this ceremony it had been their custom to disperse and reassemble later to take food of an ordinary, harmless kind.'

66 Marshall, *Commentary*, p. 170; similarly Haenchen in his *Commentary*, p. 446: 'the three day fast – best understood as a penance – demonstrates his inward transformation'.

67 *Didache* 7:4; Justin Martyr, *Apology*, 1:61; Tertullian, *De Baptismo*, 20.

68 Lake and Cadbury, op. cit. (n. 23), p. 102.

69 The two episodes, the storm on the sea and the reviving of the boy Eutyches, raise serious objections against the claim that 'Luke' was a physician. It has been shown conclusively that the author does not use more specifically medical language than what could be expected from a Hellenistic non-medical writer; H.J. Cadbury, *The Style and Literary Method of Luke*, Harvard Theological Studies 6, 1919–20. When he uses medical terms, he tends to misuse them (cf. 9:18) (Lake and Cadbury, p. 104). The narrative itself throws strong doubts on the author's medical knowledge. No doctor in his right mind would report Paul leaning on and embracing someone who had just fallen out of a high window, for he would know that this procedure would endanger the person's life by impaling him on his own broken bones. And no physician would believe that people could survive on a stormy sea for fourteen days without eating anything, let alone work, as the ship's crew must have worked.

CHAPTER 5

1 Henry Chadwick, *The Early Church*, 1967, p. 94. R.B. Tollington's two-volume massive work, *Clement of Alexandria: A Study in Christian Liberalism*, 1914, is the most extensive attempt to fill the gaps and provide a biography for Clement, including family background and early education in Athens. Tollington even imagines his initiation, first into the 'lesser mysteries by the banks of the Illyus', after which, having completed two years' discipline, 'he would carry his lighted torch along the sacred way to Eleusis' (p. 9). In his *Protrepticus*, Clement attacks the 'immorality' of the mysteries, but this no more provides sure testimony of firsthand experience than the accusation of Thyestian feasts levelled against Christians provides proof of eyewitness reporting on the part of pagans.

2 Eusebius, *Ecclesiastical History* 5:10–11; 6:6,13,14.

3 Epiphanius, *Panarion* 32:6.

4 Cassius Dio, *Roman History* lxvii:14. Asebeia means impiety, which in ancient Rome could cover a multitude of behaviours, all having in common a disrespect for rules of moral conduct that were assumed to have been handed down by the ancestors, the *'mos maiorum'*. With the rise of Christianity the word gradually acquired a distinctly religion-related meaning. Suetonius, *Domitian*, 15, mentions Domitilla as the wife of Clemens, with no suggestion as to either of them being Christian.

5 Eusebius, *Ecclesiastical History*, 3:18, claims Flavia Domitilla to have been the niece of Flavius Clemens, banished for her Christianity; Tollington, op. cit. pp. 1–2, and John Ferguson, *Clement of Alexandria*, 1974, p. 13, follow Eusebius.

6 *Paidagogos* 1:1; 2:8.

7 *Stromateis* 1:11; 2:8.

8 Bishop Melito of Sardis died *c.* 190. He wrote an *Apology*, and a work on baptism.

9 Bardesanes, or Bardaisan of Edessa (AD 154–222) was a docetist who denied the resurrection of the body.

10 Tatian was the founder of the Encratites, and the writer of the *Diatessaron*, and a defence of Christianity and attack on Greek culture.

11 Elizabeth A. Clark, *Clement's Use of Aristotle: The Aristotelian Contribution to Clement of Alexandria's Refutation of Gnosticism*, 1977, p. 89; Peter Brown, *The Body and Society: Men, Women, and Sexual Renunciation in Early Christianity*, 1988, p. 122.

12 Eusebius, *Ecclesiastical History*, 5:10.

13 Modern scholars frequently question the nature of this institution in Clement's time: for example, Gustave Bardy, 'Aux origines de l'école d'Alexandrie', *Recherches de Science Religieuse* 27, 1937, 87–8; H.I. Marrou, *A History of Education in Antiquity*, English trans. 1956, p. 372. Both writers argue that the Alexandrian catechetical school became official only in the time of Origen and that there is no evidence of church control or succession of teachers before him. We do not know who Origen's predecessor was, if he had any.

14 On the Severan persecution see T.D. Barnes, 'Legislation against the Christians', *JRS* 58, 1968, 32–50, at pp. 40–1.
15 Ibid. p. 41.
16 *Ecclesiastical History*, 6:14. Eusebius himself claimed to be a student of a student of Origen. Scholarly genealogies were popular among pagan sophists, e.g. Eunapius, *The Lives of the Philosophers and Sophists*.
17 Tollington writes that Clement received the priesthood sometime during his stay in Alexandria (op. cit. (n. 1 above), p. 20). John Ferguson asserts that it was bishop Julian of Alexandria who ordained Clement (op. cit. (n. 5 above), p. 15). P. Brown goes a step further and asserts 'Clement became a priest. In 202–203 he left Alexandria to serve the bishop of Jerusalem' (op. cit. (n. 11 above), p. 136). Hugo Koch argued that Clement remained a layman throughout his life ('War Klemens von Alexandrien Priester?', *Zeitschrift fur Neutestamentliche Wissenschaft* 20, 1921, 43–8, cited by Elizabeth A. Clark, op. cit. (n. 11 above), p. 90). Henry Chadwick in *Early Christian Thought and the Classical Tradition: Studies in Justin, Clement, and Origen*, 1966, pp. 64–5, and in *The Early Church*, 1967, p. 99, accepts the view that Clement was a layman, an independent teacher of 'the Christian philosophy', instructing pupils in grammar, rhetoric and etiquette, as well as in specifically religious matters. For his teaching grammar and rhetoric there is no evidence; his work the *Paidagogos* may serve as evidence for his teaching of etiquette.
18 *Ecclesiastical History*, 6:13.
19 τὶς ὁ σῳζόμενος πλούσιος, but generally referred to by its Latin title.
20 There are some shorter works, the *Excerpta ex Theodoto* and the *Eclogae Propheticae*, which may represent other people's writings with Clement's comments, and some shorter fragments. The authenticity of some of these fragments has been questioned by modern scholars, such as E.F. Osborne, *The Philosophy of Clement of Alexandria*, 1957, p. 190.
21 Ibid., p. 4.
22 Werner Jaeger, *Early Christianity and Greek Paideia*, 1962, ch. 5. W.H.C. Frend, *Martyrdom and Persecution in the Early Church*, 1965, in Chapter 12 traces the eventual break between Eastern and Western Christianity to the differences discernible already at the end of the second century between the Carthaginian and Alexandrian 'mentality' as exemplified by Tertullian and Clement respectively.
23 Even Frend, who appears to be certain that 'the Christian community in the Egyptian metropolis was long established, comparatively wealthy, and intellectually active' (op. cit., p. 351) bases this hypothesis on Clement's own writings.
24 'There is a general though indisputable similarity of tone between his intellectual qualities and the genius of Alexandrian culture. . . . even Origen belongs more definitely to the Church and less characteristically to Alexandria' (Tollington, op. cit. (n. 1 above), p. 51).
25 Salvatore R.C. Lilla, *Clement of Alexandria: A Study in Christian Platonism and Gnosticism*, 1971, shows convincingly Clement's close dependence on Philo and on the so-called Middle Platonists (Albinus, Apuleius, Plutarch, etc.), with respect to his views concerning the

origin and value of Greek philosophy and also with respect to his ethics and theology. The very close correspondence between Clement and Philo is seen in their insistence on the compatibility of Greek philosophy and the Old Testament. Plato learned his philosophy from Moses. The mixture of Platonic, Aristotelian and Stoic elements that characterizes Clement's ethics, as Lilla argues, was not produced by Clement himself, but was taken over by him from Philo. A more limited view of Clement's indebtedness to Philo is held by H. Chadwick (*Early Christian Thought* (n. 17 above), pp. 40–2, see especially the long note 65 on pp. 141–2).

26 Osborn, op. cit. (n. 20 above), p. 171.

27 Henry Bettenson, *The Early Christian Fathers*, 1969, p. 17.

28 Walter Bauer, *Rechtglaubigkeit und Ketzerei im altesten Christentum*, 2nd edn, 1964, pp. 49–64; R.M. Grant, 'The New Testament Canon', in P.R. Ackroyd and C.F. Evans (eds), *The Cambridge History of the Bible*, vol. 1, 1970, pp. 284–308, at p. 298.

29 Frend, op. cit. (n. 22 above), p. 351.

30 Jules Lebreton, 'La Théorie de la connaissance religieuse chez Clément d'Alexandrie', *Recherches de Science Religieuse* 18, 1923, 457–88.

31 Colin H. Roberts, *Manuscript, Society and Belief in Early Christian Egypt*, 1979, pp. 71–2.

32 Brown, op. cit. (n. 11 above), ch. 6; Clark, op. cit. (n. 11 above); Chadwick, *The Early Church* (n. 1 above), ch. 6, and *Early Christian Thought*, (n. 17 above), ch. 2.

33 In its more specific meaning, Gnosticism denotes a dualistic religion that regarded the world as a tragic product of a battle within the deity itself, and regarded humans as strangers to the world who, through 'gnosis', may recognize their true self and return to their rightful place (H. Koester, *History, Culture and Religion of the Hellenistic Age*, Eng. trans. 1982, paperback edn 1987, pp. 382–3). For a different view, one that regards Gnosticism not as a kind of doctrine but a distinct social group or professional school of thought, see Bentley Layton, 'Prolegomena to the study of ancient Gnosticism', in L.M. White and O.L. Yarbrough (eds), *The Social World of the First Christians: Essays in Honor of Wayne A. Meeks*, 1995, pp. 334–50.

34 Discussed in detail in Elaine Pagels, *The Gnostic Gospels*, 1974.

35 *Stromateis* 4:26.

36 Irenaeus, *Against Heresies* 24.

37 Ibid. 3.

38 Ibid. 26.

39 Ibid. 28.

40 Robert McL. Wilson calls attention to the fact that, if one may judge on the basis of Gnostic tracts found in the Nag Hammadi library, evidence for Gnostic libertinism is due almost entirely to the writings of their enemies ('Alimentary and sexual encratism in the Nag Hammadi tractates', in Ugo Bianchi (ed.), *La Tradizione dell'Encrateia*, 1982, pp. 317–39). The same is held by Bentley Layton (n. 33 above).

41 Tollington, op. cit. (n. 1 above); Chadwick, *Early Christian Thought*; W.E.G. Floyd, *Clement of Alexandria's Treatment of the Problem of Evil*,

1971; Clark, op. cit. (n. 17 above); Lilla, op. cit. (n. 25 above); Olivier Prunet, *La Morale de Clément d'Alexandrie et le Nouveau Testament*, 1966. This is far from an exhaustive, only an illustrative list of writers who attempt to place Clement's religious orientation. Among these, Tollington and Chadwick regard him as a 'Christian liberal', Lilla as a Christian Gnostic Platonist, Floyd and Clark as a true Christian, albeit not quite orthodox, but a fighter against Gnosticism, and finally Prunet claims him for orthodoxy.

42 Werner Jaeger, *Early Christianity and Greek Paideia*, p. 47.

43 'The eclectic philosophy paves the way for divine virtue' (*Stromateis* 1:7).

44 Robin Lane Fox, *Pagans and Christians*, 1986, p. 306; Ferguson, op. cit. (n. 5 above), pp. 17–20.

45 Helmut Koester, *History, Culture and Religion of the Hellenistic Age*, 1982, p. 108.

46 *Stromateis* 2:3; 6:151, and Chadwick agrees with him (*Early Christian Thought*, pp. 34–6).

47 Ibid. p. 36.

48 Osborn, op. cit., pp. 7–8; Clark, op. cit., p. 8.

49 Most modern defenders of Clement are eager to point out that his use of the term 'Gnostic' exploits its intellectual appeal without necessarily embracing its more specific meaning. In Clement's use the term 'Gnostic' meant only an educated orthodox Christian who, as Chadwick puts it, 'was not afraid of philosophy; he could use it for his purposes, to understand what he had come to believe within the church, and to refute any adulteration' (*The Early Church*, p. 97). Not all of his readers shared this view. Photius, the ninth-century Christian bibliophile, for example, wrote: 'In some passages he appears to teach quite correctly, but in others he allows himself to be carried away entirely into impious and fictitious assertions. For he holds that matter is eternal, and he seeks to derive something like a doctrine of ideas from certain passages of scripture, and he reduces the Son to the status of a creation. Moreover he drivels on about transmigration of souls and many worlds before Adam. And with reference to the origin of Eve from Adam he does not agree with the teaching of the church, but expresses his opinion in disgraceful and outrageous fashion. . . . And on and on endlessly he prattles and blasphemes' (J.H. Freese, *The Library of Photius*, 1920, p. 200).

50 Clark, op. cit., p. 93; Osborn, op. cit., pp. 5–7, summarizes the various views on this problem.

51 *Paidagogos* 1:7.

52 Philo of Alexandria, *Spec. Leg.* 2:201.

53 A fact often pointed out by students of Clement. This observation is used to good advantage by Ramsay MacMullen in his article, 'What difference did Christianity make?', *Historia* 35, 1986, 322–43.

54 T.E. Knight writes about Clement's method of work: 'in pursuit of a thought he cites passages in free association (often from memory), in a desultory progression which frequently blurs the distinction between lemma and text' (in a review of D. Dawson, *Allegorical Readers and Cultural Revision in Ancient Alexandria*, 1992, in *AJP* 115, 1994, 132–6).

55 Chadwick, *Early Christian Thought* (n. 17 above), pp. 36–7. Two massive compendia, Diogenes Laertius's survey of the lives and sayings of ancient philosophers and Athenaeus's *Deipnosophistae*, compiled in Clement's time, still survive, which may indicate the interest and popularity of this type of literary production (discussed in Chapter 2 of this volume, pp. 44, 47).

56 *Stromateis* 1:5, and repeated at 2:20 and many other places.

57 Philo, *Spec. Leg.* II, 32, and other places.

58 *Stromateis* 1:7. Eclecticism implies a conception of the other as substantively other, as Knight pointed out (op. cit., n. 54 above), while Clement's borrowing from philosophers often forces these into a Christian mould or at least into 'prefigurations' of it.

59 *Paidagogos* 2:1.

60 Plato, *Republic*, 559.

61 *Paidagogos* 2:1.

62 See Chapter 2 of this volume, pp. 44–5.

63 Diogenes Laertius, *Lives of Eminent Philosophers*, III:78–80; VII:90, 106, 107, 109.

64 *Paidagogos* 2:2. He reinforces this in *Stromateis* 7:4, 'Then by the practice of temperance men seek health; and by cramming themselves and wallowing in potations at feasts, they attract diseases'.

65 Hostility to athletes was probably as old in Greece as their adoration, see Chapter 2 of this volume, pp. 45–6, n. 74.

66 Philo, *Spec. Leg.* II.99; *Som.* II.9; see Chapter 2 of this volume, p. 46.

67 Porphyry, *De Abstinentia*, I.27; I.51; II.3.

68 *Paidagogos* 2:2.

69 Seneca, *Epistulae morales* 108:18.

70 This concern about the effects of variety in foods, voiced by guardians of public morality, must have been based on the observation that variety indeed tends to increase appetite. However, a monotonous diet, especially a meatless one, can lead to serious deficiency diseases in humans. See the discussion of the biological bases of nutrition in the Introduction, pp. 10–13.

71 Whether the Sextius or Sextus referred to by Seneca is identical with the one Origen mentions is not certain; however the opinions and sentiments expressed by the two as these are represented in these two writers are highly compatible.

72 See Chapter 2 of this volume, pp. 48–50.

73 Plato, *Timaeus*, 72.

74 The idea that the belly was the seat of sexual desire as well as of the appetite for food is thought to go back to Democritus (fragm. 235 B. Diels-Kranz; R.B. Onians, *The Origins of European Thought*, 1951, p. 88).

75 See Chapter 2 of this volume, p. 56.

76 Chadwick, *Early Christian Thought*, p. 35, detects a 'bookish flavour' in his writings with echoes of Juvenal, Seneca, Petronius and others.

77 *Paidagogos* 2:1:3–4.

78 Ibid. 2:1:3.

79 See Chapter 3 of this volume, p. 68, on Paul's 1 Corinthians.

80 *Paidagogos* 2:1:6; 2:1:7.

81 Clement even remarks that Pythagoras prefigured the church in the common dining hall he maintained; *Stromateis* 1:15.

82 Ibid. 2:9.

83 Echoing the Roman Stoic, Musonius Rufus, see Chapter 2 of this volume, p. 55, n. 127. This view was, however, very popular and repeated by many. It provides a rather flexible yardstick: when I eat a steak it is for my health, when you eat it, it is for your pleasure!

84 *Paidagogos* 2:1:5.

85 Ibid. 2:1:8; 2:1:9.

86 Ibid. 2:1:10.

87 Ibid.

88 Ibid. 2:1:12, a paraphrase of Musonius, see Chapter 2 of this volume, p. 55.

89 *Paidagogos* 2:1:13.

90 *Stromateis* 7:6. On ancient vegetarianism, see Chapter 2 of this volume, p. 58, n. 143.

91 Romans 14:21, in *Paidagogos* 2:1:11.

92 Seneca, *Epistulae morales* 108.

93 *Paidagogos* 2:1:11.

94 Seneca, *Epistulae morales* 108.

95 *Paidagogos* 2:1:15.

96 Ibid.

97 There may even have been some justification to this hostility, on realistic grounds. A tasty and well-spiced sauce could disguise warning signs that the food under the sauce is not fit for eating. It would be interesting to know how many of the wicked sauces had acquired their bad reputation from the gastric upset caused by the meat that lay beneath them.

98 A long literary tradition on this topic is collected by Athenaeus, a contemporary of Clement, in his *Deipnosophistae*.

99 A philosopher of the Academy, younger contemporary of Plato and a famous Greek sophist of the early second century AD are here called by Clement as witnesses. Their views may be just as reliably reported here as the reasons given for the Jewish refusal to eat pork!

100 *Stromateis* 7:6.

101 It appears that in Alexandria some Gnostic Christians were vegetarians for ascetic purposes; this same assertion will crop up again in the writings of another Alexandrian, Origen, as we shall see below. Origen showed less enthusiasm than Clement for vegetarianism.

102 See Chapter 8 of this volume.

103 *Paidagogos* 2:1:15.

104 Acts 10:10–15.

105 Matthew 5:11.

106 *Paidagogos* 2:1:16. Aristotle's dictum: 'useless nourishment which contributes nothing further to the natural organism and which if too much of it is consumed causes very great injury to the organism' (*Generation of Animals*), seems to underlie Clement's thinking.

107 *Paidagogos* 2:1:17.

108 Ibid. 2:1:15.

109 Ibid. 2:1:17. Since this comes associated with the discussion of the virtue in the mean, it may remind us of Aristotle's often quoted dictum: 'Speaking generally for the majority of men, the sequel to sexual intercourse is exhaustion and weakness rather than relief' (*Generation of Animals*, 725b). The tenor of Clement's discussion throughout his treatment of food echoes not Aristotle but Philo with his repeated warnings against the dire consequences of pleasure, especially pleasure in food, as expressed, for example, in *On the Creation*, 156; 158; *Spec. Leg.* 1:94; 1:148; 3:9–11; *On the Contemplative Life*, 4:37; 9:74.

110 *Paidagogos* 2:1:17, compare it to Philo's 'physiology': 'Immoderate eating is by its nature deadly and poisonous, for what is eaten has no chance of being assimilated, owing to the rush of the fresh viands which takes place before those already swallowed have been digested' (*Op.* 157); or, 'a brief stoppage in the influx (of food) which passes into the receptacles of the body... would ensure that the stream from the fountain of reason should flow pure and crystal-clear... because the constantly repeated administration of foodstuffs which submerge the body sweep the reason away as well, whereas if they are checked, that same reason [is] stoutly fortified' (*Spec. Leg.* 2:32:201).

111 *Stromateis* 2:20.

112 Cf. *Didache* 8:1, see Chapter 1 of this volume, p. 23, n. 65.

113 See Chapter 1 of this volume, pp. 25–6.

114 Isaiah 58:4–5 is the text most often used by early Christian writers who want to allegorize Leviticus.

115 *Stromateis* 6:12. This view that goes back to Isaiah and the prophets is articulated again in Christian literature by the *Epistle of Barnabas*, an early second century Christian document that is thought by some to have originated in Alexandria.

116 *Stromateis* 7:11.

117 Roberts, op. cit. (n. 31 above), p. 49.

118 Clark, op. cit. (n. 11 above), p. 117, n. 72.

119 *Stromateis* 1:15.

120 Ibid. 1:19.

121 Justin Martyr, *Dialogue* 47–8; Epiphanius, *Panarion* 30,3,13.

122 Philo, *Cont.* 9:74; *Spec. Leg.* 1:9, 1:148; etc.; but this sentiment was shared by most ancient moralists.

123 *Paidagogos* 2:2:19.

124 Ibid. 2:2:19–21.

125 See Chapter 2 of this volume, p. 50. As discussed above, according to ancient medical and philosophical speculations the human body was believed to follow a course of natural development from being hot and moist early in life to gradually becoming cold and dry in old age. Sexual intercourse was thought to have a 'drying' effect on the body, therefore it was deemed appropriate in young adulthood when the body had both heat and moisture in adequate amounts. As one grew older and the body grew cooler and dryer sexual desire was expected to diminish. Plato, *Timaeus*, 73–82; Galen, *Hygiene*, trans. R. Montraville Green, 1952, p. 133; Oribasius, *Oribasii Collectionum Mediearum reliquie*, ed. and French trans. U. Bussemaker and C. Daremberg, 1951, I, II, XIV.

126 Josephus's description of the way the Essenes dealt with the problem of excrement seem to have aroused admiration in intellectual circles. It was later repeated with approval by the third-century Platonist Porphyry, who in his treatise, *De Abstinentia*, puts forth as one of the advantages of a vegetarian diet that it produces less excrement than a meat diet – in which he was, of course, entirely mistaken.

127 *Paidagogos* 3:66.

128 Gluttony, according to Philo, causes excrement to be 'sluiced in a steam through the genital organs, and creates in them irritations, itchings and titillations without ceasing' (*Spec. Leg.* 3:10–11). Philo in turn is dependent on Plato's *Timaeus*.

129 *Paidagogos* 2:2:22.

130 1 Timothy 5:23. Many medics used wine in therapy. Asclepiades of Bithynia, the most famous among them, who practised in Rome in the second century BC, but whose work and ideas were still widely known and debated in Galen's time, based his treatment on the judicious use of food, wine, baths and exercise, and was even nicknamed 'the wine-giver' (Oinodotes). E. Rawson, *Intellectual Life in Late Republican Rome*, 1985, ch. 12.

131 *Paidagogos* 2:2:23–9. While Dionysus, the pagan god of wine, was called 'health-giver', the pleasures and dangers of wine constituted a sizeable part of literary commonplace. The advice on how much to drink, attributed to Eubulus by Athenaeus (II.40), was well known and its variations often repeated. It went like this: one should drink three cups of wine, one to health, the second to love and pleasure and the third to sleep. When this is drunk up the wise guests go home, for the fourth belongs to violence, fifth to uproar, sixth to drunken revel, the seventh to black eyes and so on until after the tenth cup madness takes over with the hurling of furniture. Clement saw the dangers as starting with the second cup.

132 *Paidagogos* 2:2:31.

133 If they could not be made to disappear altogether, for Clement believed that 'women should be completely veiled; for her appearance will be dignified only when she cannot be seen' (ibid. 2:3:79).

134 Ibid. 2:2:33–4.

135 Ibid. 2:2:90. The Stoic sage credited with the saying was Chrysippus, *Frag. moral.* 730.

136 J.W. Trigg sees Clement as one of the great formative influences on Origen during his youth (*Origen: The Bible and Philosophy in the Third-century Church*, 1983, p. 54).

137 According to a sympathetic modern critic, Chadwick, the great display of erudition in Clement was due to being 'over-anxious to show how learned a Christian can be'. He continues by saying that in Clement's works there is a certain amount of name-dropping. 'But that fault is not a mark only of the *demi-monde*' (*Early Christian Thought* (n. 17 above), p. 37).

138 *Paidagogos* 2:2:33; 2:7:60.

139 Frend, op. cit. (n. 22 above), p. 354, talks about a 'Christian elite', 'comparing themselves mentally to the Guardians whom Socrates was

discussing'; and, on p. 359, about Clement's 'wealthy and educated congregation'. Brown, op. cit. (n. 11 above), pp. 137–8, suggests that Clement wrote for the rich and cultivated. Ferguson, op. cit. (n. 5 above), p. 85, sees 'upper-class church members'. Even Ramsay MacMullen, op. cit. (n. 53 above) thinks that the *Paidagogos* was written to persons of the slave owning leisured classes. It is true that Clement devotes some effort to advise on how to treat servants, but owning a few slaves would not have put his Christians into the top 5 percent of the population.

140 Thomas N. Habinek, 'An aristocracy of virtue: Seneca on the beginnings of wisdom', *Yale Classical Studies* 29, 1992, 187–203.

141 Chadwick, *Early Christian Thought*, p. 36.

142 Brown, op. cit. (n. 11 above), p. 135.

143 *Paidagogos* 2:3:37.

144 Ibid. 2:3:51; 2:3:64.

145 Compare Seneca's *Epistulae morales*, 108 and 110: 'preach against greed, preach against high living' (108:12). Stoic philosophers like Seneca's teacher Attalus denounced sin, error and the evils of life, praised poverty and claimed that everything that passed the measure of necessity was useless and dangerous. They 'castigated our pleasure-seeking lives, and extolled personal purity, moderation in diet, and a mind free from unnecessary, not to speak of unlawful, pleasures' (ibid. 13, 14).

146 A similarity of attitudes to marriage between Clement and the Roman Stoic Musonius is often suggested. Like Musonius, Clement too condemns adultery and any transgression of the strictest sexual ethic. But unlike Musonius, who extolled the love of husband and wife for each other as the highest form of love, Clement rarely speaks of love between man and wife. As Parker pointed out, Clement's interest was focused on describing and warning against evil, while the pagan Stoic delighted in the good and pointed to its attractions (Charles Pomeroy Parker, 'Musonius in Clement', *Harvard Studies in Classical Philology* 12, 1901, 191–210).

147 Tollington's comments in Volume 1 of *Clement of Alexandria*, pp. 272, 274, are a quaint testimony to cultural changes with respect to what is considered in scholarly circles as 'fit to print'.

148 Chadwick, *Early Christian Thought*, p. 63.

149 *Paidagogos* 2:2:94. This seems to hark back to Aristotle's complaint that the outcome of sexual intercourse is fatigue (see n. 109 above).

150 *Stromateis* 6:9.

151 Ibid. 5:11.

152 Ibid. 6:14.

153 Ibid. 7:11.

CHAPTER 6

1 Peter Brown, *The Body and Society: Men, Women, and Sexual Renunciation in Early Christianity*, 1988, p. 78.

2 Timothy D. Barnes, *Tertullian: A Historical and Literary Study*, 1971, p. 55.

3 Eusebius, *Ecclesiastical History* II.2:4, 'Tertullian who had an accurate knowledge of Roman law, a man especially famous among those most distinguished in Rome'; trans. Kirsopp Lake, LCL, 1926 (repr. 1980), p. 113.

4 Jerome, *De Viris Illustribus*, 53, PL 23. 697–8AB.

5 Among others, C. Dodgson, Preface to *Tertullian, Apologetic and Practical Treatises*, in *A Library of Fathers*, vol. 10, 1854; James Morgan, *The Importance of Tertullian in the Development of Christian Dogma*, 1928; W.H.C. Frend, *Martyrdom and Persecution in the Early Church*, 1965.

6 Barnes, op. cit., p. 29.

7 Ibid., ch. 14.

8 Jerome, *Adversus Helvidium* 17, PL 23. 211B.

9 Eusebius, *Ecclesiastical History*, V:4.3; V:16.6–20. Modern commentators also reveal a range of opinions concerning Montanism. On the one side, some regard it as 'a Christianity perverted by fear of learning', debased into a 'coarse revivalism' or 'naked fanaticism, which tried to stampede the Church into greater severity' (R.A. Knox, *Enthusiasm: A Chapter in the History of Religion*, 1950, ch. 3). On the other side, some regard Montanism as a reaction against the growing authority of the episcopal structure, a prophetic movement that 'revived several features of primitive Christianity – an intense eschatological expectation and reliance on charismatic gifts working outside the established hierarchy' (H.W. Attridge, 'Christianity from the destruction of Jerusalem to Constantine's adoption of the new religion: 70–312 C.E.' in H. Shanks (ed.), *Christianity and Rabbinic Judaism*, pp. 151–94, at p. 160).

10 Barnes, op. cit., p. 42. P. de Labriolle, *Les Sources pour l'Histoire de Montanisme*, 1913.

11 If the claims that he was born *circa* 155, and that his extant writings are datable to the short span of sixteen years, from his forties to his early fifties, are all justified, then his turning to Montanism would fall in his early fifties, not an age at which one would be expected to become an extremist radical and turn from an accepted and comfortable Christianity to an extremely rigorous one. This kind of conversion is more characteristic of young men in late adolescence.

12 Fasting is also mentioned in *De Baptismo* and other tracts, but these repeat the same rationale for it that is extensively discussed in *De Ieiunio*.

13 B. Altaner–A. Stuiber, *Patrologie* 7, 1966, p. 149; Introduction to *The Writings of Tertullian*, vol. 3 (Ante-Nicene Christian Library, 1895, vol. 18), pp. xi–xiii; and Barnes (op. cit.: ch. 5), who establishes a tentative chronology of Tertullian's writings, dating *De Spectaculis* and the *Apologeticus* to before or around AD 198, *De Poenitentia* and *De Patientia* between 198 and 203 and *De Ieiunio* to 210 or 211. The detailed and rigorous discussion of the problems of the chronology of the various treatises in Barnes reduces to four the possible bases for dating; after pointing to the shortcomings of three of these, i.e. allusions to historical events, references to earlier writings, and style, he puts the weight on doctrine. This last, of course, hinges on the assumption that Tertullian

started as 'orthodox' but became a Montanist in his early fifties, or at least, that after the age of forty he became increasingly Montanist in his doctrine.

14 Barnes, op. cit., p. 196.
15 As discussed in Chapter 2 of this volume, pp. 55–6.
16 These are mentioned by his older contemporary and collector of philological material, Aulus Gellius, *Noctes Atticae* 2:24.
17 *Apologeticus* 6.
18 Ibid. 35.
19 Tacitus, *Annales* 15:37.
20 *Apologeticus* 9:9–12.
21 Ibid. 9:13, echoing the Apostolic decree of Acts 15:20,29.
22 Ibid. 39.
23 A number of church councils attest that the *agape* was still practised by communities even in the fourth century; decisions of these same synods also hint at the controversies surrounding these community meals. See, for example, Canons 27, 28, 37, 38, 39, of the Synod of Laodicea (sometime between AD 343 and 381); or Canon 11 of the Synod of Gangra (c. AD 325 and 381).
24 Barnes, op. cit. (n. 2 above), p. 117.
25 Mishnah, *Berakhoth*, 3:4; 5:1; 6:5–6; Dom Gregory Dix, *The Shape of the Liturgy*, 1945, p. 84.
26 W.H.C. Frend, *The Donatist Church: A Movement of Protest in Roman North Africa*, 1952, repr. 1970, ch. 7. Frend, following H. Lietzmann, *Die Geschichte der alten Kirche*, 4 vols, 1937–44; trans. B.E. Woolf as *The Beginnings of the Christian Church*, 4 vols, 1947–53, vol. 2, p. 220, holds the view that Christianity came to Carthage from Rome.
27 *Apologeticus* 16.
28 Barnes, op. cit., pp. 92–3.
29 See Chapter 2, pp. 37–9 above. Confraternities of tradesmen and burial societies held banquets for their members. 'The sodalities and clubs, which were constantly holding feasts under pretext of sacrifice in which drunkenness vented itself in political intrigue ...', wrote Philo of Alexandria (*In Flaccum* 5), reflecting the unease and suspicion felt not only by moralists or pious Jews but also by the authorities. Time and again the clubs were dissolved or were allowed only by special permission. They seem to have been popular, and were often supported by rich patrons.
30 See the discussion of *patronatus* in R. Sherk, *The Municipal Decrees of the Roman West*, 1970, pp. 76, 84, 89.
31 Paul Veyne, *Bread and Circuses: Historical Sociology and Political Pluralism*, trans. Brian Pearce, 1990, p. 95. For these, a study of the motivation of present-day large contributors to the support of charities would be sobering. Giving generously, now and in all times, is a good deed that buys renown and respect, and pleases the giver.
32 For documentation of prices for dinners and outlays for gifts in the empire see Richard Duncan-Jones, *The Economy of the Roman Empire: Quantitative Studies*, 1974, p. 138 – and with reference to the African provinces, pp. 80–2.

33 Veyne, op. cit., pp. 33–4.
34 The character of the parasite, borrowed from New Comedy, seems to have been still quite popular in the time of the Second Sophistic (second and early third century AD), appearing in many of the works from the period. Alciphron, like other writers of this period, wrote literature on literature; using the literary form of the epistle, he left us four types of letters: those of fishermen, farmers, parasites and courtesans. In over thirty of these imaginary letters the 'parasites' describe – in terms quite similar to Tertullian, but in even more unhappy detail – the various humiliations they had to endure for a good dinner.
35 Singing hymns was not an exclusively Christian custom; pagan banquets also started with invocation of deity and ended with hymns; for example, the closing of the *Deipnosophistae* of Athenaeus. See also Martin P. Nilsson, 'Pagan divine service in late antiquity', *HThR* 38, 1945, 63–9. The *agape* may have replaced for some new converts to Christianity the pagan banquets of *sodalitates*, burial associations, etc.
36 In Rome, the *Liberalia* were celebrated from early Republican times on 17 March, with sacrifices, games and banquets. Originally the festival seems to have included rites for the fertility of the fields; later it was the day when a boy's coming of age was celebrated by the family. Whether it was celebrated with outdoor banquets in Carthage in Tertullian's time or whether this is just a literary reference is uncertain.
37 *Apologeticus* 40:14.
38 Mishnah, *Taanith*, 1:4–7; 2:1–9. The Mishnah mentions rabbis from the late first and early second century in connection with this ritual, suggesting that the ritual or its particular form may be post-biblical. See Chapter 1, p. 25.
39 Barnes, op. cit. (n. 2 above), pp. 92–3.
40 Leviticus 22:8. Not all scholars share Barnes's view concerning Tertullian's relationship to Judaism. Frend, *Martyrdom and Persecution*, p. 374, writes that Tertullian's Christianity was 'rapidly becoming a baptised Judaism', and that 'much in African Christianity was tending in that direction. Some Christians were in the habit of keeping the Jewish Sabbath (*De Ieiunio* 14), and the ritual abstinence from animal food whence the blood had not been drawn could also be interpreted as Judaistic.'
41 Frend, *The Donatist Church* (n. 26 above), ch. 6, citing J. Toutain, *Les Cultes païens dans l'Empire romain; 1ère partie: Les Provinces latines*, 1920, argues that the ancient African cult of Saturn and Caelestis provided a strong background for the development of African Christianity. This Semitic cult, according to him, bears a strong resemblance to certain aspects of Jewish rites, including fasting and expiatory sacrifices. The closest parallel to Tertullian's description of the fasting for rain is in the Mishnah and for the physical effects of the fasts in Psalms 109:24. Despite the dearth of evidence, one may suppose that these share roots with Carthaginian ancient Semitic practices. It is much more likely, however, that customs that bore such strong resemblance to contemporary Jewish habits were in fact influenced by them.
42 *De Ieiunio* 16:6.

43 *De Spectaculis* 13.

44 Cf. Plato, *Timaeus*.

45 As was noted earlier (Chapter 2, pp. 38–9), wealthy pagan families organized grand public funerals for their dead. These served as occasions to affirm the importance of the family and its dynastic longevity, and also provided opportunity for public feasting.

46 Nilsson, op. cit. (n. 35 above).

47 *Confessions* VI:2(2).

48 *De Spectaculis* 30.

49 *De Patientia* 13:2.

50 Ibid. 13:3.

51 See Chapter 1 of this volume, pp. 20–4.

52 *De Poenitentia* 9.

53 Barnes, op. cit. (n. 2 above), p. 135.

54 This regimen seems to have aimed to 'dry out' the body both inside and out, a procedure that, according to ancient medical views, would lead to a reduction of sexual drive and potency. Interestingly, Tertullian does not stress this aspect here at all.

55 If Barnes is right; op. cit., p. 135.

56 *De Ieiunio* 1:2–4.

57 And the seat of both is the belly! Democritus, fragm. 235 Diels-Kranz.

58 *De Ieiunio* 1:1–2.

59 Ibid. 3:3.

60 The reference is probably to the commandment in Leviticus concerning the Day of Atonement, and to Psalms 51:17.

61 *De Ieiunio* 3:4.

62 Ibid. 4.

63 This will be repeated later by Jerome for his own peculiar arguments, as will be discussed. Both seem to have ignored the story of Cain and Abel, possibly for its uncomfortable implication that God himself preferred the meat producer to the grain grower.

64 *De Ieiunio* 4:3.

65 Ibid. 5:1,4. A similar explanation of the rules of *kashruth* was proposed by Philo.

66 *De Ieiunio* 6:1.

67 Exodus 32:6.

68 Philo's fear of gluttony, as was noted earlier, is attested in almost all of his works, see for example: *Cont.* 9:74; *Spec.Leg.* 1:94, 1:148; *Op.* 156, etc.

69 *De Ieiunio* 6:2. The texts he cites for support are again from the Bible, Deuteronomy 32:15, 8:12.

70 *De Ieiunio* 6:7. It is worth putting his own words down, lest the peculiarity of the view be attributed to the translation: 'Tanta est circumscripti victus praerogativa, ut deum praestet homini contubernalem, parem revera pari. Si enim deus aeternus non esuriet, ut testatur per Esaiam, hoc erit tempus, quo homo deo adaequetur, cum sine pabulo vivit.'

71 Philo, *Cherubim* 107.

72 His remark concerning Seneca as 'saepe noster' has been variously interpreted. The maximalist view has it as 'almost ours', while the minimalist as 'sometimes on our side'. In any case the Christian who wanted to see Seneca as a Christian sympathizer would be sympathetic to his views.

73 Seneca, *Epistulae morales* 110:18–20.

74 Tosefta *Taanith* 2:12.

75 *De Ieiunio* 7.

76 Ibid. 8:1.

77 Ibid.

78 Ibid. 8:2.

79 Justin Martyr, *Apology* 1:61.

80 *Didache* 7:4. This document is regarded as the oldest Christian church order, written in Syria at the end of the first or early second century. Its indebtedness to Jewish influences is generally acknowledged (H. Koester, *History and Literature of Early Christianity*, pp. 157–60). Similar use of fasting is seen in *Didascalia* 12:22. This later church order is believed to be also of Syrian origin, dating probably from the early third century, but based on some earlier sources. Because it advocates fasting before Easter as an expression of mourning, and fasting before baptism for expiation of sins, both being Jewish practices, the document is thought to be, like the Gospel of Peter, influenced by Jewish-Christianity or Judaizers (Walter Bauer, *Orthodoxy and Heresy in Earliest Christianity*, trans. of 2nd German edn, with added appendices by Georg Strecker, edited by Robert A. Kraft and Gerhard Krodel, 1971). See also Chapter 1 of this volume, p. 23, n. 65.

81 Among third- to fifth-century writers who advocated fasting as preparation for baptism, see the so-called *Clementine Recognitions*, 3:67, 7:34–7; Gregory Nazianzen, *Orations* 40.31; Augustine, *De Fide et Oper.* 6, *Epistulae* 118, *Sermo 210 in Quadr.* 6:2. Others may not have shared the view that fasting, 'watching, tears, lying on the ground' and other ostentatious acts of repentance were necessary as preparation for baptism: 'The grace of God in Baptism seeks not groans or mourning, or any other act, but only profession from the heart. For the gift of God freely remits sins in baptism', wrote Ambrosiaster in the late fourth century (*Ad Rom.* 11:29).

82 *De Ieiunio* 8:2.

83 Ibid. 8:2–3: 'Praestituit exinde ieiuniis legem sine tristitia transigendis. Cur enim triste, quod salutare?'

84 Ibid. 9:1.

85 Ibid. 9:2.

86 Ibid. 9:4.

87 Ibid. 9:6.

88 Ibid. 9:9.

89 When or where the Christian practice originated is not clear. The earliest evidence for the practice (and for its Jewish roots) in Christian literature is the *Didache*. Justin Martyr does not mention these fasts. *The Shepherd of Hermas*, written at Rome around 160 AD, mentions the term

Station as a private fast undertaken by an individual (Simil. 5:1). Dix, op. cit. (n. 25 above), p. 342.

90 Some other early Christian writers echoed Isaiah 58:4–5 on the true meaning of fasting, notably the *Epistle of Barnabas* 3:3; Justin Martyr, *Dialogue* 15; *The Shepherd of Hermas*, Simil. 5:1:4, 5:3:6.

91 *De Ieiunio* 10:8.

92 Ibid. 11.

93 Ibid.

94 Ibid. 12.

95 The attitude he expresses here is different from that of his treatise *Ad Martyras* 1, a change that is often attributed to his lapsing into Montanism (Rudolph Arbesmann, 'Fasting and prophecy in Pagan and Christian antiquity', *Traditio* 7, 1949–51, 1–71, n. 41), rather than, more plausibly, to the different aims of the treatises.

96 *De Ieiunio* 13:3.

97 Ibid.

98 Ibid. 13:6.

99 Apparently, these councils were not yet common in Carthage in his time.

100 *De Ieiunio* 14:4

101 That is, of keeping Jewish customs, from Paul's letter to the Galatians.

102 1 Timothy 4:1–6.

103 *De Ieiunio* 15:1.

104 Ibid. 15:2.

105 Tertullian's four tracts against remarriage used also these same deceits: tendentious translations of the Greek New Testament into Latin, distortions of proof texts in St Paul and mistaken references to a non-existent passage in the Old Testament. See Robin Lane Fox, *Pagans and Christians*, p. 364, where he argues that Tertullian's wish proved too strong for the natural sense of Scripture; and that most of his resulting 'errors' were deliberate, to suit his own argument.

106 *De Ieiunio* 15:3: 'Bonum est carnem non edere, et vinum non potare. Nam qui in istis servit, placabilis et propitiabilis Deo nostro est.'

107 Lane Fox, op. cit., p. 364.

108 *De Ieiunio* 3;4: '... ieiunium mandet et animam conquassatam proprie utique cibi angustiis sacrificium appellet.' Another example of a distorted proof text (see n. 105 above), Leviticus 23:27–8, both in the Hebrew and in the Septuagintal version, specifies the sacrifice of the total burnt offering by the priests, while the people are prohibited to work and enjoined to 'constrict' their 'person' or 'soul' on the Day of Atonement. Neither in the Hebrew nor in the Greek is the 'constricting of the soul' identified with the sacrifice.

109 *De Ieiunio* 16:4.

110 Ibid. 16:5.

111 Ibid. The *locus classicus* of Tertullian's example of pagan self-abasement with sackcloth and fasting is Jonah 3:6–10. The same passage is used by the rabbis of the Mishnah to explain the need for sackcloth and ashes when fasting for rain.

112 Ibid. 16:8: 'Deus enim tibi venter est, et pulmo templum, et aqua-
liculus altare, at sacerdos cocus, et sanctus Spiritus nidor, et condimenta
charismata, et ructus prophetia.'
113 Ibid. 17:2–3: 'Apud te agape in cacabis fervet, fides in culinis calet, spes
in ferculis iacet. Sed maior his est agape, qui per hanc adolescentes tui
cum sororibus dormiunt.'
114 Eusebius, *Ecclesiastical History* V 16–19.
115 *De Ieiunio* 17:6–7.
116 The concept developed by E.P. Sanders for the description and
comparison of how religions function. Discussed in the Introduction
to this volume, p. 8.
117 In his *De Pudicitia*, Tertullian gives the impression that he repudiated
the society of the orthodox, i.e. that he left the Church.
118 Lane Fox, op. cit., p. 368.
119 See Chapter 1 of this volume, pp. 25–6.
120 Brown, op. cit., pp. 77–8.
121 *De Ieiunio* 6:1.
122 *De Exhortatione Castitatis.*
123 Ramsay MacMullen estimates that roughly one hundredth of one
percent of Christians died for their faith, while great numbers complied
with the authorities or fled ('Ordinary Christians in the later persecutions', in *Changes in the Roman Empire: Essays in the Ordinary*, 1990, pp.
156–61). The problem of how to receive the '*lapsi*' back into the fold
was far from trivial.

CHAPTER 7

1 Concerning the dating of the *Ecclesiastical History*, T.D. Barnes in his
article 'The editions of Eusebius's *Ecclesiastical History*', *Greek Roman and
Byzantine Studies* 21, 1980, 191–201, and in his book *Constantine and
Eusebius*, 1981, ch. 8, argues for a much earlier date, claiming that the
first edition of the work contained originally only seven books written
in the 290s. Robin Lane Fox's reasoning is more convincing, since it
rests on internal evidence from the *Ecclesiastical History* itself, showing
that the work was born in the wake of Constantine's conversion. In
Pagans and Christians, 1986, pp. 607–8, he puts the most likely date for
its composition to late 313. Concerning Origen, Pamphilus, *Apologia
pro Origene* (the first book of this is extant in Rufinus's Latin translation),
Gregory Thaumaturgos, *Panegyric*, Jerome, *De Viris Illustribus* 54 and
61, *Letters* 33 and 44, Photius, *Bibliotheca* 118, Epiphanius, *Panarion*
64, and Porphyry, *Contra Christianos*, are additional texts that contain
references to his life and career. These are generally less extensive than
Eusebius and are often contradictory and unreliable.
2 Eduard Schwartz, *Eusebius: Die Kirchengeschichte*, GCS, 9 1909, in vol. 1,
p. 31, calls attention to the apologetic nature of Eusebius's treatment of
Origen. Jean Daniélou, *Origène*, 1948 (trans. W. Mitchell, 1955)
accepted Eusebius's account of the life as historical. J.W. Trigg writes
that Eusebius 'suppressed some evidence that did not place Origen in

the best possible light, accepted hearsay evidence that a modern historian would reject, and made questionable inferences from the information he did have' (*Origen: The Bible and Philosophy in the Third-century Church*, 1983, p. 9); H. Chadwick, *Early Christian Thought and the Classical Tradition: Studies in Justin, Clement, and Origen*, 1966, p. 67, agrees that when Eusebius depends on oral tradition his accuracy is no better than that of a 'reasonably conscientious gossip-writer'. M. Hornschuh, 'Das Leben des Origenes und die Entstehung der alexandrinischen Schule', *Zeitschrift fur Kirchengeschichte* 71, 1960, 1–25, 193–214, suggests that Eusebius's portrait of Origen is wholly invented.

3 Patricia Cox, *Biography in Late Antiquity: A Quest for the Holy Man*, 1983, p. 72.

4 R.P.C. Hanson, *Allegory and Event: A Study of the Sources and Significance of Origen's Interpretation of Scripture*, 1959, p. 162.

5 T.D. Barnes writes: 'Origen was not a biblical scholar, either by instinct or by training; he was a philosopher who used biblical exegesis as a vehicle for expressing views not derived from sacred text but read into it' (*Constantine and Eusebius*, p. 93). H. Chadwick, in *Early Christian Thought*, sees Origen primarily as a biblical scholar, who is familiar with the eclectic Platonism of his time, which incorporated Stoic ethics within a Platonist metaphysics, who may express Christian ideas in Platonic idiom and who is able to use current philosophic ideas in defence of Christianity. Origen's surviving writings lend support to Chadwick's views.

6 Karen Jo Torjesen, 'Pedagogical soteriology from Clement to Origen', *Origeniana Quarta: Die Referate des 4. Internationalen Origeneskongresses (Innsbruck, 2–6 September 1985)*, 1987, pp. 370–8.

7 *Contra Celsum* 5:39.

8 *De Principiis* 1:7:1; 3:5; 1:8; 3:5:4.

9 Ibid. 2:10:4; 2:2:2; 2:3:2; 3:6:4.

10 Ibid. 1:6; 2:10:6.

11 Chadwick, op. cit., p. 66.

12 Eusebius, *Ecclesiastical History* 6:36:2. For modern views on the date of *Contra Celsum* see pp. xiv–xv in H. Chadwick's Introduction to his 1953 translation of Origen's *Contra Celsum*.

13 *Contra Celsum* praef. 4.

14 Ibid. 5:49.

15 Ibid.

16 Ibid. 7:48.

17 As noted earlier (Chapter 5 of this volume, p. 107), in early Christian writings heretics are the ones accused of rejecting marriage and preaching 'abstinence from food which God created to be received with thanksgiving by those who believe and know the truth' (1 Timothy 4:1–6). Irenaeus (*Against Heresies*, c. 182–8) uses both food abstinence and the opposite of it, the complete rejection of the rules of the Apostolic Council, and the eating of meat sacrificed to idols as sure signs of heretic practice, but does not suggest that the heretics abstained from meat in order to strengthen their resistance to sex.

18 As in the *Homily I in Ezekiel* 12: 'What, indeed, is it that must be rooted out and overthrown? It is any evil rooted in the soul, any heretical doctrine.... How I wish I could demolish whatever Marcion has built in the ears of those deceived, to uproot, and to undermine and to destroy such things...'.

19 *Contra Celsum* 8:55.

20 *Homily 1 in Ezekiel* 3. Similar sentiments are expressed in *On Prayer* 31:4; *Homily in Jeremiah* 20:4; *Homily in Genesis* 5:4.

21 Irenaeus, *Against Heresies* 24.

22 *Contra Celsum* 8:29–31.

23 Ibid. 8:32.

24 Ibid. 8:30.

25 Ibid., quoting Romans 14:21:15, and 1 Corinthians 8:13.

26 He is not consistent in his opposition to the transmigration of souls, expressed in *Contra Celsum* 8:30; while he did not accept the rationality of animals, in his *De Principiis* 1:4:1; 1:8:4, he seems to entertain the possibility of transmigration of human souls into animals and even reincarnation in a plant.

27 Plato and Carneades attributed rationality to animals and defended vegetarianism on a moral basis, as justice owed by people to animals who themselves possess rationality. For philosophical arguments concerning meat eating and rationality of animals see Chapter 2 of this volume, pp. 58–9.

28 *De Principiis* 2:11:2.

29 Ibid. 2:11:3, a reference to Proverbs 9:5–6.

30 *De Principiis* 2:10:5.

31 *Homily in Leviticus* 10:2.

32 Chadwick, *Early Christian Thought*, p. 91.

33 *De Principiis* 3:2:1–2; *Contra Celsum* 7:50.

34 Patricia Cox, op. cit. (n. 3 above), p. 91, quotes the letter fragment, preserved in Pamphilus's Apology for Origen, and calls attention to the fact that Eusebius used it to describe Origen's zeal and asceticism but, as she points out, Origen's own words clearly show that the strict routine was due not to his own but to Ambrose's motivation, thus showing Origen 'as a more human figure'.

35 Philo's work is the only surviving evidence for Jewish attempts to mix the Torah with Platonic speculations. It is hard to believe that he was absolutely unique among Jews in a Hellenistic environment.

36 Justin Martyr, *Dialogue* 47–8; Epiphanius, *Panarion* 30, 3, 13. Karl Baus, *History of the Church: From the Apostolic Community to Constantine*, trans. and ed. Hubert Jedin, 1980, pp. 155–6.

37 *Commentary on Matthew* 16:7; Trigg, op. cit., p. 196.

38 *Homily in Leviticus* 2:4.

39 Gregory Thaumaturgos, *Canonical Epistle of the Archbishop of Neocaesarea and the Panegyric on Origen*, edited by Alexander Roberts and James Donaldson, *Ante-Nicene Christian Library*, vol. 20, 1871.

40 For the historical background of the *Canonical Epistle* of Gregory, together with an English translation, see Peter Heather and John Matthews, *The Goths in the Fourth Century*, 1991, Chapter 1.

41 This part of the *Epistle* is believed by some scholars to be a later insertion because of its similarity to the penitential rules of Basil of Caesarea; Heather and Matthews, op. cit., p. 10.

42 Eusebius, *Ecclesiastical History* 6:2.

43 Ibid. 6:3:4.

44 Ibid. 6:3:7. This, indeed, is what Gregory said about him in his *Panegyric* 9, but he did not refer to self-mortifications, nor to the producing of martyrs.

45 Ibid. 6:3:9–13.

46 Ibid. 6:8:1. Epiphanius, the great hunter of heresies, does not seem to believe in Origen's self-castration (*Panarion* 64).

47 Ibid. 6:18:2.

48 Eusebius was not the only one who regretted that Origen was denied the crown of martyrdom. 'This is unfortunate since if Origen had died in prison it would have been much harder for subsequent generations to condemn him', writes a modern follower of Eusebius in the best hagiographic tradition (Trigg, op. cit., p. 243).

49 Cox, op. cit., p. xiv.

50 Ibid., p. 72.

51 Ibid., p. 70.

52 *Commentary on Matthew* 15:3.

53 See Chapter 2 of this volume, p. 50.

54 Trigg, op. cit., p. 245.

55 Examples are the many jibes of Lucian in *The Cynic, Philosophies for sale*, and others, at the long-haired, bare-footed, body-mortifying 'philosophers' leading 'antisocial and bestial' lives; or the disapproving remarks of Philo in *Det.* 17–20, concerning those who refuse food and bath, who are careless about their clothing, and sleep on the ground, fancying that this kind of fruitless and wearisome behaviour constitutes self-control.

56 *Ecclesiastical History* 2:17. Frugality in food was an important signifier of piety for Eusebius, leading to claims that all of Christ's disciples avoided meat and wine (*Demonst. Evang.* 3:5:74).

57 Eusebius, *Ecclesiastical History and the Martyrs of Palestine*, trans. H.J. Lawlor and J.E.L. Oulton, 1927, pp. 331–3. For the biological problems arising from this regimen see the discussion in the Introduction to this volume, pp. 10–13.

58 A. Cushman McGiffert, Prolegomena to *The Church History of Eusebius*, Nicene and Post-Nicene Fathers, 1890, repr. 1976, p. 26.

59 Barnes, *Constantine and Eusebius*, p. 82.

60 Ibid., p. 94.

61 At the Council of Nicaea Eusebius, as bishop of Caesarea, found his pre-eminence as metropolitan of Palestine potentially endangered, for the Council, although acknowledging the status of Caesarea as the metropolitan see in Palestine, also decreed that Jerusalem should receive due honour (Barnes, *Constantine and Eusebius*, p. 219). The rivalry between the two sees may have originated earlier than this Council.

62 *Homily in Leviticus* 9:5; *Homily in Jeremiah* 4:3, and others; Henry Chadwick, 'Christian and Roman universalism in the fourth century', in L.R. Wickham and C.P. Bammel (eds), *Christian Faith and Greek*

FROM FEASTING TO FASTING

Philosophy in Late Antiquity, Essays in Tribute to George Christopher Stead, 1993, pp. 26–42.

63 R. Lane Fox, *Pagans and Christians*, 1986, p. 556.

64 *Ecclesiastical History* 8:1:7.

65 Ramsay MacMullen, 'What difference did Christianity make?', *Historia* 35, 1986, 322–43.

66 Henry Chadwick, 'The attractions of Mani', in E. Romero-Pose (ed.) *Pleroma: Salus Carnis*, Homenaje a Antonio Orbe, S.J., 1990, pp. 203–22.

67 *Vita Antonii*, PG 26 835–976. Attributed generally to Athanasius, the Arian-fighting bishop of Alexandria, on the basis of Gregory Nazianzen, *Orations* 21:5; Jerome, *De Viris Illustribus* 87; and Palladius, *Historia Lausiaca* 8. For a dissenting view, see T.D. Barnes, *Athanasius and Constantius; Theology and Politics in the Constantinian Empire* (1993), p. 240, n. 64 (see also Chapter 8 of this volume, p. 159, n. 21).

CHAPTER 8

1 For modern biographies of Jerome, see J.N.D. Kelly, *Jerome: His Life, Writings, and Controversies*, 1975; Georg Grützmacher, *Hieronymus, Eine biographische Studie*, 3 vols, 1901–8; Ferdinand Cavallera, *Saint Jérôme, sa vie et son oeuvre*, 1922. Kelly, following the chronicler Prosper of Aquitaine, puts his date of birth in the year 331 (op. cit., p. 1). Others, like F.A. Wright, in the Introduction to *Select Letters of St. Jerome*, LCL, 1958, put the date as late as 345. For a discussion of the uncertainties see the Appendix in Kelly (pp. 337–9).

2 Kelly, op. cit., p. 3.

3 Jerome, *De Viris Illustribus* 135.

4 *Letters* 82:2.

5 Ibid. 66:14.

6 The fact that Jerome is unique among the Church Fathers in the frequency and vehemence of his condemnation of family attachments may indicate that the topic had personal importance for him. He writes that piety towards one's family is impiety towards God, hatred of one's family is piety towards God. This harsh sentiment is expressed in a number of letters, e.g. 14:2–3; 22:21; 24:3; 38:5; 108:6. The same is expressed in a number of commentaries, e.g. *Haggai* 1:2; *Ecclesiastes* 3:8; *Matthew* 1:10,37.

7 An impressive amount of scholarly research has been devoted to the analysis of the Classical sources of Jerome's writings, among these: Harald Hagendahl, *Latin Fathers and the Classics: A Study on the Apologists, Jerome and Other Christian Writers*, 1958; Aemilius Luebeck, *Hieronymus Quos Noverit Scriptores et Quibus Hauserit*, 1872; Ernst Bickel, *Diatribe in Senecae Philosophi Fragmenta*, 1915; D.S. Wiesen, *St. Jerome as a Satirist: A Study in Christian Latin Thought and Letters*, 1964.

8 Hagendahl, op. cit., pp. 92–3.

9 *Letters* 45:3.

10 His sojourn in Trier, where Valentinian I and Gratian established their imperial court, may have been motivated by rather worldly ambition (Kelly, op. cit., p. 28); here too he may have become aware of the increasing authority that a reputation for asceticism bestowed on churchmen like Athanasius, Hilary of Poitiers – whose writings he copied during this period (*Letters* 5:2) – and others. On the Trier of Jerome's time, see E.M. Wightman, *Roman Trier and the Treveri*, 1970.

11 Bonosus, Rufinus, Niceas, Heliodorus and others.

12 *Letters* 3:3.

13 Ibid. 17. Jerome complains about the harsh treatment he received from the monks, who, it appears, doubted his orthodoxy.

14 His letters deeply contradict each other concerning the life he led in the 'desert'. As Kelly writes in his sympathetic biography: 'his self-imposed seclusion must have had some highly unusual features... he had brought his ever growing library with him (his cave must have been roomier than most) and evidently spent a great deal of time reading books... and also having them copied. Reading, biblical studies, and book production apart, Jerome was busily employed learning or improving his knowledge of languages' (Kelly, op. cit., pp. 48, 49).

15 As opposed to the monks of Chalcis, who, as it appears from *Letters* 17, refused to accept him.

16 Kelly, op. cit., p. 101. It seems that Damasus also encouraged Jerome's work of biblical translations. Most of his writing of this Roman period, apart from the translations and biblical interpretations, dealt with asceticism and especially with virginity.

17 Most of what we know about the ancestry and social position of these women is from Jerome himself. The number of women is not as large as is often implied: Paula and her daughters, Marcella and her mother, and two or three others to whom letters suggesting real personal acquaintance were addressed. Paula was undoubtedly wealthy, for she built their monasteries in Bethlehem and supported their life there until her wealth ran out. Jerome liked to refer to Marcella's house as a monastery, but if one takes into account all that Jerome reports about her then it seems more likely that she ran a 'salon' where Christian dignitaries often met each other.

18 Peter Brown, *The Body and Society: Men, Women, and Sexual Renunciation in Early Christianity*, 1988, p. 366.

19 Kelly, op. cit., p. 331; Cavallera argues for 419 as the date of his death (op. cit., pp. 56–63).

20 That early Egyptian monasticism was different from and more complex than the models presented by the literary evidence of Jerome and Cassian is shown, based on papyrological evidence, by James E. Goehring, 'Through a glass darkly: diverse images of the Apotakti-koi(ai) of early Egyptian monasticism', *Semeia* 58, 1992, 25–45. For varieties of female asceticism see now Susanna Elm, *Virgins of God: The Making of Asceticism in Late Antiquity*, 1994.

21 Attributed in antiquity to the pen of the Arian-fighting orthodox bishop of Alexandria, Athanasius. Some modern scholars, including the most recent biographer of Athanasius, T.D. Barnes (*Athanasius and*

Constantius: Theology and Politics in the Constantinian Empire, 1993), question this (for others see the references given in H. Musurillo, 'The problem of ascetical fasting in the Greek patristic writers', *Traditio* 12, 1956, 1–64, at p. 27, n. 19). Jerome's friend Evagrius translated it into Latin *c.* 371, 'but a crudely literal version was in circulation some years earlier' (Kelly, op. cit., n. 22 to p. 30). Augustine relates in the *Confessions* (VIII:6,14) how the reading of this book converted to the ascetic life some courtiers at Trier.

22 *Vita Pauli* (PL 23.17–30); *Vita Hilarioni* (PL 23.29–54). 'Neither in ambition nor in influence, however, can the lives that Jerome wrote for others be compared with the one that he invented for himself', writes Mark Vessey in 'Jerome's Origen: the making of a Christian literary persona', *Studia Patristica* 28, 1993, 135–45. In this Vessey focuses on just one of the various facets to the persona of the saint that Jerome promoted for himself in his letters and prefaces, on that of the Christian writer.

23 There may have lived a Hilarion in Palestine, but 'outside of Jerome's Life, no evidence for Paul of Thebes survives and doubts have been cast on his very existence by modern scholars, as they were (to his intense irritation) by Jerome's own contemporaries' (Kelly, op. cit., p. 61). Jerome himself complained (*Vita Hilarionis* 1) that people thought that Paul never existed. There are some modern scholars who like to think 'that The Life of Paul was not pure fiction'. For this view see Philip Rousseau, *Ascetics, Authority, and the Church in the Age of Jerome and Cassian*, 1978.

24 E.A. Judge, 'The earliest use of *monachos* for "monk" (P.Coll.Youtie 77) and the origins of monasticism', *JAC* 20, 1977, 72–89, at p. 78, n. 20, cites the work of H. Dörries, who, by comparing the thirty-eight apophthegmata attributed to Antony with the *Vita*, demonstrates that the teaching and life style reflected in these differed in important ways from that presented by Athanasius, 'who had axes of his own to grind'.

25 Patricia Cox, *Biography in Late Antiquity: A Quest for the Holy Man*, 1983, pp. 5, 20.

26 Ibid., p. 25.

27 Five dried figs (80–100 grams) provide approximately 210–240 kilocalories of energy. It needs no argument that a human being cannot survive long on this diet.

28 *Vita Pauli*, 6.

29 Which Jerome's hero managed to sustain for 113 years (*Vita Pauli*, 7)!

30 There must be something psychologically very satisfying in these stories, for even some modern writers seem to want to suspend disbelief. Aline Rousselle, discussing stories in which monks in the Egyptian desert fasted for forty days, and others for three weeks, writes: 'this is not impossible, and in fact the body, particularly the brain, suffers less from a total fast than from excessive restriction of the daily rations' (*Porneia: On Desire and the Body in Antiquity*, trans. Felicia Pheasant, 1988, p. 169). She cites V.R. Young and N.S. Scrimshaw's report, 'The physiology of starvation', *Scientific American* 225(4), 1971, 14–21, as evidence, failing to note that the research summarized by these writers was

conducted on pathologically obese people, whose body during the long fast utilized their own enormous surplus of fat for energy (not to mention that they were maintained in a temperate environment with adequate daily fluid intake!).

31 *Letters* 22:8: 'Si autem haec sustinet illi qui exeso corpore solis cogitationibus oppugnatur, quid patitur puella, quae deliciis fruitur.'

32 It is interesting to note that in his letter to Rusticus on good and bad monks he uses the same story (*Letters* 125:12). However the aim here is to encourage the monk to study, so the outcome of the familiar tale is different; instead of fasting Jerome took up the study of Hebrew with a teacher in order to chase the lewd thoughts out of his mind.

33 *Vita Pauli*, 17.

34 Kate Cooper, 'Insinuations of womanly influence: an aspect of the Christianization of the Roman aristocracy', *JRS* 82, 1992, 150–64, at p. 157.

35 The description of Jerome's sojourn in the desert is questionable for a number of reasons. It bears too close a resemblance to the routine stories repeated about hermits, how they starve themselves and still are pursued by the demon of fornication. This goes against medical research, which shows that in healthy young men all sexual motivation disappears with a near subsistence diet of about 1,600 to 1800 kilocalories per day, and that is a lot more than five figs! Moreover the claim in *Letters* 17:2, that he supported himself by the daily labour of his own hands and by his own sweat, presumably like the Egyptian monks, tilling a small plot of land or weaving mats, does not square with the picture that is reflected from his other correspondence (*Letters* 7:1; 15:5; 5:2), of the frequent visits and support of his influential friend Evagrius, with his extensive library, assistants, studies, book production, and so on.

36 *Vita Pauli*, 10.

37 Ibid. 16.

38 Mark 9:23. Edward Gibbon's view is worth repeating: 'The only defect in these pleasing compositions is the want of truth and common sense'; *The History of the Decline and Fall of the Roman Empire*, 1776–88, repr. 1869, ch. 38.

39 John Chrysostom, *On Virginity*, 9:1 (trans. Sally Rieger Shore 1983); *De Studio Presentium* 3 (PG 63. 488).

40 *Homily 14 in 1 Timothy* 3 (PG 62. 575).

41 Diogenes Laertius, *Lives of Eminent Philosophers*, VI:20–87.

42 'Cynic epistles', trans. Leif E. Vaage, in V.L. Wimbush (ed.), *Ascetic Behavior in Greco-Roman Antiquity*, 1990, p. 119.

43 See Chapter 1 of this volume, p. 31.

44 Philo, *Det.* 19.

45 *Letters* 17:2. Of course, the Saint is describing other monks, not himself!

46 *Vita Malchi* 1 (PL 23.55–61). R. Syme thought that writing about the decline of Christian virtue 'would have been congenial to his (Jerome's) idiosyncrasy. The monk who encountered disappointment in his aspiration to place and honour, and had been chased out of Rome, incurring in the sequel much hostility and sundry feuds, was not

disposed to spare the princes of the Church or abate that ferocity which so eagerly arraigned the doctrines or diet of persons he happened to dislike' (*Ammianus and the Historia Augusta*, 1968, p. 210).

47 As Averil Cameron writes: 'while celibacy was enjoined on men and women alike, it was women who were above all the object of this repressive discourse'; 'Virginity as metaphor: women and the rhetoric of early Christianity', in A. Cameron (ed.), *History as Text: The Writing of Ancient History*, 1990, pp. 184–205, at p. 189.

48 Even by his sympathetic biographer Kelly; see for example op. cit. (n. 1 above), pp. 64, 65, 75, 89.

49 The modern literature on Jerome's 'aristocratic' or 'senatorial' women friends and their alleged role in the 'Christianization' of the Roman aristocracy is extensive, e.g. A. Yarbrough, 'Christianization in the fourth century: the example of Roman women', *Church History* 45, 1976, 149–65; J.W. Drijvers, 'Virginity and asceticism in late Roman Western elites', in J. Blok and P. Mason (eds), *Sexual Asymmetry*, 1987, pp. 241–73. See, however, the salutary remarks of Elizabeth A. Clark in her study, *Jerome, Chrysostom, and Friends*, 1979. The view that aristocratic Roman women were the important movers of Christianization has now been successfully challenged by M.R. Salzman, who, using a statistical analysis based on epigraphic evidence, demonstrated that the view that Christianity was embraced by a large proportion of aristocratic women and that women constituted a larger proportion of fourth-century aristocratic Christians than men is untenable ('Aristocratic women: conductors of Christianity in the fourth century', *Helios* 16, 1989, 207–20).

50 See for example Mercedes Serrato, *Ascetismo Femenino en Roma*, 1993, which is a history of female asceticism based almost entirely on Jerome's letters, taking these at face value. Similarly, the discussion of female asceticism in Gillian Clark, *Women in Late Antiquity: Pagan and Christian Life-styles*, 1993.

51 Mark Vessey shows how important the collection of *Letters to Marcella* was in Jerome's self-promotion as the best and best-qualified expounder of the Bible. He throws some doubt on the historical existence of Marcella: 'she is essentially Jerome's creature, attached to the documentary history of her time only by the slender thread of an alleged offer of marriage from a Roman senator, and even that anecdote occurs in a letter written by Jerome after her death, at a time when its veracity was unlikely to be challenged' (Vessey, op. cit. (n. 22 above), p. 144).

52 'In fact, as first editor and publisher of his letters it would seem that we can name the Saint himself', writes T.C. Lawler in his Introduction to the translation of the letters in *Ancient Christian Writers* 33, vol. 1, 1963, p. 8.

53 P. Brown's charitable view is that while Jerome assumed the 'persona of Origen' towards his spiritual lady friends, he still 'did not encourage woman to become theological authors in their own right'. This he claims 'meant no more than that he, like all other late antique males, wished to keep for himself the dubious privilege of being aggressive to other men' (Brown, op. cit. (n. 18 above), p. 370). But it is still curious

that, while he says that all these women wrote to him and that Marcella wrote also letters on his behalf and against his enemies, not one of these was found in his correspondence.

54 *Letters* 45, 22, 107, 54, etc.

55 D.S. Wiesen argues that Jerome attacked the corruption that he saw around him in Rome. The satirical devices that he took over from writers like Persius, Juvenal, Terence and others, coupled with his own 'brilliant powers of observation and description', helped him to expose women's failings based on his own observation of their behaviour (*St Jerome as a Satirist*, pp. 119–33). No woman, however, as long as she remained a sexual being, even a devoted wife or mother, was for Jerome anything but potential temptation. Even consecrated virgins were often used by him as screens onto which to project his overheated sexual fantasies (e.g. *Letters* 22:14;16;29).

56 *Letters* 22:8–10, 11, 13, 14, 16; 64:21; 123:4, 125:6 and many more.

57 Ibid. 22:14, 27–9.

58 Ibid. 45:3.

59 Wiesen, op. cit., p. 130.

60 See Chapter 6 of this volume, pp. 127–31.

61 *Letters* 22:10; an echo of Tertullian, who sees Adam's eating the apple as the 'original sin' (*De Ieiunio* 3:2–4). On Jerome's indebtedness to Tertullian, see Neil Adkin, '"Istae sunt, quae solent dicere", three Roman vignettes in Jerome's "Libellus de virginitate servanda" (Epist. 22)', *Museum Helveticum* 49, 1992, 131–40.

62 Tertullian, *De Ieiunio* 3:4. see Chapter 6 of this volume, p. 124.

63 *Letters* 22:11 (italics added): 'Non quo Deus . . . intestinorum nostrum rugitu et inanitate ventris pulmonumque delectetur ardore, *sed quo aliter pudicitia tuta esse non possit*.'

64 Ibid. 22:30.

65 Hagendahl is of the opinion that most of Jerome's references to Greek medical writers are second-hand, with the exception of Galen whom he read (op. cit. (n. 7 above), p. 223).

66 *Letters* 54:9.

67 See Chapter 2 of this volume, pp. 48–52.

68 See, for example, *Commentary on Amos* II prol. (CCL 76:263–4) and Kelly's comments on it in *Jerome*, op. cit. (n. 1 above), p. 295.

69 Robert Montraville Green, *A Translation of Galen's Hygiene*, 1952.

70 A phrase much favoured by Philo and Clement, and put into Latin by Jerome to describe women: 'nulla illis nisi ventris cura est et quae ventri proxima' (*Letters* 22:29).

71 Philo, *Spec. Leg.* 3:9–11.

72 Ambrose, *Letters* 63:26, trans. H. de Romestin, in *Nicene and Post-Nicene Fathers*, second series, vol. X, repr. 1955.

73 Jerome, *Letters* 22:22.

74 See his prefaces to *Didymus on the Holy Spirit* (PL 23.105), and to Origen's *Homilies on Luke* (GCS 49.1); Kelly, op. cit., pp. 143–4; Hagendahl, op. cit., pp. 115–17.

75 *Letters* 54:8.

76 Ibid. 45, 22, 107, 54, etc.

77 Ibid. 54:10 (italics added). These instructions suggest a somewhat confused echo of Basil of Ancyra's treatise, *De Virginitate* (PG 30. 669–810); both the writer and the treatise are listed in *De Viris Illustribus* 89. The dietary advice given by Basil (*c.* 336–58) is based more closely on Hippocratic medical principles, and he also seems to take into account the individual's physical disposition. Food should be consumed in such a way as to keep the balance of the four elements. Basil, who is believed to have been a physician before becoming a bishop, warns equally against excessive fasting and gluttony. (Basil's treatise is discussed in Elm, op. cit. (n. 20 above), p. 115.)

78 Again this seems to echo Philo: 'for wine is a drug of madness, and costly meat inflames the most insatiable of wild beasts, desire' (*Cont.* IX.74). Jerome refers to Philo's contemplatives in describing monastic practices in *Letters* 22:35.

79 *Letters* 54:9; 22:9.

80 Romans 14:21. It is instructive to see what Paul actually said in Chapter 14 of his Epistle to the Romans, with respect to food: 'Let not him who eats despise him who abstains, and let not him who abstains pass judgement on him who eats.... Everything is indeed clean, but it is wrong for anyone to make others fall by what he eats. It is right not to eat meat or drink wine or do anything that makes your brother stumble.' See a discussion of this in Chapter 3 of this volume, p. 67.

81 Brown, op. cit. (n. 18 above), p. 376.

82 See Chapter 3 of this volume.

83 Tertullian, *De Ieiunio* 6:1; Clement, *Paedagogus* 3:66.

84 Rousselle, op. cit. (n. 30 above), p. 172.

85 See Chapter 2 of this volume, p. 50, n. 101.

86 Hagendahl, op. cit., p. 124.

87 *Letters* 22:17.

88 Ibid. 22:29.

89 Ibid. 107:11.

90 *De Virginitate* I.7:32 (italics added); trans. H. de Romestin in *Nicene and Post-Nicene Fathers*, second series, vol. X, repr. 1955.

91 *Letters* 130:6.

92 Hagendahl, op. cit., p. 196. As Kelly has pointed out (op. cit. (n. 1 above), pp. 273–4) the *Letter to Laeta* has often been admired for Jerome's 'sensitivity' to children and their educational needs. The pedagogical insights paraded in the letter, however, are straight paraphrases of Quintilian's *Inst. orat.* I,I:24–9. See also Hagendahl, pp. 199–201.

93 *Letters* 107:8;10;11.

94 Ibid. 38, 39; she is mentioned also in *Letters* 54 and 66, and in the Preface to the *Commentary on Ecclesiastes*.

95 *Letters* 38:2.

96 Ibid. 39:1.

97 Ibid. 38:3.

98 Ibid. 38:4, 39:1.

99 *Adversus Jovinianum* II 7, see Origen, *Contra Celsum* 5:49, from where this echo of expressions put together from Romans 8:13, 1 Corinthians 9:17 and Colossians 3:5, is taken.

100 *Letters* 52.

101 See Chapter 6 of this volume, p. 125.

102 *Letters* 41, written to Marcella to educate her against Montanist propaganda.

103 Ibid. 107:10: 'when week is added to week and even oil in food and fruit are banned' seems to refer to this practice.

104 Ibid. 52:12.

105 Ibid. 125:7.

106 James E. Goehring, op. cit. (n. 20 above) shows how the description of the three types of monastics of Egypt in the writings of Jerome and other churchmen, intended for a non-Egyptian audience, may have imposed on Egyptian asceticism the writer's own theological and political views. See now also Susanna Elm's study, *Virgins of God*, tracing the various types of monastic formations as influenced by theological and political power struggles (op. cit., n. 20 above).

107 *Letters* 125:9; 15.

108 Ibid. 22:35.

109 Ibid. 22:34.

110 Ibid. 125:9.

111 Ibid. For the sake of fairness it should be mentioned that he was not unique in this. John Chrysostom, his Greek contemporary and fellow champion of starving virgins with chains around their necks, also ridiculed those who performed ascetic tricks for money: 'Some chew the soles of worn-out sandals; others drive sharp spikes through their heads; others jump naked into waters frozen with cold' (*Homily 77 in Matthew* 6; PG 58. 710, quoted in Musurillo, op. cit. (n. 21 above), p. 25).

112 Gregory of Nyssa, *Vita Gregorii Thaumaturgi* (PG 46. 933). On the social class of bishops see A.H.M. Jones, *The Later Roman Empire 284–602*, 3 vols, 1964, repr. in 2 vols, vol. 2, pp. 920–9; F.D. Gilliard, 'Senatorial bishops in the fourth century', *HThR* 77, 1984, 153–75.

113 See Daniel Callam, 'Clerical continence in the fourth century: three papal decretals', *Theological Studies* 41, 1980, 3–49.

114 Cooper, op. cit. (n. 34 above), p. 155.

115 Ibid., p. 162.

116 'Before I became acquainted with the household of the saintly Paula, all Rome was enthusiastic about me. Almost everyone concurred in judging me worthy of the highest office in the Church' ('dignus summo sacerdotio decernebar', *Letters* 45:3).

117 PL 23.221–353.

118 For the history and background of this treatise, see Chapter 17 in Kelly, op. cit. (n. 1 above), and Callam, op. cit. (n. 112 above).

119 In addition to Jerome, Pope Siricius, *Ad Diversos Episcopos, Ep.* 7 (Coustant 663–8); Ambrose, *Letters* 42 (PL 16 1123–9) and 63,7–45 (PL 16 1191–201) witness the opposition to Jovinian. Callam, op. cit., p. 9, points out that Augustine gained his information about Jovinian

at second hand, and that his sources may have been hearsay and not restricted to writing still extant.

120 Grützmacher, op. cit. (n. 1 above), vol.2, p. 148.
121 Kelly, op. cit., p. 180.
122 Hagendahl, op. cit., pp. 147–8.
123 Discussed in Chapter 2 of this volume, pp. 58–9.
124 Acts 10:9–15.
125 For example, Romans 14:21.
126 *Adversus Jovinianum* II 1.18. The whole biblical history repeats Tertullian, without naming him. It has been pointed out that Jerome used in *Adversus Jovinianum* not only *De Ieiunio* but also *De Monogamia* of Tertullian, both considered strongly Montanist treatises (Kelly, op. cit., pp. 183–4, n. 21).
127 Paul is misquoted here, just as in *Letters* 54 and 22.
128 *Adversus Jovinianum* II 6.
129 Porphyry, *On Abstinence from Animal Food*, trans. Thomas Taylor, 1965, 1:27; 1:51; 2:3.
130 Syme remarks that this is 'Jerome's own contribution, and a fraudulent autopsy'; op. cit. (n. 46 above), 1968, p. 22, with the delicious quotation on cannibalism from Gibbon's ch. 25, in n. 3.
131 *Adversus Jovinianum* II 7.
132 *Letters* 22:13, 38; 133:9; *Adversus Jovinianum* I 3, I 5.
133 For an extensive study of Manichaeism see Samuel N.C. Lieu, *Manichaeism in the Later Roman Empire and Medieval China* 1992; on the charges of Manichaeism in Jovinian's condemnation in Rome and Milan, see pp. 186–7.
134 'Coptic Manichaean: Kephalaia of the Teacher', ch. 80; trans. Michael H. Browder, in V.L. Wimbush (ed.), *Ascetic Behavior in Greco-Roman Antiquity: A Sourcebook*, 1990, p. 191, lines 7–13.
135 Ibid. 80:29–30.
136 Ibid. 79:14.
137 See the important discussions of the rhetoric in the debate on virginity in Averil Cameron, op. cit. (n. 47 above), and *Christianity and the Rhetoric of Empire*, 1991, p. 171.

CHAPTER 9

1 *Confessions* X:1.
2 P. Courcelle, *Recherches sur les Confessions de Saint Augustin*, 1950, pp. 21–6; R.S. Pine-Coffin, Introduction to *Saint Augustine, Confessions*, 1961, p. 15. Vast amounts of scholarship have been devoted to this text and to Augustine's life. For a bibliography of studies to 1963 and a brief survey of some more recent work see Gerald Bonner, *St Augustine of Hippo: Life and Controversies*, 2nd edn, 1986; also J.J. O'Donnell's massive introduction and commentary in 3 vols, 1992, and H. Chadwick's translation, 1990.
3 Peter Brown, *The Body and Society: Men, Women, and Sexual Renunciation in Early Christianity*, 1988, p. 388.

4 Pine-Coffin, op. cit., p. 11.
5 1 Corinthians 15:53.
6 *Confessions* X:31(43–4).
7 Ibid. X:30(42).
8 Ibid. X:31(43).
9 Ibid. X:31(44). Compare with Seneca, *Epistulae morales* 59:13.
10 *Confessions* X:31 (44–5).
11 Ibid. X:31(46).
12 Ibid.
13 Ibid.
14 Ibid. Using the same method and sources as the earlier great Latin Christian, Tertullian, Augustine comes to an entirely different conclusion; a state of affairs not at all unusual among scholars!
15 1 Corinthians 8:8; Titus 1:15; Romans 14:20; 1 Timothy 4:4; Colossians 2:16, etc.
16 L. Ferrari, 'The gustatory Augustin', *Augustiniana* 29, 1979, 304–15.
17 *Confessions* I:7(11).
18 An observation applicable not only to an ascetic like Augustine but to all individuals; one may live without sex but one surely dies without food!
19 P. Brown, *Augustine of Hippo: A Biography*, 1967, p. 179, seems also to take Augustine at his word. He says that greed was 'a far more acute and revealing source of disquiet for him' than sexual dreams (referring to the time of the writing of the *Confessions*). Brown contradicts himself somewhat, however, on p. 389, where he writes: 'But of all the appetites, the only one that seemed to Augustine to clash inevitably and permanently with reason, was sexual desire.'
20 H. Chadwick, 'The attractions of Mani', *Pleroma Salus Carnis*, ed. E. Romero-Pose, 1990, p. 205.
21 *Vita Antonii* 68 (attributed to Athanasius): 'Nor did he have any friendly dealings with the Manichaeans or any other heretics, except only to admonish them to return to the true religion' (trans. R.T. Meyer, in *Ancient Christian Writers*, 1950).
22 Michael H. Browder, 'Coptic Manichaean: Kephalaia of the Teacher', in *Ascetic Behavior in Greco-Roman Antiquity: A Sourcebook*, ed. V.L. Wimbush, 1990, pp. 187–212, at p. 187.
23 Lane Fox, *Pagans and Christians*, 1986, p. 568.
24 Ibid.
25 S.N.C. Lieu, *Manichaeism in the Later Roman Empire and Medieval China*, 1992, p. 184. See also Brown, *Augustine* (n. 19 above), pp. 46–60, and Chadwick, op. cit. (n. 20 above).
26 *De moribus Manichaeorum*, XIV.31; XV.36–7; XVII.59–64. As Chadwick has noted, 'a substantial portion of anti-Manichee polemic in Augustine is given to the argument that in practice they are often inconsistent with their principles, which are impressive' (op. cit., p. 206).
27 Even at his consecration as bishop, the senior bishop of Numidia created a scandal by accusing Augustine of being a crypto-Manichaean (Brown, *Augustine*, p. 203).

28 Brown, *Augustine*, p. 261.

29 *De Sermone Domini in Monte*, I:15.

30 *De Peccato Originali*, 33:38; 37:42.

31 *De Bono Coniugali*, 9:9.

32 *De Peccato Originali* 33:38. Even more extreme in this respect than his predecessors, he saw the married couple who felt the need for sexual intercourse as sick people. In his *Sermon on the Good of Marriage*, dated AD 397 (ed. F. Dolbeau, *Review Bénédictine* 102, 1992), he uses words like *aegrotus* and *infirmitas* when talking about a couple in their marriage bed. He appeals to the apostle Paul as authority, who comes to the couple as a physician as 'salubri sermone, medicina diuina humana cubicula intrauit – ad coniugarum lectos accessit, iacentes aspexit – et tamen dedit consilium infirmitatis' (ibid. 4). As a result in large measure of Augustine's efforts, from his time not only St Paul but bishops and preachers would stand over the good Christian's marriage bed proffering medication against the sickness of desire.

33 Uta Ranke-Heinemann, *Eunuchs for the Kingdom of Heaven: The Catholic Church and Sexuality*, trans. Peter Heinegg, 1990, p. 75. Augustine's attitude to sex and marriage and his concept of the 'original sin' are discussed by many authors; for a less hostile view, but one that comes to a similar conclusion, see Bonner, op. cit. (note 2 above), pp. 368–79; also Brown, *The Body and Society*, ch. 19.

34 As Chadwick argues, what Augustine renounced was the Manichee mythology, while 'something in Manichee ethical attitudes was to stay in his bloodstream. The attraction of Mani was never quite lost' (op. cit. (n. 20 above), p. 222).

35 Brown, *Augustine*, p. 389.

36 For example, Julian of Eclanum, who opposed Augustine's concept of the Original Sin in a long series of writings from 418 to Augustine's death in 430. Julian clearly accuses Augustine of Manichaeism. The evidence for the controversy is only extant in Augustine, *The Unfinished Work Against Julian*; Book II of *On Marriage and Concupiscence: Against Julian*. See Brown on Augustine's fight against Julian of Eclanum (*Augustine*, pp. 381–97).

37 Brown, *Augustine*, pp. 61, 200–2, especially n. 6 to p. 202. On Augustine's monastic community in Hippo see ibid. pp. 138–45.

38 The term ἀκηδία often appears in the desert hermit literature, describing a state akin to clinical depression; S. Wenzel, 'Akedia: additions to Lampe's Patristic Greek Lexicon', *VigChr* 17, 1963, 173–6. Self-starvation, like starvation from other causes, leads to behavioural disorders and social disruptions, some a direct consequence of energy deficiency, others linked to mental disturbance. Finally, starvation by lowering resistance to infections leads to epidemic diseases ('Famine and disease', *The Cambridge World History of Human Disease*, ed. K. Kiple, 1993, 157–63).

39 Maria Dembinska, 'Diet: a comparison of food consumption between some Eastern and Western monasteries in the 4th–12th centuries', *Byzantion* 55, 1985, 431–62.

40 Basil of Caesarea, *Letters* 22. Gregory of Nyssa, *De Virginitate* 22, following Basil, warns against extremes of fasting and mortifications of the body. See the discussion in Susanna Elm, *Virgins of God: The Making of Asceticism in Late Antiquity*, 1994, p. 198.

41 Basil, *Regulae fusius tractatae* 16.1 (PG 31.957B).

42 *Confessions* X:31(47).

43 *De Utilitate Ieiunii* 4 (PL 40.707).

44 S. Freud, *New Introductory Lectures on Psychoanalysis*, trans. J. Strachey, The Standard Edition, vol. 22, 1964.

45 There are both male and female anorectics, but the condition is today more common among females, in the proportion of about 7:1.

46 Sheila MacLeod writes: 'The anorectic perceives her body as a "thing" distinct from her "self" and so fights it on two planes: as the source of impotence and anxiety because it represents the unacceptable part of herself; and as an alien force because she considers it an all-powerful invader of herself' (*The Art of Starvation*, p. 19).

47 *De Utilitate Ieiunii* 5.

48 See the Canons of the Synod of Gangra (between 325 and 381), especially Canons II, XI, XV, XVIII; cf. Augustine, *De Utilitate Ieiunii*, Basil of Caesarea, *Regulae fusius tractatae*. 16.1 (PG 31.957B).

49 *Sermo* 198.2 (PL 38.1025).

50 *Adversus Ebriosos* I (PG 50.453), quoted in Musurillo, 'Ascetical fasting', p. 42.

51 Maria Dembinska (op. cit., n. 39 above), after compiling the rather meagre evidence for the early centuries, estimates that in coenobitic monasteries the daily food intake corresponded with the normal requirements for physically active adults.

CONCLUSION

1 See n. 65 to Chapter 1 and n. 64 to Chapter 4 of this volume.

2 Mary Douglas, *Natural Symbols: Explorations in Cosmology*, 1970, p. 81. In this and her other works Douglas elaborated an anthropological view that sees doctrines that use the human body as their metaphor as being especially concerned with social relationships. The human body, according to this view, is never treated as a body without at the same time being seen as an image of society; 'body-symbols represent condensed statements about the relation of society to the individual' (ibid., p. 195).

3 Owsei Temkin, *Hippocrates in a World of Pagans and Christians*, 1991.

4 Robin Lane Fox, *Pagans and Christians*, 1986, p. 338.

5 Cf. Mary Douglas, *Purity and Danger*, 1966; *Natural Symbols* (n. 2 above). See also Jean Soler, 'The semiotics of food in the Bible', in R. Forster and O. Ranum (eds), *Food and Drink in History, Selections from the Annales: Economies, Societies, Civilisations*, vol. 5, 1979, pp. 126–38.

6 Robertson Smith, *The Religion of the Semites: The Fundamental Institution*, 1957, p. 126.

NOTE ON THE SOURCES

The following list sets out for convenience the most frequently used ancient sources. It does not refer to works mentioned in passing once or twice, which are given in standard form in the notes. All discussions of classical and patristic authors are based on standard editions; translations also are quoted from standard series, unless otherwise specified in the notes.

1 BIBLICAL REFERENCES

The New Oxford Annotated Bible; New Revised Standard Version (eds B.M. Metzger and R.E. Murphy, 1991).
The Greek New Testament, Fourth Revised Edition (eds K. Aland, M. Black, C.M. Martini, B.M. Metzger and A. Wikgren, 1990).
The Hebrew Old Testament חזוהנביאיםובחובים (Kittel), and *The Septuagint* (C.L. Brenton).

2 RABBINIC LITERATURE

The Mishnah, trans. H. Danby, 1933; J. Neusner, 1988.
The Tosefta, trans. J Neusner, 1979–86.
The Babylonian Talmud, Soncino ed. I. Epstein, 1935–52, repr. 1961.
The Jerusalem Talmud (The Talmud of the Land of Israel), J. Neusner, general editor, 1982–9.
For a detailed description see E.P. Sanders, *Paul and Palestinian Judaism*, 1977, pp. 557–9.

3 CLASSICAL SOURCES

Apuleius, *Metamorphoses*, ed. and trans. J.A. Hanson, LCL 1989.
Athenaeus, *The Deipnosophists*, trans. C.B. Gulick, LCL 1927, repr. 1969.
Celsus, *De Medicina*, trans. W.G. Spencer, LCL 1979.

NOTE ON THE SOURCES

Diogenes Laertius, *Lives of Eminent Philosophers*, trans. R.D. Hicks, LCL 1925.

Galen, *De Alimentorum Facultatibus Liber III*, in *Claudii Galeni Opera Omnia*, C.G. Kühn, 20 vols, repr. 1964, vol. 6; to my knowledge this treatise is not available in English translation. For English translations of other treatises of Galen see bibliography below under the name of the translator; *Hygiene*, trans. R. Montraville Green; *On Bloodletting*, trans. P. Brain; *On the Therapeutic Method*, trans. R.J. Hankinson.

Hippocrates, trans. by W.H.S. Jones, P. Potter and E.T. Withington, LCL 1923–88.

Philo of Alexandria, trans. in ten volumes and two supplementary volumes by F.H. Colson, G.H. Whittaker, R. Marcus and A. Wilkgren, LCL 1926–63 (see vol. 1, pp. xxiii, xxxv for the abbreviated titles of Philo's treatises).

Porphyry, *De Abstinentia*, in *Porphyrii philosophi Platonici opuscula selecta*, ed. A. Nauck, B.G. Teubner, 1886; *On Abstinence from Animal Food*, trans. T. Taylor 1827, repr. 1965.

Seneca, *Epistulae morales*, trans. R.M. Gummere, LCL 1917–25.

4 PATRISTIC TEXTS

Ambrose, PL 14–17; trans. of relevant tracts in H. de Romestin, *The Nicene and Post-Nicene Fathers*, second series, vol. 10, repr. 1955.

Athanasius, *Vita Antonii*, PG 26, 835–976; *The Life of Saint Antony*, trans. R.T. Meyer, in *Ancient Christian Writers* 10, 1950.

Augustine, *The Confessions*, ed. J. Gibb and W. Montgomery, Cambridge Patristic Texts 1908; trans. R.S. Pine-Coffin, 1961; H. Chadwick, 1990. Tables listing Augustine's writings and their English translations are available in P. Brown, *Augustine of Hippo*, 1967.

Basil of Ancyra, *De Virginitate*, PG 30, 669–810.

Clement of Alexandria, *Protrepticus und Paedagogus*, ed. O. Stählin, GCS 12, 1909, repr. 1972; *Stromata*, ed. O. Stählin, GCS 15, 1906, and 17, 1909. English trans. W. Wilson, *Ante-Nicene Christian Library*; *Paedagogus*, trans. S.P. Wood in *Fathers of the Church*, vol. 23, 1954.

Eusebius, *Ecclesiastical History*; *Eusebius: Die Kirchengeschichte*, ed. E. Schwartz, GCS 9, 1909; trans. K. Lake and J.E.L. Oulton, LCL, 1926–32; also in *Nicene and Post-Nicene Fathers of the Christian Church*, trans. A.C. McGiffert 1890, repr. 1976.

Gregory Thaumaturgus, *Canonical Epistle of the Archbishop of Neocaesarea and the Panegyric on Origen*, eds A. Roberts and J. Donaldson, *Ante-Nicene Christian Library*, vol. 20, 1871.

Jerome, *Letters*, ed. I. Hilberg, 1910, CSEL 54–6; *Vita Pauli, Vita Hilarionis, Adversus Jovinianum*, and *De Viris Illustribus* in PL 23.

Origen, *Contra Celsum*, ed. P. Koetschau, GCS, 2 vols, 1899; PG 11, 641–1632; trans. Frederick Crombie, *Ante-Nicene Christian Library*, 23, 1885, repr. 1976; trans. and with an introduction and notes by Henry Chadwick, 1953. *De Principiis*; *On First Principles*, trans. F. Crombie in *Ante-Nicene Christian Library*, vol. 4., 1885, repr. 1976. *Commentary on Matthew*, trans. J. Patrick, *Ante-Nicene Christian Library*, vol. 10 (original supplement to the American edition, 1974). *On Prayer*, trans. J.J. O'Meara, *Ancient*

Christian Writers, vol. 19, 1954. *Homily in Genesis*, trans. R.E. Heine, *Fathers of the Church*, vol. 71, 1982.
Tertullian, *De Ieiunio*, A. Reifferscheid et G. Wissowa, CCL II, 1257–77. *Apologeticum*, E. Dekkers, CCL I. 77. *De Spectaculis*, E. Dekkers, CCL I, 225. English trans. *The Writings of Tertullianus*, in *Ante-Nicene Christian Library*, trans. P. Holmes and S. Therwall, 4 vols, 1868–70; *Apologetic and Practical Treatises*, in *A Library of Fathers*, trans. C. Dodgson 1854.

BIBLIOGRAPHY

The following select bibliography contains a list of modern authors and their books and articles that are mentioned in the footnotes. The list does not include general histories and standard reference works.

Adkin, N., '"Istae sunt, quae solent dicere"; three Roman vignettes in Jerome's "Libellus de virginitate servanda" (Epist. 22)', *Museum Helveticum* 49, 1992, 131–40.

Altaner, B.–Stuiber, A., *Patrologie* 7, 1966.

Anderson, G., *The Second Sophistic*, 1993.

Arbesmann, R., *Das Fasten bei den Griechen und Römern*, 1929.

—— 'Fasting and prophecy in Pagan and Christian antiquity', *Traditio* 7, 1949–51, 1–71.

Attridge, H.W., 'Christianity from the destruction of Jerusalem to Constantine's adoption of the new religion: 70–312 C.E.', in H. Shanks (ed.) *Christianity and Rabbinic Judaism*, 1993, pp. 151–94.

Bardy, G., 'Aux origines de l'école d'Alexandrie', *Recherches de Science Religieuse* 27, 1937, 87–8.

Barnes, T.D., 'Legislation against the Christians', *JRS* 58, 1968, 32–50.

—— *Tertullian: A Historical and Literary Study*, 1971.

—— 'The editions of Eusebius' *Ecclesiastical History*', *Greek, Roman and Byzantine Studies* 21, 1980, 191–201.

—— *Constantine and Eusebius*, 1981.

—— *Athanasius and Constantius: Theology and Politics in the Constantinian Empire*, 1993.

Bass, M.A., Wakefield, L.M. and Kolasa, K.M., *Community, Nutrition and Individual Food Behaviour*, 1979.

Bauer, W., *Rechtglaubigkeit und Ketzerei im altesten Christentum*, 2nd edn, 1964; trans. as *Orthodoxy and Heresy in Earliest Christianity*, with added appendices by G. Strecker, eds R.A. Kraft and G. Krodel, 1971.

Baus, K., *History of the Church: From the Apostolic Community to Constantine*, trans. and ed. H. Jedin, 1980.

Beard, M., review of A. Rousselle, *Porneia*, in *JRS* 81, 1991, 180.

Beard, M. and North, J. (eds), *Pagan Priests: Religion and Power in the Ancient World*, 1990.

Berger, P.L. and Luckmann, T., *The Social Construction of Reality*, 1966.

Bettenson, H., *The Early Christian Fathers*, 1969.

Bickel, E., *Diatribe in Senecae Philosophi Fragmenta*, 1915.

Black, J.S., 'Fasting', *Encyclopedia Britannica*, 13th edn, vol. 10, 1926, pp. 193–8.

Bonner, G., *St Augustine of Hippo: Life and Controversies*, 2nd edn, 1986.

Bowersock, G.W., *Greek Sophists in the Roman Empire*, 1969.

Brain, P., *Galen on Bloodletting*, 1986.

Brothwell, D. and Sandison, A.T., *Diseases in Antiquity*, 1967.

Browder, M.H. (trans.), 'Coptic Manichaean: Kephalaia of the Teacher', in *Ascetic Behavior in Greco-Roman Antiquity: A Sourcebook*, ed. V.L. Wimbush, 1990, pp. 187–212.

Brown, P., *Augustine of Hippo: A Biography*, 1967.

—— *The Body and Society: Men, Women, and Sexual Renunciation in Early Christianity*, 1988.

Bruce, F.F., *The Acts of the Apostles: The Greek Text with Introduction and Commentary*, 3rd edn, 1990.

Bruch, H., *Eating Disorders; Obesity, Anorexia Nervosa and the Person Within*, 1974.

Bultmann, R., *Theology of the New Testament*, trans. K. Grobel, 2 vols, 1959.

Burkert, W., *Homo Necans: The Anthropology of Ancient Greek Sacrificial Ritual and Myth*, trans. P. Bing, 1983.

—— *Greek Religion*, trans. J. Raffan, 1985.

—— 'Craft versus sect: the problem of Orphics and Pythagoreans', in B.F. Meyer and E.P. Sanders (eds), *Jewish and Christian Self-definition*, vol. 3, 1982, pp. 1–22.

Bynum, C. Walker, *Holy Feast and Holy Fast: The Religious Significance of Food to Medieval Women*, 1987.

Cadbury, H.J., *The Style and Literary Method of Luke, 1. The Diction of Luke and Acts*, Harvard Theological Studies 6, 1919–20.

Callam, D., 'Clerical continence in the fourth century: three papal decretals', *Theological Studies* 41, 1980, 3–49.

Cameron, A., 'Virginity as a metaphor: women and the rhetoric of early Christianity', in A. Cameron (ed.), *History as Text: The Writing of Ancient History*, 1989, pp. 184–205.

—— *Christianity and the Rhetoric of Empire*, 1991.

Campbell, T.H., 'Paul's missionary journeys as reflected in his letters', *Journal of Biblical Literature* 74, 1955, pp. 80–7.

Cavallera, F., *Saint Jérôme, sa vie et son oeuvre*, 1922.

Chadwick, H., *Early Christian Thought and the Classical Tradition: Studies in Justin, Clement, and Origen*, 1966.

—— *The Early Church*, 1967.

—— 'Philo and the beginnings of Christian thought', in A.H. Armstrong (ed.), *The Cambridge History of Later Greek and Early Medieval Philosophy*, 1967, repr. 1991, pp. 137–95.

—— 'The attractions of Mani', in E. Romero-Pose (ed.), *Pléroma Salus Carnis*, Homenaje a Antonio Orbe, S.J., 1990, pp. 203–22.

—— 'Christian and Roman universalism in the fourth century', in L.R. Wickham and C.P. Bammel (eds), *Christian Faith and Greek Philosophy in Late Antiquity*, Essays in Tribute to George Christopher Stead, 1993, pp. 26–42.

Clark, E.A., *Clement's Use of Aristotle: The Aristotelian Contribution to Clement of Alexandria's Refutation of Gnosticism*, 1977.

—— *Jerome, Chrysostom, and Friends*, 1979.

Clark, G., *Women in Late Antiquity: Pagan and Christian Life-styles*, 1993.

Conzelmann, H., *I Corinthians: A Commentary on the First Epistle to the Corinthians*, trans. J.W. Leitch, 1975.

—— 'Luke's place in the development of early Christianity', in L. Keck and L.J. Martyn (eds), *Studies in Luke-Acts*, 1980, pp. 298–316.

—— *Acts of the Apostles: A Commentary*, trans. J. Lindburgh, A.T. Kraabel and D.H. Juel, ed. E.J. Epp with C.R. Matthews, 1987.

Cook, M.J., 'The mission to the Jews in Acts: unraveling Luke's "Myth of the 'Myriads'"', in J.B. Tyson (ed.), *Luke-Acts and the Jewish People: Eight Critical Perspectives*, 1988, pp. 102–23.

Cooper, K., 'Insinuations of womanly influence: an aspect of the Christianization of the Roman aristocracy', *JRS* 82, 1992, 150–64.

Courcelle, P., *Recherches sur les Confessions de Saint Augustin*, 1950.

Cox, P., *Biography in Late Antiquity: A Quest for the Holy Man*, 1983.

Cox Miller, P., 'Desert asceticism and "the body from nowhere"', *Journal of Early Christian Studies* 2, 1994, 137–53.

Cumont, F., *Oriental Religions in Roman Paganism*, English trans. 1911, repr. 1956.

—— *The Mysteries of Mithra*, Engl. trans. 1903, repr. 1956.

Daniélou, J., *Origène*, 1948, trans. W. Mitchell, 1955.

—— *Les Manuscrits de la Mer Mort et les origines du Christianisme*, 1957.

d'Arms, J., 'Control, companionship and clientela: some social functions of the Roman communal meal', *Echos du Monde Classique, Classical Views* 28 NS 3, 1984, Special Issue, 327–48.

de Labriolle, P., *Les Sources pour l'histoire de Montanisme*, 1913.

de Ste Croix, G.E.M., *The Class Struggle in the Ancient Greek World*, 1981.

de Vaux, R., *Archaeology and the Dead Sea Scrolls*, 1973.

Dembinska, M., 'Diet: a comparison of food consumption between some Eastern and Western monasteries in the 4th–12th centuries', *Byzantion* 55, 1985, 431–62.

Detienne, M. and Vernant, J.-P., *The Cuisine of Sacrifice Among the Greeks*, trans. P. Wissing, 1989.

Dibelius, M., *Studies in the Acts of the Apostles*, trans. H. Greeven, 1956.

Diehl, E., *Pompeianische Wandinschriften und Verwandtes*, 1910.

Dillon, J.M., 'Self-definition in later Platonism', in B.F. Meyer and E.P. Sanders (eds), *Jewish and Christian Self-definition*, vol. 3, 1982, pp. 60–75.

—— *The Middle Platonists: 80 B.C. to A.D. 200*, 1977.

Dix, G., *The Shape of the Liturgy*, 1945.

Dodds, E.R., *Pagan and Christian in an Age of Anxiety*, 1965.

Dombrowski, D.A., 'Asceticism as athletic training in Plotinus', *ANRW* II.36.1, 1987, 701–12.

Douglas, M., *Purity and Danger*, 1966.

—— *Natural Symbols: Explorations in Cosmology*, 1970.

Dow, S. and Gill, D.H., 'The Greek cult table', *AJA* 69, 1965, 103.

Drijvers, J.W., 'Virginity and asceticism in late Roman Western elites', in J. Blok and P. Mason (eds), *Sexual Asymmetry*, 1987, pp. 241–73.

Dumont, L., 'A modified view of our origins: the Christian beginnings of modern individualism', in M. Carrithers *et al.* (eds), *The Category of the Person*, 1985, pp. 93–122.

Duncan-Jones, R., *The Economy of the Roman Empire: Quantitative Studies*, 1974.

Edwards, J., *The Roman Cookery of Apicius*, 1984.

Ellis, E.G., *Ancient Anodynes. Primitive Anaesthesia and Allied Conditions*, 1946.

Elm, S., *Virgins of God: The Making of Asceticism in Late Antiquity*, 1994.

Erikson, E.H., 'Identity and the life cycle', *Psychological Issues* 1, 1959, 18–164.

Esler, P.F., *Community and Gospel in Luke Acts*, 1987.

Farb, P. and Armelagos, G., *The Anthropology of Eating*, 1980.

Feldman, L.H., 'Palestinian and Diaspora Judaism in the first century', in H. Shanks (ed.), *Christianity and Rabbinic Judaism: A Parallel History of their Origins and Early Development*, 1993, pp. 1–39.

—— *Jew and Gentile in the Ancient World*, 1993.

Ferguson, J., *Clement of Alexandria*, 1974.

Ferrari, L.C., 'The gustatory Augustin', *Augustiniana* 29, 1979, 304–15.

Fieldhouse, P., *Food and Nutrition: Customs and Culture*, 1986.

Fishel, H.A., *Essays in Graeco-Roman and related Talmudic Literature*, 1977.

Fitzmyer, J.A., 'Jewish Christianity in Acts in light of the Qumran Scrolls', in L. Keck and L.J. Martyn (eds), *Studies in Luke-Acts*, 1980, pp. 233–57.

Floyd, W.E.G., *Clement of Alexandria's Treatment of the Problem of Evil*, 1971.

Forbes, R.J., *Studies in Ancient Technology*, 2nd edn, 6 vols, 1964.

Foucault, M., 'Technologies of the self', in *Technologies of the Self: A Seminar with Michel Foucault*, ed. L.H. Martin, H. Gutman and P.H. Hutton, 1988, pp. 16–49.

—— *The History of Sexuality*, trans R. Hurley, 3 vols, 1978–88.

Fowden, G., 'The last days of Constantine: oppositional versions and their influence', *JRS* 84, 1994, 146–71.

—— 'The Platonist philosopher and his circle in late antiquity', *FILOSOFIA* 7; Yearbook of the Research Center for Greek Philosophy at the Academy of Athens, 1977, 359–83.

Fraade, S.D., 'Ascetical aspects of ancient Judaism', in A. Green (ed.), *Jewish Spirituality: From the Bible through the Middle Ages*, 1985, vol. 1, pp. 253–88.

Freese, J.H., *The Library of Photius*, 1920.

Frend, W.H.C., *Martyrdom and Persecution in the Early Church*, 1965.

—— *The Donatist Church: A Movement of Protest in Roman North Africa*, 1952, repr. 1970.

Freud, S., *New Introductory Lectures on Psychoanalysis*, trans. J. Strachey, The Standard Edition, vol. 22, 1964.

Gasque, W.W., *A History of the Criticism of the Acts of the Apostles*, 1975.

Gilliard, F.D., 'Senatorial bishops in the fourth century', *HThR* 77, 1984, 153–75.

Goehring, J.E., 'Through a glass darkly: diverse images of the Apotakti-koi(ai) of early Egyptian monasticism', *Semeia* 58, 1992, 25–45.

Goodman, M.D., *Mission and Conversion: Proselytizing in the Religious History of the Roman Empire*, 1994.

Goody, J., *Cooking, Cuisine and Class*, 1982.

Gordon, R., 'Religion in the Roman Empire: the civic compromise and its limits', in M. Beard and J. North (eds), *Pagan Priests*, 1990, pp. 233–55.

Gowers, E., *The Loaded Table, Representations of Food in Roman Literature*, 1993.

Grant, R.M., 'The New Testament Canon', in P.R. Ackroyd and C.F. Evans (eds), *The Cambridge History of the Bible*, vol. 1, 1970, pp. 284–308.

Green, A. (ed.), *Jewish Spirituality: From the Bible through the Middle Ages*, 1985.

Grmek, M.D., *Diseases in the Ancient Greek World*, trans. M. and L. Muellner, 1983.

Grützmacher, G., *Hieronymus: Eine biographische Studie*, 3 vols, 1901–8.

Habinek, T.N., 'An aristocracy of virtue: Seneca on the beginnings of wisdom', *Yale Classical Studies* 29, 1992, 187–203.

Haenchen, E., *The Acts of the Apostles: A Commentary*, trans. B. Noble and G. Shinn under the supervision of H. Anderson; revised and brought up to date by R. McL. Wilson 1971.

—— 'The Book of Acts as source material for the history of early Christianity', in L. Keck and L.J. Martyn (eds), *Studies in Luke-Acts*, 1980, pp. 258–78.

Hagendahl, H., *Latin Fathers and the Classics: A Study on the Apologists, Jerome and Other Christian Writers*, 1958.

Hamel, G., *Poverty and Charity in Roman Palestine, First Three Centuries C.E.*, 1989.

Hankinson, R.J., *Galen on the Therapeutic Method, Books I and II*, 1991.

Hansleiter, J., *Der Vegetarismus in Antike*, 1935.

Hanson, R.P.C., *Allegory and Event: A Study of the Sources and Significance of Origen's Interpretation of Scripture*, 1959.

Harris, H.A., *Greek Athletics and the Jews*, 1976.

Heather, P. and Matthews, J., *The Goths in the Fourth Century*, 1991.

Hengel, M., *Acts and the History of Earliest Christianity*, trans. J. Bowden, 1979.

Hornschuh, M., 'Das Leben des Origenes und die Entstehung der alexandrinischen Schule', *Zeitschrift für Kirchengeschichte* 71, 1960, 1–25, 193–214.

Hubert, H. and Mauss, M., *Sacrifice: Its Nature and Function*, trans. W.D. Halls, 1964.

Hurd, J.C., Jr., *The Origin of I Corinthians*, 1965.

Jackson, R., *Doctors and Diseases in the Roman Empire*, 1988.

Jaeger, W., *Early Christianity and Greek Paideia*, 1962.

Jeremias, J., *The Eucharistic Words of Jesus*, trans. A. Erhardt, 3rd edn, 1966.

—— *Jerusalem in the Time of Jesus: An Investigation into Economic and Social Conditions During the New Testament Period*, trans. F.H. and C.H. Cave, 1969.

Jones, A.H.M., *The Later Roman Empire 284–602*, 3 vols, 1964; repr. in 2 vols, 1973 and 1986.

Judge, E.A., 'St Paul and classical society', *JAC* 15, 1972, 19–36.

—— 'The earliest use of *monachos* for "monk" (P.Coll.Youtie 77) and the origins of monasticism', *JAC* 20, 1977, 72–89.

Käsemann, E., *Commentary on Romans*, trans. G.W. Bromiley, 1980.

Kee, H.C., *Medicine, Miracle and Magic in New Testament Times*, 1986.

—— 'After the crucifixion – Christianity through Paul', in H. Shanks (ed.) *Christianity and Rabbinic Judaism*, 1993, pp. 85–124.

Kelly, J.N.D., *Jerome: His Life, Writings, and Controversies*, 1975.

Keys, A., Brozek, J., Henshel, A., Mickelsen, O. and Taylor, H.L. (eds), *The Biology of Human Starvation*, 2 vols, 1950.

Kittel, G. (ed.), *Theological Dictionary of the New Testament*, trans. G.W. Bromeley, 1964–76.

Knight, T.E., review of D. Dawson, *Allegorical Readers and Cultural Revision in Ancient Alexandria*, 1992, in *AJP* 115, 1994, 132–6.

Knox, R.A., *Enthusiasm: A Chapter in the History of Religion*, 1950.

Koch, H., 'War Klemens von Alexandrien Priester?', *Zeitschrift für die Neutestamentliche Wissenschaft* 20, 1921, 43–8.

Koester, H., *Introduction to the New Testament*: vol. I, *History, Culture and Religion of the Hellenistic Age*; vol. II, *History and Literature of Early Christianity*, 1982, paperback edn 1987.

—— 'Writings and the spirit: authority and politics in ancient Christianity', *HThR* 84, 1991, 353–72.

Korchin, S.J., *Modern Clinical Psychology*, 1976.

Kuhn, K.H., 'The Lord's Supper and the communal meal at Qumran', in K. Stendahl (ed.), *The Scrolls and the New Testament*, 1958, pp. 65–93.

Kümmel, W.G., *Introduction to the New Testament*, revised edn, trans. H.C. Kee, 1975.

Lake, K. and Cadbury, H.J., *The Acts of the Apostles*, English trans. and commentary in F.J. Foakes-Jackson and K. Lake (eds), *The Beginnings of Christianity*, 1933.

Lane Fox, R., *Pagans and Christians*, 1986.

—— *The Unauthorized Version: Truth and Fiction in the Bible*, 1991.

Layton, B., 'Prolegomena to the study of ancient Gnosticism', in L.M. White and O.L. Yarbrough (eds), *The Social World of the First Christians: Essays in Honor of Wayne A. Meeks*, 1995, pp. 334–50.

Lebreton, J., 'La théorie de la connaissance religieuse chez Clément d'Alexandrie', *Recherches de Science Religieuse*, 18, 1923, 457–88.

Liebeschuetz, J.H.W.G., *Continuity and Change in Roman Religion*, 1979.

Lietzmann, H., *Die Geschichte der alten Kirche*, 4 vols, 1937–44, trans. B.L. Woolf as *The Beginnings of the Christian Church*, 4 vols, 1947–53.

Lieu, S.N.C., *Manichaeism in the Later Roman Empire and Medieval China*, 1992.

Lilla, S.R.C., *Clement of Alexandria: A Study in Christian Platonism and Gnosticism*, 1971.

Lind, L.R., 'The tradition of Roman moral conservatism', in C. Deroux (ed.), *Studies in Latin Literature and Roman History* I; Collection Latomus 164, 1979, pp. 7–57.

Longrigg, J., *Greek Rational Medicine, Philosophy and Medicine from Alcmeon to the Alexandrians*, 1993.

Lonie, I.M., 'A structural pattern in Greek dietetics and the early history of Greek medicine', *Medical History* 21, 1977, 235–60.

Lowy, S., 'The motivation of fasting in Talmudic literature', *JJS* 9, 1958, 19–38.

Luebeck, A., *Hieronymus Quos Noverit Scriptores et Quibus Hauserit*, 1872.

Lutz, C.E., 'Musonius Rufus "The Roman Socrates"', *Yale Classical Studies* 10, 1947, 3–151.

Maccullogh, J.A. and Maclean, A.J., 'Fasting', *Hasting's Encyclopedia of Religion and Ethics*, 1951, vol. 6, pp. 759–71.

MacLeod, S., *The Art of Starvation*, 1981.

MacMullen, R., 'What difference did Christianity make?', *Historia* 35, 1986, 322–43; reprinted in *Changes in the Roman Empire: Essays in the Ordinary*, 1990, pp. 142–55.

—— 'Ordinary Christians in the later persecutions', in *Changes in the Roman Empire: Essays in the Ordinary*, 1990, pp. 156–61.

Malherbe, A.J. (ed.), *The Cynic Epistles*, 1977.

—— 'Self-definition among Epicureans and Cynics', in B.F. Meyer and E.P. Sanders (eds), *Jewish and Christian Self-Definition*, vol. 3, 1982, pp. 46–59.

—— *Paul and the Thessalonians: The Philosophic Tradition of Pastoral Care*, 1987.

Marrou, H.I., *A History of Education in Antiquity*, English trans. 1956.

Marshall, I.H., *The Acts of the Apostles: An Introduction and Commentary*, 1980.

Meggitt, J.J., 'Meat consumption and social conflict in Corinth', *JThS* NS 45, 1994, 137–41.

Menoud, P.H., 'The Acts of the Apostles and the Eucharist', in *Jesus Christ and the Faith: A Collection of Studies by P. Menoud*, trans. E.M. Paul, 1978, pp. 84–106.

Millar, F., 'The imperial cult and the persecutions', in *Le Culte des souverains dans l'empire romain*, Fondation Hardt, Entretiens sur l'antiquité classique 19, 1973.

Misch, G., *A History of Autobiography in Antiquity*, 2 vols, trans. E.W. Dickes, 1951.

Mommsen, T., *The History of Rome*, 5 vols, trans. W.P. Dickinson, 1894.

Montraville Green, R., *A Translation of Galen's Hygiene*, 1952.

More, C.H., 'Greek and Roman ascetic tendencies', in H.W. Smyth (ed.), *Harvard Essays on Classical Subjects*, 1912, pp. 97–140.

Morgan, J., *The Importance of Tertullian in the Development of Christian Dogma*, 1928.

Mounteer, C.A., 'Guilt, martyrdom and monasticism', *The Journal of Psychohistory* 9, 1981, 145–71.

Murray, O., 'The Greek symposium in history', in E. Gabba (ed.) *Tria Corda: Scritti in onore di A. Momigliano*, 1983, pp. 257–73.

Musurillo, H., 'The problem of ascetical fasting in the Greek patristic writers', *Traditio* 12, 1956, 1–64.

Nagy, M., 'Translocation of parental images in fourth-century ascetic texts: motifs and techniques of identity', *Semeia* 58, 1992, 3–23.

Neusner, J., *From Politics to Piety*, 1972.

—— 'Varieties of Judaism in the formative age', in A. Green (ed.) *Jewish Spirituality: From the Bible through the Middle Ages*, 1985, pp. 171–97.

—— *The Mishnah: A New Translation*, 1988.

Nilsson, M.P., 'Pagan divine service in late antiquity', *HThR* 38, 1945, 63–9.

Nock, A.D., 'The historical importance of cult associations', *Classical Review* 38, 1924, 105–9.

O'Donnell, J.J., *Augustine, Confessions*, 3 vols, 1992; I, Introduction and Text; II–III, Commentary.

Ogilvie, R.M., *The Romans and their Gods*, 1969.

O'Neill, J.C., *The Theology of Acts in its Historical Setting*, 1961.

Onians, R.B., *The Origins of European Thought*, 1951.

Orr, D.G., 'Roman domestic religion: the evidence of household shrines', *ANRW* 2.16.2, 1978, 1557–91.

Osborne, E.F., *The Philosophy of Clement of Alexandria*, 1957.

Pagels, E., *The Gnostic Gospels*, 1974.

—— *Adam, Eve, and the Serpent*, 1988.

Parker, C.P., 'Musonius in Clement', *Harvard Studies in Classical Philology* 12, 1901, 191–210.

Patrick, A., 'Ancient Greece and Rome', in D. Brothwell and A.T. Sandison, *Diseases in Antiquity*, 1967.

Perkins, J., 'The "self" as sufferer', *HThR* 85, 1992, 245–72.

Phillips, C.R., 'The sociology of religious knowledge in the Roman Empire to A.D. 284', *ANRW* 2.16.3, 1986, 2677–773.

Prunet, O., *La Morale de Clément d'Alexandrie et le Nouveau Testament*, 1966.

Ranke-Heinemann, U., *Eunuchs for the Kingdom of Heaven: The Catholic Church and Sexuality*, trans. Peter Heinegg, 1990.

Rawson, E., *Intellectual Life in Late Republican Rome*, 1985.

Reicke B., 'Die Mahlzeit mit Paulus auf den Wellen des Mittelmeers Act. 27,33–38', *Theologische Zeitschrift* 4, 1948, 401–10.

Roberts, C.H., *Manuscript, Society and Belief in Early Christian Egypt*, 1979.

Robertson Smith, W., *The Religion of the Semites: The Fundamental Institutions*, 1957.

Rousseau, P., *Ascetics, Authority, and the Church in the Age of Jerome and Cassian*, 1978.

Rousselle, A., *Porneia: On Desire and the Body in Antiquity*, trans. F. Pheasant, 1988.

Russell, G.F.M., 'Anorexia nervosa', *Oxford Textbook of Medicine*, 1987.

Salmon, M., 'Insider or outsider? Luke's relationship with Judaism', in J.B. Tyson (ed.), *Luke-Acts and the Jewish People: Eight Critical Perspectives*, 1988, pp. 76–82.

Salzman, M.R., 'Aristocratic women: conductors of Christianity in the fourth century', *Helios* 16, 1989, 207–20.

Sanders, E.P., *Paul and Palestinian Judaism: A Comparison of Patterns of Religion*, 1977.

—— *Jewish Law from Jesus to the Mishnah: Five Studies*, 1990.

—— *Judaism, Practice and Belief 63 BCE–66 CE*, 1992.

Scheid, J., 'Sacrifice et banquet à Rome', *MEFRA* 97, 1985, 193–206.

Schürer, E., *The History of the Jewish People in the Age of Jesus Christ, 175 B.C.–*

A.D. 135 (a new English version revised and edited by G. Vermes, F. Millar and M. Goodman 1986).

Schwartz, E., *Eusebius: Die Kirchengeschichte*, GCS 9, 1909.

Scullard, H.H., *Festivals and Ceremonies of the Roman Republic*, 1981.

Segal, A.F., *Rebecca's Children: Judaism and Christianity in the Roman World*, 1986.

Selvini Palazzoli, M., *Self-starvation: From the Intrapsychic to the Transpersonal Approach to Anorexia Nervosa*, 1974.

Serrato, M., *Ascetismo Femenino en Roma*, 1993.

Shanks, H. (ed.), *Christianity and Rabbinic Judaism: A Parallel History of Their Origins and Development*, 1993.

Sherk, R., *The Municipal Decrees of the Roman West*, 1970.

Simoons, F.J., *Eat Not This Flesh*, 1961.

Slater, W.J. (ed.), *Dining in a Classical Context*, 1991.

Smith, M., 'Palestinian Judaism in the first century', in H.A. Fishel (ed.), *Essays in Greco-Roman and Related Talmudic Literature*, 1977, pp. 199–214.

Smith, R. and James, W.P.T., 'Nutrition', in D.J. Weatherall, J.G.G. Ledingham and D.J. Warrell (eds), *Oxford Textbook of Medicine*, 2nd edn, 1987.

Smith, W.D., *The Hippocratic Tradition*, 1979.

Soler, J., 'The semiotics of food in the Bible', in R. Forster and O. Ranum (eds), *Food and Drink in History, Selections from the* Annales: *Economies, Societies, Civilisations*, vol. 5, 1979, pp. 126–38.

Sorabji, R., *Animal Minds and Human Morals: The Origins of the Western Debate*, 1993.

Sparkes, B.A., 'The Greek kitchen', *JHS* 82, 1962, 121–37.

Sparks, H.F.D., review of J.C. O'Neill, *The Theology of Acts*, in *JThS* NS 14, 1963, 457.

Sperling, D., 'Israel's religion in the ancient Near East', in A. Green (ed.), *Jewish Spirituality: From the Bible through the Middle Ages*, 1985, vol. 1, pp. 5–31.

Stambaugh, J.E., 'The function of Roman temples', *ANRW* 2.16.1, 1978, 554–608.

Stern, M., *Greek and Latin Authors on Jews and Judaism*, with introductions, translations and commentary, 3 vols, 1974–84.

Stiegman, E., 'Rabbinic anthropology', *ANRW* II.19.2, 1979, 487–579.

Stone, M.E., *Fourth Ezra*, 1990.

Strack, H.L. and Stemberger, G., *Introduction to the Talmud and Midrash*, trans. M. Bockmuehl, 1991.

Stroumsa, G.G., 'Caro Salutis Cardo: shaping the person in early Christian thought', *HR* 30, 1990, 25–50.

Sumney, J.L., *Identifying Paul's Opponents: The Question of Method in 2 Corinthians*, 1990.

Sutcliffe, E.F., 'Sacred meals at Qumran?', *Heythrop Journal* 1, 1960, 48–65.

Syme, R., *Ammianus and the Historia Augusta*, 1968.

Szemler, G.J., *The Priests of the Roman Republic: A Study of Interactions Between Priesthoods and Magistracies*, Coll. Lat. 127, 1972.

Talbert, C.H., *Luke and the Gnostics: An Examination of the Lucan Purpose*, 1966.

Tannahil, R., *Food in History*, 1973, repr. 1988.

Temkin, O., *Hippocrates in a World of Pagans and Christians*, 1991.

Thiessen, G., *The Social Setting of Pauline Christianity: Essays on Corinth*, ed. and trans. J.H. Schütz, 1982.

Thomson, W.A.R., *Black's Medical Dictionary*, 1974.

Tollington, R.B., *Clement of Alexandria: A Study in Christian Liberalism*, 1914.

Torjesen, K.J., 'Pedagogical soteriology from Clement to Origen', in *Origeniana Quarta: Die Referate des 4. Internationalen Origeneskongresses (Innsbruck, 2–6 September 1985)*, 1987, pp. 370–8.

Toutain, J., *Les Cultes paiens dans l'Empire romain; Ière partie, Les Provinces latines*, 1920.

Trigg, J.W., *Origen: The Bible and Philosophy in the Third-century Church*, 1983.

Tsekourakis, D., 'Pythagoreanism or Platonism and ancient medicine? The reason for vegetarianism in Plutarch's Moralia', *ANRW* II.36.1, 1987, 366–93.

Vallance, J.T., *The Lost Theory of Asclepiades of Bithynia*, 1990.

van der Ploeg, J., 'The meals of the Essenes', *JSS* 2, 1957, 163–75.

Vermes, G., *Jesus the Jew*, 1973.

——— *Jesus and the World of Judaism*, 1983.

——— *The Dead Sea Scrolls in English*, 3rd edn, revised and augmented, 1987.

Versnel, H.S., 'The Festival of Bona Dea and the Thesmophoria', *Greece and Rome* 39, 1992, 31–55.

Vessey, M., 'Jerome's Origen: the making of a Christian literary persona', *Studia Patristica* 28, 1993, 135–45.

Veyne, P., *Bread and Circuses: Historical Sociology and Political Pluralism*, trans. B. Pearce, 1990.

——— (ed.), *A History of Private Life*, vol. 1, trans. A. Goldhammer, 1987.

Ward, B., *Harlots of the Desert: A Study of Repentance in Early Monastic Sources*, 1987.

Wenzel, S., 'Akedia: additions to Lampe's Patristic Greek Lexicon', *VigChr* 17, 1963, 173–6.

Wiesen, D.S., *St. Jerome as a Satirist: A Study in Christian Latin Thought and Letters*, 1964.

Wightman, E.M., *Roman Trier and the Treveri*, 1970.

Wilkens, U., *Die Brief an die Römer*, 1978–82, vol. 2.

Williams, C.S.C., 'The date of Luke-Acts', *Expository Times* 64, 1953, 283–4.

Williams, M.H., 'The Jews and Godfearers Inscription from Aphrodisias: a case of patriarchal interference in early 3rd century Caria?', *Historia* 41, 1992, 297–310.

Wilson, R. McL., 'Alimentary and sexual encratism in the Nag Hammadi tractates', in U. Bianchi (ed.), *La Tradizione dell'Encrateia*, 1982, pp. 317–39.

Wimbush, V.L. (ed.), *Ascetic Behavior in Greco-Roman Antiquity: A Sourcebook*, 1990.

Winston, D., 'Philo and the contemplative life', in A. Green (ed.) *Jewish Spirituality: From the Bible through the Middle Ages*, 1985, vol. 1, pp. 198–231.

Yarbrough, A., 'Christianization in the fourth century: the example of Roman women', *Church History* 45, 1976, 149–65.

Young, V.R. and Scrimshaw, N.S., 'The physiology of starvation', *Scientific American* 225(4), 1971, 14–21.

Ziesler, J., *Paul's Letter to the Romans*, 1989.

INDEX